FIELD OF GOURDS
A Guide to Intellectual Rebellion

BY ROBERT M. FISHER AND BELLA THE DOG

ISBN-10:   1479156493

EAN-13:   9781479156498

Library of Congress Control Number: 2012915247
CreateSpace, North Charleston, SC

PRODUCT WARNING

This is a radical book; it is not for those who are more comfortable with convention. The term "radical" is used here not in the political sense, but in its broader meaning. To be "radical" is to go to the root of a problem. It is to think for oneself and to think well. This book encourages you to do just that, and provides an intellectual toolkit to facilitate it. But thinking for oneself almost always defies convention, including both social and political convention. It upsets people. And this is not without a cost. History is chock full of stories of those who have been shunned and punished for thinking for themselves—that is, thinking differently. This is as true today as it ever was, and it is certainly true of society in the US. Most of us develop keen radar for this; we learn to avoid open explorations of ideas in our discourse with others, lest we give offense. Intellectual timidity provides the path to safety and social coziness. In this manner, we lose the impulse to think deeply. One simply tows the party line. If you aspire to be a polite, socially-conditioned, highly successful automaton who thinks what he or she is supposed to think and who meets society's every expectation, then dispose of this book quickly and quietly. Clear, analytical, creative thinking is inherently radical. And it is not always appreciated. On the other hand, it is entertaining! One final note of caution: do not rely on anything I tell you in this book. I am not taking responsibility for your life. Take yourself seriously. I am simply a curmudgeonly philosopher. You, on the other hand, have a life to lead, full of attendant opportunities, risks and rewards. Make your own decisions.

DEDICATION

I dedicate this book to my daughters—Roxy, Kate, Sammy and Grace. My wife—Lisa—and I have home-schooled our daughters. This has not been out of some philosophical or religious predisposition, but because we thought it might provide them with a better education. Although home schooling is not for every family, it has served us well. While Lisa has done the bulk of the work, I have tried to assist where I can. It has turned out to be a grand intellectual adventure. The challenges of determining the best curriculum and manner in which to develop young minds are not only enormous, but personally rewarding. Through tracking my daughters' intellectual pursuits and interests, and working closely with them, I find myself rediscovering what is most meaningful and beautiful in life. I thank my daughters for this. Their energy, earnestness and deep curiosity inspire me. They are—each one of them—wonderful people who have a great deal to offer the world. I wrote this book for them in the hope that it may provide some modest assistance and stimulus as they seek to fulfill their individual and unique potential. Manifesting one's full capabilities and dimensions brings happiness. But this requires that one think for oneself. That is my simple hope for my daughters. Adventures of the mind—enabled by independent thought—will carry them to heights from which they can see beyond themselves and experience the joy of comprehending that each of us is part of a meaningful whole that is ultimately beyond our full comprehension. That is my hope for you too. Intellectual adventures are, in their very essence, spiritual adventures.

ACKNOWLEDGMENTS

Thanks first to Lisa, my wife, and to Roxy, Kate, Sammy and Grace, my children, for their ideas, advice, comments, editing, sacrifice, encouragement and love that made this book possible. Special thanks are due also to Larry Fisher, my brother, who has been an intellectual sparring partner throughout my life and has taught me a great deal. Essential thanks are also due to my Mom and Dad, shockingly rebellious thinkers themselves, who started me on the path to independent thought, and who then had to put up with it. My Dad died when I was 15, but I think he would be pleased with this book.

The many people who have shaped my thinking are due thanks, though no blame. In particular, my political views—which are hard to categorize—may be quite different than theirs, so please don't associate my eccentric thinking with them. The views expressed herein are uniquely mine, and reflect my journey, not theirs. By far, my most important teacher was a Jesuit priest—Father William Sampson. He honed my critical thinking skills, sharpened my writing, broadened my mind and taught me the power of critical questioning. In economics graduate school, it was in discussions with fellow student Rod Maddock that I became fascinated with the study of scientific methodology. I broadened my understanding of creative processes by working with Lynn Kremer, a colleague from the Theater Department at Holy Cross College, with whom I co-taught a course on "Political Economy through Performance Art." At Harvard Law School, I sharpened my legal, political and policy analyses in constant debate as well as collaborative projects with fellow student Barack Obama. (One of the more remarkable events of my life was having the privilege of becoming good friends with a man who would become the President of the United States.) As I reflect on these and other relationships that have defined my intellectual life, I realize how blessed I have been.

In developing the ideas in this book, I have relied on works of well-known and truly great thinkers. These include among others: Karl Popper,

Imre Lakatos, Paul Feyerabend, Thomas Kuhn, Milton Friedman, Friedrich von Hayek, Adam Smith, Karl Marx and Joseph Schumpeter. These thinkers captured my imagination in undergraduate and graduate school. To be sure, they don't all agree with one another—indeed, some are polar opposites. But they do have one thing in common; they are all bold, deep thinkers. And I admit it—that is what I admire. I don't pretend to claim these thinkers as authority for what I say, but I do want to emphasize that my best ideas are derivative. I read these authors at a formative stage, and have incorporated their insights into my own thinking. Thus, I may replicate some of their ideas and examples here without being aware of it. If I do so without attribution, it is unintentional.

I thank the following people for reading parts or all of the manuscript and providing helpful comments: Lisa Fisher, Roxy Fisher, Kate Fisher, Sammy Fisher, Grace Fisher, Gail Fisher, Larry Fisher, Arjo Klamer, Rod Maddock, John May, Cindy Moore, Ken Rothwell and Glenn Stern. There are also others who provided important assistance or comments and whom I thank.

TABLE OF CONTENTS

Part II
Collective Rationality (or Democracy as Discovery)

Part III
The Sound of a Flower Blooming

MEET MY COUNTERFOIL

You may notice as you read this book that I have a companion named **Bella.**
She helps me tell the story. She is pictured below.   Just by looking at her,
you can tell she was a big help.

Photograph by Roxy Fisher 1

The Nose Knows!

PREFACE

Bella: I never read prefaces; I like to get right to the meat of the matter.
Rob: Well, please read this one; it is integral to the book.
Bella: But I am a dog; I can't read anyway.
Rob: I sometimes wish you couldn't talk.
Bella: Be quiet. The book is beginning.
Rob: But it's my book!
Bella: Hush.

> *Long live impudence! It is my guardian angel in this world.*

> ALBERT EINSTEIN

INTELLECTUAL MISCHIEF—THE GREATEST ADVENTURE

This book is for the rebellious who want to use their minds, perhaps to stir up trouble or maybe just to have some fun—that's you, isn't it?

Bella: *No, I am just a dog.*

But you like mischief, don't you?

Bella: *Sure. Mischief is my middle name. But what kind of mischief do you mean?*

I mean the grandest kind of all—intellectual mischief. This book is an instruction manual on how to be playful with your mind. The great thing about such intellectual mischievousness is that it renders the universe your playground. And, perhaps surprisingly, it turns out that it is the most important ingredient to rationality. Embrace such playfulness. Not only will it provide you with a capacity for greater understanding, but it will make you happier. If the only thing I succeed in doing in this book is to convince you of the importance of playfulness to rationality, I will have accomplished a great deal. It is a key ingredient in thinking, creating and working constructively with others. Indeed, it provides the very essence of thinking.

Bella: *But perhaps the reader thinks she already knows how to think, as proven by the fact that she is now thinking that.*

Yes. It's kind of like the French philosopher Rene Descartes, who said "I think, therefore I am," only the reader has amended this to say, "I think I think, therefore I think!"

Bella: *Descartes once walked into a restaurant. The waiter said: "Rene, would you like something to drink?" Descartes replied "I think not"— and disappeared.*

Thank you—Bella—for that bit of mischief. Of course, when I say that I will be providing you—the reader—with a theory of how to think, I am not talking about the mere act of thinking, but rather a dynamic way of using questions, ideas and arguments to explore the world. If you begin to use these tools as active implements of exploration, you will have launched yourself on the greatest of adventures. With these tools you can explore just about anything, whether it be science, religion, art, history, love, revolution or spirituality. Such are the powers of rational thought when properly applied.

Rationality has the power of radical transformation. Indeed, it is the means by which we are empowered to change ourselves. With each new concept you acquire, you see things in a different way. And the journey never ends. Rationality carries you to ever new shores of thought. You are Magellan about to circumnavigate the globe—who knows what you will see?

Bella: *That is a bad example. Magellan didn't go around the world; he was killed in the Philippines. It was his crew that made it around the world.*

Good point, Bella.

Rational discourse, as epitomized by the historical development of science, is the most powerful discovery of humankind. These tools began to find their expression with the ancient Greeks, but faded during the Dark Ages. They were then reborn in the Renaissance (which means re-birth) and flourished with the Enlightenment. They were developed to free individuals to think for themselves and to question authority in all forms. They were developed to empower us to change ourselves. Their proliferation marks the beginning of an era of phenomenal progress in human affairs. These tools form the basis of the scientific revolution, the protestant revolution, the founding of the United States of America and modern capitalism. They constitute the foundation of individual and spiritual freedom. It all begins and ends with questioning authority. Unfortunately, as a society, it may be a set of tools we are on the verge of losing—but more on that later.

This book is an exploration in the nature of rationality. How does knowledge grow across time? What is it, if anything, that makes science special and different from other pursuits? What does it mean to be rational? And what are powers, scope and limits of rationality? Can the tools of rationality be wielded by anybody, or are they restricted to experts? Is there such a thing as non-scientific knowledge? If so, how does it grow? Where does rationality fit in with democracy, politics and economics? What is the relationship between scientific knowledge and the spiritual? How does rationality give us the power to change ourselves? That is our agenda for this book. The purpose of the book is to hand these tools on to you, so that they may proliferate—so that you can wield them better than I have.

Bella: *Is this really a political book in disguise? Are you a left-wing or right-wing ideologue trying to infect my mind? Because I can tell you right now, I am only in my comfort zone when I am reading dog-centric authors, and I am not sure you are dog-centric enough for me.*

I admit from the start that my book is insufficiently dog-centric. Moreover, I do not pretend that this is not a dangerous book from a political perspective. No—let's be clear. This is a dangerous book to anyone who wants to remain myopically dog-centric. I will argue in this book that epistemology—which is the study of how we know things—and politics and economics are intricately interrelated. I believe that if your epistemology changes, so too may your politics. A lot of politics is driven by what we think we know and what processes we trust from an epistemological perspective.

That being said, the "politics" of this book is hard to categorize. As you are probably aware, politics has a spectrum that is divided into "Left" and "Right", which I'll talk about later in the book. People from either end of the political spectrum are likely to find things in this book with which they disagree and also with which they agree. I do believe that—regardless of your politics—the epistemological perspective that I am trying to convey in this book will make you a more powerful thinker. I am not trying the change your politics, but your epistemology.

My own politics has shifted during my lifetime—back and forth across the political spectrum—so I find it hard to categorize myself with simplistic labels, but let me put it this way: I do admit to being a fervent believer in freedom of speech, the importance of questioning authority in all forms, the beauty of science and technology, the power and efficacy of allocating resources through markets, the preeminent importance of fully democratic institutions, the centrality of liberty, property and tolerance to a healthy society that embraces individual freedom, the guiding role that spirituality should play in our lives as well as the notion that there is a struggle between good and evil in the world in which each of us needs to pull our weight. I have no idea where that puts me on the political spectrum, as I find I usually upset people with my views regardless of their placement upon the political spectrum. At times they say to me, "I don't believe that you believe what you are saying." I assure you that, generally, I do believe what I am saying. But since people like labels, I think the above set of beliefs should have one, so I am going to call myself a Fisherite. Nay, you can call me a radical Fisherite, if you like. If you believe all those things I enumerated, then you are a Fisherite too.

As you read this book, you will find that I have quite strong views on some things, and I will happily share those with you. It is my book, after all. In general, however, I believe that formulating bold positions, and expressing and sharing them in a bold form, is one of the keys to deepening your own knowledge, as it is the best way to evoke the constructive criticism by which one grows in knowledge. I will speak as boldly as I would hope you do. However, in doing so, I am not trying to convince you that my general views are correct. Indeed, I am sure I am mistaken about many things, and that there is much error in this book. But I do have an ambitious goal; it is to help you build your own intellectual tool kit with which you can figure out the world out for yourself. I am trying to convince you to adopt a particular way of approaching knowledge—an approach that entails assessing evidence, crafting bold guesses, seeking and embracing criticism, formulating and reacting constructively to argument and collecting and wielding fruitful ideas. Most importantly, it is an approach that demands that you place yourself at the center of the discourse—that is, that you enter into the knowledge process and make it your own. In sum, I want you to think for yourself and I want you to think boldly.

THE SAND TRAP OF SCIENTISM

I have a friend who takes science as the ultimate arbiter of reality—or, at least, that is how I read him. From that position, he appears to conclude—with a visceral certainty—that there is no God. I think my friend is caught in an intellectual trap shaped by a misunderstanding of both science and God, leaving him lost to the wonders of each. If life were a golf fairway, you might say he is stuck in a sand trap. This particular sand trap—a misapplication of the scope of science—is called "scientism". It is the view that science is the final arbiter of all true and meaningful things. I wondered: what kind of an intellectual wedge is needed to lift him out of that sand trap?

As I continued to mull this over, I started to think about the many intellectual traps that are inherent in modern thought. I realized that I had something to say on the topic and that I wanted to convey an intellectual toolset to my daughters with which they might address these conundrums. I believe there is something fundamentally wrong with the modern mindset. It is an oddly subservient mindset that sees the essence of rationality merely as embracing the pronouncements of experts. In this same vein, it has a way of approaching ideas and knowledge that excludes normal people from the process. Indeed, this exclusion of normal folks from important discourse is the very hallmark of modern mindset. In this light, the modern mindset sees democracy not as playing any particular role in rational discourse, but rather being at tension with it. While democracy is, of course, seen as a "good thing", it is nonetheless viewed as something that needs guidance and to be cabined and informed by the more educated among us—that is, the elite. The modern mindset also seems to bias our thinking toward an empty view with respect to the meaning of our lives, as if life—and the great choices we confront in each of our lives—were all a matter of mere preferences and myopic hedonism with nothing more to it than that. It is a mindset that suppresses mystery. In reflecting upon these things, I realized that I am not a modern person.

Bella: *Neither am I.*

Indeed, this is not a modern book. You have been warned. I also realized, upon reflection, that my disagreements with the modern mindset entail a complicated set of interrelated arguments that would require careful articulation if it were to serve successfully as both as an antidote for the limited bandwidth of modern thought and an entrée to the true powers of discovery—for both an individual and a democracy—embodied in the application of rationality, so I wrote this book. This book is like a big puzzle. All of the parts relate to one another. And some of the parts are difficult. I hope you will patiently work through some of the technical details that I provide. I hope you take the time to put the pieces together. Ultimately, I am making an argument about how you should relate to the world. I don't think you will find this argument—in its entirety—anyplace else. That is why I felt compelled to write the book for you.

In my view, the false confidence of scientism blinds us to the mysteries and the meaning of life, and thereby impoverishes us—leaving us feeling alone in an empty and meaningless universe. Yet, ironically, the tools of science that purportedly shape the modern mindset, when properly grasped and employed wisely, have the potential to propel each of us into ever more joyful journeys of discovery, taking us beyond ourselves and deeper into the mysteries that surround us. I want my daughters to be free of the intellectual shackles that confine what passes for modern thinking. I want them to be open and courageous critical thinkers who use rationality to explore the world around them creatively, but who ultimately understand there is much in the world that science, with its utilitarian yet valuable insights, is too limited to encompass—things such as love, beauty, joy, sacrifice, duty, meaning and truth itself. I want them to understand that the invisible is real. I want them to be unconstrained by the false emptiness of the modernist horizon and bold enough to make independent and thoughtful choices that will shape meaningful journeys in their own lives. I want them to ask hard questions of everyone—including themselves—and with respect to each and every body of thought they encounter. And I want them to recognize that there is not only good, but also evil in the world—a thought that the modernist cannot fathom—and yet a reality with which we each of us must personally grapple if we are to be good people. I want that for you too.

There is a struggle in every human heart between good and evil. We greatly disadvantage the potential for good if we do not explicitly recognize that struggle, and it is the very lack of recognition of the existence of that struggle that accounts for much evil. In sum, I want my daughters to love and embrace both science and God. Indeed, in my experience, it has been through the very application of rationality that I occasionally catch a glimpse of the sacred. Rationality—when properly applied—blurs the boundaries of our individuality and renders us part of something larger. It not only enhances our thinking, but also ennobles our spirits.

MY FIRST FIELD OF GOURDS

I grew up on a tobacco and cattle farm. One year, I decided to cultivate a half acre of gourds. That is a pretty big piece of land from a suburban point of view; about the size of a very large lot. With my parent's permission, I plowed the land myself, pounded the stakes in the ground, ran wire between the stakes, planted the gourd seeds, weeded my vast garden, guided the vines up across the wires and, ultimately, harvested a large quantity of gourds—indeed, they filled about 20 sacks. My parents and older brother were a little skeptical about the whole project, but not critical of it. They knew I was an eccentric kid, after all.

Now, as you may know, you can't eat gourds, and while they do come in all kinds of fantastical shapes and colors, they don't have the grace and elegance of, say, flowers. In other words, at first blush, they appear pretty useless. But you can cure them, in which case they last almost forever, and you can paint them as well. The long-handled ones make very elegant dippers, if you happen to have a well in need of a dipper. One can make Christmas decorations out of them. (I did.) One can make very nice birdhouses out of them. (I did.) One can even balance them on one's head or juggle them. (I did.)

Bella: *Are they good for chewing?*

Oh yes.

🥒 I left my field of gourds and went on to spend a great deal of my life studying and collecting abstract ideas—from mathematics, philosophy of science, economics, political theory, theater and law—many of which, at first blush, can seem useless as well. But the manner in which abstractions can suddenly and surprisingly yield useful and powerful insights has always 🥒 allured me. This book is my second field of gourds. It is my collection of the beautiful odds and ends of thought that I have collected across a lifetime. You'll find that some of them have odd shapes and colors. Like my first field of gourds, these ideas are a garden of discovery. But you will find that the roots of the plants in my garden are all interconnected. It is a garden with a theme. The theme is the means by which we explore ideas and make discoveries. Those are my roots.

I have always had this intuitive notion that to go deeper into anything, one had to come at it from a variety of unexpected angles. While I am very concerned with the solutions to practical problems, I have always felt that to develop creative solutions one had to go to the intellectual roots that shape the way we think about problems in the first place. I believe the fresh answers lie in a field of gourds. Indeed, sometimes the only thing that will do is a gourd. That is my faith, although my mom is still shaking her head and saying (as comedian Bill Cosby might put it) "What's wrong with that boy?" Welcome to my field of gourds.

As you will have gleaned from the dedication and the above, I wrote this book primarily for my daughters—but I am delighted that you are reading it as well! You may also note that, in general, I will use the pronoun "she" as opposed to "he" in this book when I am describing a generic person. In providing editorial comments on the book, my brother commented that he found this "jarringly feminist" and that it tended to "disrupt the reader's train of thought ... unless intended specifically for [my] daughters", in which case I should say so. I admit that I sometimes find such usage jarring as well, but I assure any reader that might otherwise have her train of thought disrupted by my generic use of the pronoun "she" that I am not trying to change the world and that such usage is specifically intended for my daughters.

My daughters and I grew a new field of gourds this summer and we are currently in the process of curing them. I think some of them may end up on our Christmas tree this year. I highly recommend growing a field of gourds yourself.

PART I

RATIONAL PURSUITS (OR HOW THE NOSE KNOWS)

in which we explore the nature and limitations of knowledge. Epistemology constitutes theories about how we know things and what we can know. It matters more than you might think. Our epistemological views shape us in profound ways—sometimes to the good and sometimes to the bad. I will argue that they determine how each of us thinks about ourselves as well as our role in the world. Epistemological views influence our views on economics, art, politics, democracy and religion. Because most people's epistemological views are muddled, their views on these other topics are also sometimes muddled.

1

AN ANCIENT TREASURE HUNT

Blind respect for authority is the greatest enemy of truth.
ALBERT EINSTEIN

*No one can be a great thinker who does not recognize that as a thinker
it is his first duty to follow his intellect to whatever conclusions it may
lead. Truth gains more even by the errors of one who, with due study and
preparation, thinks for himself, than by the true opinions of those who
only hold them because they do not suffer themselves to think.*
JOHN STUART MILL

*Sic Semper Tyrannis
("Thus Always to Tyrants")*
Virginia State Motto

You are invited on a treasure hunt—the hunt for the keys to knowledge. A Jesuit priest once told me a fascinating tale involving this ancient treasure hunt. The Jesuits are an order of Roman Catholic priests who are well known as thinkers and teachers. Indeed, the adjective "jesuitical" has come to mean clever thinking, although sometimes with a connotation of excessive analysis and manipulation. Historically, the Jesuits have been sometimes controversial, although always formidable. I was educated by Jesuits in high school, and throughout my life I have been influenced by the way that they ask tough questions and encourage one to think for oneself. I was told by one Jesuit priest that the Jesuits used to have a specific method for teaching people how to think analytically—not what to think, mind you, but how to think cleverly about anything. What intellectual gold that must have been! He also told me that this intellectual treasure had been lost. As a religious order, the Jesuits were specifically founded to directly serve the Pope. However, there was a brief period of time when the then-current Pope decided to suppress the Jesuits. It was during this period of disruption that the method that the Jesuits had developed for teaching people how to think was lost.

I have always been fascinated by this story. I don't even know if it's true, but that doesn't really matter for my present purposes. It is the idea that I love. I am in search of that lost treasure—not the specifics of what the Jesuits may have developed (although that would be nice), but rather its substance and spirit—its main ingredients. What is the most powerful approach to thinking that enables us to advance our understanding of the world? And by the "world" here, I don't mean just the physical world, but our total environment, including our social world. It should be noted that there is nothing peculiarly Roman Catholic in seeking such treasure, even if the Jesuits were on the same mission. Indeed, my ideas about thinking come not from that bit of history, but from the study of science, and how it grows.

The essence of rational thought—at its most powerful—can be identified by looking at the way in which science advances. I'll talk extensively in this book about how science works—what we can know, and what we cannot know, and how it is that we know what we know, or don't know what we think we might know. This is called "epistemology." The word epistemology comes from the Greek word episteme, which simply means knowledge. I will argue in this book that the rational core of science, when properly understood, provides us with a broader theory on how to think more critically, how to be creative and how to work more constructively with others. This rational core can be applied well beyond science. It teaches us how to explore ideas generally. It also teaches us something about the nature of economic systems, when they are working well, and, indeed, even about democracy as an ideal. I will argue in this book that epistemology, economics, politics, and even your personal and spiritual development are all wrapped together and interrelated in a rather unexpected way. What links them is the process of discovery—at least, when those processes are working well and at their best. We will seek that ancient treasure in this book—how to explore the world of ideas in the most powerful way.

SCIENCE HAS BEEN BOTH OVERSOLD AND UNDERSOLD

Everybody has a view about what science is, even if she is not consciously aware of it. We are inundated with views on science—and on what is knowable and not knowable—from when we are toddlers. It is built into how we talk about things. And what we think about science shapes our view of what it means to be rational. It shapes what we believe, what we think is possible, and what we think is nonsense. It shapes who we trust and do not trust. Indeed, it shapes a person's philosophy of life and her spirituality. Ideas about the nature of science permeate our world view, yet often in ways that are unexamined and even unwarranted.

In fact, most people do not have a firm grasp on what science is and how and why it works as it does. As a consequence, given the deep influence of science in shaping our thought, their thinking is confused not only about the nature of science, but much more broadly. By doing some careful thinking about the nature of science, we can both free our minds from false traps and yet take full advantage of its rational core.

Bella: *But that doesn't sound any fun. Rationalism is so dry and boring. Where is the passion? Where is the excitement of, say, pursuing a furry little creature?*

Bella, you are wrong about that. You will see that the notion of rationality that I offer in this book has passion at its very core. Discovery is a creative process that requires the participation of the full person.

Bella: *Or dog?*

Or dog, of course. It is fully as fun as chasing little furry creatures, I assure you.

But, as I was saying, science has been both oversold and undersold in terms of what it can teach us. It has been undersold in that its approach is thought to be restricted to "scientific" topics, construed narrowly. I will argue in this book that the rational core of science can be fruitfully applied well beyond the range of topics we normally deem to be "science." That doesn't mean that we will be applying the scientific method per se to everything, but rather that we will be applying the concept of rational interactive discourse more broadly—even to art! When we grasp the rational core of science, we will see that it is based on a peculiar interaction of questions, bold guesses and probing evidence. We will also come to see that this method of discovery—driven by the interaction of questions, guesses and evidence—can be applied beyond science. Whether or not you want to be a scientist, you need to understand how science works, because it will give you a much deeper appreciation of both the possibilities and limits of thought generally as well as expanding, I believe, your sense of your own possibilities.

But science has also been oversold in the sense that it is often taken as the final arbiter of all truths—and of reality itself. It is taken as the final measure of what is possible. The view is that: if science doesn't say it's so, it cannot be so. Scientific knowledge is treated as constituting the full sum and substance of valuable human thought, beyond which nothing can be known. The rest of human mental activity is deemed as mere preferences, tastes, and eccentricities, but not deemed to have much substance or import beyond that. Indeed, the haughty conclusion by some that we have an empty, amoral and Godless universe—and that anyone who thinks differently is ignorant and unsophisticated—is driven by the mistaken view that what is knowable is only knowable through science. This view misconstrues science, and what it can do for us.

Bella: *But what about philosophy and religion and the arts and the humanities, including history? Those aren't exactly science, but don't some people take those seriously?*

People do. But many people also look at those pursuits as dominated by tastes and preferences. There is deep-seated belief that those activities lack the kind of authority that science is believed to possess. Science is viewed as "about reality" while the other activities are viewed as mere entertainment or at least as highly personalized judgment-laden perspectives that lack the objectivity of pure science. Non-scientific pursuits are seen as lacking the epistemological seriousness of science. In short, science is king. While not everyone thinks about it this way, it does reflect the tone of our times. This tone is important and, I believe, misleading. Among other things, it discourages people from pursuing seriously the kind of deep understanding that results from the non-scientific—yet interactively rational—explorations that characterize history, literature, the arts and religious or philosophical contemplation. Indeed, I believe that this dichotomization of explorations into scientific and non-scientific is itself false and misleading.

Now, don't get me wrong. Science is extremely useful and important, and it is (largely) driven by rational processes. But the modern perspective takes science as a body of established truth. This static view of the nature of science is mistaken. The prowess of science lies not in its authority, but in the process by which it continues to challenge authority. Rationality lies not in believing established truths, but rather in the evidentiary based manner by which one questions and challenges seeming truths to ultimately replace them with yet deeper insight. It is not a "body" but rather a process. It is dynamic. By its very nature, science is neither comprehensive in its scope, nor completely authoritative in its content. Indeed, science often, and in fact typically, has not really proven what it thinks it knows. That is, scientific results typically do not constitute knowledge in the specific sense of constituting proven truth.

Bella: *How can that be?*

First, we know that science can't prove with absolute certainty because science lacks any method to do so. You may find that surprising. We will explore this point thoroughly in the following chapters. We will find that science, as valuable as it is, constitutes no more than tentative guesses, and simply does not have the power to exclude many "non-scientific" views of reality. Second, however, we know that scientific knowledge is not certain by virtue of the fact that the history of science is constituted by a never ending series of revolutions in which one set of purported scientific truths is overturned by another. We will explore some historical examples of this.

There is no reason to think we are at a point in history where the scientific revolutions will cease. Indeed, we may be on the verge of great discoveries in physics that will challenge and overturn long-held and fundamental scientific beliefs. We just don't know. Indeed, recently, we were hit with some tantalizing science news. For about 100 years physicists have maintained that nothing can travel faster than the speed of light. In 2011, some scientists appeared to have discovered particles that did travel faster than that. They ran the experiments repeatedly, and continued to obtain the same result. The evidence was so disturbing that it made world news and continued to be assessed. As it turned out, someone eventually figured out that the observations were due to some sort of measurement problem. What was important, however, was that science was open to the possibility of another revolution. Our scientific beliefs are not maintained because they are established truth, but rather because they are the best explanations that we currently have. Great scientists are always open to the possibility that we may have it wrong. We never know for sure what new developments in science will bring us, and turn what we thought we knew on its head. Indeed, as this example attests, even what we think of as "observations" in science are themselves dependent on other theories and on equipment that may turn out to have problems. We will see that nothing is certain in science—even if it often feels that way and even if it makes eminent sense to rely on scientific results in our decision-making—at least, for the time being. I will argue in this book that a false sense of authority in science leads not only to bad science, but also to an impoverished view of the possibilities of the universe.

Indeed, in my view, precisely because many people (mistakenly) view science as the absolute authority on the nature of reality, they turn away from religion and spiritual pursuits. Yet there is nothing in science—and there never could be anything in science given its nature—that demonstrates that there is no God. Nor could science ever demonstrate that, say, God does not actively intervene in the world in answer to prayer. There is simply nothing in the scientific process that speaks to those issues. Of course, scientists as scientists prefer not to explain things in terms of divine intervention. But this is not because that may not be the case, but rather simply because that approach doesn't yield explanations that humans can do much with. That is, it is an important discipline within the scientific community to try to explain everything in non-spiritual terms, because that constitutes the most likely path to developing knowledge that will give us power over our environment. In other words, it is a very practical assumption from a methodological perspective in that it will stimulate the greatest progress in yielding usable knowledge that can be applied to imminently practical problems. But it is nonetheless just that—an assumption to guide our methods. Spiritual explanations, of course, do not yield the same predictable power over the world of our senses that scientific explanations do. That is not their purpose.

I have to say that I am always shocked by the manner in which many people make the illogical leap that just because science can make a prediction about something it has a lock on the full nature of the underlying reality—and that somehow this excludes the spiritual. Just because some scientist has come up with an equation that makes useful predictions about some complex aspect of the universe does not mean that we have grasped the full reality. In general, scientific tools aren't designed to tell us much if anything about the ultimate nature of things or about, say, the myriad possible meaningful and spiritual connections among people. From a purely logical perspective, there is nothing in science that crowds out mystery, spirituality or God from the universe.

As noted above, the fact that spiritual explanations and prayer are not part of the scientific method makes perfect sense. But it would be foolish to conclude from the very practical set of assumptions that undergirds scientific discourse that they somehow imply that the spiritual realm does not exist or does not harbor its own meaning and reality. For very practical reasons stated above, we don't want scientists explaining the world in terms of God's interventions. That is not their job. On the other hand, the fact that religious beliefs are not a sensible starting place for science doesn't speak to spiritual truths in any way. Scientists as scientists have no business—literally—telling us what is possible in religious terms, just as priests, ministers, rabbis, imams and others who promote religious views have no particular advantage in telling us what is possible in terms of scientific explanation. At its best, science sheds light on how the world works—in a very superficial but also extremely useful way. It facilitates useful predictions. But it sheds no direct light on the ultimate meaning of our lives or the deep connections that may lie beyond our scientific toolkit. Other than on the most superficial level, the supposed conflict between science and religion is a false one. As you begin to understand better how science actually works, this will become clear.

THE CULT OF EXPERTISM

As we will see in this book, concomitant with the many successes of modern science, the ideal of rationally-derived knowledge has been turned on its head and become an instrument by which independent thought is suppressed. Science is viewed as static and authoritative. As such, its results are not to be questioned. Cadres of trained experts, bureaucrats and academics are the new oligarchs who earn their keep by wielding "knowledge." To be "rational" is to follow their dictates, for they are the keepers of knowledge. The success of science proves it. Individual citizens are not to be trusted with such responsibilities. There is a new set of high priests in town—a new feudalism.

The dominant epistemology of our time propagandizes us to believe that it is the "experts" who have all the knowledge. They are the ones who are supposed to do the thinking! They take the results of their expert analysis and convey it to us, and we pay them for this service. It is their job to produce knowledge and our position is to consume it. Just like we generally find it more efficient to buy vegetables at the grocery store rather than grow them for ourselves, so too—according to the modern mindset— we are supposed to give up the province of thought itself to specialists and experts. This modern view constitutes a new kind of feudalism—with everyone put in their epistemological place. It is important to understand that certain epistemologies—and ways of thinking about the nature of knowledge and science and who should control them—actually constitute methods for controlling people.

Now, mind you, controlling people is not always bad, and there are many times, places and situations to defer to others' thinking, expertise and wisdom. I don't want you thinking naively that, say, a poison is not a poison simply because you have decided to think for yourself about it. That would be monstrously foolish. Arsenic is arsenic no matter what you think about it, and its power to poison is unaffected by your opinions. There is a reality out there and it is generally unforgiving. Indeed, there is no doubt that a lot of independent thinking is simply bad thinking. Suggesting that you begin to think for yourself is not meant to preclude you from having the thought that, on occasion, it might be best to defer to the expertise of others, or even to the wisdom of your elders. A goal of this book is to enhance your sense of how you can use your own intelligence and thinking capacity in an intelligent way.

I was taking a walk one day on the Mall in Washington, DC, and thinking about how to encourage independent thinking. I encountered a man who was mumbling about various conspiracies, and who held up a sign concerning an imminent invasion by aliens. I thought to myself: this is certainly an independent thinker. Yet, he was not exactly what I had in mind. I realized that it's not independence per se that is important. What is important is critical independent thought—that is, thought that is both imaginative in seeing possibilities while simultaneously tightly focused on evidence as a means of sorting among possibilities. And it is thinking that takes full advantage of the great thinking that has come before. This is not to say that aliens might not invade—but I doubt whether this man had any good evidence of the imminence of such an invasion.

Bella: *Very few people are aware of this, but Martians actually look a great deal like Great Danes.*

I certainly am aware of that fact, as the evidence stands before me.

While there are innumerable times, places and circumstances in which you do want to defer to an expert, nonetheless, I shall argue in this book that the authoritarian view of knowledge, with its attendant cult of expertism, is not only palpably wrong in its purported epistemology (that is, its theory of knowledge), but is essentially corrupt; it creates inefficient flows of income to those who haven't really earned it and don't really deserve it. Unfortunately, this epistemology—even though quite mistaken—has become the "common sense" of our time. It is a trap from which few escape.

It does us great harm. The proponents of "expertism" are myopic, oppressive, egotistical and driven by self-interest. But the harm runs far deeper than their expropriation of power and economic returns that go beyond their genuine contributions and merit. This authoritarian view of knowledge infiltrates our minds, fragments and impoverishes our intellectual capacity and robs us of our freedom of thought. It thereby weakens not only our thinking, but also our personal capability to explore and enjoy what the world has to offer. Indeed, by biasing whose expressions of ideas are taken seriously, expertism undermines democracy itself and thereby undermines our collective capacity to address our most serious challenges with the best ideas. It renders citizens less knowledgeable, less fruitfully engaged with the world, less fulfilled and ultimately less capable of navigating modern life and pursuing happiness. It leaves us with an empty and amoral universe, taking away the capacity for wonder that brings us closer to God. In this book, I refute this authoritarian view of knowledge. In its stead, I share with you a simple intellectual toolkit which will empower you to explore the world for yourself.

THREE KEY COMPONENTS TO INDEPENDENT THINKING

In this book, I argue that there are three key components to independent thinking: (1) mastering what I will call the "logic of discovery", (2) collecting fruitful concepts or ideas that can be applied broadly and wielded creatively, and (3) committing yourself to exploratory processes thereby taking responsibility for the active construction of your own understanding of the world.

THE LOGIC OF DISCOVERY

To identify the "logic of discovery"—that is, the secret to how knowledge grows—we will look at the history of science as well as draw heavily from many excellent works in the philosophy of science. The vision of science as entailing a dynamic logic of discovery was developed most extensively by two philosophers of science—Karl Popper and Imre Lakatos—and I have been heavily influenced by their thinking. I will argue that this logic of discovery can be applied well beyond the realm of science. There are six essential elements to the process:

(1) A defined **question**, purpose, task or mission;
(2) Conjectures—that is, educated **guesses** consistent with what has been observed so far—that are intended as potential answers to a question, or intended actions to fulfill a purpose, mission or task;
(3) Criteria—or at least a **sensibility**—for what constitutes im-provement in answering a defined question or in accomplishing a defined task, mission or purpose;
(4) **Criticism** (with specificity) of those conjectures as to the manner in which they do or do not answer a particular question or accomplish a task, mission or purpose;

(5) **New conjectures** responsive to the criticism; and

(6) **New questions, directions** or purposes in light of the criticism and new conjectures.

In essence, these steps will constitute our theory of how to think productively and creatively about anything. At this stage of the book, I don't expect you to fully grasp or appreciate these steps, which can be found in all fruitful knowledge processes. In the context of a scientific inquiry, however, let me briefly expand on them.

In science, we start with a question. We make guesses as to the best answer to the question, keeping our guesses consistent with what has been observed thus far. We criticize our tentative guesses to see where those guesses fail in their mission. This may be done through experimentation. Having identified failures in our tentative answers, we then try to improve upon them through further conjecturing. In this manner, the process continues, and we continue to strive to improve our scientific understanding of the world.

I will expand on this considerably, of course. But there are a couple of things worth noting. First, this is a dynamic theory of knowledge. That is, the focus is not on proving propositions, but rather on the process by which knowledge is improved. Second, this theory of knowledge emphasizes the importance and constructive role of both conjectures—that is, educated guesses—and criticism to the growth of knowledge. The first component in becoming an independent thinker is mastering this logic of discovery, grasping the importance of both imagination and criticism to the growth of knowledge and developing the ability to apply this "logic" to all things.

FRUITFUL CONCEPTS

The second component to becoming an independent thinker is to collect and master concepts that are sufficiently powerful in their scope and application that they may justly be deemed "fruitful". By a "fruitful" idea, I mean fundamental concepts or structures or sets of interrelated concepts that find repeated application across different applications, disciplines or areas of knowledge. In other words, it is a tool of thought that can be applied widely. In science, such sets of interrelated fruitful ideas are sometimes called research programs, as we will see in later chapters. As we will see, Newton's universal law of gravitation and his three laws of motion constitute such a research program. More generally, a fruitful idea goes beyond the facts, and gives you a way of framing many different phenomena. Fruitful ideas are generally associated with the recognition of deep-seated structures or patterns that have repeated application. The power of this approach is rather obvious.

Bella: *Precisely what is it that makes an idea fruitful?*

Two things: First, and crucially, as I just noted, the idea must have wide application beyond the context in which you find it. It must be an idea or set of interrelated ideas that give you a tool with which you can actively explore the world—a structure you will be able to recognize and exploit in different contexts. The odd thing about fruitful ideas is that you see them crop up again and again in different situations that may at first seem dissimilar, but the fruitful concept allows you to see the hidden similarity. That kind of an idea changes how you think about things, and in so doing changes you. Indeed, it has the potential to change the world. Great concepts are like fruit trees—that is, they continue to bear fruit over and over again. The most fruitful ideas are those that cut across disciplines, or that permit wide application within a discipline.

The notion of fruitful concepts or structures that cut across disciplines, or have surprisingly wide application, is best captured in a passage from the anthropologist Gregory Bateson:

> I picked up a vague mystical feeling that we must look for the same sort of processes in all fields of natural phenomena – that we might expect to find the same sort of laws at work in the structure of a crystal as in the structure of society, or that the segmentation of an earthworm might really be comparable to the process by which basalt pillars are formed.

> I should not preach this mystical faith in quite those terms today but would say rather that I believe that the types of mental operation which are useful in analyzing one field may be equally useful in another—that the framework ... of science, rather than the framework of Nature, is the same

in all fields. But the more mystical phrasing of the matter was what I vaguely learnt, and it was of paramount importance. It lent a certain dignity to any scientific investigation, implying that when I was analyzing the patterns of partridges' feathers, I might really get an answer or a bit of an answer to the whole puzzling business of pattern and regularity in nature. And further, this bit of mysticism was important because it gave me freedom to use my scientific background, the ways of thought that I had picked up in biology and elementary physics and chemistry; it encouraged me to expect these ways of thought to fit in with very different fields of observation. It enabled me to regard all my training as potentially useful rather than utterly irrelevant to anthropology.[1]

The poet William Blake put this notion more simply:
To see a world in a grain of sand
And heaven in a wild flower
Hold infinity in the palm of your hand
And eternity in an hour.
Or as Walt Whitman captured it:

I believe a leaf of grass is no less than the journey-work of the stars.

The collection of concepts with the most general application include epistemology itself and, of course, mathematics. No one is truly well educated unless they have been exposed to and mastered a good dose of mathematics. The theory of rational discourse that this book explores itself embodies a set of interrelated "fruitful" concepts—that is concepts that can be applied across many disciplines. Economics has many ideas that cut across disciplines, and is thus also a font of fruitful ideas. That is why I love it so. The arts often deal in ideas with an element of universality—that is why they are so fruitful within our lives and have the capacity to inspire. In sum, the first criterion of a fruitful idea is wide and perhaps unexpected applications.

Second, a fruitful idea should have beauty to it. That is, it must tickle the mind. I know that this is surprising and doesn't seem like it should be an important epistemological criterion, but it is.

Bella: *Why is beauty important?*

I honestly don't know, but it is. Perhaps it's because beauty helps you remember a concept, and see it reflected in the world. But I think it is deeper than that. I think we are wired to see beauty in the ideas we need. I have tried in this book to introduce some fruitful ideas from my personal collection of favorites. Enjoy their beauty.

In order to give you a clear understanding of what I mean by a fruitful idea, I will provide you with an example from economics. In economics, the idea of "opportunity cost" involves the insight that the true cost of anything is not the resources, time or money you expend on it, but rather the benefits lost by not doing the best alternative thing that you might have done with the resources, time or money. Let's say exam week is coming up and you decide to keep studying history for an extra hour—simply because you like history so much—even though you already know it well. And let's also say that what you really need to be studying is your math. In that scenario, the cost of that extra hour of study of history is not the hour of time per se, but the foregone benefit you would have received by studying your math instead, since that would have been the best thing to do with that time.

In 1748, Benjamin Franklin captured the idea of opportunity cost in his Advice to a Young Tradesman.

Bella: *Did he ever write any Advice to a Young Dog?*

Not that I know of.

Bella: *Another humanist no doubt. You humans are so human-centric! Did you ever think that a dog may have opportunity cost as well. For example, if I am chewing a bone, I can't be chasing a squirrel. Life is cruel in its trade-offs.*

Yes. At any rate, Mr. Franklin states:

> Remember, that time is money. He that can earn ten shillings a day by his labor, and … sits idle, one half of that day … has really spent, or rather thrown away, five shillings … Remember, that credit is money. If a man lets his money lie in my hands after it is due, he gives me the interest, or so much as I can make of it during that time.

Franklin is expressing here the concept of opportunity cost. If you are idle, and you could have been making 5 shillings with your time, then that is the cost of your idleness. If you let money sit idle and you <u>could</u> have been earning interest on it, then that is the cost of not employing that money to earn interest.

The idea of opportunity cost finds application in numerous situations and disciplines, and thus it may be deemed a fruitful idea. Engineers who design things have to think about the fact that a design intended solely to address one particular type of structural challenge may, in fact, create other types of challenges or problems. In such a case, you may think of the opportunity cost of one particular design in terms of the design benefits foregone in the best alternative design.

For example, we could certainly design a car in which almost no one would ever die from a crash. This could be done by armor-plating cars, placing an automatic fire extinguisher under the driver's seat and rigging the vehicles to go no faster than 10 miles per hour and not to run unless the driver is wearing a helmet, a cross-shoulder harness and a fire-resistant suit. Of course, such a car would deliver you to your destination much more slowly (generating the opportunity cost associated with that lost time) and would cost a fortune (generating the opportunity cost associated with that expenditure) and would be ugly (generating the opportunity cost of foregone visual pleasure) and uncomfortable (generating the opportunity cost of the foregone comfort) and less fuel efficient (generating the opportunity cost of less fuel use and less pollution) and would be much more dangerous on impact for pedestrians and bicyclists (generating the opportunity cost of forgoing less severe injuries and fewer deaths for others).

In sum, opportunity cost is a simple but powerful idea that can be applied to many things. It is a fruitful idea. An independent thinker looks for such concepts and collects them—indeed, cherishes them. We will also find that, at the end of the day, science is really about collecting and applying fruitful ideas as well. In science, they are known as research programs—that is, sets of interrelated concepts that have predictive power and are susceptible of wide application, further development and improvement in terms of their predictive content. And they certainly are beautiful.

In this book, I will try to introduce some fruitful ideas from the realms of economics, politics, law and the arts, although the scope of this book limits what I can do in that regard, of course. It is really your job—as you study different disciplines—to look for such ideas and incorporate them into your thinking processes. I do hope to give you a sense of how to recognize them.

A CALL TO INDEPENDENT THINKING

The third ingredient to independent thinking is to realize that you are the agency and catalyst of discovery. Your mission in life—should you decide to accept it—is to go where you have not gone before—to enter into the wonderful exploratory activities that surround you, and to partake of them by contributing to them. It is crucial that you grasp this. Your understanding of the world isn't a commodity to be purchased, or to be handed to you by someone in a position of authority. It is not something that you can buy off a shelf, or that is the responsibility of your parents, teachers or professors. Your understanding of the world is something that must be constructed actively—by you!

I remember when I was a professor. Many of the students had an attitude that it was my job to give them knowledge, since they (that is, more typically, their parents) had paid for it. They were quite mistaken. Their error was to think that knowledge can be commoditized. Knowledge is not for sale, as such. It must be earned by each of us. My role as a professor was to provide students with the concepts, conditions, materials, tools, criticism, feedback and encouragement conducive to the growth of their knowledge—but gaining that knowledge was something that only they could do. As the saying goes: "You can lead a dog to water, but you can't make him drink it."

Bella: *Isn't that supposed to be a horse?*

I sometimes think it would be nice to pay someone to do exercise on my behalf.

Bella: *I don't think that would work. I think you should take me for a walk! We could hunt for squirrels together.*

Yes, perhaps you are right. If I want to be healthy, I have to do the exercise myself.

Bella: *And can you not see that it is the same for knowledge?*

You have me convinced. If you want to be knowledgeable, you must explore the world of thought for yourself. This implies that you must think for yourself.

18

Bella: *And if you want to chase squirrels, you have to do it yourself.*

There are some real challenges here however. First, it does matter how you approach this. Not all modes of thinking are created equal; some are more powerful than others. And there are also traps in thinking—places where you can get stuck. And, of course, there are many mistakes that may be made along the way. In this book, we will explore how to think in the manner that has proven to be the most adventurous and powerful—to think in a way that brings you into the process of discovery.

Second, it takes great courage to think for oneself. In a way, it is a wild thing to do.

Bella: *Yes! What gives you the right? Who are you to think for yourself? Are you worthy? And what if you get it all wrong?*

The problem is, however, that there is no other way; no one can do it for you. So you must be bold, if you are to explore and understand the world.

Bella: *I like the wildness of it. I think I'll go run around in circles.*

You do that.

Third, it makes some people very nervous when you start thinking for yourself. You will not always be encouraged to do so. Indeed, despite much lip service to the idea of independent thinking, it is generally discouraged. Other folks have strong ideas about what you should be thinking. They want you to think what they want you to think. We are often taught that our own thinking has no legitimacy—that we are not worthy to think for ourselves. Thinking for yourself—and expressing those thoughts—is not occasionally without cost, and sometimes comes at a very high cost. Independent thinking always requires courage.

Bella: *As does defending the house against postmen—standing as a lonely sentinel, ever ready to bark at their daily and inscrutable descent upon our home.*

The special value of independent thinking is that it explores things afresh for each individual. But this does not imply that one should ignore the foundations for great thinking built by others—quite the contrary. A truly independent thinker doesn't rebel for rebellion's sake. She is educated about what others have thought. Just as we do not set out to reinvent language, so too there is no need to reinvent thought. The thought that has gone before you provides a foundation for your explorations in the same way that language itself provides a foundation. Independent thought does not imply a return to "Year Zero". The independent thinker is brave enough to realize that conventional thought—often built into the language itself—is very often right, and she stands ready to proclaim it so, if that is the case. The true rebel does not rebel for rebellions sake, but rather in the name of pursuing truth, justice and beauty.

Bella: *And the American way!*

Yes, at its best, it is the American way, and I will get to that. While ever vigilant and skeptical of abuses of knowledge processes by supposed authorities—and ever aware of the profound limitations of human knowledge—an independent thinker uses her abilities as best she can to choose among and contribute to productive and joyful thought and activity and promote changes in thinking where it appears fruitful to do so. A truly independent thinker is both radical and conservative at the same time—radical in always questioning, going to the root of an issue for herself and in seeking the truth afresh, but conservative in utilizing the tools and evidence that have been provided before her. That being said, she never supports the status quo simply because it is the status quo; she is not conservative in that sense. Where change constitutes improvement, she pushes for that. An independent thinker is constructive and engaged in the world, and she believes that rational open discourse has the power to transform the world (which is not to say that rational open discourse is always permitted in every society, of course!)

In the United States today, many people are trapped in an intellectual prison. They consume ideas and culture—like they are eating some macaroni and cheese their mom has cooked for them. They believe that knowledge, culture, art, science and religious belief are things to be received from others. They may find some of these consumables somewhat interesting, and others boring, but they do not explore any of them for themselves. They do not wield their own intellectual prowess.

Bella: *We have a mental obesity problem. They need to exercise their minds more!*

They do not construct their knowledge, or even realize that they have an active and critical role to play in constructing their own understanding of things. They do not take responsibility for what they think, believe or feel. They do not embrace knowledge and culture as their own. Rather, they passively digest other people's vision of the world—and in the cacophony of viewpoints that characterize modern life they wonder that they are left in confusion, with no sense of purpose. They do have a sense, however, that they have been excluded from the real action. And they have been.

20

The irony, however, is that—trapped in a false idea of the nature of knowledge—they have excluded themselves.

If this is your approach to life—one of passive consumption and looking to others to sort it all out for you—then your life will be impoverished. You will not create as much, you will not know as much, and you likely will not even love as much or as deeply as you otherwise might have, because you will not be as deeply engaged in the world around you. And—to top it all off—you will be boring. You will not be you, in fact—at least, not the you that could have been, not the largest and most vibrant version of you. No, you will be the pawn of others—a passive cipher to events, rather than an actor in the world. Indeed, you will be the victim of an epistemological tyranny—a tyranny driven by the viewpoints, whims and desires of others. In this book, I ask you to throw off that tyranny and think for yourself. *Sic Semper Tyrannis. Thus Always to Tyrants.*

I am not inventing a new way of thinking about things here, by the way, but rediscovering an old way—the way of the Enlightenment, the movement in thought that lifted us out of the dark ages. The Enlightenment's most powerful insight was that to best understand the world one had to think for oneself. Immanuel Kant captures this well when he writes:

> Enlightenment is the emancipation of man from a state of self-imposed tutelage ... of incapacity to use his <u>own</u> intelligence without external guidance. Such a state of tutelage I call 'self-imposed' if it is due, not to a lack of intelligence, but to <u>lack of courage</u> or determination to use one's own intelligence without the help of a leader. ... Dare to use your own intelligence! This is the battle-cry of the Enlightenment.[2]

It is a remarkably radical thought, and remains so today.
Bella: *Radical thought seems to be an old idea.*
Indeed, it is.

TRAPPED IN FIXED PATTERNS OF THOUGHT

Michel Foucault, a French author, views one's epistemological presumptions as a trap. He believes that culturally-bound fixed patterns of thinking and static ways of categorizing the world shape our observations and thoughts in ways in which we are <u>not</u> typically fully aware. That is, we see the world in terms of preconceptions that always remain tacit (that is, unspoken and unarticulated) and therefore trap us. Below I quote Foucault, who is quoting an author named Borges, who is quoting a certain ancient Chinese encyclopedia in which it is written that:

> animals are divided into: (a) belonging to the Emperor, (b) embalmed, (c) tame, (d) sucking pigs, (e) sirens, (f) fabulous, (g) stray dogs, (h) included in the present classification, (i) frenzied, (j) innumerable, (k) drawn with a very fine camelhair brush, (l) et cetera, (m) having just broken the water pitcher, (n) that from a long way off look like flies.[3]

Bella: *What a weird quote!*

That is exactly Foucault's point. He comments:

> In the wonderment of this taxonomy ... the thing that ... is demonstrated as the exotic charm of another system of thought, is the limitation of our own, the stark impossibility of thinking *that*.[4]

Bella: *But I don't get the point.*

Foucault is saying that if we are from different eras and cultures, we will think about and categorize things so differently that we can't even imagine how someone from the other era or culture would think about things the way they do. He calls it a "stark impossibility." The reason we can't understand how one another thinks is simply because we have such different approaches to categorizing the world. Foucault's idea is that deep-seated epistemological views and preconceptions shape our thinking so profoundly that we lose the capability of stepping into another system of thought. Because our epistemological assumptions and preconceptions will always be tacit, we can never truly escape them. Indeed, in Foucault's view, this is such a powerful trap that one cannot even comprehend what other people mean if they are employ a different set of preconceptions.

Foucault is right that epistemology, combined with the preconceptions with which we categorize our world, shapes both our interpretation of the world and our sense of truth, falsity and coherence. He is also right that these preconceptions can be a trap. Our epistemological view and general preconceptions do determine what kinds of ideas and statements people trust, what sources they trust and ultimately what they think. Moreover, it is generally true that people are <u>not</u> fully aware of the foundations for their own views. Indeed, many people are trapped in preconceptions that muddle their thinking on a broad array of topics.

But Foucault is wrong in some important ways. First, we are not trapped by the preconceptions that define and often constrain us. Rather, at any one time, there can be, and there typically are, competing and clashing ideas of knowledge and clashing ways of categorizing the world, and it is this very clash that points the way out.

Bella: *I've met some clashing ideas in my time.*

I do believe that clashing frameworks and pre-existing presumptions play some part in many of the most fervent disagreements and misunderstandings within society, which we will address later in the book—particularly political disagreements. But it is the very co-existence of such clashing frameworks that serves to give us hope, for it is in their very contrast—in the <u>differences</u> among our viewpoints—that we may begin to think more carefully about what we think we know and thereby become open to new ideas. That is, different viewpoints generate criticism, and, as we will see, criticism is crucial to the growth of knowledge. Through argument, questions, criticism, guesswork and evidence, we can begin to escape our presumptions.

Foucault believes that we can never ultimately escape from our epistemological blinders. In contrast, I believe that there <u>is</u> a way out. The tools of rationality—if understood and wielded properly—are not a limitation, but the very means to our freedom. Precisely because the tools of rationality are not <u>static</u> in nature—that is, merely reinforcing our preconceptions—but rather dynamic, they permit us to change ourselves and improve our understanding of the world. Their very strength is that they continue to challenge and pressure-test everything we believe.

RATIONALITY WILL SET YOU FREE

This book is about why Foucault's epistemological pessimism is wrong. Put another way, this book is about how to break out of intellectual traps. More particularly, it is about breaking out of the traps that have been set by our modern, but false, view of science. Only by doing so can you fully become yourself. The tools of rationality are the keys to your freedom. Are you ready to have the keys? To get them, you need to understand what rationality is, and how and why it works as it does. That is, you need to have an explicit, as opposed to tacit (i.e., unspoken and inarticulate), understanding of epistemology.

If you make an awareness of epistemological biases part of your intellectual toolkit, and learn to wield criticism and conjecture in order to develop ideas and concepts in constructive interaction with others, you can come to understand better what it is that can be known, how it is we come to know it, and the limitations on what we think of as knowledge. You also come to understand people much better—what they think, why they think what they think, and how and why they might be mistaken. You also come to understand how and why you might be mistaken yourself. Most importantly, however, you come to understand how you can contribute to the development of knowledge and actively explore ideas. You join in the adventure that the modern mindset would otherwise deny you.

A study of epistemology will render you both bolder and more humble. Your humility will be based in your understanding of how tentative knowledge is, how subject to error it is and, ultimately, how shallow, limited and partial your understanding will always be with respect to our true nature, the meaning of our existence and the ultimate nature of the universe. Human knowledge is frail and weak compared to the challenges of comprehending reality. This humility is crucial, because it opens you mind.

I look at my daughter's beta fish. His name is King Arthur. He is a delightful, sentient little creature that seems to enjoy his food as well as the daily round of piano playing that occurs nearby. Yet, I am pretty confident that King Arthur has very little idea of the complexities of the world in which I operate and the things in which I believe. He is a small fish in a little bowl with a very limited set of experiences.

Bella: *And so are we all.*

Indeed, I have no doubt that reality itself—that is, the true and absolute nature of the universe and its ultimate meaning—is further beyond me

24

than my world is beyond that of King Arthur. We live our lives engulfed in a fog of unfathomable mysteries—and that is part of the great delight of this life. A study of epistemology fosters the kind of humility that will help you appreciate and embrace the mysteries of life.

But epistemology will also make you bold. Your boldness will be based in an understanding of the interactive nature of the discovery process. You will come to understand that boldness is the key to advancing your own knowledge as well as contributing to society. It takes boldness to escape from the epistemological traps that Foucault has highlighted and, indeed, to truly begin to understand the world for yourself and to understand the viewpoints of others. Knowledge is not some item to be received passively from others. You will come to appreciate the thrill of being bold in your thinking. And there is another side benefit of studying epistemology. You can always rock someone's world by asking: "How do you know that?" You'll rile a lot of people up if you keep asking that question. I always like to do that.

Bella: *Is that as fun as barking at fluffy little white dogs?*

Yes, Bella. Epistemology gives you the tools to go on the attack. Please do. If there is anything of which the world needs more, it's people asking hard questions. And, oh, the glory of it! To ask hard questions is to dedicate your efforts to a knowledge process that is bigger than yourself. It is, indeed, the only way by which society can stumble toward important truths. But the greatest benefit of studying epistemology is that it reveals the rational core of discovery. This rational core can be applied well beyond the traditional realms of science. The rational core of discovery will make you free.

Science is just a small part of who and what we are. If you are to lead a rich life, it is essential to understand the limits of science, and, more importantly, not to let a naïve view of science prevent you from broadening your mind and fully educating yourself as to the possibilities, beauty and meaning that this life holds for us all. This requires the exploration and understanding of myriad non-scientific realms of knowledge. That being said, the tools of rationality can help deepen all of these explorations. As an integrated person, always remember that there is much more to you than science can ever encompass. Do not be trapped by the narrow confines of scientism.

2

SCIENCE AS THE ACCUMULATION OF PROVEN TRUTH

I was like a boy playing on the sea-shore, and diverting myself now and then finding a smoother pebble or a prettier shell than ordinary, whilst the great ocean of truth lay all undiscovered before me.

ISAAC NEWTON

POSITIVISM AND THE SACK OF SCIENCE

Imagine a girl collecting very special pebbles on a beach; the girl is our scientist and these special pebbles are truth. She carries with her the "sack of science." In it, she wants to place only truths, and keep out anything that is false. Her puzzle is this: which pebbles to place into the sack as truth, and which to reject as false? She wants to make sure she collects only those that are <u>proven</u> "true," so that science—that is, her sack of pebbles—will be authoritative. In this manner, everyone will be assured that they can rely on anything that comes from the sack of science. As a good scientist, she wants to be scrupulously careful to keep nonsense out of the body of scientific knowledge.

Philosophers would call this girl a positivist. "Positivism" is a fancy word for a certain way of thinking about science. Positivists believe that science involves the <u>accumulation of proven truths</u>, with the truths being proven mainly through observation. In fact, positivism is the most prominent view of how science works. Science is seen as a process of demonstrating and collecting truths that have been proven through careful observation, and being skeptical of all other things.

As long as we are careful about including only proven truth, then science can become a cumulative process—that is, a collection process where our knowledge builds over time—and to which people across different ages and cultures can contribute. Thus, we must be very careful to preserve the epistemological integrity of science. We must not be led astray by nonsense or mere speculation. If you can't prove something, it is <u>not</u> going to go into the sack of science!

Bella: *Woof! So how does one go about proving? That seems kind of important.*

THE WHITE SWAN OF INDUCTION

There are basically two ways to prove propositions—induction and deduction. Induction involves proof through repeated observation, and deduction involves proof through logic. Induction is the primary means of proof, so let's look at that first. Induction is the process by which you prove something through repeated observations. This is the core concept of positivism. For example, suppose you want to prove that: "The Sun rises every day." How might you go about proving that through induction?

Bella: *You could wake up early each morning and watch the Sun rise.*

Exactly. After having observed the Sun rise on many mornings—each and every time and without fail—at some point it seems reasonable that we can declare that it has been proven that the Sun rises every morning. So let's put that proposition in our sack of science! That is the essence of induction. If you observe something over and over again, then—at some point—you can declare the general proposition to be true. As positivist psychologist B.S. Skinner observed: "[Science] begins, as we all begin, by observing single episodes, but it quickly passes on to the general rule, to scientific law."[5]

Let's take another example just to make sure you have grasped this important idea. Suppose our proposition is that: "Water boils at 212 degrees Fahrenheit." How would you prove that through induction?

Bella: *You could buy a bunch of pots, little stoves, and thermometers, hire many assistants, have each of them heat up some water and record the temperature at which it boils, and collect these observations. If the water is found to boil at 212 degrees Fahrenheit in these many observations, you have proven that "water boils at 212 degrees Fahrenheit."*

That's correct. The most famous example of proof by induction—and my favorite—is when Aristotle, an ancient Greek philosopher, said "all swans are white" and declared that we could know this because every swan anyone had ever seen was white. Indeed, down through the ages, the white swan continued to provide the classic example that induction serves us well as a guide to truth.

Bella: *I get it. I am picturing a gaggle of 15th century Monty-Pythonesque Englishmen strolling along the river Cam saying: "There is a white swan." "Oh, there is another one." "See that swan over there, it's white." "I declare, I think they are all white." "You have to hand it to that Aristotle!" "Oh, he knows what he is talking about when it comes to swans." And then a big dog named Bella—that's me—barks at them, scaring both Englishmen and swans!*

Bella!

Bella: *Sorry. But I agree that positivism and induction do seem eminently sensible. Carefully proceed with science and only allow in the proven truths. I like it. I am glad that our scientific knowledge is based on such a firm foundation.*

THE BLACK SWAN OF COUNTEREXAMPLE

Induction would be great if it worked. But there is a big problem here. It doesn't work as advertised. Induction doesn't and can't prove anything. Worse than that, induction can be misleading. This can be captured in one image, a black swan, which is pictured above. As you can see for yourself, Aristotle was wrong. Not all swans are white. This is despite the fact that for about 2000 years every swan that anyone had ever seen was white (unless you happened to be an Aboriginal Australian or an early visitor to that continent!) Indeed, it was not until Europeans came to Australia that they found <u>black</u> swans—birds that were like white swans in every way, except that they were black![6]

    Bella: *What an embarrassment for induction and Aristotle! British inductivists—punting on the river Cam—humiliated.*

    This is an important epistemological idea: no matter how many times a proposition is seemingly confirmed through observations, it is never

31

proven. In contrast, note that it only takes one counterexample—that is, one black swan, if you will—to disprove a proposition!

Bella: *But why doesn't induction work? It seems so very ... well ... scientific.*

The problem with induction is that it is always possible that there is some condition or influence that can change the outcome you are observing, but that you don't know about. As a consequence, no matter how many times you observe a phenomenon under a given set of conditions, it doesn't necessarily tell you that it will hold true under all conditions. Indeed, you cannot even be sure that you have held all relevant conditions constant within your experiments or observations. Thus, no matter how many times a proposition has been confirmed by observations, <u>it doesn't tell you that the next observation will also confirm the proposition</u>.

The only way to know that a proposition is true under all conditions would be to observe it under <u>all</u> conditions and to know that you have done so. In general, that is impossible, since you don't typically know what all the relevant conditions are in the first place—science is about discovery after all—and, typically, you cannot observe all possible applications of the proposition.

In the first example above, we tried to prove through induction that "The Sun rises every day." But if we changed the conditions under which we are making this observation, we might find that the proposition is no longer confirmed. Suppose we went to the North Pole. There it turns out to be false. At the North Pole, there are extended months of darkness in which the Sun does not rise at all (when the Earth is in the phase of its orbit in which the northern hemisphere is tilted away from the Sun) and there are also extended months of light in which the Sun does not rise at all (when the Earth is in the phase of its orbit in which the northern hemisphere is tilted toward the Sun.) The point is that no matter how many times we had observed the daily sunrise in, say, the state of Virginia, it does not prove that the proposition is true under all circumstances—say, for example, at the North Pole. In our second example above, we tried to prove through induction that "water boils at 212 degrees Fahrenheit." Let's suppose we had, in fact, confirmed this proposition 1,000,000 times through repeated experiments.

Bella: *Wouldn't that finally prove it?*

No. In fact, the proposition turns out to be false, if you change the experimental conditions, say, by moving away from sea level. If you climb up a mountain, and try to boil an egg, you will find that water does <u>not</u> boil at 212 degrees Fahrenheit. As it happens, water only boils at 212 degrees Fahrenheit at a certain air pressure. Since air pressure varies with altitude, the boiling temperature will be different at the top of a mountain. The key point is that no matter how many times you confirmed your proposition at sea level, it doesn't tell you that it would remain true under other conditions.

Let's look at an example that was originally suggested (as I recall) by the philosopher Bertrand Russell. Suppose there is an inductive chicken that lives with other strictly non-scientific chickens in a chicken coop surrounded by a fence. Every morning, the farmer comes, opens a squeaky gate, and tosses chicken feed on the ground. The inductive chicken notices this pattern. She wants to be the first chicken to greet the farmer, so she can get as much food as possible. She employs the power of inductive reasoning. After observing the pattern—(1) farmer opens gate, and (2) food on ground soon thereafter, she concludes through inductive reasoning that this must always be the case. Thereafter, she is always the first chicken to arrive just after the farmer opens the gate. She gets lots of food and becomes very plump.

Bella: *It sounds like induction works pretty well.*

Yes, that is how it seems to the chicken too until one day a relevant condition changes that the inductive chicken doesn't know about. One day the farmer is particularly hungry and he has decided to have a chicken dinner. Of course, he grabs the first chicken that runs toward him when he opens the gate, and, of course, that is our friend—the inductive chicken. In sum, induction doesn't actually prove anything (and can be dangerously misleading!)

Bella: *I got it. Induction's prone to error; it's a fraud, a con. It is all hat and no chicken.*

Yes. Moreover, the failure of induction to prove means that positivism, as a vision and explanation of the nature of science, fails. Science cannot involve the accumulation of proven truths if induction does not, in fact, prove. This is not just an idle philosophical point; it has great practical significance—particularly if you were relying on induction to ensure that you had captured the truth in your sack of science! The failure of induction is not a new idea. It has been well understood at least since the 18th century when the philosopher David Hume explained it.

Nonetheless, it remains big news. For the most part, Hume is ignored. Many folks still pretend that induction proves. Indeed, people talk all the time as if science can prove through repeated observation. Young people are constantly propagandized with the specious idea that science can prove propositions. It just seems too hard to accept that induction doesn't work.

Bella: *If induction doesn't work, what is the role of observation in science? Surely, observation remains important.*

Please stop calling me Shirley. Of course, I am not saying that observation is not central to science. Certainly, we want our scientific theories to be <u>consistent</u> with what we observe. That is of profound importance. Moreover, as we will emphasize later, a single observation has the power to disprove a scientific proposition. So it's not that observations are not important to science; it's just that they can never constitute a proof for scientific propositions. Our scientific propositions <u>may</u> well be absolutely true; it's just that we can't <u>know</u> for certain that they are true based on any series of observations.

Bella: *But if science cannot prove through observation, how do we account for all the scientific progress that we observe? Shirley, we have more scientific knowledge today than we did, say, 100 years ago. How did we gain that knowledge if science cannot prove? And even if induction is flawed, don't we have to rely on it anyway?*

Science does have a rational core that explains its progress. We will get to that in later chapters, but that rational core to science is <u>not</u> induction.

Bella: *What about that other method for proof you mentioned?*

THE TRUTH TRANSFERENCE OF DEDUCTION

While induction was always deemed <u>the</u> great scientific method of proof, deduction was thought to be an important complement to it. Deduction is a process in which you apply the rules of logic to propositions that are assumed to be true, or deemed to be true by virtue of their intuitive appeal, to demonstrate or "prove" other propositions.[7] The most famous example of the use of this technique is by the ancient Greek mathematician Euclid in his book on geometry. Euclid's book was the primary text for learning geometry from his time all the way up to and including Einstein, who was deeply influenced by it.

Bella: *All dogs are four legged creatures. I am a dog. Ergo (fancy Latin term for "therefore"), I have four legs and can run faster than you. I love deduction.*

Deduction is, indeed, an important analytic tool, but it doesn't have the capacity to fulfill the positivist vision either. The limitation of deduction, and it is a severe one, is that it only has the power to <u>transfer</u> truth—from one set of propositions to another—it doesn't have the power to establish truth. That is, with deduction, if you know your assumptions to be true, then you can know that your conclusions are true. The problem is, however, that you can never know that your assumptions are true. This is a severe limitation simply because there is no one set of assumptions that we can agree on as definitely true for anything other than very limited purposes. In other words, for the most part, we don't really know what those first truths are from which other important scientific propositions might be deduced.

For example, although Euclid's assumptions, upon which he based his geometry, are broadly seen as useful in many contexts, and are certainly intuitively appealing, mathematicians have developed numerous non-Euclidean geometries that have also been found useful. These non-Euclidean geometries have assumptions that are inconsistent with Euclidean geometry, which means that both Euclidean and non-Euclidean geometries can't be true at the same time for the same things.

The danger of relying on deduction is that the <u>assumptions</u> themselves have not been demonstrated. The history of science shows us that even if assumptions are intuitively appealing, that doesn't necessarily render them true. Indeed, many of the major developments of science in the 20th century are based on premises that are not only not intuitive, but disturbingly counter-intuitive. In Einstein's physics, time and space are not absolute, but relative concepts. As a particle increases in its speed, time itself slows down for that particular particle and space itself contracts in the direction of the motion. Moreover, objects exerting a gravitational field curve space itself. These propositions hardly seem intuitive, but they are, in fact, not only accepted by modern physics as truth, but are also confirmed through experimentation. Whether a proposition is intuitively appealing is not a good test of truth.

Bella: *But you are saying that there is <u>no</u> way to prove scientific propositions!*
That's correct.

Bella: *Doesn't that make the word "science" itself meaningless? What is the nature of scientific rationality, if not in proving?*

By the 20th century, many philosophers and scientists had come to realize that science cannot prove anything, and were asking exactly those same questions. One of our goals in this book is to answer them.

PROBABILISM

Bella: *Eureka! I have the answer! We have been trying for too much here. So what if we can't prove scientific propositions with 100 per cent certainty? We know when things are probably true, don't we? How about thinking of science as the accumulation of <u>probable</u> truths? That seems like a pretty firm foundation.*

That is one of the possible answers to the puzzle. That approach is called "probabilism." Probabilism waters down the positivist standard of the accumulation of proven truths to one of the accumulation of probable truths. That is, when the girl on the beach, that we spoke of earlier, is trying to decide which pebbles go into the sack of science, the criterion is no longer that the item is proven, but rather that it is merely probable.

Bella: *Probabilism sounds very sensible and moderate. I like it.*

Although probabilism does sound like a promising approach, it turns out that it is also fundamentally flawed. The problem is that there is no conceptually coherent way to determine the probabilities of competing scientific theories, at least not without making various <u>assumptions</u> that themselves cannot be proven, (and which may, in fact, turn out not to be true.) And without a sensible way to determine the probabilities of competing theories, the notion of science as the accumulation of probable truths is rendered meaningless. Below, I am first going to tell you a bit about probability theory, and what it <u>is</u> good for. Second, I will explain why probability theory runs into trouble if you try to use it as a criterion to choose among competing scientific theories.

PROBABILITY THEORY

Probability theory is a good way to deal with uncertainty in some well defined situations. Suppose you have a box of marbles. Twenty of them are black and ten are white. If you reach into the box, but don't look while you are reaching, probability theory suggests that you are twice as likely to pick a black marble as a white marble. Indeed, on average, and after many trials, one would expect that approximately two-thirds of the time you will pick a black marble and one-third of the time you will pick a white marble.

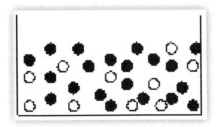

This is very sensible analysis and a quite useful approach in many types of situations. The question is whether this same type of probabilistic analysis can be applied coherently to identify which scientific theories are more probable than others, and which are sufficiently probable to deem worthy of inclusion in the "sack of science." A famous philosopher of science, Karl Popper, has argued that the answer to this question is "no". More specifically, he argues that it is impossible to develop a coherent probabilistic theory that would enable you to choose among competing scientific theories. It turns out that scientific theories are not like marbles in this sense. Let's see why.

Probabilities are ratios. In our above example, we noted that there was a two-out-of-three probability that one would pick a black marble. The numerator—the number on the top of the ratio—was "two" and the denominator—the number on the bottom of the ratio—was "three." The ratio was determined by putting the number of <u>black</u> marbles that one might pick on the numerator and the total number of marbles (both black <u>and</u> white) that might be picked on the denominator—that is:

$$20 \div 30 = \frac{2}{3}$$

In that example, 2/3rds is the probability that you will pick a black marble.

More generally, it is clear that to determine a probability you have to be able to establish both the numerator and the denominator of such a ratio. The numerator represents the event you are looking for and the denominator represents the full field of possibilities. You cannot determine a probability unless you can figure out <u>both</u> parts. One insurmountable problem with applying probability theory to the selection of competing scientific theories is that you cannot determine the denominator that would form the probability. To determine the probability that any one theory is true, the <u>denominator</u> should include <u>all</u> possibly true theories. That is, this should include all theories consistent with what has been observed thus far. But we are not in a position to identify the full set of theories that would be consistent with known observations for three reasons. First, our current observations may not reflect all the relevant conditions that determine the outcomes we are observing. That is, we may neither be aware of which variables are actually relevant, nor of the true relationship among them. As a consequence, it is impossible to determine our denominator—that is, the set of theories that <u>could</u> be true—because some of those theories may relate to variables that we haven't even thought of yet.

Bella: *Isn't that really the same problem that you ran into with induction?*

Exactly. If there may be relevant variables that we are unaware of, it undermines both proof by induction <u>and</u> probabilism. Second, even assuming we could determine the full set of theories that could be true, we also cannot know that all of the competing theories are <u>equally</u> probable, which would be required to use the kind of analysis we applied to the marbles problem. For example, suppose that your fingers were magnetic and the white marbles were attracted by magnetism and the black marbles were not. In that case, the probability of any one marble being selected would likely not be the same, and the formula we used above would not give an accurate answer. That is, if you are applying that formula, you have to be able to presume that the probability of selecting any one marble is the same as selecting any other. Yet, there is no way we can say that all the theories that fit the data are equally probable. How would we know that? Nor can we know <u>a priori</u> what the relative probabilities of the competing theories are to one another—since that is what we are trying to figure out in the first place!

Third, from a purely mathematical point of view, for any finite number of observations, there are—in fact—an infinite number of theories that could be true; that is, there are an infinite number of <u>possible</u> relationships that would fit the data. (This is the point that the philosopher Karl Popper focused on.) To grasp this, just imagine three points on a plane, as in the graph below. Think of these three points as your observations. I have labeled them as points A, B and C. Each point stands for an ordered pair in the X-Y plane, which reflects a hypothesized relationship between the variables X and Y. Now, think of your possible explanatory theories as any line or curve that runs through all three points. I have provided two such curves—one with a dashed line and one with a solid line. Each of these theories is consistent with the observations—that is, the observed pairings of X's and Y's—precisely because each curve runs through all three points. It is easy to see—as long as you include curved lines as possibilities—that there are an <u>infinite</u> number of lines that <u>could</u> be drawn through these points. Thus, if we were trying to calculate the probability of these competing theories in this case, our denominator would be infinite.

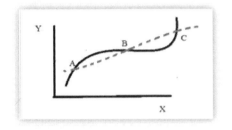

Of course, as the denominator of a fraction gets bigger, the size of the fraction itself gets smaller. Thus, as the denominator tends toward infinity, the fraction tends toward zero. Similarly, since there are an infinite number of possible "theories" that could connect those three points in the example given above, the probability of any <u>one</u> of those theories being true has to be approximately zero.[8] This analysis demonstrates that there is simply no way to make the leap from pure observations to placing probabilities on competing theories—at least if you are dealing with a finite number of observations that do not include every possible instance of the application of the theory.

The bottom line is this: if you don't know whether or not something is true, you also don't know the universe of possibilities that would inform you as to its probability. As a consequence, there is no conceptually sound method for determining the probability that any given theory is, in fact, true, and therefore no way of comparing the probability of one theory with another. Probabilism sounds plausible as a way to save the positivist vision of science, but it fails because there is no coherent way to accurately gauge the probability that a particular theory is true. The problems of accurately defining the numerator and denominator in such a calculation cannot be surmounted.

Bella: *But scientists and analysts do calculate probabilities as to whether various theories are true or not, don't they?*

I am not saying that one cannot set up an analytic framework that makes various <u>assumptions</u> about reality, and <u>given</u> those assumptions places a probability on some particular hypothesis or statement. The point, however, is that such analysis is always based on the assumptions, which themselves cannot be proven and which themselves may well prove inaccurate. There is no non-controversial and non-problematic method for placing probabilities on competing theories. When people talk about a scientific theory "probably" being true, they are either speaking very loosely, as informed by their beliefs and judgments, or are basing what they say on certain unproven (and usually undisclosed) assumptions, or they are simply talking non-sense. This isn't to say that one should never use the language of probabilities in talking about scientific beliefs, but rather that you should realize that those statements are really a reflection of personal judgment and are not firmly established by science itself—or, as indicated above, they are based on a set of unproven assumptions that the speaker has not identified for your benefit.

Science is not, and cannot be, any more about the accumulation of <u>probable</u> truths than it is about the accumulation of proven truths. Ultimately, the same problems that we have with proofs also haunt the realms of probability. Still, many scientists and laymen alike will talk about science as containing probable truths. And while there is no sound basis for such statements, it is not unreasonable to do so. These folks are simply conveying to you their belief about the truth of the scientific statements and perhaps also that the scientific statements may be the best that science has to offer in terms of capturing the evidence. I am not saying here that the best that science has to offer should not be embraced, but rather that our tentative embrace of the best of science is <u>not</u> based on a probability calculus by which competing theories have been fairly compared and weighed.

THE FAILURE OF POSITIVISM

To summarize where we have come at this point, we first showed that science cannot be the accumulation of proven truths, because it cannot prove (through either induction or deduction.) Next, we argued that you cannot successfully water down this idea to the notion of science as the accumulation of <u>probable</u> truths. Positivism fails. It is <u>not</u> what science is all about.

Positivism is to be rejected not only because it has no logical foundation, but also because it's not an accurate description of what science does. An examination of the actual history of science reveals that it is not characterized by the accumulation of proven truth, but rather by <u>revolutions</u> in which one set of supposed truths are found to be false and are replaced by another set of tentatively held beliefs. For example, Einstein's theories showed that Newtonian mechanics did not constitute universal truths, but, in fact, were inaccurate depictions of reality in many contexts. Indeed, our very conception of the nature of reality itself keeps evolving with rapidly changing theories in physics. So let's get one thing straight: the actual history of science looks nothing like the simplistic, cumulative story told by the positivists! I will give you some more examples of this in the next chapter.

But despite the evidence against the positivist view of science—based both upon epistemological arguments as well as the actual history of science—the positivist view still holds a strong sway. So before exploring more fully the actual rational core of science, let's flesh out a bit more fully the way positivists think about the world, as we will encounter this viewpoint and set of attitudes again and again—and not just in science. Positivism entails a certain attitude—and a muddled one at that—about what is knowable and who can know it. We will see that it has the capacity for great harm.

The positivist view of knowledge is pretty simple; let's return to our metaphor of a girl collecting pebbles of truth in the sack of science. Knowledge is that which is <u>in</u> the sack of science. This view makes science education seem pretty simple too. One focuses on teaching what is <u>in</u> the sack of science. Positivism tries to play it safe by avoiding speculation and allowing into science only that which is proven true. The problems with this approach are six-fold.

First, as we have seen, the accumulated "truths" can never, in fact, be proven, and may <u>not</u> turn out to be true after all. Thus, while this approach plays for epistemological safety and certainty, <u>there is no safety or certainty to be had</u>. Second, in this play for safety, much is given up. This is perhaps the more important point. There may be much that is knowable in science, but that requires bold conjecturing to reach it. Einstein's idea of a time-space continuum could not be reached without bold, and indeed, playful conjecturing. Intellectually reaching <u>beyond</u> that which we can know with certainty is a crucial step that can provide insight and knowledge, even if imperfect. We do this through bold conjecturing, not epistemological timidity. This is particularly true in the "social sciences" and economics where there isn't anything that can be known with certainty, and yet there is much knowledge to be gained. While that knowledge may be judgment-laden and prone to error, it is far better than the entirely empty contents which a positivist approach will yield.

Third, positivism does not describe what scientists actually do. Conjectures often, and even typically, run ahead of empirical verification. As we will see later in this book, there is a complex interaction of conjectures, refutations, and further responsive refinements through yet more conjecturing that the positivist account of science completely misses.

Fourth, the positivist account of science is simply boring—and this is a serious problem. Under the sway of positivism, scientists are little more than clerks recording observations and rendering them as general truths when they cross a numerical threshold of repetition. Where is the passion that characterizes the real scientists we meet in life? Science is, in fact, a passionate and creative pursuit. Real scientists—and particularly good scientists—are passionate and creative people who bring the quirks of their individuality to the scientific process. Positivism does not recognize the role of creativity in science. Even worse, it doesn't recognize the real people at the core of science who are conducting the activity—the scientists themselves. Science is a human process, not a machine.

Fifth, positivism turns science into a commodity—that is, in portraying scientific truth as like a collection of discrete tangible objects it renders it speciously rigid and exclusionary. For the positivists, the teaching of science therefore involves handing the "sack" of this knowledge to the student, who receives it <u>without question</u>. Where is there any role for questions? It has all been proven. There is no need for questioning. Nor is there any need for criticism. Why criticize something that has been proven? There is no need for independent thought. Positivism excludes the young scientist from entry into the discourse of science, whereas a proper education in science should draw the young student <u>into</u> the discourse.

Indeed, within positivism, there is little or no role for the <u>history</u> of science, or even the history of ideas. Within positivism, the only sensible historical questions to ask are: "Who first discovered a particular proven truth?" and, somewhat less interestingly, "What did the early scientists have wrong?" It is because of the dominance of positivism that history plays little or no role in the training of scientists. There is no reason to look at history if present scientific knowledge contains all that is proven. It is only when you come to recognize science as a dynamic voyage of discovery that its history becomes of deeper interest. Indeed, to fully grasp scientific ideas, and to contribute to the discovery process itself, knowledge of the "journey" taken thus far is extremely helpful.

Sixth, within positivism, the supposed authority of science serves to suppress both criticism and conjecturing, <u>and by doing so actually retards the advance of science</u>. According to a positivist viewpoint, science has the authority that comes with harboring proven truth. It follows that a reasonable person cannot but accept its dictates, for to not do so would be to ignore that which has been proven. The question of what should be considered as science and what should not is known as the "demarcation question". The demarcation question takes on the highest importance in the authoritative atmosphere generated by positivism, for to be considered as science is to be perceived as bearing proven truth. Science thereby becomes the sheriff of our thoughts and beliefs, and although non-science might not be considered the equivalent of nonsense, it is pretty close. Purported provability becomes the hallmark of serious thought. Other types of mental activity might be amusing occasionally, but they must always remain on the periphery of the "scientific" understanding.

Positivists have a deep bias against that which hasn't been proven true (or, at least, against anything which they don't consider to have been proven), and you can see why; they want to keep science pure. They are very skeptical of the unobservable and of speculation in any form. Many scientists today have this attitude, and it is the legacy of positivism that accounts for it. Yet, ironically, it is an odd bias that does not itself have any basis in science. Because something is unobservable does not mean it does not exist, or is not important. Indeed, there are many variables in science that are not directly observable, such as gravity. While the <u>effects</u> of gravity are observable, gravity itself is not. Yet, we do postulate that it exists. And, as we noted previously, new theories often formulated <u>before</u>

43

we find many of the observations that confirm them and which convince us of their value. Despite the presence of many unobservables in science itself, positivists still have an odd bias against them. For example, you may not be able to prove that a dog has a sentient awareness of the world in the same way that a human does, but failure to prove that does not mean it is not so.

Bella: *Oh, this is too much! My sentient awareness is perfectly keen; thank you very much!*

To me, to assume that dogs do not feel and think as we do is as absurd as a person thinking that she is the only person in the universe who thinks and feels—a philosophical condition called solipsism—simply because she cannot prove that anyone else has sentient awareness. Yet many people with scientific training really do think that anything that they cannot directly observe and prove through their methods does not exist, even though they have no evidence for the lack of existence of whatever is under consideration.

Bella: *GRRRRRRRRRRRR. That is all I have to say to those who do not believe in canine sentience.*

In this chapter, I introduced a philosophy of science known as positivism. Positivism views science as the accumulation of proven truths. I talked about induction and deduction as potential methods of proof, but showed how neither can lead to proof with certainty. I then talked about probabilism, which views science as an accumulation of highly probable truths. I argued that there is no coherent, non-controversial method for placing probabilities on competing theories.

Suggested Readings

- Joy Hakim The Story of Science: Einstein Adds a New Dimension Smithsonian Books (2007)

3

SCIENCE AS A COMEDY OF ERRORS

If you think science is certain—well that's just an error on your part.
RICHARD FEYNMAN

*Textbooks ... being pedagogic vehicles for the perpetuation of normal
science, have to be rewritten in whole or in part whenever the language,
problem-structure, or standards of normal science change. In short, they
have to be rewritten in the aftermath of each scientific revolution, and, once
rewritten, they inevitably disguise not only the role but the very existence
of the revolutions that produced them.*
THOMAS KUHN

Everyone was against me, but I knew I was right.
BARRY MARSHALL, NOBEL PRIZE WINNER IN MEDICINE

In the last chapter, we developed the logical and philosophical arguments for why it is not possible to prove within science. In this chapter, we will look at a few situations from the actual history of science where scientists were: (1) quite mistaken in their views (at least, as it appears in retrospect); (2) quite convinced that their then-current views constituted the absolute and certain truth; and (3) were quite resistant to clearly superior theories that constituted an improvement in science. This is, in fact, the norm in science. It is how science advances—in fits and starts with bursts of creativity and the correction of previous errors and mistakes by virtue of theories with superior predictive and explanatory content. By looking at the actual history of science, this chapter reinforces the point that whatever science is—and whatever is special about it—it is not the accumulation of proven truths. If science is the history of mistakes being corrected, then those earlier mistakes cannot be viewed as having been proven.

HELICOBACTER PYLORI: A PAIN IN THE STOMACH

Peptic ulcers, which are bleeding sores in the stomach, can be extremely painful, debilitating and recurrent. For a long time, the medical profession believed that such ulcers were caused by a combination of stress and excess acid in the stomach. However, in the early 1980s, Dr. J. Robin Warren and Dr. Barry Marshall noticed a mysterious microorganism—helicobacter pylori—that was found in the stomachs of ulcer patients, but generally not found in others.[9] They hypothesized that this bacteria was causing the ulcers. If they were right, there might be an easy cure for ulcers through antibiotics. On its web site, the Academy of Achievement describes the situation as it stood at the time:

> Practitioners of gastroenterology and the pharmaceutical industry were both heavily invested in the theory that peptic ulcers were caused by emotional stress and stomach acids, and could only be treated with repeated courses of antacid medication. While the reduction of stomach acid often alleviated the existing ulcer, inflammation of the stomach lining usually persisted, and most patients found themselves returning in a year or two with another ulcer.

Patients were routinely advised to seek psychiatric counseling, find less demanding employment or make other
drastic lifestyle changes to address the purported cause of
the disease. Volumes were published detailing the alleged
psychological causes of gastric ailments ... In this environment, the possibility that the ailment was directly caused
by a single microorganism that could be completely eliminated with a two-week course of antibiotics was a threat
to the status quo. While many of Marshall's critics had
serious scientific questions about his hypothesis, others
may have had economic motives in disputing his findings,
and Marshall was not shy about saying so. The targets of
his criticism soon sought to discredit him and his research.
One prominent gastroenterologist dismissed him as "a crazy guy saying crazy things."[10]

Despite the fact that Dr. Marshall was having success in treating patients,
there was considerable resistance by the medical profession to accepting
Marshall's new hypothesis. Dr. Marshall became so frustrated that he
decided to conduct an experiment on himself. First, he did an endoscopy
on his own stomach to demonstrate that he had no ulcers. Next, he drank
the contents of a Petri dish swarming with helicobacter pylori, much to the
distress of his lab partners and wife.[11]

Bella: *Not to mention his stomach!*

He soon developed symptoms, and quickly established the fact of the
damage to his stomach lining. He then cured himself with a treatment of
antibiotics, and published an article on his findings. The battle to have
the new successful treatments recognized was long and hard. Indeed,
despite the fact that the bacterium had been identified in 1982 by Dr.
Marshall and Dr. Warren, it wasn't until 1996 that the US Food and Drug
Administration officially approved a course of treatment for peptic ulcer
disease consistent with Marshall's findings.[12] In 2005, Dr. Marshall and
Dr. Warren received the Nobel Prize in medicine for their work on helicobacter pylori. The Nobel Committee states: "Thanks to the pioneering discovery by Marshall and Warren, peptic ulcer disease is no longer a chronic,
frequently disabling condition, but a disease that can be cured by a short
regiment of antibiotics and acid secretion inhibitors."[13]

There are a couple of important lessons here. First, as I will reiterate again and again, at no point in time is the current body of scientific knowledge authoritative—despite the many authoritative statements that will emanate from its practitioners. Medical science was clearly wrong in its views as to the causes of peptic ulcers. Not only was medical science wrong, but it was very slow to adjust to the mounting evidence that it was wrong. The point is very simple. Scientific views can turn out to be wrong, and often are. The history of science is not one of gradual accumulation of proven knowledge, but of rebellion and revolution. Incorrect views can prevail at times, and the fight over whose view is correct can be long and hard. And the fights never end. That is the nature of scientific advance. While it is based on evidence, it is not based on conclusive proof.

Now, this is not to say that you shouldn't follow the advice of your doctor. Heeding the best that science has to offer at any point in time is, of course, eminently practical. Nonetheless, it can also be quite useful to understand that science <u>can</u> be wrong, is often in a state of flux and that there may be returns to educating yourself on the current state of a science if you are in a position where you have to rely upon it.

Second, resistance to better scientific ideas is sometimes generated by the vested interests that many may have in the current body of thought, as appears to have been the case here—at least in part. A lot of people were making a lot of money off the older viewpoint. And nobody likes to rewrite their textbooks and admit they were wrong. As a consequence, science was slow in this case to adapt a view that had stronger evidence supporting it, and from which many would ultimately greatly benefit.

BREAKING THE UNIVERSAL SPEED LIMIT

According to Einstein and modern physics, the speed of light—which is approximately 186,000 miles per second—stands as the speed limit for the universe. Nothing in the universe—including light—can ever go faster than that.

Bella: *They haven't seen me run!*

According to the equations, if something did go faster than that, very strange things would have to happen—such as time going backward or the object weighing more than the universe.[14] That's why Einstein, who announced this speed limit in his special theory of relativity in 1905, said it couldn't happen.[15]

Bella: *That was all the way back in the days of the horse-and-buggy!*

Einstein expanded on this theme in his general theory of relativity in 1915, and modern physics has relied on this speed limit ever since. But, as we noted previously, recent experimental observation brought this all into question for awhile.

Bella: *They <u>have</u> seen me running.*

The experiment is a joint project being conducted by CERN in Switzerland, which is the European Organization for Nuclear Research, and the Gran Sasso National Laboratory, which is located in Italy.[16] As I understand it, they have an underground tunnel—almost a mile down—running between the lab in Switzerland and the lab in Italy, which is about 500 miles away. The lab in Geneva sends a beam of neutrinos, which are subatomic particles, to the lab in Italy, at which point they measure the time of arrival.[17]

Bella: *They must have quite a catcher's mitt.*

They do. It's very fancy. But the problem was that the neutrinos, which are supposed to travel at the speed of light, were arriving 60 nanoseconds earlier than they should have been—that is, they appeared to be travelling faster than the speed of light! The scientists at CERN expressed shock at this result. They repeated the experiment over and over again, but they couldn't find anything wrong. Finally, they announced it to the world and asked scientists around the world to double check their work.

In his blog, theoretical physicist Michio Kaku highlighted what was at stake here. He noted that if the recent CERN experiments were correct, it would imply that both the special and general theories of relativity were wrong. Kaku stated:[18]

> Not only is cosmology, nuclear physics, atomic physics, laser physics, etc., all in doubt, but also the fundamental theories of particles physics ... The Standard Model of particle physics (containing quarks, electrons, neutrinos, etc.) is also based on relativity ... String theory has relativity built in from the start ... So you can see why physicists are breaking out in a cold sweat contemplating the demise of relativity.

Kaku highlighted that this one set of observations had the potential to refute much of what physics thought it knew. He stated that "Einstein's theory has withstood the test of time for almost a century" but "if there's one data-point out of place, we would have to throw the entire theory out." Kaku believed that "there is the slim chance that the result holds up" under scrutiny, but if it does "[t]hen relativity may fall and we will have to await the coming of the next Einstein who can make sense out of it all." He closed, however, with the observation that "this is how science is done."[19]

As it turned out, it appears that the observations were indeed problematic. Something turned out to be wrong with the equipment. Kaku called it correctly. But what is noteworthy here is the open mind that an excellent physicist like Kaku displayed with respect to the possibility that Einstein's theory might be turned on its head. The point is that we can never be sure that any particular scientific statement is true, no matter how long it has guided science and no matter how long it has been held to constitute knowledge. The history of science is fraught with cases where we thought we knew something, but it turned out to be wrong. And good scientists do recognize that this is the case—even for their most cherished theories. The history of science is not a cumulative process—even though science does progress—but one marked by revolutions where some scientific notions are falsified, rejected and replaced by altogether different ideas. Good scientists like Kaku are ever ready and watchful for the next revolution on the horizon.

Another take-away from the CERN experiment is that there are also many false revolutions. What may appear at first take to be a new dawn in science sometimes turns out itself to be misleading or wrong. For example, there have been a number of announcements over the years of the discovery of a new cheap source of energy through "cold-water fusion." Thus far, these have turned out to be false leads. Science is fraught with false steps, and, indeed, as we just saw false or misleading "observations". Our scientific skepticism should extend not only to established theories, but also to the new competitors as they appear on the horizon.

SEEING ORDER IN A QUASI-CRYSTAL BALL: EYN CHRA KAZO!

In 2011, the Nobel Prize in Chemistry was awarded to Daniel Shechtman for his discovery of quasi-crystals.[20] In general, the structure of a crystal is both orderly and periodic. That is, in general, crystals are based on molecular structures that form geometric patterns that are repeated. In 1982, however,

Daniel Shechtman rapidly cooled a molten metal and observed what had heretofore been thought impossible—namely a crystalline structure that was orderly, but not periodic—that is, it did not repeat its pattern.[21] Upon seeing this, Dr. Shechtman exclaimed in Hebrew: "Eyn chra kazo", which means "there can be no such creature."[22]

In more technical terms, what Dr. Shechtman observed did not have "translational symmetry", but it did have what is known as icosahedral symmetry. As one tome described the situation:

> A fundamental 'law' of crystallography declares icosahedral symmetry to be impossible in the crystal kingdom. This law, based on the long-established hypothesis of periodicity and taught in every textbook, had been confirmed in all known instances: instructors delighted in pointing out how examples of *apparent* icosahedral symmetry (dodecahedral pyrite, 'fivelings' of silver or gold) could be shown to be irregular or an artifact of twinning.[23]

When your observations conflict with "fundamental laws" and "long-established hypotheses" that have been confirmed in all known instances, you can expect trouble, and trouble is what Dr. Shechtman got. When Dr. Shechtman announced his discovery to the world, his colleagues agreed with his initial assessment that what he had seen was, indeed, impossible and they treated him very poorly as a consequence. The Guardian (which is a British newspaper) reported that:

> In an interview this year with the Israeli newspaper, Haaratz, Shechtman said: "People just laughed at me." He recalled how Linus Pauling, a colossus of science and a double Nobel laureate, mounted a frightening "crusade" against him. After telling Shechtman to go back and read a crystallography textbook, the head of his research group asked him to leave for "bringing disgrace" on the team. "I felt rejected," Shechtman said.[24]

Bella: *Don't try to tell scientists that their pretty crystals are less periodic than they thought they were.*

Exactly. As it turned out, Dr. Shechtman prevailed fairly quickly, although not before losing his job. As Marjorie Senechal describes it:

> Unlike some other famous examples of 'headline physics', this phenomenon did not fade away on close inspection. Just the opposite: not only was this 'phase' quickly reproduced in laboratories throughout the world, but many other examples of 'noncrystalline crystals' were found as well. It soon became clear that aperiodic metallic phases are not rarities but, on the contrary, are very widespread.[25]

In fact, Dr. Shechtman went on the win the Nobel Prize in Chemistry in 2011. Once again, it turned out that the experts didn't know what they thought they knew.

CATCHING THE DRIFT OF THE CONTINENTS

Alfred Wegener, the discoverer of continental drift, had to wait a very long time before his controversial theories were accepted—indeed, it didn't happen until <u>decades</u> after his death.

Bella: *That is a long wait.*

Alfred Wegener lived from 1880 to 1950. He was a meteorologist and explorer with broad scientific interests. Among other things, he explored the icy recesses of Greenland. In fact, he died on one of these explorations, a day after his 50th birthday. He was also a bit of an adventurer; he and his brother Kurt set a record for a manned balloon flight. Wegener's big idea was that the continents are not fixed in position, but rather—over very long periods of time—drift. Wegener provided expansive evidence for this theory in a book entitled <u>The Origin of Continents and Oceans</u>, the first edition of which appeared in 1915.[26]

Bella: *Are you saying continents are like big boats floating around?*

Yes, it's something like that.

Bella: *Well, no wonder nobody believed it.*

Among other things, Wegener noted in his book that biologists and geologists held theories that were mutually inconsistent. On the one hand, the <u>biologists</u> saw from the types of plant and animal species in different continents that the continents must have had land bridges at one time. The <u>geologists</u>, however, did not believe that such land bridges could have existed. Wegener's resolution of this puzzle was that the continents themselves had once been together, and were in a process of drifting. His book collected together biological, geological and climatic arguments for his thesis.

While Wegener was largely correct in most of his arguments and conclusions, it wasn't until more than 50 years after his first edition, and 35 years after his death that plate tectonics, the successor to his theory, was fully embraced. Lisa Yount, who wrote a book on Wegener's scientific contributions, notes that while "Alfred Wegener's continental drift is not the same as the theory of plate tectonics", nonetheless "plate tectonics evolved from continental drift."[27] Lisa Yount describes the reactions to Wegener's theory as follows:

> Wegener gathered from a wide range of geological fields what he felt was an impressive quantity of evidence to support his theory—but it was not enough. His critics were quick to point out that some of his information was inaccurate and some could be, or even had to be, interpreted in ways other than the ones he suggested. He (and the scientists that ridiculed him) lacked the data that would later provide such convincing support for plate tectonics. Some of that data came from fields such as paleomagnetism, which did not even exist in Wegener's time.[28]

It wasn't until 1966 and 1967 that: "Three key scientific meetings bring together the lines of research that support the new theory of plate tectonics and convince most earth scientists to accept the theory."[29] One takeaway here is that an accurate scientific hypothesis can arrive before its time—that is, even though a theory is correct as originally stated, it may take other theoretical, empirical and technical advances in complementary fields before a theory is more fully supported and finally embraced. The lesson: science grows in fits and starts, and a superior hypothesis may be around for a long time before being accepted.

EVEN MATHEMATICAL PROOFS DON'T ALWAYS PROVE: EULER'S CONJECTURE

In sum, the problem with proofs is that they don't actually prove anything. This, of course, doesn't mean that they are not important or useful. The philosopher of science Imre Lakatos wrote a wonderful book called <u>Proofs and Refutations</u>, which explores the nature of proofs in the context of mathematics.

Bella: Even from the title you can see he means to stir up trouble. How can a proof be refuted?

Exactly. In his book, Lakatos focuses on a mathematical proof of Euler's conjecture. (By the way, "Euler" is pronounced like oiler.) By examining the history of this particular proof and the various criticisms of it, Lakatos shows that even mathematical proofs don't actually "prove" in the sense of establishing certain knowledge. But despite the fact that proofs don't actually prove, it turns out that they are quite useful. In his book, Lakatos shows that mathematical knowledge grows and continues to <u>improve</u> through a dynamic process that includes: (1) efforts at proof; (2) criticism (and even refutation) of the proof; (3) adjustments to the proof in light of the criticism; and (4) new efforts at proof.[30]

Let's take a look at Euler's conjecture and his proof, and see what we learn. By the way, another great source for reading about Euler's conjecture and proof is in a children's mathematics book entitled <u>One, Two, Three ... Infinity</u> by scientist George Gamow. Gamow provides an easy exposition, and this is where I first encountered Euler's ingenious and elegant proof. I highly recommend Gamow's version of the proof.[31] My exposition below is based on the work of these two authors.

To examine Euler's conjecture, you first have to know what a polyhedron is. I presume that you already know that a polygon is a multi-sided two dimensional figure. Triangles, squares, pentagons and octagon are all examples of polygons. A polyhedron is a multi-sided <u>three</u> dimensional figure. Examples would include a cube or, say, a tetrahedron.

Bella: A tetra-what?

You need to know what a tetrahedron is, because we will use it in an example below. A tetrahedron is a three dimensional shape made from four triangles put together as its sides. It looks vaguely like a pyramid, but there are important differences—whereas a pyramid has a square base with four triangles placed along its edges and meeting at a point at the top, <u>all</u> the sides of a tetrahedron are triangles. Instead of having five sides like a pyramid, the tetrahedron only has four sides. More specifically, imagine that you have two perfectly square pieces of paper, and you fold each one across the diagonal. If you put those pieces of paper together along the edges, you would have a tetrahedron. I have placed a picture of one immediately below, with the dashed line representing an edge that you can't see.

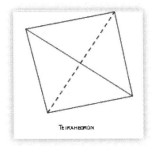

TETRAHEDRON

Now that you have the concept of a tetrahedron in your back pocket, let's get back to Euler's conjecture.

Bella: *I don't have a back pocket.*

Euler's conjecture is that for any polyhedron, the number of vertices minus the number of edges plus the number of faces always equals 2, or, in symbols:

$$V - E + F = 2.$$

"Vertices" means the end points—the parts that could poke your eye. "Edges" means, well, edges—that is, the lines where the triangles meet. And "faces" means the flat sides of the object. To see how this formula works, let's look at an example. Take the tetrahedron, which is a four-sided three-dimensional figure such as the one pictured above. If you look at the picture above, you can readily see that the tetrahedron has:

4 vertices, 6 edges and 4 faces.

Euler's conjecture says that:

$$V - E + F = 2.$$

Thus, in the case of the tetrahedron, that would mean that:

$$4 - 6 + 4 = 2$$

which it does, of course. Thus, we can see that Euler's conjecture holds at least for the tetrahedron. Let's do one more example of Euler's conjecture. Get yourself a cube and have a look at it. You will notice that it has eight vertices, twelve edges and six faces. Here, once again, we see that Euler's conjecture holds—that is, for the cube:

$$V - E + F = 2$$

since

$$8 - 12 + 6 = 2.$$

Bella: *How on Earth did he come up with this conjecture?*

If you played around with shapes enough, and started trying to systematize and categorize them, you might come up with that—assuming you had a lot of time on your hands, that is. But Euler didn't just come up with the conjecture, he also proved it. It's a very elegant proof. We will look at it here because it can teach us something important about how knowledge grows. As we work through the proof, let's keep a specific polyhedron in mind, so that you can visualize it. Specifically, we'll think of a cube. As you already know from your analysis above, a cube has six faces, eight vertices, and twelve edges. Thus:

$$V - E + F = 8 - 12 + 6 = 2.$$

Now imagine removing one of the faces of the cube. Since you are subtracting one face, your equation will now read:

$$V - E + F = 8 - 12 + 5 = 1.$$

Next, imagine that the remaining faces of the cube are elastic. Using the opening where one of the faces has been removed, imagine that you stretch the sides of the figure out so that it is now flat on a plane. It would look like the following diagram:

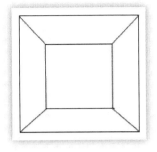

Notice that, when you stretch out the figure, you do not change the numbers of faces, vertices or edges. The next thing you do with the figure is to triangulate all the faces by drawing a diagonal across each face (that is, one line segment connecting opposite corners of each face.) The new figure should look something like that pictured below:

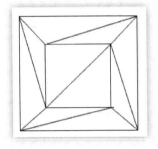

The key thing to notice about this figure is that it now has 10 faces instead of 5 and it has 17 edges instead of 12. As a consequence, it <u>remains</u> true that:

$$V - E + F = 1$$

since both V and E have increased by 5, and thus cancel each other out in terms of the effect on the sum on the right hand side. Now, imagine removing the triangles one by one.

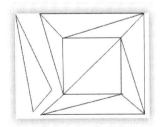

You will see that there are only two possibilities with each triangle that you remove; either you are eliminating one edge and one face—as in the example portrayed just above—or you are eliminating two edges, one face and one vertex—as in the example just below.

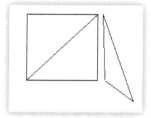

If you examine the effect of either of these on the equation, it always leaves the sum on the right hand side unchanged. That is, it continues to remain true that:

$$V - E + F = 1$$

After you have removed all of the triangles except the last one, you can then count the number of vertices, edges and faces on that final remaining triangle and see that it is remains true that:

$$V - E + F = 1$$

The proof of Euler's conjecture simply involves reversing all these steps! That is, start with a triangle, for which:

$$V - E + F = 1$$

Next, build up your polyhedron using triangles, for which, as we have seen, it continues to remain true for the constructed figure that:

$$V - E + F = 1$$

Finally, add one final triangle to complete the polyhedron, thereby adding only one face, but no new edges or vertices, and you have:

$$V - E + F = 2$$

Bella: *Brilliant!*

It's one of the most famous proofs in mathematics. There is only one problem with it, and that is that later mathematicians came up with counterexamples to the proposition—that is, polyhedrons for which:

$$V - E + F \neq 2.$$

Bella: *But how could that be; Euler proved that:*

$$V - E + F = 2$$

So how could we end up with anything other than that?

It would seem that his proof didn't prove what it set out to.

Bella: *So what was the counterexample?*

Actually, there were quite a few. But we'll just look at one to give a sense of how it was dealt with. The counterexample we will look at is called the twin tetrahedron. Now, we already know that:

$$V - E + F = 2$$

for a tetrahedron. (Recall the picture of the tetrahedron earlier in this chapter.) Imagine taking a tetrahedron and connecting it to another tetrahedron along one of the edges. It would look something like the following:

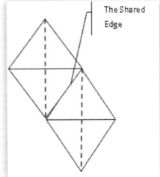

Since you already know that for each tetrahedron:

$$V - E + F = 2$$

You can now infer that if the two tetrahedra are added together, to form the twin tetrahedron, but also share an edge, then, for the new figure:

$$V - E + F = 3$$

You can double-check this by counting the number of vertices, edges and faces on the new figure, and you will find that there are 6 vertices, 11 edges and 8 faces. And, of course:

$$6 - 11 + 8 = 3$$

Bella: *That's an abomination; that's not what we meant by a polyhedron.* That is what some people said. But let's see if we can learn more if we take the criticism serious. Euler's conjecture said that:

$$V - E + F = 2$$

We know that for the twin tetrahedron this is not true. But Euler had a proof that seemed pretty convincing. The best way to utilize this criticism is not to ignore it. Rather, what we should do is examine the proof, and figure out why it did not prove <u>in this particular case</u>. We can then figure out how to adjust the conjecture that Euler thought he had proven to take account of this counterexample. Put differently, we can use the criticism to help us figure out how to improve Euler's conjecture. This is more easily seen by walking through these steps, of course, so let's do that. First, it is important to ask: <u>why</u> doesn't Euler proof cover the twin tetrahedron? Well, if we examine the twin tetrahedron, we can ask ourselves: is it susceptible to <u>each step</u> of Euler's proof? For example, we might ask: can its faces be triangulated?

Bella: *The answer to that is trivial. The faces are already triangles, so there is no problem there.*

You are right. We might also ask: can the triangles be removed one at a time?

Bella: *Of course they can. There is no problem there.*

You are right again. So we can say with confidence that those steps in the proof can be successfully applied to the twin-tetrahedron. Thus, those parts of the proof are not the source of our problem. But we might also ask:

After we remove one of the faces, is the remainder of the figure stretchable out onto a plain?

Bella: *Aha! The answer to that is clearly "no".*

You are correct. If we remove a face, we still have the problem of that shared line. That is, you could <u>not</u> stretch the figure out onto a plain without breaking that line, and thus changing the nature of the figure. What we have discovered is that one of the steps of Euler's proof cannot be done. That is the reason the twin-tetrahedron provides a counterexample and the proof does not prove in this case. We need a name for the special class of polyhedra that—unlike the twin-tetrahedron—<u>can</u> be stretched out onto a plain when a face is removed. Let's call such polyhedra "simply connected", and by that term we will include any polyhedra where an un-broken line can be drawn from any point on the polyhedron to any other point—without having to cut across any other lines. You can readily see that the twin-tetrahedron is not simply connected, and that any polyhedron that is simply connected is stretchable out onto a plain when a face is removed. By looking at our proof more carefully in light of the criticism we were able to narrow the class of polyhedra to the group for which the proof really proves—that is, the group of polyhedron for which the set of sub-arguments that constitute the proof appear to provide insights. But, of course, if we are to do this, we must adjust the conjecture that we claim to be proving. Previously, Euler's conjecture was that:

For <u>all</u> polyhedra:

$$V - E + F = 2.$$

Now we need to adjust the conjecture to read:
For <u>simply connected</u> polyhedron:

$$V - E + F = 2.$$

LESSONS LEARNED ABOUT PROOFS AND CRITICISM

There are some important lessons here. First, we see that Euler's original proof didn't really prove. At least, it did not prove in the sense of precluding the possibility of a later counterexample—that is, the twin-tetrahedron. Nonetheless, the proof has demonstrative power. It teaches us something about the terrain in which we are operating. It just doesn't give us certainty. Second, we note that if one takes counterexamples seriously, one can improve the rigor of the proof, as we did above. Third, improving of the proof involved a twofold analysis. The first step was to figure out the aspect of the proof that the counterexample violated. The second step was to see how that aspect of the proof could be more tightly tied to the statement of what it was that was being proven. Finally, and most importantly here, the story of Euler's conjecture highlights that there is an explorational aspect even to mathematics. It too grows through a process of criticism and fruitful response thereto. And it shows us the importance of being open to fruitful criticism.

Suggested Readings

- George Gamow <u>One, Two, Three ... Infinity: Facts and Speculations of Science</u> Dover Publications, Inc. (1988)
- Imre Lakatos <u>Proofs and Refutations: The Logic of Mathematical Discovery</u> Cambridge University Press (1976)

4

SCIENCE AS REVOLUTION

Led by a new paradigm, scientists adopt new instruments and look in new places. Even more important, during revolutions scientists see new and different things when looking with familiar instruments in places they have looked before.

THOMAS KUHN

THE ROUTINIZATION OF CHARISMA

Sociology is the study of human societies. One of the great sociologists of the 19th century—indeed, one of sociology's founding fathers—was a man named Max Weber. Among other things, he studied religion, and, in particular, how religion changes. In this context, he came up with two fruitful ideas: (1) the charismatic leader, and (2) the "routinization" of charisma.

Bella: *Cool. You mean like an alpha male or alpha female.*

First, let's look at the idea of the alpha ... I mean ... the charismatic leader. Weber said that sometimes—and especially when a society is confronting new needs, challenges or pressures—a religious leader would appear who was charismatic. To have charisma is to have a special power to charm people. The charismatic leader is the right person at the right time and place. In the context of religion, he or she has recognized the spiritual needs of the people and met them squarely with a new formulation of religious ideas. Charismatic leaders draw forth a large following of people. They change the world in this way.

Of course, eventually the charismatic leader retires from his or her leadership role or dies. The charismatic leader is typically replaced by an individual, or more likely a group of individuals, who are not as magnetic or creative as the original leader. They want to keep things going in the direction that was established by the charismatic leader, but they don't have his or her leadership skills and instincts. They also tend to revere the leader and want to preserve carefully the insights and the processes associated with him or her. Given this, they try to create routines, practices and documentation thereof that fully capture the former leadership's brilliance. This is called the <u>routinization of charisma</u>—that is, the effort to infuse the insights of the now departed charismatic leader into the routines that define his or her followers.

Bella: *It is all those beta males and beta females. They just don't have that alpha thing going.*

The problem is that when you make something routine, it doesn't usually capture the magic of the original moment, nor the manner in which the leader's words and actions had informed that moment. The initial leader had seen what the people needed spiritually at a given point in history and crafted a message that directly and specifically addressed those needs.

Bella: *If an idea is developed just because people need to hear it, does that mean it isn't true?*

Of course not. I am not saying that there may not be universal truths in the charismatic leaders initial words, but rather that those words and images were crafted and shaped with a view to move those in a particular time and place to see certain truths. In contrast, the bureaucracy that

64

follows—that is, the group that routinizes the leader's charisma—tends not to be as talented as the original charismatic leader. Nor are they as responsive to the changing needs, language and culture of the society. Typically, they are not able to keep the message as alive and directly relevant as did the original charismatic leader. This generates tension, as the message seems to lose direct relevance. Over time, the society does change. New technologies are developed. Different social relations and classes evolve. There may be immigrations of new and different peoples and emigrations as well. As the society changes, the message of the original leader, crafted to address the needs of a different time, becomes ever less relevant to the current spiritual needs and challenges of the people. The bureaucracy that was set up to keep the leader's initial message alive gets further and further out of touch with the changing spiritual needs of the people, and ever more interested in simply replicating itself. This provides a situation ripe for change. Eventually, the tension between the out-of-date, routinized bureaucracy and the spiritual needs of the people becomes so great that a new charismatic leader emerges with a new spiritual message to address the situation. This might be presented as a wholly new approach, or alternatively as a return to original principles. Either way, this new charismatic leader will attract a large following, because they have a fresh message that is well targeted at the current needs and modes of the people. And so the cycle continues.

Bella: *But isn't the most important thing about religion whether it is true or not? I find the notion that it simply changes to meet changing needs rather disturbing.*

The fact that a formulation of spiritual ideas meets a specific set of human needs, and is alluring for that reason, does not indicate that those ideas are false. There can be little doubt that God's ways are a mystery to humans. If God inspires a particular religious leader to meet the needs of a population with a particular spiritual message, the fact that the people, in fact, had a need for that spiritual guidance in no way affects its possible truth.

Bella: *And what does all this have to do with understanding the nature of science?*

Weber's ideas of charisma, routinization and social change can be applied not only to religion, but also to other areas of social interaction and change—including science, economics and even art. More particularly, a philosopher of science named Thomas Kuhn applied this same structure to science. And an economist named Joseph Schumpeter applied very similar ideas to economics. Indeed, there are many variants of Weber's fruitful idea to be found in many different disciplines. In this chapter, we'll take a quick look at Thomas Kuhn's application of Weber's notion of charisma and routinization to science, and see what we can learn from it. In a later chapter, we will look at Schumpeter's brilliant application of the idea to economics and the world of business.

ROUTINE AND REVOLUTIONARY SCIENCE

Thomas Kuhn applied Weber's ideas to science in a famous book entitled The Structure of Scientific Revolutions. (Note, however, that Kuhn didn't frame his book as being an application of Weber, and he may well have arrived at the ideas independently—but the structure of the ideas is essentially the same.) In his book, Kuhn argues that there were really two kinds of scientists: revolutionary scientists and normal scientists.

The revolutionary scientist is the equivalent of Weber's charismatic leader—these are the Newtons and Einsteins of the world. The "normal scientists" are the routinizers, who simply try to apply the theories that have been developed by some revolutionary scientist, but do not question it. Kuhn's "normal scientists" correspond to Weber's routinizers of charisma. For Kuhn, "normal scientists" are those who are trained in the application of a particular dominant scientific theory, but who are not inclined to question that theory or even test it. Rather, their task is simply to go out and find more things to explain in terms of the theory.

Imagine a young woman seeking to receive her Ph.D.—the highest degree—in, say, physics, and let's say we are still in the Newtonian world (that is, Einstein hasn't come along yet). She does some research and experimentation and uncovers a phenomenon that cannot be explained—indeed, appears to represent a counterexample—to the very theories that her professors have made their reputations on, and which they get paid handsome salaries to teach. Let's say that she finds that the planet Pluto is following a path that is not quite what it should be in terms of the theory. She comes to a panel of her professors to "defend" her research—that is, answer questions about her research as the final hurdle in receiving her degree. She enthusiastically explains to them she has disproven their beloved Newtonian physics through a counterexample. She shows the professors her evidence that Pluto isn't quite where the theory predicts it should be. She declares: "It's time to reject Newtonian mechanics, and banish it from the realm of science!" She figures her name is soon going to be up in the lights with Newton's.

As you may well imagine, it doesn't take long for her professors to start asking whether she has considered the possibility that there might be <u>other</u> gravitational forces pulling on Pluto that would account for its position. Indeed, they are likely to conclude not that she has refuted their cherished theory, but simply that she is not very good at applying it. They will be dismayed that she couldn't think of any conjectures regarding the observation that would save and protect Newtonian mechanics. For the <u>normal scientist</u>—who is, say, being trained in Newtonian mechanics—the fact that Pluto is not where it is supposed to be is not a test of Newtonian mechanics <u>but rather a test of her ability to apply the theory</u>. The theory is simply assumed to be true.

Whatever the dominant theory is in a particular scientific discipline at any one time, Kuhn calls a "paradigm". According to Kuhn, what scientists normally do is learn the paradigm and apply it—not question it. That's why he calls it "normal science". In Kuhn's portrayal of science, counterexamples—as such—do <u>not</u> play a big role. Indeed, "counterexample" is a very strong word. It suggests that an observation runs <u>counter</u> to the theory, and therefore refutes it.

Bella: *With a word like that, you are going to think: "Hey, we better get rid of the theory; we have a counterexample. It's counter to the theory!"*

In contrast, folks who don't think counterexamples should necessarily lead to the rejection of a theory may want a gentler word. That word is "anomaly." An anomaly is an observation that doesn't fit your theory. Of course, an anomaly is simply a counterexample—but it's a counterexample that we think we might be able to eventually explain <u>in terms of the theory</u>, perhaps through some additional minor adjustment to the theory. In that hope, normal scientists like to think of a counterexample as merely a problematic observation—something that we feel is in need of explanation if we are going to keep our theory, but one we think we will eventually be able to figure out in terms of the theory. Anomalies are observations that are looked at more as the key puzzles that the practitioners of the science should take on. By addressing and resolving these anomalies through the application of the current theory the up-and-coming young scientists have an opportunity to prove their worth. The observation of Pluto not being quite where it is predicted to be in terms of the theory would be something that would normally be viewed as an anomaly—a puzzle to solve, not the end of the line for the theory.

Bella: *If everyone is simply learning the current paradigm and applying it, how does science develop and embrace new paradigms?*

For Kuhn, the big changes in science come through revolutionary scientists. (These correspond to Weber's charismatic leaders, of course.) The thing about anomalies is that usually they <u>can</u> be solved. That is, usually they can be explained in terms of the theory. Sometimes, however, they cannot be explained. Within a scientific discipline, when an anomaly is initially noticed, as we have noted above, it is simply seen as an intriguing puzzle. But if the anomaly stubbornly resists being explained in terms of the theory, then it will become more famous within the discipline. It will at first become seen as a particularly challenging puzzle. Eventually, if it resists resolution in terms of the current theory for long enough, it will start to be seen as a problem with the theory. Perhaps a number of such counterexamples accumulate, none of which has been explained by the theory. At this point, some scientists will begin to re-think and re-examine the theory itself. That is, we finally reach the moment where the anomaly is seen as potentially a counterexample—one to be taken seriously. But note that this is an exceptional situation—not the norm. We may reach a point of crisis, where the scientists come to doubt the truth of the current theory. It no longer seems as powerful of an explanatory framework as it once did.

At this point, some great scientist—Kuhn calls him or her a revolutionary scientist—makes a breakthrough. He or she develops a new theory that explains much of what the old theory covered, but which also explains the highly problematic counterexample. Often this new theory will render the old theory as simply a "special case." This means that the old theory is no longer seen as universally true, but rather as simply capturing an aspect of reality in certain special situations—a useful model, but not the truth. In other instances, the new theory will completely replace the old theory, and banish it to the history of science books (where we can all wonder at how anyone could have once thought that!) This is a scientific revolution, and the actual history of science is full of them.

A scientific revolution introduces a new paradigm—that is, a new theory (or interrelated set of theories) along with prominent observations and celebrated examples of application of the new theory. Students of the science will accept these as truth, just as they did the dominant paradigm that preceded this one. Students and practitioners of the science will apply the new theories to whatever challenges they encounter. And, of course, problematic observations will be seen not as counterexamples, but merely as anomalies—puzzles to be explained in terms of the new theory. And so the cycle of revolutionary science, normal science, crisis and then back to (new) revolutionary science continues. That is how Kuhn sees science advancing—in fits and starts—with big leaps followed by periods of consolidation and unquestioning application.

Clearly, Kuhn's revolutionary scientist plays a role analogous to Weber's charismatic religious leader and, as we will see in a later chapter, to Schumpeter's entrepreneur. And, similarly, Kuhn's normal scientist plays a role analogous to the routinizers found in these other kinds of movements. Kuhn portrays science as a very human process. His description of alternating periods of scientific normalcy and revolution fits much of what we observe in the history of science.

Suggested Readings

- Thomas Kuhn The Structure of Scientific Revolutions Second Edition, The University of Chicago Press (1970)

5

SCIENCE AS INTELLIGENT GUESSWORK

No great discovery was ever made without a bold guess.

ISAAC NEWTON

If we knew what we were doing, it wouldn't be called Research.

ALBERT EINSTEIN

{T}hey have failed to solve the great problem: How can we admit that our knowledge is a human—an all too human—affair, without at the same time implying that it is all individual whim and arbitrariness?

KARL POPPER

Field of Gourds

{T}he advances in scientific thought come from a <u>combination of loose and</u> <u>strict thinking</u>, and this combination is the most precious tool of science.

GREGORY BATESON

Truth emerges more readily from error than from confusion.

FRANCIS BACON

As we saw in the previous chapters, science cannot prove its propositions, nor even definitively determine the probabilities of competing theories. Science is <u>not</u> an accumulation of proven truth. Indeed, the history of science is a history of revolutions—and thus it cannot be an accumulation of proven truth. On a regular basis, what was once thought to be scientific truth is rejected and replaced by something new.

Bella: *If science can't prove anything, then what is the difference between, say, astronomy—the study of the stars and planets—and astrology—forecasting one's personal fate in terms of the stars and planets? Most people—and dogs too—would agree that one is science and the other is not, and that there is a difference between them. But if the difference is not in the capacity to prove, then what is it? Is there no basis on which to deem one person's view of reality as better than another's? Is truth merely relative? Is anyone's theory on anything to be considered just as good as anybody else's regardless of the facts? Surely there is still something that is special about science—something that explains the technological progress we have experienced. We did land men on the moon after all, and they couldn't have done that in the 19th century. Our day-to-day experience of technology tells us that we know more now than we used to know. So how do you explain that? Woof! Woof! Woof!*

In this chapter, I try to answer your questions.

Drawing by Kate Fisher 1

CONJECTURES AND REFUTATIONS

The philosopher of science Karl Popper explained how and why science can progress even though it can't prove anything. Like you Bella, he wanted to identify what was special about science—what made it different than other activities—and to explain why it was so successful. But Popper does this in a rather surprising way. He focuses on disproof rather than proof as providing the special hallmark of science. From a logical perspective, disproof is much more powerful than proof. As we saw in an earlier chapter, while one can never prove a proposition—no matter how many observations one collects—it only takes one counterexample to disprove it. That is, no matter how many white swans you see, you haven't proven that "all swans are white," yet it only takes one black swan to disprove the proposition. Popper uses this fact—that it only takes one counterexample to disprove—as the basis of a dynamic kind of rationality, which he calls "falsificationism". According to Popper, scientific progress is generated through a bold, vibrant and open-ended process in which competing conjectures are tested against observations, with falsifications constantly narrowing the field while also generating new, more interesting observations in need of explanation.

For Popper, then, science is not about proving, but rather about conjectures and refutations. "Conjectures" are educated guesses that are consistent with the evidence that we have encountered thus far—that is, tentatively held propositions. The word "tentative" implies that we always remain aware that these propositions are unproven and may eventually be shown to be false. For Popper, at any point in time, what we consider as scientific knowledge is always maintained only tentatively. We do not consider it proven (which doesn't mean that it isn't perhaps true, of course). "Refutations" involve empirical observations that disprove propositions. In other words, they are criticisms based on observation. A refutation highlights that something is wrong or incorrect about a theory. That is, there is something the theory was meant to explain, but doesn't.

In sum, for Popper, science involves the interactive, ever evolving and fruitful dance of conjectures and refutations. While scientists cannot prove, they can propose guesses that are consistent with what has been observed. Science, according to Popper, is advanced through a two-step process in which: (1) conjectures—that is, tentative guesses—are forwarded in an effort to explain what has been observed up to that point in time, and (2) the competing conjectures are then criticized and refuted through further observation. What remains after this two-step competition for survival are the tentative guesses that might be true. And that is the best that science can do (and, in fact, that is pretty good).

Popper's vision of science is a bit like Darwin's theory of evolution. The scientific conjectures are like the species competing for continued existence within an ecosystem. Observations provide the environment within which they try to survive—with just one counterexample resulting in the extinction of a conjecture. New conjectures are like mutations that result in new species that compete to survive within the ecosystem. At any given point, of course, just as we don't know which species will survive and which will not, so too we do not know which conjectures will survive and which will not. Over time, observations (more specifically, counterexamples) refute some of the new conjectures, so that only the fittest survive. At any given point, we can only say that the survivors have not been refuted. We cannot say that they are true, only that they <u>may</u> be and that they are <u>consistent with the evidence that we have so far</u>.

THE GROWTH OF KNOWLEDGE THROUGH CRITICISM

Thus, Popper argues that science is not so much about proving as about disproving. Indeed, in his view, it is the disproving that generates the progress, which evolves from the interaction of conjectures and refutations. The good scientist tries to disprove her theories.

Bella: *What! This turns everything on its head. I thought scientists tried to* <u>*prove*</u> *their theories, not disprove them. How can the growth of scientific knowledge be explained by disproof?*

An example will help you see the power of Popper's vision. Let's go back to our conjecture that "water boils at 212 degrees Fahrenheit." While a good scientist will want to run some experiments, and confirm that the water does, in fact, boil consistently at this temperature, we have seen that there is no point in trying to prove it through induction; that is really just a waste of resources. Rather, according to Popper, what the good scientist should do is try to <u>disprove</u> it.

What might a scientist do to try to disprove the proposition that "water boils at 212 degrees Fahrenheit"? Instead of simply running the experiment a very large number of times under the same conditions—which is a useless exercise—the scientist could instead try to see if the proposition still holds under different conditions. A good scientist will try to test the proposition under as many different conditions as she can think of. She is really trying to find out <u>not</u> when it works, but rather when it doesn't work—as this is kind of the information that will raise more interesting scientific puzzles. It is these puzzles that will force new questions and trigger further scientific advance. For example, she might try boiling the water while moving along rapidly on a train. If she did, she would find that the water still boils at 212 degrees Fahrenheit. But she should keep trying to disprove it. She should try it under any conditions she can think of.

Bella: *I get it. It's like Dr. Seuss. She should try it on a plane, in a train, with a fox and in a box!*

Perhaps she thinks of climbing a mountain and trying to boil water at a high altitude. It's at that point that she will find that water does not always boil at 212 degrees Fahrenheit. Under those circumstances, the proposition is falsified. She will be forced to stop and think, and ask herself why. This is the great moment of science. She must ask: what is special about these circumstances? This is a new and very valuable question that she is unlikely to have come across, or to have come across as soon, without her efforts to disprove the proposition. Here we arrive at a crucial step in the advancement of knowledge. The falsification of the proposition has brought the scientist to a new question, and therein resides the potential for the advancement of knowledge.

She asks herself: why was the proposition refuted at a high altitude? She must find a new, and more refined, conjecture that targets and explains this counterexample—that is, the failure of the water to boil at 212 degrees Fahrenheit when high up on the mountain. This is where the bold conjecturing comes back into play. More specifically, she needs a new conjecture that is consistent with water boiling at 212 degrees Fahrenheit at sea level, but that also encompasses the observation that water boils at a different temperature high up on the mountainside. Perhaps her new conjecture is that air pressure has something to do with it. If she can formulate this new conjecture in a testable form—perhaps an equation that relates the temperature at which water boils to air pressure—then she has a new conjecture that is consistent with not only past observations, but also with these new observations on the mountainside. That is scientific progress! And it wouldn't have happened without a focus on the counterexample. Thus, surprisingly, we see that the discovery comes not through proof, but through disproof. This view of science is called "falsificationism"—because it places the spotlight on empirical criticism and the opportunity for the advancement of knowledge that is so intimately tied to criticism and the process of falsification.

Through our example, we can see that science really involves a four-step process—thus, we are fleshing out the two-step description we gave above in this chapter. First, conjectures are proposed in an attempt to explain some phenomenon. Second, there is the criticism—that is, an attempt to disprove the conjecture. In this way, empirical counterexamples are discovered. (Counterexamples are instances where the original conjecture is falsified.) Third, a set of more interesting questions are raised by the counterexamples. Fourth, there are new, bold conjectures that are proposed to explain both the former observations <u>and</u> the new problematic observations. Most importantly, note here that while one has not proven the theory, one has <u>improved</u> it through this discovery process. That is, the more refined conjectures that result from this process explain <u>more</u> observations than do the earlier less refined conjectures. That is the essence of scientific progress and provides the foundation for technical progress.

Bella: *So that is the answer to my puzzle with which I introduced the chapter!*

Yes. It is this dynamic process of conjectures and criticism that constitutes the explanation for how science can rapidly advance and support technological progress <u>without</u> ever proving anything—for while proving is impossible, <u>improvement</u> is not. <u>We can recognize when a theory explains more than it did before.</u> Popper's idea that knowledge grows through criticism is a dramatically different view of science than that presented by the positivists. While some important refinements will be added below, this is the theory of knowledge that this book embraces. I will argue that this theory of knowledge provides us with a core understanding of rationality itself, and that it also has broad application beyond science <u>per se</u>; it can be used to explore just about anything. Indeed, I believe it can provide a foundation for a philosophical approach to your life, and a key to the meaning of life.

Bella: *Whoa, that's heavy.*

Life is heavy with meaning. But we will get to that later in the book.

POPPER'S DEMARCATION CRITERION

For Popper, it is this possibility for refutation that keeps science honest. Indeed, the potential for falsification provides Popper's demarcation between science and non-science. "Demarcation" is a fancy word for drawing a line.

Bella: *Philosophers like to use words like "demarcation" because it makes them sound smart.*

Well, you have to admit that the "line drawing" debate about science vs. non-science doesn't sound as elegant as the demarcation debate. According to Popper, what is special about science is the fact that it works with conjectures that are susceptible to being falsified. That is, they lend themselves to making predictions that we can check against observable things in the real world. Popper argues that if a body of thought doesn't lend itself to propositions that have the potential to be refuted, then it isn't really scientific. For example, Popper would argue that astrology (as opposed to astronomy) isn't a science because it doesn't lend itself to testable propositions.

Bella: *But something is amiss here. Popper's ideas can't be both a way to distinguish science from non-science and also a theory of how to think about anything and everything.*

Popper's demarcation criterion—that is, the drawing of this line between science and non-science—was of central importance to him as a philosopher, and there is certainly something to it. But, as we will see later in this book, his demarcation criterion doesn't fully hold up—at least, not in my view. To be sure, some topics—like physics and chemistry and biology—do lend themselves to a much more robust type of empirical progress than others. At the same time, I will argue that the dynamic interaction of conjecture and criticism <u>does</u> provide a foundation for a broader type of rationality, which we will explore in later chapters. We haven't finished building our theory yet, so you have to be a little bit patient.

But while we will make a few amendments to Popper's ideas, he basically has it right. The essence of rationality is in the dynamic interaction of conjecture, criticism, new questions and further conjecturing. This constitutes a complete break with the positivists and the positivist's mindset. With Popper, we reject the metaphor of the scientist as collector of pebbles of truth to be placed in the sack of science. And while we recognize that there is something special and powerful in the scientific discovery process, we also come to understand that science is not authoritative—it is not proven truth. To join Popper in this puts you at odds with much of modernity—indeed, it will put you at odds with much of the conventional thinking that characterizes our era. What Popper makes us realize is the idea of proof itself is a red herring.

Bella: *What is a red herring?*

It's a smelly fish. But what people mean when they say "red herring" is that it's a distraction that leads you down the wrong path. Suppose there are dogs—like you Bella—using their sense of smell to track a person, and the person wants to mislead the dogs so she can escape. She might drag a red herring—a smelly fish— across the path. The dogs come to this point, smell the scent of the fish, and are lured to follow that scent instead of following the person.

Bella: *Oh, that is sneaky!*

And so is positivism with its specious claims to authority. The idea of "proof" in science is a red herring, because scientists end up mistakenly putting their resources into proving, which is not possible, rather than into efforts at disproof, which—as we saw above—provides the key to advancing knowledge by generating counterexamples, new questions and ever more refined conjectures with expanding empirical content.

In sum, at the heart of the scientific process is not proof, but two intertwining components: (1) boldness and creativity in conjecturing—that is, educated guesses that are consistent with past observations and (2) tough criticism that seeks counterexamples combined with an attitude that takes those counterexamples seriously. While we can never know whether our scientific propositions are true, we <u>can</u> know whether they are consistent with what has been observed <u>so far</u>. Thus, we can hold them as <u>possibly</u> true up to the point at which they are disproven by some observation. This is what scientific knowledge is. Through criticism, this knowledge is advanced. We'll occasionally refer to this dynamic process as the "logic of discovery".

THE ROLE OF OBSERVATION IN SCIENCE

The role of observation in Popper's view of science is central, but quite different than it is with positivism. With positivism, the idea was to use observations as a basis for proof. This simply is not possible. In contrast, in Popper's view, science uses observations as a lever of further discovery. The true role of observation is, first, to limit our conjectures to those that are consistent with what has been observed so far. That is a pretty tough constraint, of course. But note that we are not saying that our conjectures must be true, just that they must fit what has been observed so far. Second, observations are used to try to disprove our conjectures. Third, counterexamples, which are a type of observation, once found, must be taken seriously. We try to account for them with additional new, bold conjectures. As noted above, it is precisely this building process that explains how science could advance so rapidly, while at the same time not having the capacity to prove anything. Indeed, as we saw in the example of efforts to disprove the proposition that water boiled at 212 degrees Fahrenheit, this Popperian dance of conjectures and refutations provides the most direct and aggressive path to knowledge. It also explains how one can be a rationalist—a believer that some approaches to knowledge are superior to others—while at the same time not believing that science has the capacity to prove.

The fact that our scientific conjectures—even if tentatively held—are consistent with what has been observed in the past renders the information extremely useful (even if not necessarily true). With Popper's logic of discovery, we see not only that proof is not essential for scientific progress, but rather that excessive efforts at proof are apt to actually slow down the discovery process. It is through criticism—and efforts at disproof—that we dig deeper and uncover new improved conjectures that capture yet more of reality (even if inevitably unproven). The tentative nature of scientific propositions renders them no less useful in terms of developing technology. No one cares that the propositions are unproven, so long as they work! By acknowledging the tentative nature of scientific knowledge, we are merely embracing the more fundamental truth that we can never know them to be true. But recognizing this is very important as it opens our minds and our scientific process to further discovery through criticism and conjecture.

Thus, Popper's view fully explains the rapid progress of technology. What impresses us all about modern technology and science is not, in fact, its status as truth but rather the fact that it appears to work. We do rightly sense that there is something special and progressive about science. We can know that the medical breakthroughs that provide cures for some cancers, or the technology that produces the computer I am typing on at this moment do, in fact, appear to work, and that the scientific propositions upon which they are based are good working tools in order to get such things done. That is, we can know that the tentatively held propositions of science have worked with respect to what we have observed so far. But in no way does this imply that scientific propositions are necessarily true, and, indeed, will not be falsified at some future point in time. Indeed, as we saw in previous chapters, the history of science shows us that what we once thought was true is often later refuted.

It turns out that proof is simply not necessary for scientific and technical progress.

Technology, after all, is not about proven truth, but about practical usefulness. Ideas can be quite useful, even if not proven to be true, or even, in fact, if they are false. They are useful so long as they happen to fit the terrain and the topics within which one is operating. Thus, when I am reading a street map of a city, and trying to find my way to a particular address, I may well assume that the world is flat, and that assumption is good enough for my purposes even if it is not true. On the other hand, if I am trying to navigate a flight from New York to Mumbai, it is best that I not rely on that assumption. Similarly, we know that many of the propositions of Newtonian physics are false, if they are taken as <u>general</u> propositions about all of reality. At the same time, they remain excellent tools with which to develop certain technologies. That is, within certain realms, they remain a good approximation to reality. The point is that proven truth and technological usefulness are not the same thing.

Bella: *So should we give up on the idea of truth altogether?*

THE QUEST FOR TRUTH

There are quite a few thinkers who reach this point in their analysis and then leap to the conclusion that we should focus only on usefulness and give up on the quest for truth. I disagree with that idea. I think the <u>quest</u> for truth—and the belief that there is a truth—remains of fundamental importance. The problem with the notion of usefulness is that—as a criterion of theory choice—it is always tied to some particular set of usages. Thus, it is intrinsically short-sighted. It does not carry you to new ideas. In contrast, the driving force behind Popper's conjectures and refutations is, indeed, an effort to find universal truths. It is our refutations that tell us we have not done so, but our desire to find those universal truths leads to the further conjecturing. In contrast to the rich discourse that is driven by a quest for truth, there is no arguing with an idea if one is simply proposing it as <u>useful</u> for some narrow set of purposes. One person says: "The world is flat!" The other says: "That can't be true because it doesn't explain how a ship could slowly appear over the horizon." And the first person then replies: "My assumption is good enough for my purposes." Clearly, that approach doesn't lead to a growth in knowledge. Moreover, actual truth is important, even if we can't necessarily know when we have found it. The truth will always prevail in terms of the ultimate reality we confront. For example, there may be a high degree of uncertainty associated with the question of how many jobs a particular governmental economic stimulus program might create, or alternatively, destroy. But whatever the answer to that question is, we will, in fact, incur the consequences of whatever the truth is, even if we can't know for sure what that impact is. Truth matters. The fact that it is incredibly difficult to establish should not lead us to conclude otherwise.

The weirdness of the Popperian view—and I think it is right in its weirdness—is that growth of knowledge results from combining a quest for universal truth with the recognition that we can never know if we get there. As I noted above, Popper's dance of conjectures and criticism is sometimes referred to as the "logic of discovery". The metaphor that captures this idea is not one of collecting, but rather of a journey of discovery. Science is a ship of discovery, and we are all invited along to partake in the journey. Its beauty lies not in its authority, but in its invitation that we all partake actively within, and contribute to, the adventure. Its very essence is anchored in a community of discourse and argument, without which it cannot exist. Popper's logic of discovery is dynamic and takes us to the heart of the actual discovery process. It is bold, clear conjectures that render criticism and refutation possible. It is criticism and refutation that unearth yet more interesting observations and stimulate yet further conjecturing. As we will see below, this, indeed, provides the essence not only of science, but of rationality itself.

POSITIVISM AND FALSIFICATIONISM COMPARED

Notice how the values of science—that is, what is to be celebrated—shift with the adoption of a Popperian perspective. With the positivists, speculation was to be avoided at all costs. We have to keep unproven nonsense out of the realm of science! Only proven truths need apply. With Popper, speculation—albeit speculation driven by an effort to account for observations—is no longer to be avoided, but rather is to be embraced. Indeed, it is at the very heart of the scientific process.

The positivist view of science is that it involves accumulating proven truths—like an agglomeration of pebbles. The key is to let in only proven items, so that we can rely on scientific truth. The problems with this approach are twofold. First, the accumulated "truths" have not been proven, and thus may not turn out to be true after all, and so the progress is not as sure as it seems. Second, and perhaps more problematic, there may be much that is knowable to some degree, and graspable by science, but that remains beyond the scope of this approach. That is, some scientific knowledge may only be reachable through bold conjecturing.

With Popper's falsificationism, we have to change our guiding metaphor. Instead of collecting pebbles of truth in the sack of science, we must think of throwing our fishing nets wide—those are our bold conjectures. The wider we throw our nets, the more fish we are apt to catch. And so it is in science. There is a great deal of content we cannot reach by playing it safe. Instead, we must be bold in our conjecturing. We sometimes have to go beyond the facts that lie before us. With such bold conjecturing, however, the following step is <u>not</u> to try to prove the conjectures, of course, but to attempt to falsify them. And then, of course, having spotted the counterexamples, the good scientist attempts to develop further conjectures that account for them as well. And so the dynamic process of bold conjecture and refutation continues—never resulting in either proof or certainty, but nonetheless providing for the most rapid and efficient growth of knowledge.

Bella: *The proof of the pudding, so-to-speak, is in the history of science.*

EINSTEIN'S CURVED SPACE

An examination of the history of science reveals that great advances in science are not always driven by observation, but rather—quite often—through bold new conjectures that are only corroborated after the fact. To see how important bold conjecturing is to the development of scientific knowledge, let's look at one of the more famous examples from the history of science—Einstein's notion of curved space. Einstein hypothesized that gravitational forces had the effect of curving space itself.

Bella: *Now that is a bold conjecture!*

And it is certainly counterintuitive. In our everyday lives we experience curved things, but not a curvature of space itself.

Bella: *How would one ever test such a hypothesis?*

Einstein thought of a way. He argued that if it were true that space is curved by gravitational forces, then when light from distant stars passed by our Sun that light would itself take on a curved trajectory—that is, its path would be bent—as it travelled though the space that has been curved by the gravitational force of the sun. As a result, the light from those stars would have been curved prior to the point at which that light strikes our eyes—that is, prior to the point when we see it. Normally, when light strikes our eyes, our minds interpret the light as emanating from a source that is directly (that is, straight) in the direction from which the light strikes us. To us, then, if Einstein were right, it would appear as if the stars have been shifted outward from their normal positions—that is, away from the sun—because the angle at which the light hits our eyes would be shifted out by the curvature of space. (The diagram below—in combination with the text that follows—should help make this clear.)

Bella: *But that's silly. We wouldn't be able to see that starlight at all because the brightness of the Sun would block it out.*

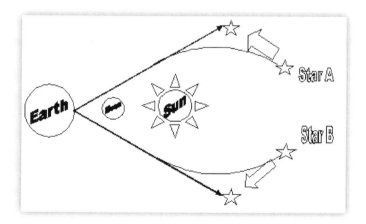

Einstein had an answer for that too. He said if we wait for an eclipse of the sun—that is, the next time that the moon blocks the light from the sun—we would be able to see the star light, even though the Sun is lined up with them. He predicted that we would then observe that the stars will have appeared to shift outward, due to the now curved trajectory of their starlight as bent by the gravitational force of the sun. Looking at the diagram above, begin your analysis by looking at Star A and Star B, as labeled. The curved lines (sorry that they are a little squiggly) represent the light emanating from Star A and Star B, as it is curved by the gravitational force of the Sun. When that light reaches the Earth, it hits our eyes at an angle that does not reflect the actual position of those stars (precisely because the light has been curved.) As noted above, however, when light strikes our eyes, our mind imagines that the light is emanating from something that is directly behind the light—that is, in a straight line. Thus, on the diagram, if you follow the straight lines back out from the Earth, you can see where the stars will appear to be located from the perspective of a viewer on Earth, even though that is not the actual location of those stars. Of course, when we look at these same stars at night—that is, when no Sun is placed near their path—the light will not be bent in this fashion. As a consequence, normally the stars will appear to be in their actual positions.

Bella: *Did this movement in the apparent location of the stars really happen just as Mr. Einstein predicted?*

When an eclipse did come, everyone was ready to see if Einstein was right. And it happened exactly as he predicted, making him very famous. Indeed, his name became synonymous with genius.

Bella: *You're an Einstein.*

Thank you. No one had ever noticed such a thing before. Einstein predicted it solely on the basis of his speculative and unconfirmed theories. And what a bold prediction it was! This was bold conjecturing leading the way. Einstein's theories were also a major blow to the notion of proof by deduction from assumptions that could be known intuitively. There was no denying that Einstein's theories had led to new, interesting and confirmed predictions about the world. Yet, its theoretical assumptions were counterintuitive. His work also shows how theory may well advance ahead of observation. It was not through induction that Einstein arrived at his brilliant discoveries. Rather, his work displayed the power of bold conjectures. He cast his fishing nets wide, and found new truths that would have always remained beyond those steeped in, and trapped by, inductive and deductive reasoning.

Bella: *I am going to be bold in all my conjecturing from now on!*

Well, do keep in mind that many bold conjectures turn out to be flat out wrong and are, ultimately, falsified. For example, Plato conjectured that the four elements of which all matter is constituted are all based on different regular geometric solids.[34] Needless to say, this is a little different than the periodic table of today. Boldness is a good quality for a conjecture, but not the only one that matters. And, yet, it all begins with boldness.

INTELLECTUAL PLAYFULNESS COMBINED WITH DISCIPLINE

In a way, Einstein's approach was like that of a very young child—playful. Intellectual playfulness is often the key to great discoveries. Indeed, a young child is a machine of discovery. How does a young child discover the properties of the world? Do they use deductive and inductive reasoning? No. They play. Imagine a very young child sitting on a carpet holding a rubber ball. What are its properties? What is it for? What is fun about it? The child will try all kinds of bold conjectures—through play. How does it taste? (Not so great.) Can I stick it in my ear? (No.) What happens if I smash it against my noggin? (Doesn't feel so great.) Can I squeeze it? (Oh, that is sort of interesting.) Can I throw it? (Yes.) Does it bounce? (Yes.)

Bella: *Can I play too? Give me that ball.*

Playing is a mode of discovery. Playing, in its essence, is conjecturing—trying things out. Science is not so very different than that. To play is to explore. To play is to discover. To play is to experiment. Children have this deep drive to play.

Bella: *And dogs too!*

That is how they discover the world. We all have that same drive, although it is often suppressed in adults. If you want to make discoveries about the world—if you want to probe it deeply and fully grasp it—you must be playful—playful with ideas, playful with bold conjectures, playful in your thinking. All great thinkers and scientists are playful in this way. Indeed, they can't help themselves anymore than children can. Playing is essential to discovery because it generates the conjectures. And playing with the conjecture itself can generate the refutations. The logic of discovery is little more, and nothing less, than playing with ideas. And, yet, here is the paradox or, perhaps, I should say the difficult challenge. In the midst of this playfulness there must also be discipline. The discipline is needed in terms of the follow-through and focus required to keep an exploration on a fruitful track and consistent with observations. That is, as a scientist is attempting to advance our knowledge, not just any conjecture will do. We need conjectures that address former counterexamples and refutations, and bring them into the scope of what the ideas can successfully explain. To put this more simply, science is also a discipline and a lot of hard work. We have to keep our eye on the prize—the key anomalies we are trying to explain. Thus, the "play" of science is neither random, nor undisciplined. And it is finding the right balance between playfulness and discipline that makes a scientist truly great.

And so it is with all things. A great dancer must have worked extraordinarily hard, and disciplined her mind and body to perform, to reach the point where she can experiment with movement in a manner that results in a beautiful and innovative dance—to reach the point where she is in free flight, yet fully within the parameters and language of the dance. And so it is with an actor, who must work extraordinarily hard on the script and the character to reach a point where she can be fully and freely exploring a moment in that character's story with the audience, and yet be fully grounded in the text of the play and connected to the character.

Bella: *And so it is with a dog leaping through the air to catch a Frisbee.*

Freedom within the discipline, discipline within the freedom—therein lies the magic of discovery.

IT'S NOT THE PEOPLE, IT'S THE PROCESS

Scientists are human beings, and they have the same failings and strengths as the rest of us. They can be brilliant, creative, clever, productive, passionate, diligent, truthful, open minded, tolerant, loving, wise, spiritual and humorous. They can also be narrow minded, biased, greedy, dull, unkind, proud, selfish, untruthful, manipulative, shallow and profoundly ignorant. They are people. As such, in fact, they tend to be a complex mix of all of the above. Indeed, one of the profound puzzles of science is how such lovely and terribly flawed creatures—as humans are—can regularly advance scientific knowledge. The answer to that puzzle is not that scientists constitute an elite who simply are better than most of humankind—though many scientists would like to believe that, and there are many who are ready to join in the worship of scientists. The answer to the puzzle lies in something that transcends the flaws of individual humans—and that something is the logic of discovery. We do not reach truth through purity, but rather through a complex interactive process that transcends our impurities. The logic of discovery results <u>not</u> in people who are superior, but with ideas which are improved. Indeed, the dynamic process of conjectures and criticism uses our human flaws to best advantage. Our conjectures may be driven by irrational, biased or aesthetic considerations, yet they may still be quite worthy of the scrutiny that is provided through criticism. It is not the source of an idea that matters—or the emotional motivation behind it—but rather whether it can withstand criticism.

Historian of science Paul de Kruif makes this point in the context of the debate in the 18th century about the then prevalent belief that the spontaneous generation of life was a common occurrence. Spontaneous generation is the idea that living creatures can come into existence without predecessors of any sort. As historian de Kruif describes: "The English naturalist Ross announced learnedly that: 'To question that beetles and wasps were generated in cow dung is to question reason, sense, and experience.' Even such complicated animals as mice didn't have to have mothers or fathers …"[35] according to the beliefs at the time. De Kruif tells the story of how the Italian scientist Lazzaro Spallanzani challenged these beliefs regarding spontaneous generation through a series of experiments. Pointedly, however, de Kruif notes that Spallanzani's starting point—that is, his initial conjectures—were no more nor less based in fact or science than those of his opponents. As he describes:

> Spallanzani heard all of these stories which so many people were sure were facts, he read many more of them that were still more strange, he watched students get into brawls in excited attempts to prove that mice and bees didn't have to have fathers or mothers. He heard all of these things—and didn't believe them. He was prejudiced. Great advances in science so often start from prejudice, on ideas got not from science but straight out of a scientist's head, on notions that are only the opposite of the prevailing superstitious nonsense of the day.[36]

This is a key point. It doesn't matter from where we get our conjectures or what motivates them; what is important is the role those conjectures play in advancing the process of discovery.

FALSIFICATIONISM AT WORK

The story of Lorrenzo Spallanzani—our protagonist above who refused to believe that the spontaneous generation of life was a regular occurrence—provides an excellent example of falsificationism at work.[37]   In the 18th century, one Father Needham provided a "demonstration" that microscopic life could be generated spontaneously. He put some gravy in glass containers, sealed the containers with cork—to keep out any microscopic creatures that might enter from the air—and then heated the containers to kill any microscopic creatures that might be in them. He left the containers to sit for a number of days. He then opened them, put the contents under a microscope and saw microscopic creatures. He also reached the same result when he used mashed up seeds in water. He concluded that the microscopic creatures must have come into being spontaneously, since the conditions of his experiment had assured that there were no microscopic creatures originally within the containers. He hypothesized that these microscopic creatures were the result of something he called the "Vegetative Force", which, according to him, accounted for the spontaneous generation of life. Father Needham's discovery was highly celebrated.

Father Spallanzani—he also happened to be a priest—set out to falsify Needham's propositions. Spallanzani figured that the microscopic creatures had entered through the corks, which are somewhat porous in nature. He conducted Needham's experiment, but instead of sealing the glass containers with corks, he sealed each by fusing the glass at the mouth of the container. He also heated up the containers for a longer duration of time than had Needham. When Spallanzani broke open the containers, he found that there were no microscopic creatures. It appeared that he had falsified Father Needham's results. But the story doesn't end there. Father Needham countered that the extended duration of time over which Spallanzani had heated the glass containers had killed the "Vegetative Force." In response, Spallanzani conducted the experiment again, and heated the glass containers for the same extended duration of time again, only this time he sealed the containers with cork. Despite the extended duration of the heating, when the corks were used as a seal—instead of sealing off the glass itself—the microscopic creatures did return. Paul de Kruif describes what happens next (in falsificationist terms!):

> Spallanzani was triumphant, but then he did the curious thing that only born scientists ever do—he tried to beat his own idea, his darling theory—by experiments he honestly and shrewdly planned to defeat himself. That is science! That is the strange self-forgetting spirit of a few rare men, those curious men to whom truth is more dear than their own cherished whims and wishes. Spallanzani [thought] ... "maybe there is some mysterious force in these seeds that strong heat might destroy." Then he cleaned his flasks again, and took some seeds, but instead of merely boiling them in water, he put them in a coffee-roaster and baked them until they were soot-colored cinders. Next he poured pure distilled water over them, growling: "Now if there was a Vegetative Force in those seeds, I have surely roasted it to death."[38]

He once again sealed the flasks up with corks. When he checked back days later, the microscopic creatures were back again. Spallanzani's work provides a good example of how efforts to disprove fuel the logic of discovery. Eliminating possibilities can be quite powerful in the pursuit of knowledge. Popper's work makes us realize that rationality really resides in the interaction of the essential components of conjectures and criticism—and thus, in a sense, emanates from a certain kind of interaction among people. That is, the process of discovery can be quite rational, even if the people are not! Just as the source or motivation of a conjecture does not matter, neither does the motivational, inspirational, aesthetic or emotional drivers behind criticism. We might criticize a conjecture simply because we don't like the person who is forwarding the conjecture. Nonetheless, our criticism may prove valuable in that it highlights a counterexample and thereby facilitates the development of an improved set of conjectures that explains more than the previous conjecture.

THE MISSING BOLD CONJECTURE

Sometimes the boldness necessary to carry science forward is missing. For example, in the second half of the 17th century, a Dutchman named Antony Leeuwanhoek discovered and documented the existence of microscopic organisms.[39] He was particularly good at grinding lenses, and so his microscopes were the best. In the midst of his explorations, he also discovered that very hot water would kill the microscopic organisms. Indeed, he accidentally discovered this by testing the plaque from his teeth for microscopic organisms just after drinking some very hot coffee. He didn't find the tiny band of creatures that were normally there. Thus, as early as the late 1600s, it was known that microscopic organisms can be found in a person's mouth and that hot water kills those organisms. And yet, in 1831, about 150 years later, as a very young Louis Pasteur wondered why people bitten by a mad dog soon thereafter die, no one had yet conjectured that it was microscopic organisms that cause disease. Imagine how many lives could have been saved if someone had made the bold conjecture that—just perhaps—diseases might be caused by these tiny creatures.[xii] If they had, then the idea that we should clean, say, medical instruments with boiling water—would likely have followed on quickly. But Leeuwanhoek—an extremely careful observer—was not one for bold conjectures. Nor for that matter was Spallanzani, our hero above who defeated the theory of spontaneous generation, and who had continued to pursue microscopic creatures in the intervening century leading up to Pasteur.

Suggested Readings

- Karl R. Popper Conjectures and Refutations: The Growth of Scientific Knowledge Routledge and Kegan Paul (1972)
- James Robert Brown The Laboratory of the Mind: Thought Experiments in the Natural Sciences (Routledge 1993)
- Paul de Kruif Microbe Hunters Harcourt, Inc. (1996) (originally published in 1926)

6

THE FALSIFICATION OF FALSIFICATIONISM

A new scientific truth does not triumph by convincing its opponents and making them see light, but rather because its opponents eventually die, and a new generation grows up that is familiar with it.

MAX PLANCK

Galileo claimed the he could 'observe' mountains on the moon and spots on the sun and that these 'observations' refuted the time-honored theory that celestial bodies are faultless crystal balls. But his 'observations' were not 'observational' in the sense of being observed by the— unaided—senses: their reliability depended on the reliability of his telescope—and of the optical theory of the telescope—which was violently questioned by his contemporaries.

IMRE LAKATOS

Scientists do not, in fact, typically go around trying to disprove their own conjectures. Indeed, you have probably noticed that most people do not, in fact, go around touting which of their own ideas they have disproven. Imagine: your friend walks in the door and says: "I came up with a new idea today, and then I disproved it! Want to hear all about it?" That doesn't happen. The same goes, more or less, for scientists. This is a serious problem for Popper's ideas about science, because if scientists don't really do what he says they do, then his ideas about how science progresses would appear to be wrong.

Bella: *Indeed, falsificationism would have been falsified! I thought you said Popper was right!*

Popper is basically right. But we are going to apply a bit of falsificationism to falsificationism. And it turns out, Popper is not completely right. We need to challenge his ideas a bit, to arrive at a more sophisticated understanding of the scientific process. One of the problems with Popper's falsificationism is that scientists typically do, in fact, try to prove their conjectures, and to convince others of their truth in any way they can. Even if proof with certainty is not possible, they nonetheless spend their time aggregating what they believe to be convincing evidence. Moreover, as we noted just above, scientists tend not to spend their time in self-criticism and attempts to disprove (albeit with some notable exceptions). What is even more problematic with Popper's ideas is that scientists often, and even typically, do not reject their scientific propositions even when confronted with a counterexample! This is extremely troubling, as it undermines Popper's logic of discovery. Even worse for Popper's vision, as we will see below, there may—on occasion—even be good reasons for ignoring counterexamples.

So while falsificationism may have some elements that are more historically accurate than positivism—for example, in recognizing that scientists do engage in creative leaps—and while it may accurately portray the centrality of criticism to the growth of knowledge—there does appear to be something missing from Popper's account in terms of explaining how and why actual scientists behave as they do and how that behavior would result in the growth in scientific knowledge. In sum, Popper's falsificationism has some flaws or gaps and is in need of further development if we are to develop our full blown theory of rational discourse. As noted above, in this book we will, in fact, adopt most of Popper's insights about conjectures and criticism, and, in particular, the key role that criticism plays in the growth of knowledge. In this chapter, however, we will provide a critique of Popper's vision. And then in the next chapter, we will improve Popper's vision in a manner that addresses these critiques. Let's first see why it sometimes makes sense to reject the <u>counterexample</u> rather than the theory—a most un-Popperian approach.

SAVING A THEORY FROM THE CLUTCHES OF A COUNTER-EXAMPLE

Suppose we are living in a Newtonian world—that is, Einstein's physics have not yet been developed. (By Newtonian physics, I mean his three laws of motion, which we don't need to go into here, and his law of gravity.) Newton's physics allows one to predict where a planet will be at any point in time. Further, let's assume that Newton's physics has been wonderfully successful at explaining many things, (which, of course, is true.) Finally, let's suppose that an astronomer notices that the planet Pluto is observed to be slightly <u>off</u> the course that Newtonian physics has predicted for it.[43]

Bella: *Hey, wait. Didn't they recently declare that Pluto wasn't a planet?*

Yes, you're correct. Some committee of scientists has declared that Pluto is no longer deemed a planet—now it's just an icy rock way out there that orbits the Sun with the status of former planet.

Bella: *I don't know how some self-appointed arbitrary group of people figures it has the right to set the parameters for the English language as to what we call a planet. Who do they think they are—Webster? If they want to play around with different definitions of "planet" for their mutual amusement—to create fodder for additional publications to list on their resumes to generate a bubble reputation— that's fine, but don't involve me! And don't even get me started on that whole business about changing the name of the Brontosaurus—the Great Thunder Lizard—to Apatosaurus.*

Listen, Thunder Dog, let's get back to our example, which we introduced earlier in the book with our PhD candidate. Assume that we have observed that Pluto is not quite where it should be according to Newtonian physics. If we were strict falsificationists—that is, if we followed Popper's advice to immediately reject a theory if we observe a counterexample— then we would now <u>reject</u> Newton's physics. That is, we would eject it from the body of scientific knowledge. But it might quite reasonably be argued that this is too tough a standard. First, given that Newtonian physics has been successful in explaining so many things, it doesn't make sense to reject it based on one anomalous observation. It is still a useful theory. The defenders of the theory would say: "Let's not throw out the baby with the bathwater," by which they would mean that we should try to retain the beneficial knowledge contained in Newtonian mechanics, despite the existence of this one counterexample. They might reasonably ask: "what would we replace it with?" They would argue: "Retaining a flawed theory, which has had some success, is better than having no theory at all." Indeed, we aren't really going to stop using Newton's theory for the other things that it seems to work well on, just because it doesn't work in this one instance—at least <u>not until we have a better theory to replace it</u>. Of course, we may now have to admit that the theory is flawed, and clearly doesn't represent the full truth. On the other hand, it remains useful, and we have nothing else with which to replace it.

Second, the scientists may attempt to save Newton's theory by criticizing the <u>observation</u>, rather than the theory. One sees this strategy used quite often in science. More specifically, Newtonian mechanics could be saved from this counterexample by reinterpreting the significance of the observation in terms of the theory itself. That is, scientists could argue that the reason Pluto is not where it is predicted to be is because of some <u>other</u> hidden gravitational influence causing this. This would then render the observation consistent with Newtonian physics, and suggest that we start looking for the other gravitational influence that is pulling Pluto out of the precise orbit that we would otherwise predict. The scientists might reasonably conjecture that, for example, there is some <u>other</u> planet further out than Pluto and that our current telescopes—given their limitations—are not powerful enough to see.[44] They would assert that it must be the gravitational force of this other planet—heretofore unknown—that accounts for Pluto being pulled out of the orbit in which Newtonian physics would otherwise predict. Instead of rejecting Newtonian mechanics in the face of a seeming counterexample, they think of a new conjecture that renders the observation consistent with Newtonian physics. Thus, <u>Newtonian scientists aren't testing Newtonian physics through observation, but rather interpreting those observations in terms of Newtonian physics</u>. They don't test Newtonian physics, they apply it.

Bella: *This is starting to look like Kuhn's description of normal science.*

That's right. And, indeed, at this point the scientists who are defending Newtonian physics might set about securing funding to build bigger telescopes. Three years later they may have constructed a huge telescope—far larger and more powerful than any other telescope heretofore seen. They aim this new telescope at the spot where they think the new planet tugging on Pluto might be located. If they spot the new planet up there, then they would celebrate this as a wonderful achievement for Newtonian science.

Bella: *I think they should name the new planet "Bella".*

If they don't find a new planet, then they will come up with some new conjecture to save Newtonian science, such as, perhaps, that there is some cloud of space dust up there that is blocking our view. If we send up a space probe, and it detects the space dust, then we celebrate it as a huge success for Newtonian science. If not, we come up with some other saving conjecture.[45] The fact that scientists generally have the option to choose to attack and criticize <u>the observation</u> rather than the theory presents a big problem for Popper's ideas about science. To put it simply, scientists not only confront severe challenges in trying to prove statements—as we argued in earlier chapters, but also severe challenges to disproving them. The purported asymmetry between proof and disproof is not as neat, clean and easy as Popper suggests, or as I suggested in earlier chapters.

OBSERVATIONS ARE THEORY-LADEN

Indeed, in truth, there is no such thing as a pure observation. Observations are "theory-laden", which is to say that they are typically bundled up with supplemental theories, and it is hard to separate the supplemental theories that tell us what the observation means from the observation itself. For example, when we see something, we take whatever we think we see to be what it looks like to us. However, in doing so, we are making a number of assumptions about the nature of light, and how it strikes our eyes and the relationship of that light to the object we believe we are observing, and how our mind interprets that light. These kinds of supplemental theories that are intimately tied to an observation are typically not important. But on occasion they can be quite important, and they are not always well-founded.

To take another example, let's consider Galileo's discovery that the moon had geological features and was not a "faultless crystal ball", as captured in the quote from the philosopher of science Imre Lakatos with which we began the chapter. As Lakatos notes, Galileo's critics challenged his observation and argued it was dependant on this new-fangled telescope and we had no way of knowing whether this device provided accurate representations when targeted at the celestial sphere. It was, in fact, a pretty good argument, despite the fact that it turned out to be wrong. When scientists are confronted with what appears to be a counterexample to their theory, they often, and sometimes for good reason, find a way to argue that it's not the theory that is the problem, it is the observation itself, or the way in which we are interpreting the observation, that is the problem. Observations are never as clean and clear of trouble as we would like.

This was, of course, the big question with respect to the recent observations at CERN of particles going faster than the speed of light. Scientists were asking themselves whether to throw out 100 years of Einsteinian-based physics in an instance where there was no developed body of thought (with the same predictive powers) to replace Einsteinian-based physics or, alternatively, whether perhaps it was the "observation"—which was quite complex and technology-driven itself—that was the problem. As you can imagine, this "observation" did, in fact, receive a lot of scrutiny and turned out to be mistaken! The point here is that while criticism remains central to science—as Popper has taught us—scientists can choose to direct that criticism not only at the theories but also at the so-called observations—all of which are theory-laden and, indeed, judgment-laden. And, at times, it will turn out that the observations are themselves wrong. For example, let's take propositions that the planet is getting warmer—by specified amounts and over various particular time-frames.

Bella: *Are you going to try to tell me that global warming is not caused by humans?—because I am sure that it is you humans. You are a blight on the planet, I tell you. If dogs were running things, it would be different, I assure you. Not only would our energy sources be clean—we wouldn't produce any at all!*

Let's not get into the debate as to whether global warming is caused by human activity for the moment. I am talking about something simpler—just the question of whether the planet has gotten warmer at all and, if so, by how much. Let's take a careful look at the "observation" itself and what is involved in it. In the 20th and 21st centuries, data on temperature around the world has been based on thermometer readings, and in very recent decades on satellite readings as well. To get a "global" temperature, however, one has to give different thermometer readings from around the world a certain weight—to determine some kind of an average. For example, if you had a cluster of thermometers in one place, and only a few thermometers in some other far-away place, you might <u>not</u> want to take a simple weighted average of all the temperatures, because you would be effectively double-counting—or multiple-counting—the readings in one place, and thus overweighting it. As you can see, even the concept of an observed "global" temperature is not a simple one.

Suppose some scientists posit that over, let's say, a thirty year period, the global temperature has risen by, say, ½ degree Fahrenheit. Other scientists might challenge that observation, and ask "did you weight the thermometer readings properly?" Or, more critically, they might ask: "did the immediate environment around each thermometer stay the same?" For example, they might ask: were any of your thermometers near, say, where a nuclear power plant or steel plant were constructed during those thirty years, or perhaps near black pavement that absorbs heat from the Sun at a much greater rate than would, say, a forest? Urban areas tend to retain more heat simply because asphalt and concrete absorb heat whereas plant life, by using energy from the Sun, tends to keep things slightly cooler. Thus, if there were an increase in urbanization near the thermometers (that was beyond the average degree of urbanization for the Earth's surface overall), then the thermometer readings would likely give an artificially high increase in temperature. Industrial operations and urban growth might artificially heat up the immediate environment and therefore give you a false reading in terms of changes in "global" temperature.

Others may counter that, yes, but you can tell there is warming because glaciers are receding and ice shelves in the Arctic are melting. But what if there are ice shelves elsewhere (perhaps in the Antarctic) that are increasing in size? This might not indicate a change in <u>global</u> temperature but rather merely a re-arrangement of temperature patterns—with some areas getting warmer and others getting cooler. That is, what if the observed melting is due to a change in currents or weather patterns generating a different distribution of heat, but not necessarily more heat on average? This could suggest that there has <u>not</u> been a global change in temperature, but rather a localized change. Taken in isolation, the fact that <u>some</u> ice is melting doesn't tell you it is getting warmer across the globe; nor does it tell you how much warmer it is getting, if, indeed, it is getting warmer. If we go to earlier centuries, the "observations" of temperature become even more theory-laden and judgment-laden. Let's see why. In these earlier centuries the scientists are relying on various proxies—that is, natural phenomenon that give us a sense of what the temperature must have been in the past. The importance of these past observations is that they give us a sense of whether current postulated changes in temperature are unusual or normal from a broader historical perspective. If we are experiencing degrees of warming that are unprecedented it would raise different kinds of concerns than if this amount of variation in temperature is normal—from the broader perspective of history, that is.

Bella: *So where do we get this earlier data that can cover periods of time before we had thermometers scattered about the planet?*

One of the ways to measure temperature in earlier eras is to look at tree rings. More specifically, one takes a horizontal slice of a tree trunk and looks at how far apart the tree rings are. If two particular tree rings are far apart, that means the tree grew more in that year. If the two tree rings are closer together, it means the tree grew less in that year. The theory, then, would be that in warm years the tree grew more and in colder years the tree grew less. As a consequence, one can look at the distance between the tree rings and estimate the temperature at an earlier point in time. But there are many potential problems with such "observations". What if there are other things that affect the rate of growth of the trees other than temperature? For example, perhaps the amount of moisture or rain would change the growth rate of the tree. We may think we are measuring temperature when we are really measuring the impact of rainfall. Perhaps overcast skies affect the rate of growth of the tree, and we are measuring that as opposed to temperature. Perhaps the number of parasites affects the growth rate of the trees on an annual basis—as they eat leaves and this reduces the ability of the tree to grow. And we should ask whether all types of trees are affected the same by these other factors, or whether some types of trees may be better proxies for temperature than others. And it may be that trees in some specific geographic locations or altitudes are more likely (or less likely) to have temperature as the key constraint on the rate of growth, and thus the primary determinant of ring width. And then one may also question whether the relationship between temperature and ring width is linear. That is, the degree to which temperature changes affect the tree's growth may vary depending on how much growth has occurred that year already, as induced by temperature. Growth may also depend on how extended the periods of warmth are, rather than the average temperature for the year. The point is that in taking tree ring width as a proxy for temperature, one must be making many other assumptions.

Bella: *And how would one determine all these relationships between tree rings and other variables?*

Of course, one would study trees growing today to see how trees respond to these different factors. But conditions today may not be like conditions in the past. For one, we know there is more air pollution today. How does that affect the results? There is probably a different distribution of parasites today. How does that affect the results? There may well be different weather patterns today. How does that affect the results?

Bella: *Can we ever be sure that what we observe about tree rings today—and the relationship between their width and these other variables—holds for the time period in the past we are looking at?*

No. We cannot be sure. Of course, scientists should study such evidence, but we can't be sure the relationships are the same. Finally, one would want to look at the selection of tree rings from the past that we have available to examine. Is the sample biased for some reason? That is, do all our samples come from a few particular places? If so, can we be sure that what was going on in these places reflected broader trends for the globe as a whole? And if we have a sample that is clustered in certain geographic locations, how do we weight these observations vis-à-vis one another to come up with a global temperature? The point here is not whether or not there is global warming. Rather, the point is a very simple one: observations themselves are <u>theory-laden</u>, and as susceptible to reasoned argument and criticism as are the theories themselves. Observations are inevitably intimately linked to a number of supporting theories, and cannot really be separated from those theories. This renders Popper's view that we test theories against observations as a little naïve. In reality, we are testing theories against each other, and arguing about which we find more convincing. The process is evidence based—certainly—but, in general, observations often do not have the power to knock out a theory. If observations are theory-laden—and they are—then they are as difficult to prove as theories themselves. It is often the case that observations don't so much disprove a given theory, as provide an alternative and competitive challenge to the original theory.

THE POTENTIAL BENEFITS OF OCCASIONALLY IGNORING COUNTER-EXAMPLES

Indeed, if we look at the history of science, we see that great advances are often developed in the face of seeming counterexamples. The counterexamples are simply ignored until they can be dealt with. Let's take an example. This one comes from the philosopher E. A. Burtt writing about the Copernican revolution. Nicolai Copernicus hypothesized that the Earth orbits the Sun rather than the Sun going around the Earth. Now if you think about it, taking the proposition just on the face of it, it seems kind of silly.

Bella: *After all, the ground under our feet feels pretty secure. And it certainly looks like the Sun* rises *in the morning. And it looks like it sets at night. It seems as if it is the Sun doing the moving, not us.*

But Copernicus said no. Even though it looks like the Sun is going around the Earth, he said it is really the other way around: the Earth is going around the Sun! There is a fancy word for this theory; it's called heliocentric, which is another way of saying sun-centered.[47] The old view—that the Earth was at the center—is called the Ptolemaic view.

Bella: *And the view held by most dogs to this day!*

It is named after the ancient astronomer Ptolemy, who, of course, thought that the Earth was at the center of things. The astronomers Kepler and Galileo picked up on Copernicus' new heliocentric theory, and it grew from there. And, of course, today we accept the heliocentric theory as the truth—at least, I hope you do!

Bella: *I'm considering it.*

Indeed, now we think this is a rather obvious truth. But at the time there was a lot of sound evidence that seemed to weigh against it. Indeed, Burtt notes, quite correctly, that this heliocentric theory was developed in the face of contrary evidence, which was simply ignored. Let's see what the evidence was. Both the Ptolemaic system and the heliocentric system tried to track and explain celestial phenomenon—that is, they tried to predict where things would be and when they would be there. Under the Ptolemaic system, they assumed that the path of an object supposedly orbiting the Earth was circular. If that assumption didn't match with what was observed, however, they would assume there was a circular path around a point that was itself taking a circular path around the Earth. That is, they would hypothesize circles on circles, and, indeed, circles on circles on circles if they had to.[47] These are famously called "epicycles"—which is Greek for "on the circle."

Bella: *They definitely were into circular reasoning.*

Actually, the Ptolemaic system worked well in terms of explaining what was observed. Its predictions were pretty accurate. As Burtt notes: "there were no known celestial phenomena which were not accounted for by the Ptolemaic method with as great accuracy as could be expected without more modern instruments."[48] Now, the new heliocentric system explained the seemingly daily journey of the Sun across the sky by means of the hypothesis that <u>the Earth was spinning</u>. But there were some observations that seemed contrary to the notion of the Earth spinning. For one, why didn't things simply fly off the surface of the Earth if it were spinning around? Also, if the Earth was spinning toward the East, why didn't a ball that was dropped from a tower fall toward the West? Indeed, from the point of view of the early critics of the heliocentric theory, these would have been pretty compelling arguments. We didn't yet have Newton's theories of gravity and motion that would explain these things. For example, using Newton's (and Galileo's) first law of motion—which tells us that an object in motion has a propensity to continue in motion unless a force acts on it to the contrary—would help explain why a ball dropped from a tower wouldn't fall toward the west. However, in Copernicus' time, without these complementary theories, such phenomenon really appear as counterexamples to the heliocentric—or Sun-centered—system. Indeed, you can see from this how theory-laden observations truly are. It is only with a Newtonian view of the world that these counterexamples to the Copernican system become explainable. There was an even more powerful observation that ran against the heliocentric theory—namely that if the Earth were on a journey around the Sun with an orbit that is well in excess of 100,000,000 miles from one end to the other—that is, from the apogee (furthest point from the sun) to the perigee (closest point to the sun)—then there should be an apparent <u>shift</u> in the position of the stars relative to the Earth. Such a shift is called a "parallax." Yet, no parallax was observed. Seemingly, under Popper's falsificationist perspective, this lack of observed parallax should have led to a <u>rejection</u> of the heliocentric theory. But the theory was not rejected, and, indeed, as you know, the theory turned out to be correct. We can say today that it would have been a mistake to reject it.

Bella: *There must be something wrong with Popper's falsificationism, if it would have us re-writing the history of science and <u>having great scientists of the past rejecting theories that we now think are absolutely compelling</u>.*

103

Yes. We know today that the lack of observed parallax was due to the fact that the stars were much further away than people thought at the time. If you think about it, you can see that if the stars are <u>very</u> far away, the degree to which they appear to shift as the Earth travels from one end of its orbit to the other will be less than it would be if the stars were closer. Eventually, with more refined modern equipment, a parallax was, in fact, observed. But at the time, the lack of an observed parallax argued against the notion that the Earth was orbiting the Sun.

Bella: *Why was the heliocentric theory adopted at the time, given that the Ptolemaic system was as good at keeping track of the journeys of planets through the sky?*

Burtt suggests that it was embraced because it was a simpler system. A system that was mathematically simpler—and therefore more elegant—was thought by some to be more likely to be true.

Bella: *But couldn't it be the case that physical reality is complicated and messy? Simpler doesn't necessarily mean true.*

You are right. But simpler is a virtue, of course. A simpler system is apt to be easier to use. But that is not an argument that it is true. Given the other seeming evidence against the heliocentric theory at the time, it might have seemed that the more objective view belonged to the Ptolemaics. Perhaps this is why Copernicus presented his heliocentric theory as merely a convenient hypothesis useful in calculating celestial movements, but not to be considered as truth.

Bella: *Yet, for all that, the heliocentric theory* <u>was</u> *correct.*

The point here is that theory often advances not only ahead of observation, but even advances in the face of seemingly contradictory evidence—with that evidence only much later being encompassed into the new viewpoint, given its further and ultimate development. Thus, it seems that, not only do scientists <u>not</u> try to falsify their theories, as Popper argued, but sometimes even end up <u>advancing knowledge by ignoring seemingly contradictory evidence</u>, at least for a time.

Bella: *It doesn't sound like scientists are really falsificationists. Nor does it sound like* <u>strict</u> *falsificationism would always be the best way to advance knowledge.*

That's right. However, we will find Popper wasn't too far off the mark. We need to add just a few more components to Popper's approach and we will have our core theory of rationality that we will apply far and wide.

Suggested Readings

- Paul Feyerabend <u>Against Method</u> (Verso Press 1978)
- Benjamin D. Wiker <u>The Mystery of the Periodic Table</u> Bethlehem Books (2003)

7

SCIENCE AS IMPROVEMENT

*The idea that we live and die in the prison of our 'conceptual framework'
was developed primarily by Kant; pessimistic Kantians thought that the
real world is for ever unknowable because of this prison, while optimistic
Kantians thought that God created our conceptual framework to fit the
world. But revolutionary activists believe that conceptual frameworks can
be developed and also replaced by new, better ones; it is we who create our
'prisons' and we can also, critically, demolish them.*

IMRE LAKATOS

Bella: *Popper says that criticism is at the heart of the growth of knowledge. But Kuhn and others argue that scientists often ignore criticism. And, in the last chapter we saw that it can even sometimes be beneficial to the progress of science to ignore seeming counterexamples. How can we resolve these two contrary views of science?*

In my view, the philosopher Imre Lakatos, proclaiming himself a follower of Popper, reconciled the views of Popper and Kuhn, and built a theory of rational discourse capturing the best insights of each. In this chapter, we will see how he does this. Lakatos agrees with Popper that proving cannot be the rational core of science—because, as we have seen, science can't prove anything. However, Lakatos also recognizes that science cannot disprove, because observations are theory-laden; you can always choose to attack the observation rather than the theory. And we have even seen that sometimes it makes sense to ignore counterexamples until your theory—or other complementary theories to your theory—have been sufficiently developed to address them. As a consequence, falsificationism cannot provide a rigorous core to science, because disproof is not always possible. In this, Lakatos clearly disagrees with Popper (and for this reason Popper himself did <u>not</u> see Lakatos as following in his footsteps). Finally, Lakatos also recognizes—like Kuhn—that scientists often do, in fact, resist criticism—at least with respect to whatever set of core assumptions they are trying to develop as a theoretical framework. Lakatos shows how this can be rational.

Bella: *So if the rational core of science is not proof or disproof, what is it?*

According to Lakatos, the rational core of science is not provided by proof or disproof, but by the fact that we can recognize when a theory has been <u>improved</u>. This is a subtle, but important, distinction. We will see that with Lakatos, criticism remains the key to the growth of knowledge, but he also shows how and why, in certain limited circumstances, it is rational to temporarily shun direct criticism of certain presumptions you are working with.

Bella: *So how does Lakatos do all that?*

Lakatos thinks science advances through what he calls a "scientific research program." We'll call it a <u>research program</u> for short. A research program is a series of models, which are based on some specific concepts, ideas or "laws." Typically, a group of scientists are exploring and explaining some aspect of the world, and making predictions about that world, through the use of this series of models. A research program is defined by three things: (1) the "hard core", (2) a "negative heuristic", and (3) a "positive heuristic." We'll first define these key terms and then provide an example to give you a sense of what they mean.

Bella: *What is a "heuristic"?*

"Heuristic" is just a fancy term for a way of approaching something.

Bella: *Is that like when I want to find out about something, first I sniff it, and then—if it seems to be of interest—I nibble at it, and then if it squeals, I bite it.*

Precisely. That is a heuristic.

Bella: *I got it.*

The "hard core" of a research program is constituted by the core ideas, or assumptions, that define the program.

Bella: *That's really hard core, man.*

Yes, dog. If you are working on the research program, the hard core includes the ideas that you <u>assume</u> to be true. The hard core is <u>never</u> challenged, at least not from within the ranks of those working on the elaboration of the research program. The reason for this is not because these assumptions are necessarily true, but rather simply because the point of the research effort is to see how much can be explained in terms of these assumptions.

As noted above, the word "heuristic" simply means a way of approaching something. The "negative heuristic" is very closely related to the hard core of a research program. The negative heuristic includes anything that the scientific research program <u>precludes</u> from being criticized or being considered. The negative heuristic says, first of all, that you don't attack the hard core assumptions that define the research program. That is, we have a certain set of assumptions with which we are going to try to explain certain phenomena. Thus, the idea is not to challenge those assumptions, but to see how much we can explain in terms of those assumptions.

In practice, however, the negative heuristic is a bit broader in its role than just protecting the hard core set of assumptions. Although Lakatos does not focus on this, the negative heuristic also precludes <u>other</u> ways of explaining the phenomena one is looking at. That is, it defines what is <u>not</u> included as part of the program of research. For example, if you are an economist, and your mission is to try to explain as much human behavior as you can in terms of rational incentives that are characterized by personal preferences, constraints on choices and production and technological possibilities, then you are <u>not</u> going to be using Freudian psycho-analysis to explain that same behavior. This is not to say that Freudian psycho-analysis might not be true, but rather that it is just not part of your program of research.

Similarly, as we have alluded to above, spiritual explanations for phenomena are generally precluded from research programs—not because they might not be correct, but simply because the point of the research program is to see how much of reality can be explained with the hard core assumptions that define the program.

The "positive heuristic" of a research program involves a series of theoretical models that provide ever better approximations of reality and the vision of where you want to take your theory and what you want to try to explain. Thus, the envisioned series of models corresponds to a series of aspects of reality—anomalies if you will—that have not <u>yet</u> been incorporated into the program, but which the program seeks to explain through further refinement and adjustment. In essence, the positive heuristic is the set of all the things you are going to try to explain with your hard core set of assumptions.

Bella: *I am not sure I really get all this.*

It will make much make more sense with an example.

NEWTON'S RESEARCH PROGRAM

Let's take the greatest research program of all time as an example: Newtonian mechanics. Suppose a fellow named Isaac Newton decides he wants to try to explain as much of the world as he can through his law of gravity and his three laws of motion. That is his "hard core". Within his research program, he is not really testing the law of gravity and his three laws of motion. Rather, he is assuming them to be true, and he wants to see how much of the world he can explain through ever more refined applications of that hard core. Newton might launch his research program by building a very simple mathematical model of the solar system. In this model, for the sake of simplicity, he might assume that the Sun and the planets are mere pinpoints. This abstraction turns out to be helpful, since the math involved in working with a spherical Sun and spherical planets is complicated. Let's also say that, in setting up his initial model of the solar system, he decides to ignore interplanetary gravitational influences, since they are also very complicated to deal with. That is, not only does the gravitational force of the Sun attract the planets, but the planets also affect one another with their gravitational pull. But Newton decides to ignore that, at first. After all, he has to walk before he can run—so-to-speak.

So he decides to start a simple model—that is, pinpoint Sun and pinpoint planets and no interplanetary influences—to see if the model has promise in terms of predictive content. Later, he can turn his attention to these others complications from which he abstracts, at first. That vision of the direction in which the series of models will progress is the positive heuristic. So Isaac builds his model, and finds that it gives reasonably good—although not perfect—predictions of where the Sun and planets will be at any point in time. Note that Newton doesn't dispose of the theory because the predictions are imperfect. Rather, he sees that the predictions are good enough to warrant further exploration. His next step is to take some of the aspects of his model that he knows do not fit reality, and see if he can address those. For example, he might now turn to introducing interplanetary gravitational influences into his mathematical model of the solar system.

So let's say that he works out the mathematics for this, and comes up with a set of predictions. And let's suppose these predictions are more accurate than the predictions of the previous, simpler model. Newton might now think that he is onto something good here, and he can certainly say with confidence that this later, more sophisticated model is an <u>improvement</u> over his first model. That is, although he hasn't proven that his model is true, per se, <u>he can know that this later version, with both more realistic assumptions and better predictions, is superior to the earlier model</u>. (As you may suspect, this is where Lakatos' key insight comes into play; to wit: we can recognize <u>improvements</u> within a research program, even if we can't prove or disprove it.) Next, Newton might try to incorporate a spherical Sun and spherical planets into his calculations. If he obtains yet better predictions, he might gain yet more confidence in his research. And so Newton would continue to work on his series of ever improving models. With each stage, as he introduces new aspects of reality into the model, and as his predictions continue to improve, he can say with confidence that these later models in the series constitute improvements over the earlier, more simplistic models. That is, he can declare that there has been an increase in knowledge through his research efforts. As we have seen, this vision of a series of models to be built—with (hopefully) ever better predictive content—is the positive heuristic. Lakatos says this is typical of how science progresses. The positive heuristic lays out the kinds of empirical criticism—anomalies (that is, observations that don't fit the current model)—that the research program intends to address. Thus, <u>criticism remains a key part of the process</u>. At the same time, as we have seen, Lakatos argues that not <u>all</u> parts of a theory are always to be subject to criticism—that is, the hard core of the program is off-limits in terms of criticism. This makes sense because we are trying to see how much we can explain in terms of those very assumptions.

    Bella: *So in what ways is Lakatos' vision of science like Popper's? And what is it that is rational about it?*

    <u>Within</u> a research program, the role of criticism—and anomalies—is to highlight those aspects of reality that the research program intends to try to explain, but has not yet explained. What is rational about the approach is that, as a research program is developed, its predictive content is improved and expanded. Thus, it can explain more about the world than the previous models within the program. The advancement of research programs <u>is</u> the advancement of our knowledge—at least in terms of predictive content.

PROGRESSIVE AND DEGENERATIVE RESEARCH PROGRAMS

    When a research program is being built with model after model leading to ever expanded predictive content—transforming the anomalies (envisioned by the positive heuristic) into corroborations—we call it a "progressive" research program. The predictive capacity of <u>progressive</u> research programs increases over time. This is why it makes sense to work on and improve them. They are worthy of our continued effort.

    Bella: *But what happens if the research program does* <u>not</u> *continue to grow in its predictive content?*

    If a research program does not keep growing, but rather is confronted by anomalies for which it cannot account, then scientists may begin to think this program is not worthy of their continued efforts at improvement. Let's call such a research program a "degenerative" program. When confronted with a degenerative research program, scientists may begin to search for an alternative that has more growth potential.

    Bella: *This sounds a lot like Kuhn's view of science.*

It is. When confronted with a degenerative research program, some great scientist—one which Thomas Kuhn would call a "revolutionary scientist"—comes along with a <u>new</u> set of hard core concepts that might be developed as an alternative research program. This alternative program may cover some or all of the ground that the other program covered, but if it appears more promising in terms of its growth potential then scientists will begin to work on it. Pretty soon most of the scientists are working on this more promising program.

Bella: *So what is the difference between* <u>*Kuhn's*</u> *view of science and that of Lakatos?*

The differences are subtle. The first difference is that Lakatos is focused on trying to explain how and why the manner in which scientists work on progressive research programs is <u>rational</u>, advances knowledge and explains progress. In contrast, in my view, Kuhn was a bit more focused on simply describing what scientists appear to do. Second, Kuhn's idea of scientific revolution lives on a grander scale than Lakatos' notion of a research program. Kuhn's scientific revolutions are giant events that come along on rare occasion. Lakatos' idea of a research program is smaller. At any one time, there might be numerous competing research programs within a discipline, and many more if you look across disciplines. Lakatos' idea is that science comes in clusters of interrelated ideas. And the manner in which you test those ideas is through their further development and articulation. They are developed with a view to increasing their scope and predictive content—to see how much you can do with them and how far you can run. Moreover, they compete with one another. The most profound critique of a research program is to develop an alternative program that appears more progressive in its capabilities to develop predictive content.

Bella: *And if the negative heuristic says we can't criticize the hard core—that is, the key cluster of ideas that define the research program—at least not while working within the research program, is there anything left in this vision of science of Popper's bold world of conjectures and criticism?*

Oh, yes. Under Lakatos' vision of science, conjecture and criticism remain key drivers in the process of developing these ever more articulate models based on the hard core as well as in developing new, competing research programs. The difference is that the conjectures and criticism tend to be more narrowly focused and cabined than in Popper's world. The conjectures are typically those that might advance the research program in

113

addressing the series of puzzles or anomalies that it is intended to address. And the criticism is done through pressure testing the hard core with ever new sets of anomalies to see if the model can be adjusted to account for them. But as we have already noted, <u>a different and new kind of scientific criticism</u> is now introduced by Lakatos—and that is the criticism of one research program by the development of a competitor that is more progressive. In this manner, Lakatos recognizes that scientists refuse to "throw out the baby with the bathwater." That is, they will not throw away a theory that has useful predictive content—even if it has been otherwise refuted—<u>without being presented with a superior alternative theory</u>. Thus, Lakatos teaches us that constructive criticism in the form of the development and presentation of superior alternative approaches is the most powerful sort. He also thereby rejects Popper's narrow falsificationism. That is, along with Kuhn, <u>he rejects the notion that a single counterexample will, of necessity, be enough to lead to the rejection of a scientific theory</u>.

THE GROWTH OF KNOWLEDGE AMONG COMPETING RESEARCH PROGRAMS

In sum, Lakatos' vision is one of science as competition. Research programs compete for the attention of scientists. Scientists are always tempted to pursue those programs which appear more promising in terms of growth potential. Thus, according to Lakatos, there are <u>two</u> ways in which scientific knowledge grows, and correspondingly two types of criticism that generate these respective types of growth.

First, science grows <u>within</u> a research program—that is, through the construction of ever improved models of reality with ever increasing predictive content. (As noted above, this is pretty close to Kuhn's concept of normal science.) The kinds of criticism that are permitted within the research program are determined by the positive heuristic. The type of criticism that is not permitted, of course, is of the hard core set of assumptions that define the research program. Those types of criticism that are precluded are referred to as the negative heuristic. Second, there is the progress that comes from the development of wholly new research programs that are more promising than the programs they replace. This second type of criticism involves a comparative analysis of which program appears more promising in terms of the continued growth and improvement of predictive content. So here is the really odd thing about science. You can have progress without really <u>knowing</u> anything!

Bella: *Now that sounds really strange.*

Yes, it does, but it is true in the following sense. According to Lakatos—and I think he has this right—research programs are successful because of ever increasing <u>predictive</u> content, but <u>not</u> because they are known to be based on truth. For example, Newtonian mechanics is not and was not embraced by the world of science due to him <u>proving</u> his law of universal gravitation and his laws of motion. Those can never be proven. Rather, his mechanics were embraced by science because of the predictive content of his models, and—in addition—because they appeared robust in terms of the promise inherent in the model with respect to further development to make predictions about many things. Newton's research program was alluring. But, as it turned out, there were many things that Newtonian mechanics could <u>not</u> explain nor with respect to which make accurate predictions. Newton's mechanics doesn't seem to work so well if you are working with the very fast (we are talking speed of light here) or the very big or the very small. These were the kinds of things with which Einstein was wrestling. Thus, Einstein came up with an alternative hard core of assumptions—just as unproven as Newton's and also inconsistent with Newton's—and started developing an alternative research program to make predictions about phenomena where Newtonian mechanics appeared to fail. Given a promise of increasing predictive capacity, the lines of research he began were embraced by many scientists, and Newtonian mechanics was no longer seen as universal truth, but rather simply as a special case or approximation. Where Lakatos is in full agreement with Popper is in the crucial role that criticism plays. For Lakatos, criticism—and constructive responses to criticism—play a role both <u>within</u> research programs and <u>among</u> research programs in terms of the promise of greater predictive capacity. These two types of criticism are what drive the process by which science is improved. In sum, for Lakatos, science is not about proof or disproof, but about "improof."

Bella: *Is "improof" really a word?*

No. But you get the idea. While we cannot always prove and disprove in science, what we can do is recognize that a model of the world has <u>increased</u> predictive content. This can be gauged objectively, and it is through the development of such predictive content that we have developed our modern technological capacities—all without proof or even disproof. As noted above, Lakatos' idea of a research program is somewhat similar to Kuhn's idea of a paradigm—but the difference is that Lakatos' approach focuses on the <u>rational</u> core of science, and explains how it is that such an approach would be expected to result in progress—otherwise known as an increase in predictive content.

THE COLLAPSE OF THE DEMARCATION CRITERION

As you may recall from an earlier chapter, one of Karl Popper's concerns was to demarcate a sharp divide between science and non-science. Popper drew that line with respect to falsifiability. If statements lend themselves to the possibility of falsification, then they are within the realms of science. If they do not, then they are outside the realm of science. With Kuhn and Lakatos, we realize that Popper's demarcation criterion line is not as strong as he implied. This is because, as we saw above, science does not, and should not, always reject a theory when confronted with a counterexample. Indeed, with Lakatos vision of science, we realize that there is not a strict dividing line between science and non-science. Science is nothing more, nor less, than the process of exploring interrelated assumptions for predictive content, and attempting to improve them across time. But <u>to the extent an improvement can be recognized as such, this same logic of discovery can be applied to any topic, or subject matter, or project, or even artistic endeavor</u>. As we will see in a chapter coming up soon, it can even be applied to creating theatrical performances.

Suggested Readings

- Imre Lakatos "Falsification and the Methodology of Scientific Research Programmes" <u>Criticism and the Growth of Knowledge</u> Edited by Imre Lakatos & Alan Musgrave Cambridge University Press (1970)

8

BELLA EXPLORES A HAMMOCK

Drawing by Kate Fisher 2

Drawing by Kate Fisher 3

Drawing by Kate Fisher 4

9

THEATER AS DISCOVERY

Literature begins with the telling of a tale. This tale is the representation of a sequence of events by sounds or visual signs. The events thus represented are mental events in the teller's mind. They consist of perceptions, images, ideas, emotions and other nervous processes. ... The teller strives to express his experience in order to communicate it to others, that is, to cause others to experience similar mental states and thus to establish a more intimate communion with them, to transcend the isolation of his self. Artistic expression is thus one of several ways of satisfying the integrative tendency by sharing of thoughts, emotions, sensations, imaginations.

ARTHUR KOESTLER

Literary intellectuals at one pole—at the other scientists, and as the most representative, the physical scientists. Between the two a gulf of mutual incomprehension—sometimes (particularly among the young) hostility and dislike, but most of all lack of understanding. They have a curious distorted image of each other. Their attitudes are so different that, even on the level of emotion, they can't find much common ground. … Thirty years ago the cultures had long ceased to speak to each other: but at least they managed a kind of frozen smile across the gulf. Now the politeness is gone, and they just make faces.

C. P. SNOW

Bella: *Ooof! That last chapter was kind of hard on me. So where are we now?*

As we saw in the previous chapters, scientific progress is driven by a dynamic logic of discovery. In this chapter, we will explore the idea that the same logic of discovery can be applied well beyond the realm of science. Indeed, it constitutes the very essence of rationality. The logic of discovery can be fruitfully applied to just about any human endeavor—including not only science, but areas as far afield as art or spirituality or how to run a business or developing a better governmental policy. It really constitutes a theory of how to think creatively and productively. Drawing on Popper's and Lakatos' ideas about science, using these terms in their most general meaning and taking into account that these elements overlap somewhat, we can say that the six essential elements of any logic of discovery include the following:

(1) A question or purpose;

(2) Conjectures that target the question, or are intended to fulfill the purpose;

(3) Criteria or a sensibility for what constitutes improvement in whatever one is attempting to accomplish or answer;

(4) Criticism with specificity of those conjectures as to the manner in which they do or do not accomplish or answer what was intended;

(5) New conjectures responsive to the criticism;

(6) New directions, questions or purposes in light of the criticism;

That's it. That's our theory of how to think productively about anything. We will explore it in some detail in this chapter, but we have seen these elements before in our discussion of science. While previously we referred to it as a two-step dance of conjectures and refutations, we are merely refining it here into more of a tango. As our first example, let us consider

120

the process by which Bella boldly explored the hammock in the previous chapter. That exploration was more of a two-step. I hope you laughed when you saw those three panels; I did.

Bella: *I didn't. It wasn't all that funny!*

But, Bella, it was the very universality of your exploration that generated the humor. In the first panel, we see you thinking: "Well, this looks entertaining. What shall I do with it?" There we have the Question. In the second panel, you are clearly thinking: "This seems to be a very fine perch from which to observe the world." There we have the conjecture as to the best use of the hammock. In the third panel we see the conjecture refuted, in you falling down. It is funny because it captures our universal experience of exploration as well as the occasionally unforeseen and sometimes unfortunate discoveries that occur along the way.

Bella: *Could we move on to a different example?*

Let's take the creation of a piece of performance art as an example where the logic of discovery can be applied, and walk through the six steps of our tango—one by one—to get a sense of their full generality. (I'll label them as Tango Steps One to Six, so you don't lose your footing.) Performance art, by the way, is where you use movement, gesture and language to engage an audience in some way.

TANGO STEP NUMBER ONE: A QUESTION OR PURPOSE

Suppose an acting professor walks into a class on performance art, and says to her students: "As your first assignment, using movement and sound, I want you to create and perform a solo piece that tells a story about who you are. It should use no more than five words and employ at least four dramatic gestures." The students are perplexed. They ask: "What do you mean by a dramatic gesture?" She replies: "That is up to you to decide." The students are a bit frustrated by this answer, but the teacher figures that if the assignment remains somewhat vague, it will force them to think for themselves. In addition, she has tightly restricted the number of words she wants them to employ, because she wants to ensure that they do not rely too heavily on the spoken word, but instead begin to explore the possibilities of communicating artistically with movement and sound. They now have their initial question or purpose. In this case, it is an assignment—to create a piece that tells a story about themselves within the constraints the teacher has established.

TANGO STEP NUMBER TWO: CONJECTURES

The students head home. Each one struggles to create a piece that meets the requirements set by the teacher. They return to the classroom the next week and are asked to perform their pieces. One student walks to the front of the classroom. She is ready to begin. She curls up into a ball and is motionless. She begins to slowly move out of her beginning position. Her motions are clumsy and jerky. She crawls. And then rises and stumbles. And then clumsily walks about, as she begins to say the words "Where? There." She moves about as if in search for something, and her movements become more fluid. She searches different parts of the space. Her sweeping movements begin with the question "Where?" She ends each movement with the question "There?" She moves to center stage in a ballet-like pirouette and exclaims "Here!" She does a series of ballet movements, each punctuated with "Here" and a clap of the hands. She makes one final leap, but suddenly falls with her legs crumpling under her. She slowly looks up, with her expression distraught. She begins to crawl again, slowly, and then clumsily and slowly rises. She comes to a final full, but stiff, standing position and looks directly to the audience and asks: "Where now?" She is done. Let's call this performance her artistic conjectures; it constitutes her effort to fulfill the professor's assignment. It is her beginning point for this work —a point from which the collaborative exploration can begin.

TANGO STEP NUMBER THREE: A SENSIBILITY AS TO WHAT CONSTITUTES IMPROVEMENT

In addressing this performance piece, the first thing the professor asks the student is: "what were you trying to do?" The professor knows that it is only through understanding what the artist is trying to accomplish that one can assist in the creative process. The student explains that she is trying to express the importance of discovering ballet as a pursuit in her

122

development as a person, prior to which she had felt lost and clumsy. She was also trying to express the loss associated with becoming injured and no longer being able to pursue ballet at the same level. And, in the final part of the performance, she intended to show the search for something new. An understanding of what the artist is trying to accomplish in a piece gives one a sensibility for what might constitute an improvement as it is further developed. This is a crucial foundation for constructive criticism. Now that the professor and the class understand what she is trying to accomplish with the piece, they can help her develop it through very specific questions and criticisms.

TANGO STEP NUMBER FOUR: CRITICISM WITH SPECIFICITY

Now the professor and the students are in a position to criticize the piece with specificity. They might begin with questions. "Why did you begin curled up as a ball?" "What were you trying to convey with that?" And as they get a more precise sense of what the performer was trying to do with each part, and how that was intended to relate to the piece as a whole, they are in a position to criticize in a constructive way. They may say "That didn't work for me. What I saw when you were curled up was [whatever it was they saw, or how it affected them]." And they can say "You intended this effect, but here is how it affected me, and here is what I saw." Through this very detailed and precise process, the performer begins to get a sense of what aspects of the piece "worked" and what "didn't work." This gives her a sense of which parts she should keep, and in which parts she might try something different altogether. Note that general praise of the piece, or general criticism of the piece, is not particularly useful in the process. That is, some students might say: "Oh, I loved that. It was wonderful." While that might make the performer feel good, it doesn't do anything to advance the further creative development of the piece. The performance artist needs to know, with specificity, what worked for you, and what about it made it work. And she needs to know, with specificity, what didn't work, why it didn't work, and what you saw or felt or experienced as opposed to what was intended. (By the way, this is the same kind of specificity we saw in the proof-analysis of counterexamples to Euler's conjecture and it is needed here for very much the same reason.)

TANGO STEP NUMBER FIVE: NEW CONJECTURES RESPONSIVE TO THE CRITICISM

At this point, the performer may want to try some different movements, gestures or words to substitute for aspects of the performance that didn't "work." The experimental process continues. Maintaining what has "worked" so far, she adds to, supplements or replaces the parts that didn't "work." Since the parts are interrelated, however, the piece as a whole will have to evolve as well if it is to maintain its coherence. In sum, this is the time for new conjectures to supplement what has been successful so far in the development of the piece.

TANGO STEP NUMBER SIX: NEW DIRECTIONS, QUESTIONS OR PURPOSES

As a performance piece is developed and improved through this rational process of experimentation, discoveries are made. Sometimes the discoveries are more interesting than the original direction of exploration. Just as a scientist may stumble upon an extraordinary truth or question, so too may the performance artist. She needs to stand ready to recognize this moment and exploit the power of her new discoveries.

DEVELOPING A CHARACTER

Let's take another example from the theater—the process of developing a character for a play—to further explore the application of the logic of discovery. As a preliminary to this discussion, I will provide a little background on acting methodology.

Bella: *As an actor, how does one develop a character? What kind of a process does an actor go through to permit her to step on the stage and dazzle an audience?*

Let's start with the actor and her script. The actor begins to memorize her lines. But the real work is something much deeper than this, of course. She is trying to create a character—the character who will be delivering these lines. To do that, she has to think about why this character is saying these particular lines—and the answer to that question is not some abstract

124

psychological theory. Rather, it must be answered <u>from the character's perspective</u>. With respect to each and every line, she should ask: what is this character trying to accomplish in saying this line? What is the character trying to do? What does she want?" The path to great acting is to figure out what the character is <u>trying to do</u>, and then—as a performer—use one's lines, movements, body and voice to try to do what the character wants to do. In acting lingo, this is called "playing an objective."

Suppose, for example, that a character has the line: "Be quiet." Depending on the context, the character's most likely purpose is saying such a line is, obviously, to get another person or other people to be quiet. But such an immediate purpose may be part of some larger objective as well, of course. The actor not only has to understand what the character is trying to do both with the line, but also within the scene, and, even more generally, within the play. The point of "playing the objective" of the character, of course, is that the performance comes across much more naturally and powerfully, and the lines tend to be much more convincing to the audience. "Playing an objective" taps in on a deep layer of tacit knowledge about life, and how to get what you want. By relying on this tacit knowledge, the actor is free to dedicate her whole body and self to portraying that character while they are on the stage.

In contrast to this approach, most beginning actors <u>think</u> that the best way to approach a part is to try to put a lot of feeling into their lines. In theatre parlance, this is called "playing the emotion." This is, in general, a bad approach, and typically leads to unconvincing acting. Rather, as noted above, the superior approach, in general, is for the actor to try to <u>use</u> words and motions to accomplish the character's pursuits, and let her voice and body respond accordingly. Let's try a little experiment. Let's return to our simple line above: "Be quiet." Imagine you are at a solemn event and can't hear the speaker at this event because the people sitting behind you are being noisy. You are angry with them. Try saying the line "be quiet," and attempt to put a lot of feeling into it—that is, "play the emotion." Now let's try it a different way. Imagine the same scenario, and say the same line, but this time don't worry about the emotion. Rather, focus on your objective. That is, by saying the words "Be quiet" try to get them to be quiet, and try to do it in a way that your statement itself isn't too disruptive—it is a solemn occasion, after all. In sum, "play the objective" this time. Was there a difference? My guess would be that the way you said it when you were "playing the objective" was more subtle, natural and convincing, and the way you said it the first time was a bit artificial, stiff and overdone.

In general, this indirect method by which the actor uses language to try to obtain the character's objective, rather than attempt to directly fill the line with emotion, oddly leads to <u>more</u> authentic emotions. In particular, what tends to bring out the subtle and natural emotions to the greatest degree is if the actor is playing the objective, <u>and</u> her objective is being frustrated. For example, the actor tries to get a group to be quiet using her lines, but they continue to be noisy. Believable emotions emerge out of frustrated action.

Now, interpreting a line—and most importantly—figuring out what the character is trying to do with the line is not always so simple. Suppose the line is: "You are a monster." Such a statement could have very different purposes in different circumstances. Perhaps the character is playing a game with a child and wants to amuse the child. Perhaps the character is congratulating a fellow athlete for having just scored a goal and trying to encourage her to more such efforts. Or perhaps the character saying it is trying to make another person feel remorse for what she has done and to separate herself from this person. To understand what a character is trying to do with a line, you need to fully understand the character. This involves a great deal of imaginative work. While I say that the actor must understand the character she is portraying, you should note also that the actor is, simultaneously, also actively <u>creating</u> that character.

Bella: *That's a bit paradoxical. How can you both try to understand a character and at the same time be creating that character?*

While the actor should remain fully consistent with the text, of course, to obtain the understanding necessary to play a character, she nonetheless must go beyond the text in imagining that character's life and purposes. Thus, an actor's ultimate performance is a combination of the creativity of the playwright and her own creativity. This is partly a question of understanding the text and partly an imaginative act of constructing a character that is consistent with that text. In this sense, it is the actor that constructs the character, at least in part. Indeed, it constitutes her work of art. Within this process, she must make <u>choices</u>—choices about who the character is, choices about the character's past, choices about the character's views on the world and on the other characters. So long as they are consistent with the text, the actor should begin with character choices that make sense to her.

Those are her <u>initial artistic conjectures</u>. The actor will also have to make choices about the character's physicality. How does the character walk? Does she lead with her knees? Does she walk with her feet pointing out, or in? Does she limp? Does she hold her shoulders back? Does she stand up straight, or crouch? Are her movements quick and light, or ponderous and slow?

Ideally, much of this imaginative work is done by the actor before beginning to work with the director and the other actors. As the actors begin to work on a scene, the director watches to see whether the choices the actor has made are "working." That is, in the director's view, is this character convincing? Would the character come across to an audience? Do the character "choices" make sense with the text of the play? Are the characters interacting with one another? If it is not "working," the director will intervene. This is the stage of <u>constructive criticism</u>. This is often done through questions. The director might ask the actor: "What are you trying to do here?" She will probe the actor's choices. Sometimes the director will be quite specific in the criticism. For example, the director might say: "The way in which you grab that package isn't working for me, try something different." The "try something different" is encouragement to try another <u>conjecture</u>—that is, make a different choice—about the character. Note that while a good director will provide this feedback as to what is "working" and what is "not working," most good directors do not try to specifically shape the actor's new conjectures. That is, as noted above, they generally leave it a bit open ended for the actor to "try something different." After all, the choice—that is, the new conjecture—not only has to work for the play and the production, but also for the actor herself. She is the one who will be making it happen.

At this point, we can again see the deep structural similarities with the scientific process. The actor and the director are engaged in an interactive dialogue to attempt to discover a portrayal of the character that "works" from an artistic perspective. While there are many different ways to portray any given character, some ways are much better than others. Thus, there is a kind of empiricism to the process. The director and actor, working together, try to discover a set of acting "choices" that are consistent with the text, work for this actor, and powerfully shape this character in a way that enhances the meaning of the play. It is, in its essence, an empirical process. This does not mean that there is anything definitive about it;

rather, it is understood, and recognizable, that—given what is trying to be accomplished—some ways of doing it are superior to others, and can be recognized as improvements.

THE CONDITIONS OF RATIONAL EXPLORATION

As we saw in the previous chapter, rationality is an open ended process of improvement through conjecture, criticism, analysis, theoretical adjustment and further conjecturing. Science, at its best, employs this method. As we also saw, science does not have the power to prove. Rather, it has the power to <u>im</u>prove. Thus, while science can't tell us definitively if something is true or not, it can assist us through the development of bodies of knowledge that have ever improving predictive content. Finally, we have also seen that this rational process of improving our knowledge requires: (1) asking questions; (2) bold creativity in conjecturing; (3) openness to criticism and taking criticism seriously, and (4) a certain suppleness in thought that facilitates making adjustments to theories in light of criticisms, and developing new adjusted conjectures that transform the unsuccessful aspects of a work or project into successful aspects.

Our example above on how to develop and improve a performance piece suggests that this creative process of discovery is not narrowly tied to science, but rather is a universal method that can be fruitfully applied to other areas. What are the conditions that permit the use of the logic of discovery? First, as noted above, one does need to have some sensibility of what constitutes an improvement. While in the arts, this is obviously a much more subjective standard than in, say, physics, artists do, in fact, generally have a pretty good idea of what they are trying to accomplish, and within that, what constitutes an improvement. For example, as I am writing this, I am watching one of my daughters paint a dragon on one of her sister's hands. She doesn't like the way she painted on of the dragon's legs. She wipes it off with some water, and tries it at a different angle. There—that is <u>better</u>. An artist knows an improvement when she sees it. It is this quasi-empirical sensibility that facilitates the use of the logic of discovery.

The second requirement of the operation of a logic of discovery is that there is criticism, which is constructive and specific, and the person or persons controlling the project take the criticisms seriously. This does not mean that they should reject their project in light of the criticism—though that might be an occasional outcome—but rather that they see within the criticism the possibility of, and opportunity for, improvement. The third requirement is an open-endedness to further exploration through yet more conjectures and further criticism. That is how one takes advantage of the criticism to generate growth and improvement. When these three conditions are present, the logic of discovery can be applied—no matter what the topic area or discipline.

On the other hand, anything that interferes with this process will hinder the scope and robustness of such dynamic explorations. For example, if the performance artist in the example explored above simply rejects all criticism on the basis that all art is subjective, then the logic of discovery cannot be applied. Here she is now: "I created this piece, it is my work of art and my expression, after all, and I therefore reject all criticism. You either you like it or you don't." With this attitude, which is not uncommon, there can be no dynamic, interactive improvement through a logic of discovery. In general, this kind of proprietary attitude results in impoverished works of art—works that are uninteresting. The reason for this is that the developmental process cannot go beyond the mind of the original artist. She will never be in a position to take advantage of other artists' insights to improve her work or to grow as an artist in light of these discoveries.

Many artists bristle at this notion that there is a quasi-empirical aspect to their work. Nonetheless, most serious artists do intuit that there is an exploratory aspect to their work. Their work involves not only something inside them, but something outside of them—and its dynamic essence through time entails an interactive journey between what is inside and what is outside. This is the logic of discovery at work. Artists speak of it as the "experimental" aspect of their work, or as a "language they are developing." Precisely.

10

CAPITALISM AS DISCOVERY

The essential point to grasp is that in dealing with capitalism we are dealing with an evolutionary process. ... Capitalism, then, is by nature a form or method of economic change and not only never is but never can be stationary. ... The fundamental impulse that sets and keeps the capitalist engine in motion comes from the new consumers' goods, the new methods of production or transportation, the new markets, the new forms of industrial organization that capitalist enterprise creates. ... The opening up of new markets, foreign or domestic, and the organizational development from the craft shop and factory to such concerns as U. S. Steel illustrate the same process of industrial mutation—if I may use that biological term—that incessantly revolutionizes the economic structure from within, incessantly destroying the old one, incessantly creating a new one. This process of Creative Destruction is the essential fact about capitalism. It is what capitalism consists in and what every capitalist concern has got to live in.

JOSEPH A. SCHUMPETER

It is important to foster individuality, for only the individual can produce new ideas.

ALBERT EINSTEIN

SPECIALIZATION

Economic progress and the historic growth of human knowledge are closely linked. In primitive societies, needs were typically fulfilled through hunting and gathering.

Bella: *What do you call societies like that?*

Oddly enough, they are called "hunter-and-gatherer" societies.

Bella: *Those anthropologists are a clever lot.*

Yes, they are. As society advanced, people began to domesticate animals. This reduced the need to hunt.

Bella: *Yes. That was a big bummer for their dogs.*

Folks also began to grow plants as opposed to simply gathering them as they found them. This reduced the need for gathering. With these developments, societies could settle in one area and not exhaust the food supply. As a consequence, they became less nomadic. There were, of course, conflicts between the shepherds tending the domesticated animals and the farmers raising the crops. The problem was that these different uses of land weren't always consistent with one another. If you are trying to grow a field of corn, you don't want cattle and sheep nibbling on it and stomping it down. This conflict led to the need for the concept of property—that is, rules determining who got to use land and in what way and for what purpose and at what point in time. The increased supply of food led to larger concentrations of people. This required yet more rules so that, for example, they weren't throwing their waste and refuse over each other's walls. Rules imply the need for enforcement of the rules. To enforce the rules, governments formed. The rules were recorded and, thus, laws were codified.

With large numbers of people aggregated together in growing communities, it became more obvious that some people are better at some things than others. Perhaps one person is very good at making baskets, another is good at making spear tips, and a third person is a better farmer. Recognizing these differences, people began to specialize and just produce one type of thing, and then trade that thing for the other things they might need. The basket maker would trade baskets with the farmer in return for grain and fruit. The hunter might trade a recently caught animal for a few new spear tips. Markets—that is, places where people come together to exchange goods and services—began to form. Specialization led to enhanced growth of knowledge, as specialists had the time and incentive to attempt to improve their processes. Someone who spends all their time making pots gets better at the technology. The productivity from this specialization—and the consequent growth in knowledge—was such that not everyone had to focus all their resources solely on economic necessities. Demand developed for nicer things, such as decorated pots. Civilization began to develop. With specialization, and increasing knowledge, there came the need to share and replicate that knowledge. Specialists shared with one another and replicated their knowledge through the generations. The roots of science and education are here. In the grand scheme of things, these human developments are all relatively recent—with civilization arising over the last 10,000 years or so. To put that in perspective, that is only 100 generations living to 100. Recorded history covers just over half of that.

Bella: *And dogs have been along for the whole ride.*

CAPITALISM VERSUS COMMUNISM

The modern market economy—otherwise known as capitalism—is the continuation of the arc of human development from these early origins. A market economy is an economy where decentralized market participants make the economic decisions as to what goods and services should be produced and how they should be produced, priced and distributed. In capitalism, there is private (that is, non-governmental) ownership of the means of production—otherwise known as "property"—and private decision making drives the economy. Individuals decide for themselves where to work and what work to do, what to produce, how to price those goods and services and so forth. In stark contrast to such capitalist systems stands communism. Communism was the great human experiment of the 20th century—an experiment that didn't turn out too well. The thought was that when an economy is left to the whims of private individuals it results in unfairness and occasional economic collapse. In a communist system, the government makes the vast majority of the basic economic decisions. Many people thought such a system would make the lives of the mass of the people better off. Unfortunately, it didn't turn out that way. Communist countries performed very poorly from an economic point of view. In addition, as the government controlled the details of economic decision-making, it tended also to leave little room for personal freedoms and liberty. Communist countries tended to take away basic liberties such as freedom of speech, freedom of movement within the country and even freedom of religion. Communist leaders tend not to be believers in open and critical discourse—particularly with respect to their decision-making.

In this chapter, I will refer to "market" or "capitalist" economies interchangeably, as they are pretty much the same thing. To be sure, there are hybrids—systems that fall between capitalism and communism. Also, there are various types of capitalist economies, characterized by different degrees and kinds of government intervention. But we will leave that discussion to another book. Here we will hone in on what is special about capitalism, and how it ties to knowledge processes, science and freedom. The theme of this chapter is that a capitalist economy is driven by the same rational process of conjectures, refutations and innovation as is science. Indeed, this is no coincidence. The development of human knowledge itself was driven by economic imperatives. We will see that a market economy—through the decisions of the many market participants—is like a giant rational mind, which poses economic conjectures. Moreover, just like the scientific process, the economy rejects some of these conjectures and refines others—and thereby solves complex problems with a remarkable degree of efficiency. Market economies prevail over communist economies in the long run precisely because they most effectively harness the ideas and creativity of the population in addressing and solving economic challenges. That is, taken in its totality, the market economy constitutes a rational discourse that is very much like science in the way that it progresses across time. And the most remarkable thing about a market economy is that it does this in a decentralized manner—with nobody planning the economy in its details or as a whole. In fact, it works best that way. Let's see how it works.

THE MARKET'S EFFICACY IN MEETING DEMAND

Suppose tomorrow I take a trip from my home in Virginia to Paris. It's just a spur-of-the-moment thing; I haven't planned it. I've always wanted to see the Eiffel tower. If I call a travel agent, or use the web, I can probably get a flight, even on such short notice. I can also probably obtain a hotel room for the night in Paris. When I arrive at Charles de Gaulle airport, which is near Paris, I can get a taxi to take me into the city. After getting advice from the concierge at the hotel, I could probably find a very fine restaurant to dine at and perhaps even get a ticket to the Paris opera.

Bella: *There is nothing particularly surprising in all that.*

That is precisely my point. No one on the planet knew that I was suddenly going to go to Paris. I didn't even know it myself until the impulse struck me. And yet, at each and every step of the way, there would be sufficient resources and services to meet my each and every need—assuming I was ready to pay for them, of course. And the most striking thing is that, at the same time, there would not have been a lot of waste in the process of meeting my needs. The plane and the hotel would have been relatively full and the restaurant probably wouldn't have had a lot of wasted food.

Bella: *So how is it that a system can operate with this kind of efficiency—meeting unexpected needs while at the same time not wasting much—without some central planner thinking it all through ahead of time and everyone applying to that central planner with a list of their forthcoming plans and needs?*

The answer lies in the mechanics of a market economy. A market economy is a powerful machine of discovery. Indeed, it is all about epistemology—in the most practical sense. The market discovers the needs and wants of the people and brings together resources to meet them in an efficient manner. Just the right amounts and types of goods and services are produced to meet those needs and wants. These goods and services are then delivered to people at just the right places and times. There are not a lot of wasted goods and services that go unpurchased and unused. Nor are there shortages, in general. If people are willing to pay the price, the goods and services are produced to meet their demand. The economy does this on its own. No one runs it. No one plans the details. Indeed, there is no giant panel of experts, technicians and economists working at computers in some vast subterranean building somewhere ensuring that the amount of inputs needed to produce the desired goods and services will be brought together in the right quantities at the right times and places. (The Soviet Union, a formerly communist country that no longer exists as such, <u>did</u> try to run its large economy with such central planners—and it didn't work every well.) The globalized market economy of today accomplishes this amazing feat of coordination through untold billions of independent decisions made by billions of dispersed people.

Bella: *But exactly how is it that all these individual decisions are coordinated into a coherent outcome?*

THE NEURONAL COMPLEX OF PRICE SIGNALS

There are two key elements to understanding how a market economy works: the first is prices and the second is the process of innovation. Both facilitate and manifest the logic of economic discovery in different ways, and both are closely interrelated. First, let's talk about the special role of prices in coordinating economic outcomes. Prices are like the neuronal synapses of the economy's brain. They transmit the signals that permit the economy to solve complex problems through so many decentralized decision makers. As you know, a price is what you pay for something. But from a social point of view, prices are much more than that. Prices send signals throughout the economy to <u>all</u> the potential buyers and sellers of a good or service. In doing so, <u>prices</u> coordinate behavior better than any central planner ever could. To provide an example, let's talk about "widgets." A "widget" is a fictitious good. That is, we are just going to pretend that it is a good that is produced and that people want to buy. When economists want to make an argument about markets, they often speak of widgets.

Bella: *Why is that?*

No one knows why. But I am just going to go with tradition here—so widgets it is. Suppose that, at the current price of widgets, <u>too many</u> have been produced. That is, sellers are not able to sell all the widgets they have produced at that price. Economists call this situation an "excess supply" or a "surplus." When this occurs, no central planner is needed to eliminate this surplus, or coordinate a decrease in production. Rather, the economy has a built-in mechanism for addressing and eliminating the surplus.

ELIMINATING AN EXCESS SUPPLY

When confronted with this inability to sell all of their inventory, sellers will independently lower the price of widgets in an effort to lure additional buyers and thereby sell more. The decrease in price sends a signal throughout the economy. The signal is that: "Widgets are now less expensive." In response to that signal, some buyers will decide to buy <u>more</u> widgets, since it is now cheaper to do so. At the same time, with the decreased price, some <u>suppliers</u> of widgets realize that they can no longer make as much money in the widget business as they did before. Upon this realization, some of the suppliers will shift their productive resources into other, more profitable uses and thus produce fewer widgets than they did before, or may drop out of the market altogether.

Thus, with the decreasing price of widgets, we get both an increase in the quantity that the buyers would like to buy and a decrease in the quantity suppliers would like to sell. Both of these responses serve to reduce the surplus of widgets. However, so long as there is a surplus of widgets, the downward pressure on price will continue. But the further down the price goes, the less of a surplus there will be—due to the dual influence of increased quantity demanded and decreased quantity supplied at lower prices, as described above. Through this mechanism, the downward pressure on price will obviously continue until the surplus is eliminated. Economists refer to this final point—where the quantity supplied just equals the quantity demanded—as an "equilibrium."

Bella: *They call it an "equilibrium" because they want to sound like physicists. The word makes them feel very important and scientific.*

Right you are Bella. The economists do envy the physicists. A market moving toward an equilibrium is very much like the path of a marble when it is dropped into a bowl. It will roll around for awhile, but eventually it will settle at the bottom.

Bella: *But what if the problem isn't that too many widgets are being produced, but too few? That is, what if there is a shortage?*

ELIMINATING A SHORTAGE

When <u>too few</u> widgets are being produced to meet the quantity demanded at the current price, economists call it a "shortage" or an "excess demand."

The economy has an automatic response to this as well. The sellers of widgets soon figure out that they could increase the price, since many people who would like to buy the good at the current price aren't able to get it. Imagine as the Christmas season approaches that there is some special new toy being advertized that is unexpectedly popular with kids. The kids all ask their parents to get the toy for them. The parents all try to buy it, but not enough of the toy has been produced to meet the quantity demanded at the current price. The toy manufacturers and retailers did not predict that kids would like the new toy this much! You can imagine that the suppliers of the toy would soon get the idea that they could increase the price!

As the price of the toy increases, two things happen. First, some of the people who were going to buy the toy now decide not to buy it. It has become a little too expensive for them at its now higher price. Perhaps they find some close substitute—a similar toy—and figure that that will just have to do given the now higher price for the original item. At the same time, as the price increases, suppliers realize that it is now more profitable to produce and sell the toy than it was before. The sellers will make every effort to produce more of the toy as quickly as possible, perhaps even paying the workers a higher overtime wage to stay up all night and keep producing! It is for the little kids, after all. Thusly, the sellers produce more of the good. As the price continues to increase, quantity demanded continues to decrease while quantity supplied continues to increase until the shortage is eliminated—that is, the quantity demanded just equals the quantity supplied at the now higher price. We are back in an equilibrium.

This is the mechanism by which prices send signals throughout the economy that coordinate behavior to eliminate a shortage. As a result of this mechanism, there is usually enough of a good being supplied to meet the quantity demanded in the market. This is why I can fly to Paris on an impulse, and generally secure whatever I need to make my trip a success, if I am willing to pay the market price for it. Based on past experience and price signals, businesses are constantly adjusting what they produce and what they hold in reserve to meet the demand that they predict will be there—and they tend to be pretty good at that. If they are not good at it, they go out of business. Thus, those that remain in business for the long run tend to be pretty good at it.

Economists have a short-hand way of describing the processes I have noted above—they call it "supply and demand" and it is their answer to almost any question. If you ask them, "hey, economist, why does a pack of hot dogs cost $5?" they will reply "supply and demand". And they are right, of course. It's entertaining to ask economists these kinds of questions, and always get the same answer.

Bella: *They are kind of like parrots.*

Supply-and-Demand is a very powerful idea. It is far more than just a theory to explain why a market economy has so few shortages and surpluses. First, it is a theory of price and of price change. Prices are determined by the equilibrium point where supply and demand just meet. Price changes are determined by shifts in the supply and demand, which change the ultimate equilibrium to a higher or lower price. For example, other things being equal, an increase in consumers' income might lead them to want to purchase more widgets at each and every price. This would constitute an increase in demand at each and every possible price, and thus move the equilibrium point, and therefore, the final equilibrium price to a higher point.

Bella: *Squawk! Squawk! Supply-and-Demand. Supply-and-Demand. Polly wants a cracker.*

Second, supply-and-demand is also a theory regarding the quantities of goods and services produced. The quantity that will be produced is the amount that is just sufficient to maintain the equilibrium price. Third, prices also send signals that influence economic behavior in the long run. This is pretty much an extension of the same analysis, but within a longer time frame that permits individuals and businesses to adjust not just production levels within their current productive capacity, but by investing in new plant and equipment, new software, new training for employees and even developing new technologies.

For example, let's suppose the price of oil increases dramatically and for an extended period of time. Automobile companies may begin to invest more in research and development to produce cars that use less fuel, and consumers will likely be more interested in purchasing these cars in light of higher fuel prices. Given the higher price, purchasers of oil will try to do more to economize on its use. They might invest in added insulation to their home or better windows to lower their heating bill. People may invest in equipment that uses other sources of energy, such as natural gas or solar power. As a consequence of these responses that take some time to emerge, in the long term there may be a greater reduction in the quantity demanded than would be the case in the short run. At the same time, there is a long term adjustment on the supply side as well. At this new high price for oil, methods of oil extraction that had been uneconomic may now become worth doing. New extraction technologies might be developed in light of the higher profits now available in oil. At the same time, given the higher profits available for substitutes for oil, one would expect suppliers to engage in research and development to find and improve the substitutes—that is, the rewards from the enhancement or further development of other energy sources will be higher.

Bella: *Oils well that ends well.*

Many people worry that we will run out of oil someday. After all, there is a finite amount of oil, and demand for it continues to grow. Thus, the reasoning goes, someday we must run out. Surprisingly enough, supply-and-demand analysis informs us that it is impossible for the world to run out of oil.

Bella: *How could that be? That sounds crazy!*

As the amount of oil available is reduced, its price will increase. As the price increases, <u>on the demand side</u>, people will be stimulated to find substitutes and to find ways to do without oil. At the same time, <u>on the supply side</u>, businesses will invest in new technologies and engage in more expensive extraction techniques to increase the supply of oil, all justified in light of the new higher price. These changes would occur long before we run out of oil as a planet. As the availability of oil decreased further, the price would increase yet more, which would further increase the pressure to find substitutes and to also spend more on extraction. As a consequence of these pressures, it is extremely unlikely we would ever actually run out of oil altogether. Now, note that the fact that the world is not likely to ever run out of oil does not imply that the increased price of oil might not cause great economic hardship. With an extremely high price of oil, people might have a substantial reduction in their standard of living. Thus, reaching the point at which there would be a dramatic increase in the price of oil is not a good thing. Accordingly, to say that we will never actually run out of oil is not to say that we shouldn't be concerned with conserving oil, or that we shouldn't also be concerned about the pollution associated with the usage of oil, oil products and other carbon based fuels.

But we won't run out. If someone tells you different, they simply don't grasp economics.

Bella: *That's OK. It would be boring if we were all economists.*

Amusingly, there were parliamentary hearings in Britain in the mid-1800s on what was called the "Coal Question." The concern was that, at the then-current rates of coal consumption, Britain was expected to run out of coal within the next few decades. It's now 2010, and Britain still hasn't run out of coal. Why not? The price one had to pay for coal encouraged people to find and use alternative fuels, which they did. In sum, prices are like the neuronal system of the economy. They send signals to everyone either:

> that an item is becoming more expensive, and thus, on the demand side, it needs to be economized and, on the supply side, it may offer opportunities for yet greater profit through increased production and/or innovation, or

> that an item is becoming less expensive, and thus, on the demand side, represents an opportunity to buy more and to perhaps substitute that item for other more expensive items and, on the supply side, may mean less resources are required for its production and that there may be better profit opportunities by allocating productive activities to other activities.

INNOVATION AND CREATIVE DESTRUCTION

In the midst of all these signals, people are trying to make a living. If they are business people, they try to make money on their businesses. These businesses compete with one another to offer better and cheaper products and services. In the marketplace, buyers are not forced to buy from any one seller—they can shop around. The buyers will look for where they can get the best value for each dollar spent. The businesses compete with each other not only in terms of who has the lowest price, but also in terms of the quality and usefulness of what you are getting for that price. That is, if I am a buyer, I might buy one seller's tomatoes simply because they are a lower price, but I might change my mind and buy more expensive tomatoes if they taste better.

As businesses compete, therefore, they are looking at and thinking about a lot of different variables. Is there a way they can make their product cheaper than their competitor? Perhaps they can find a cheaper source of fertilizer for the tomatoes, or a cheaper form of transport to the market, or less expensive labor. Innovative business people are always looking for a cheaper way to produce something and get it to market. If they can find a cheaper way, they can lower the price, sell more than their competitors, and make higher profits. Profits are how much money you make once you've collected what the buyers of products pay you (which is called your revenue) minus your costs. (That is, profits equal revenues minus costs.) But, as noted just above, the businesses are also competing in terms of the quality of what they offer. How can they better meet the needs and wants of their customers? Should they be bundling a different combination of goods and services to meet the needs of their customers? Could they reach different customers in a better and different way? Are they using the best technology? In sum, businesses are competing not only on the basis of price, but also on the basis of technology, product innovation and marketing innovation. To put this another way, they are competing in terms of who has the best economic ideas. They look at potential buyers and try to see what needs and wants are emerging and are, as yet, not fully met, or not met as well as they might be. They look at evolving technological developments and ask whether the goods and services being produced are taking full advantage of the latest technological breakthroughs.

Joseph Schumpeter, whom I quoted at the opening of this chapter, realized that—as important as price competition is—the more fundamental competition that drives economies is with respect to economic ideas. Economics, as a discipline, traditionally emphasizes price competition. And above we did see how very important that is. In this scenario, one business firm gains more customers by working as efficiently as possible to lower its costs, which, in turn, facilitates it in under-pricing its competitors. That is, if it's the same product, folks will want to buy the one that has the lower price. In contrast, however, Schumpeter emphasizes a different type of competition—a type of competition that he thought was more important to the economy. In the long run, Schumpeter said, what really matters to economies is not so much the fact that one firm might sell, say, tomatoes for a slightly lower price than another firm, but rather the major innovations in technology and business that replace one way of doing business, or one type of product, with something new. Let's take, for example, the market for materials with which one might wrap left-over food to temporarily preserve that food in one's refrigerator. A product that is useful for this is wax paper. One might have a number of businesses competing to produce and sell such wax paper for wrapping left-overs. But then an innovator might invent some new kind of plastic wrap that is substantially cheaper, which does a better job keeping air away from the left-overs, and which is transparent so you can see what the left-overs are. When an innovative product—like plastic wrap—appears on the scene, it tends to quickly grab a large market share.

For Schumpeter, this competition of economic ideas and innovation is driven by a special kind of business leader which he calls an "entrepreneur." The entrepreneur is the one who spots some emerging economic need that has, as yet, gone unfulfilled. She sees the possibility of using a technology and other resources in a new way to meet this need. The entrepreneur brings together these ingredients into a new business model to meet customers' needs in a way no one else has previously done. A successful entrepreneur quickly captures a big share of the market and thereby transforms the world. Sometimes they will dominate a market for quite some time, and reap a considerable reward for their economic innovation. Sometimes they will be quickly bypassed by some other entrepreneur with a yet better idea.

Bella: *Wait a second. This sounds like Weber's charismatic leader and Kuhn's revolutionary scientist!*

It is all one and the same. Economic entrepreneurs eventually either retire or die. When they do, there will be others who want to keep their successful business model going. Unfortunately, these people often tend not to be as insightful or creative as the original entrepreneur. Their task is to try to capture and replicate the special insights and processes that had been developed by the entrepreneur. These routinizers focus on simply keeping the business model going as it was, in the hopes that the profits will continue. They avoid innovation, because they think that might undermine the business model that has been profitable for so long.

Bella: *Wait! These are just like Weber's routinizers of charisma and Kuhn's normal scientists.*

Right you are again. Over time, however, the business model begins to fail. This is for several reasons. First, other businesses will see the success of the original entrepreneur and try to copy it. This will increase the intensity of price competition, and will lead to lower prices and less profits for everyone in this new line of business, which is now becoming crowded. Second, eventually other entrepreneurs may find radically new ways of addressing the needs heretofore addressed by this now old business model. Over time, economic and technological opportunities change and evolve as do the ways in which human needs and economic desires are manifested in the market. A static business model is unlikely to prosper unless it adjusts to these changes. Ironically, it is the very attempt to rigidly maintain the founder's business model by those who follow in her footsteps that leads to its demise. This sets the stage for a new entrepreneur to step in with some new idea or business model or technology that dramatically challenges the old business models, and grabs away an enormous market share. And so the cycle of innovation—or what Schumpeter would call "creative destruction"—continues.

CREATIVE DESTRUCTION

By "creative destruction" Schumpeter means the process by which old economic ideas, business methods, technologies and products are bypassed and new ones are implemented. Within this process, resources have to be moved from the old uses, methods, technologies and products to new ones, of course. This can be a difficult process, as people have to be trained or re-trained to meet these new challenges, while some regions and industries prosper as others decline. The creativity and innovation comes at an expense—hence, the term "creative destruction." There is a policy lesson here. As a government, if you want a vibrant, innovative economy, you cannot artificially support the declining industries and regions. Otherwise, the resources will not be freed up to move to their new and better uses. This Schumpeterian vision of the economy brings us to the full realization that the economy entails a logic of economic discovery.

Bella: *How does that work?*

The entrepreneur—otherwise known as the innovative business person—is like the scientists making bold <u>conjectures</u>. In the case of the economy, the entrepreneur envisions how resources might be brought together in some new way to better meet economic needs and desires, using the latest technological developments, developing new business methods and observing prices, the nature of changing demands and the changing availability of resources. In an economy, the <u>criticism</u> takes the form of whether or not the new venture is profitable. If the venture is profitable, it means that people do want to buy the new product or service that results from the innovation—or the product or services as produced under the new method or technology—and are willing to pay a price that more than covers the cost. If the venture is not profitable, it means that people do <u>not</u> want to buy the new product or service that results from the innovation—or the product or services as produced under the new method or technology—at a price that more than covers the cost. In the latter case, unless the entrepreneur wants to subsidize the new business—that is, unless she wants to transfer some of her wealth to the people consuming the new venture's goods or services—she will either discontinue the venture, or seek to improve it through further, through more refined business conjectures that are responsive to the aspect of the business that is resulting in this failure to be profitable. There may need to be further refinement in the product or service. Or perhaps the technology can be improved further. Or perhaps they haven't found quite the right market yet for the new product or service, or are failing to communicate the benefits of the new product or services to the people who would most benefit from purchasing it.

In the realm of the economy, failure of the enterprise to be profitable is directly analogous to Popper's concept of a refutation in science. An unprofitable business cannot stay in business in the long run—at least, not unless it through a transference of wealth from others in some form of subsidy. The enterprise constitutes a failed conjecture. It must either be salvaged through improvement or abandoned. In this sense, the economy itself is not so different than a scientific laboratory. As a nation—and planet—we have limited resources at any given point to meet the economic needs and wants of, respectively, the 300 million plus people in the United States and the nearly 7 billion people on the planet. How do we get that done and done effectively? In the United States, and in many other countries, we largely rely on the market to answer those questions. This chapter has been about how markets do that. It is through entrepreneurs—innovators—making bold economic conjectures by starting new ventures directed at these needs and wants. Profits, or lack thereof, and prices provide immediate feedback and, effectively, "criticism" of these conjectures. If the entrepreneurs do not adjust and respond to such criticism, then they go out of business and lose wealth. If they do respond to such signals, they prosper.

Bella: *Do you think these entrepreneurs will come up with a better dog food?*

There are some important broad policy insights tied to this vision. Once one realizes that the economy is really a knowledge process—and that if it is operating well it follows the same logic of discovery as does science—then the importance of the "conjectures" of new business ventures and ideas as well as the crucial role played by the "criticism" of either lack of profits, or in the happiest scenario, great profits, becomes crystal clear. This is why economic and personal freedom are required for economic prosperity. It is only through that freedom that "economic conjectures" put forward by enterprises and individuals may be properly implemented and tested. This also explains why central planning doesn't work very well. Central planners will never be in a position to make the many detailed conjectures about the evolving marketplace that entrepreneurs can. It is only when we have de-centralized economic decision-making by many different people with many different ideas that we, as a society, can capture the benefits of the millions of clever conjectures it takes to render an economy vibrant and innovative. Some of these people will turn out to have the right ideas and they will be rewarded with profits. Others will have the wrong ideas. Their conjectures will be "refuted" by a lack of profits. The market economy harnesses the ideas of a huge variety of people and transforms the whole economy into an engine of discovery for the betterment of humankind.

Bella: *But are profits really a good thing? If someone makes a lot of profit on their business, doesn't it mean that they are overcharging for their goods and services? Or perhaps underpaying their workers?*

Historically, there is a long tradition of seeing profits as somehow immoral or unfair. Through the ages, people have struggled with your question.

Bella: *If a merchant buys a good at $10 and then turns around and sells it to someone else for $12, isn't he really stealing $2 from the second person, given that the true value of the object is $10?*

That is one way to look at it. On the other hand, if a merchant sees that there are, say, a plethora of baskets in one town—indeed, too many to meet their needs—whereas in an nearby town there are not enough baskets, is she not providing a valuable services when she buys where the baskets are lower in price—where they are not so very needed—and then conveys them to where they command a higher price, precisely because they are more needed there? And should not that valuable service be rewarded and encouraged through profits? I believe that is the better way to look at it, because it recognizes that the entrepreneur is solving a puzzle and that there is great value in that—not only to the entrepreneur but to society. Of course, whether profits are moral or immoral is not really the point. The point is that just as criticism is essential to the growth of scientific knowledge, so too are profits central to a modern innovative economy. Profits are the scorecard that tells an entrepreneur whether she has an idea that meets needs in an efficient way or does not. If a society decides that profits are immoral or unfair, and as a consequence taxes them away or otherwise suppresses them, it can say goodbye to economic innovation and rapid economic growth.

Suggested Readings

- Joseph A. Schumpeter Capitalism, Socialism and Democracy Harper Torchbooks (1975)

11

THE EPISTEMOLOGICAL FAILURE OF MARKETS

Markets fail a lot.

KATE FISHER

Bella: *Does the free market lead to the best of all possible worlds?*

While I would like you to appreciate the wonders of markets—and their prowess as an engine of discovery—it is also important to understand their limitations and potential failures. To be sure, markets are very good at doing many important things. At the same time, it is important to understand that markets are <u>not</u> good at fulfilling every goal that we value. Moreover, markets do occasionally fail epistemologically, even in those areas in which they are usually effective.

UNFAIR OR UNDESIRABLE DISTRIBUTION OF INCOME AND WEALTH

The first and most important thing to understand about the ways in which a market economy might fail is with respect to the distribution of income and wealth. There is absolutely nothing in economic theory, or in our knowledge of how market economies operate more generally, to suggest that the distribution of income and wealth that is generated by a market economy is going to be particularly fair or desirable. Simply put, an efficient economy is not necessarily a fair one. Let's see why.

Now, it is true that, in a capitalist economy, if you work harder, you typically will make more money than you would otherwise, although it is not guaranteed. Among other things, luck can have a bit to do with how much you make as well. Indeed, there are many people around the world who work very hard from morning to night and yet remain well below the poverty line. Most of these people have very little in the way of resources or training or opportunity. So even though they may work very hard, their hard work doesn't produce much. Indeed, there is nothing in economic theory to suggest that the equilibrium wage for a particular kind of work may not be at a level at which a person starves, or at least is at near starvation. That's why Carlyle (a famous Englishman) called economics the dismal science.

No matter how hard you work, much of your ultimate productivity—and thus your income—is tied to the kind of productive capacity that already exists around you, including technology, plant and equipment and so forth. Thus, if you are unlucky enough to be born at a time, place and circumstance in which there isn't much real capital to combine with your labor efforts, you are apt to end up very poor no matter how hard you work or how smart you are. There is nothing particularly fair about that; it is simply a matter of bad luck. There is also nothing particularly desirable about it. There are billions of people in the world who live at a subsistence level, barely making it from day to day.

In a market economy, one's success is <u>not</u> just about hard work—it is also about what one starts with. Suppose a girl is born into dire poverty. And let's suppose that she is a potential Einstein in terms of her thinking power. But due to the poverty of her family, they cannot secure a good education for her and thereby expose her to the ideas and information that might permit her to manifest her talents. Indeed, her family may be so poor that she has inadequate nutrition for her brain to develop properly.

This girl is not likely ever to fulfill her potential no matter how hard she works. There is nothing particularly fair or desirable about that, and the market—for all its wonders—does not really address it or remedy it.

In contrast, suppose a girl happens to be born into a very wealthy family. As a consequence of her parents' wealth, she inherits a huge amount of money. And let's suppose she doesn't do a bit of work, or anything particularly useful with her life, and she spends the whole fortune on frivolous pursuits. She will continue to enjoy that wealth regardless of her lack of personal contribution to any constructive process. There is clearly nothing particularly fair about that. Now, it is also true that, in a market economy, if you invest in training and education, you are apt to do better. But, of course, you may not have sufficient resources to invest in that training in the first place. Moreover, if you do receive such training—and even if you did your very best to find the right training—it is not guaranteed to bring higher income. After all, you might have the misfortune to get yourself trained in the wrong thing. For example, you might have decided to become an expert at putting horse shoes on horses just as society is beginning to use motor cars instead of horses; in such a case, you might end up with very little employment and income, and certainly you are apt to get very little return on your investment in a skill set. Today, the world changes at a very fast pace. As a consequence, it is quite hard for people to know what kind of training is apt to bring them the best returns. Finally, it is true that if you are talented, you are also apt to do better in a capitalist society. Of course, you might have had the misfortune to have been born with very little talent.

Bella: *C'est moi.*

There is nothing particularly fair about that. Moreover, even if you are talented, there are no guarantees that you will be successful at garnishing returns to those talents. For example, while there are many people who have show business talents (such as singing, dancing, acting and so forth), very few of them end up able to make a living at it, even though many of them are as good as the people who do make a living at it. While talent is, no doubt, very important to becoming accomplished in such a career, there is evidence that once someone gets a "break" in the business, they are much more likely to continue to succeed, regardless of the presence of others with the same degree of talent. That is, in this profession, early success breeds continued success. Thus, luck—as opposed to fairness—plays a substantial role here and perhaps even a dominant role.

Bella: *Not that I can sing worth a lick.*

No, me neither. For a moment, let's digress to note that not only does market efficiency not imply fairness, it is also the case that what many might deem as fair does <u>not</u> imply efficiency—indeed, quite the contrary. Let's suppose in the name of fairness, we decide that each person should receive the same pay no matter what their job is. That turns out to be neither efficient nor fair. It's not efficient for a number of reasons. First, some jobs are much harder or nastier than others. Who will want to do the hard or nasty jobs if we are all paid the same thing? In such a world, too many people will want to do the easy jobs and too few people will want to do the hard or nasty jobs. As a consequence, the hard and nasty jobs will not get done—yet they may be very important. A good way to address this insufficient supply of folks to do the hard and nasty jobs would be to pay them more money—but under the system of equal pay that can't be done. Thus, equal pay for all work ends up being both unfair and inefficient.

It is inefficient for another reason as well. Some jobs may take much more investment and study than others. For example, to become a good medical doctor or medical researcher takes years of study and expensive training. If medical doctors were paid the same thing as, say, a person whose job is to sell gloves at a store, there would be an insufficient supply of people willing to work that hard and spend that much money in training to become a doctor or medical researcher. That could present some serious problems for sick people. Finally, some people just work harder and are more productive than others. If they are rewarded for this harder work by extra pay, they are apt to keep up that intensity of effort. If they are not paid more for their extra productivity, then they may decide to stop putting in such an intensity of effort. At the same time, if those who are intrinsically a bit more lazy, see higher rewards going to those who work harder, then in some instances they may decide to work harder and be more productive themselves. A lack of reward for people's extra efforts is apt to lead to less productivity, and therefore less goods and services for society as a whole.

It is a fact that societies that reward those who work harder and are more productive tend to be much more prosperous. But, of course, this leads to some people having much more money than others, and it also means some will be born into families that are advantaged while others will be born into families that are disadvantaged. This makes economic life a bit like a footrace where some people have a starting line that is way in front of others. While this is not particularly fair, it does turn out to be more efficient, since it is a ramification of rewarding hard work and investment which are essential to a prosperous society. There is no easy way around these social tradeoffs. One answer—to help level the competitive playing field and give everyone at least some opportunity to manifest his or her intrinsic abilities—has been public education provided free of charge by the government to everyone. By this means, kids born into poor families can have an opportunity to learn and to develop their talents, skills and knowledge.

In sum, while capitalist economies tend to result in a general prosperity, there is nothing ultimately fair, or even necessarily desirable, about the final distribution of income and wealth. A capitalist economy can end up with great potential talents going to waste because no one ever invests in the education and training of some of the poor people who possess those talents. This is not only bad for the poor folks, but also for everyone else who might have benefitted from their potential contributions. On the other hand, non-market economies tend to be both unfair and inefficient. Thus, society is compelled to embrace capitalism and markets, but also attempt to find ways to deal with its flaws in sensible ways.

POSITIVE AND NEGATIVE EXTERNALITIES AND PARETO EFFICIENCY

Markets often fail is due to what economists call "positive" and "negative" externalities." To understand these ideas, it is best to start with a discussion of the Italian economist Vilfredo Pareto. Pareto had a nifty way of explaining what is so great about markets. Wait! We have an interruption. Bella has just rested her big head on my computer, while I was looking into the distance lost in thought over Vilfredo Pareto. I think she wants her breakfast. At any rate, here is what she typed with her big nose (really):

Xzcv bbbbbbbbbbbbbbbbbbbbbbbbbbbbbbbbbbbbbbbbbbbbbbbbbbdsfgzzz zzzzzzzzzzzzzzzzzzzzzzzzzzzzzzzzzzzzzzzzzzzzzzzzzzzzzzzzzzzzzzzzzzzzzz zzzzzzzzzzzzzzzzzzzzzzzzzzzzzzzzzzzzzzzzzzzzxVCCCCCCCCCCCCCCCCCCCCC CCCCCCCCCCCCCC

Here's a mystery: Can you tell which side of the keyboard she had her head on?

Now back to Pareto. Pareto used a little story to indicate what was so great about markets. To wit: let's suppose two people decide to freely trade one thing for another. Indeed, let's say that Vilfredo himself strolls down the boulevard and smalls some lovely fresh donuts in Luigi's Donut Shop. He walks in to purchase one for $1. What can we say about this transaction?

Bella: *Clearly, Vilfredo prefers having the donut to having that dollar (just as I would). At the same time, clearly, Luigi prefers having the dollar to having that donut. Thus, we may say that both are made better off by virtue of the transaction.*

Correct. Now, Pareto asked, was anyone else hurt by the transaction?

Bella: *The answer to that is clearly: no.*

Correct. As a consequence, Pareto argued that we could conclude that such a transaction makes <u>society</u> better off. He argued, so long as no one else is made worse off by virtue of a transaction, and we know that the two parties to the transaction entered it willingly, we can conclude that society as a whole is better off. It follows from this—or so argued Pareto—that free markets make society better off. That is, since each and every transaction freely entered into makes the counterparties better off, so long as no one else is directly harmed, we may say that society is better off. This is sometimes known as the Pareto Principle or—once everyone has made as many beneficial trades as can be made—Pareto Efficiency. Now, rather obviously, you can extend the idea of Pareto Efficiency beyond just trading goods to also include trading services, including productive services. For example, we can think of a worker having her labor time to sell and an employer wanting to buy her labor time. If they both willingly enter into the employment arrangement, then they must both feel like they are better off. If no one has been made worse off, then we can say that society as a whole is better off.

Bella: *With Pareto Efficiency, are we now in the best of all possible worlds?*

Not necessarily. Although Pareto Efficiency is a very good thing, there are at least two problems with it. First, it doesn't address issues of distribution of income and wealth at all. That is, all beneficial trading within a time period may have occurred, but some people may still end up terribly impoverished—as we noted above—and even starving, while others have a great deal of wealth.

Bella: *How could that be?*

It may be because they don't start out with much to trade in the first place. Maybe the labor they had to sell simply wasn't worth very much. If a person happens to be an unskilled laborer, their best efforts may not command much remuneration. Indeed, it is interesting to note that a world where one person owns everything would be Pareto Efficient, simply because there couldn't be any further beneficial trading!

Bella: *In that world, I doubt that the other people—who had nothing to trade—would be very impressed with Pareto efficiency.*

The second problem with Pareto Efficiency is that it can't be said to imply that society is better off if what economists call positive and negative externalities are present, which we will define momentarily. Recall that, in Pareto's argument, he says that if two people are both made better off by a trade, and no one is made worse off, then we can say that society as a whole can be considered better off.

Bella: *Ah, but what if our transaction does lead to someone else being made worse off?*

Good question. In that case, we cannot definitively say that society is better off, of course. A situation where a transaction between two willing traders makes some third-party worse off is called a "negative externality". It is also sometimes called a "negative third-party effect". This most easily understood through an example. Suppose you produce and sell aluminum and I purchase it from you. In that case, by virtue of the same arguments we made above, it is fair to say that both you and I are better off. But is the rest of society left unaffected? Let's suppose that the production of the aluminum—in the aluminum smelter—created a great deal of river pollution. In that case, the rest of society is not left unaffected. Rather, all the users of the river are harmed. This is an example of a "negative externality." If there are important negative externalities in an economy that are unaddressed, the free market will not necessarily lead to the best of all possible worlds. That is, if the market is left to its own devices and there are important negative externalities, the market will fail as an engine of social discovery because—from a social point of view—too many of the goods or services with negative externalities will be produced.

Bella: *What do you mean by "too many" goods or services?*

I mean that more will be produced than would have been the case if the people engaged in the transactions had taken account of (and had to pay for) all of the costs (to anyone) entailed by the production and sale of whatever good or service was involved. For example, take the example of the aluminum. If the parties to the transaction had to incorporate the cost of the harm they are doing to others through the pollution (or alternatively were required to produce the aluminum in a manner that did not cause such pollution in the first place), they would end up producing and exchanging less of it.

Bella: *How do we know that?*

Because the price would be higher if the producers had to pay for the costs that they are imposing on third parties, and if the price is higher we know that folks will want to buy less of the good or service.

Bella: *Are externalities always bad?*

No. Externalities can also be good—or, as economists like to say, "positive." If an externality, or third-party effect, is a good thing, it is called a "positive externality." For example, suppose that everyone loves the smell of the donuts being cooked as they walk past a bakery in the morning, and it makes them happy.

Bella: *That's my kind of externality.*

In that case, not only are the baker and the purchaser made better off by the sale of the donut, but also all the people who walk past the bakery. Thus, they are receiving a benefit without paying for it. With a positive externality, the market, if left to its own devices, also fails as an engine of social discovery, because it ends up producing too little of the good or service.

Bella: *And exactly what do you mean by that?*

I mean that if the third-party beneficiaries of the baking activity were willing to pay some money to the baker for the benefit they are receiving, then the baker would find it profitable to produce and sell more donuts than he would without receiving such payments. The bottom line is this. We have seen that the market is a machine of discovery that leads to the production of just the right quantity and mix of goods and services to meet everyone's needs at prices they are willing to pay. But because the cost of a negative externality is not reflected in market prices, we end up having too many goods and services that produce negative externalities. That is, if we could arrange it so that the producers of the goods and services had to compensate those who are harmed by the negative externality, and thus incorporate that cost into their pricing, we would find less of these particular goods and services being produced, and those who were compensated for the negative externality would not be harmed—in net—by the activities. Conversely, with respect to goods or services that result in positive externalities, as we noted above, the market produces too few of these.

GOVERNMENT INTERVENTION

The presence of positive and negative externalities is sometimes a good argument for government intervention into the economy. The argument goes as follows: where positive or negative externalities exist, the government could and should pass laws that address these problems or opportunities. For example, let's look at the issue of pollution. The government might choose to make certain types of pollution illegal. That is, the government will declare that if you dump certain kinds of industrial waste products in the river you have committed a crime, and are subject to a fine and possibly imprisonment. For other types of pollution, they may charge a tax. For example, they might say that for a given amount of smokestack emissions from a factory, you have to pay a certain amount of money to the government. This is a way of making the producers of goods that result in pollution incorporate the cost of that pollution into their business calculations. Another thing the government might do is provide some kind of subsidy or tax rebate (or reduction in taxes) for those who produce or consume items that involve less pollution. For example, if one buys a car that emits less air pollutants, the government might correspondingly lower the taxes you might otherwise pay.

With respect to positive externalities, the government could subsidize the activity, either by sending money to anyone who engages in the activity in proportion to how much of the activity they are engaging in, or provide them with a tax break—that is, lower taxes than they would otherwise have to pay. Another possibility would be to require that those third-parties benefitting from the transactions compensate those engaged in the production of the good or service. In this manner, the government can indirectly subsidize the production of the good or service with the positive externality, and thus ensure that more is produced. A good example of this might be health research. The market, left to its own devices, might under-produce health research. Indeed, governments often subsidize research that has important social benefits.

Bella: *Should the government always intervene if a positive or negative externality is present?*

No. Addressing positive and negative externalities is not always easy, and the costs of doing so may outweigh the benefits or interfere with our sense of liberty and privacy. It also may be the case that if the government tried to address the externality, it wouldn't do a very good job and would thereby render society worse off through its failure. Finding the right points and degree of governmental intervention into the economy is also—or at least should be—a process of discovery. Among other things, the accurate "pricing" of externalities by the government tends to be difficult, precisely because the market doesn't tell us what those prices should be. For example, how would the government ever figure out what the pleasant smell of donuts is worth to third-parties? And even if it could price this pleasant experience, how could it efficiently create a transfer from the third parties to the producers of the donuts?

Bella: *The answer is that it couldn't.*

Right you are. And, finally, do we really want every aspect of our interactions with one another commoditized in this fashion?

Bella: *Clearly not!*

Thus, in practice, it doesn't always make sense to have the government intervene in the operation of markets when there is an externality. First, as noted above, there is the problem of "government failure." That is, just because the market gets it wrong doesn't mean the government will get it right. Government is a complicated business, fraught with all kinds of complicated processes simply because it is the government. Because governments are so powerful, we have special processes to ensure (or at least try to ensure) that they behave responsibly and in the interests of the people. But these processes themselves are not always particularly efficient, and certainly don't necessarily move quickly. And sometimes the government just gets the answers wrong. As a consequence, particularly if externalities are not large, it may not make a lot of sense to have the government involved.

Second, sometimes governments interfere with markets for the purposes of unfairly advantaging some of the people over others. This is a form of government failure as opposed to market failure. The government is not apt to say that it is doing this, of course. But perhaps certain people gave the politicians bigger political donations than others did. Thus, when the government tries to address externalities, it may actually—due to the biases of politicians or possibly their corruption—end up not improving market outcomes, but simply unfairly advantaging some constituents at the expense of others. This is a particularly disturbing type of government failure, of course.

Third, the government always has to somehow pay for whatever it is doing. Governments generally do this through the collection of taxes. Thus, if the government decides to intervene in a particular market to address an externality, it may end up having to collect more taxes. The very process of the collection of taxes itself has a cost to it. In addition to the direct cost of collecting taxes, there is often an indirect cost in that the manner in which the taxes are applied and collected may itself change private behavior, and often in ways that themselves generate market inefficiencies. For example, let's suppose you impose a tax on employers whenever they hire someone to help pay benefits to those who end up unemployed. Such a tax on employers would also make it more expensive for those employers to hire workers. Thus, the employers may decide to hire less workers than they would have otherwise. This creates unemployment, which is quite unfortunate for those who end up with no job, even if the tax was well intended and does serve to ameliorate some of the pain of unemployment.

Fourth, we may not want the government to address externalities because they interfere with our sense of liberty. Within a broad range of activities, we want people to feel free to take action without having to fill out 28 forms or wonder what the government thinks about it and whether the government will say it's OK. To put this another way, in the name of liberty and the pursuit of happiness, we don't really want to recognize all third-party effects as such. Let's take a trivial example, but one that will make the point clearly. Suppose I like to wear purple shirts. Suppose you genuinely find it offensive to the eye when I wear a purple shirt. In other words, there is a negative externality for you when I wear a purple shirt. That is the kind of negative externality that the government should ignore in the name of liberty. That is, I should be free to wear whatever colored shirt I want no matter how you feel about it

Bella: *And that person should get a life and start thinking about something better than the color of your shirt.*

On a more serious topic, suppose you are offended—and indeed deeply disturbed—regarding my religious beliefs, which are different than yours. And suppose I go about telling people what my religious beliefs are and trying to convert others to my faith. Your disturbance regarding my beliefs is a negative externality from your perspective, but in the name of liberty we should, of course, ignore your concerns.

Bella: *Amen.*

THE PROLIFERATION OF PERCEIVED NEGATIVE EXTERNALITIES COMPROMISES LIBERTY

For the most part, the current trend in the United States, unfortunately, is to recognize more and more such "negative externalities" that compromise our liberty. For example, some people have the sensibility that they don't like how pick-up trucks look, and thus they don't want pick-up trucks in their neighborhood. Now, there is no doubt that, from their perspective, a pick-up truck in their neighborhood makes them worse off. These people wield their power as a group to ensure that pick-up trucks are, in fact, banned in many neighborhoods. If you park a pick-up truck in these neighborhoods, you receive a fine. This myopic concern with such sensibilities does violence to those who would like to live a different lifestyle. Some folks just like to have a pick-up truck. Others may need a pick-up truck to make a living. But these fancy folks don't want to live near those people.

Bella: *They should mind their own business, and should recognize that their "own business" is cabined by the liberty interests of others. Besides—pick-up trucks are great for carrying dogs. The way in which the wind flaps your ears about and stings your eyes is lovely.*

Right you are, Bella. As another example, I am told by a friendly neighbor that the county in which I reside has a rule that you cannot hang out laundry in your back yard to dry. This makes her unhappy because she likes the smell of laundry that has been dried outside. I agree with her. Now, it's not like we live on top of each other here; I have a half-acre lot. But apparently bureaucrats somewhere think it's unseemly for me or my neighbor to save on energy by hanging our towels out to dry, even if neither of us minds the other doing so. That is not a free society.

Bella: *Have you started a rebellion by hanging out your towel?*

No.

Bella: *If you hung up towels, I would enjoy pulling them down.*

In my neighborhood, I am also not allowed to put a tall fence around my back yard, even though that would make it safer for you, Bella (in terms of ensuring that you stay in the yard).

Bella: *That hardly seems necessary.*

I suppose if you look at it from the county's perspective, they might worry; who knows what I might be doing behind a tall fence?

Bella: *You might be hanging up laundry back there!*

Bottom line: I am not free to use my own property in such a reasonable manner, simply because of the odd aesthetic of the people who live in this county and the manner in which they impose that aesthetic through the law. That is not liberty. In the US, we used to have a broader kind of tolerance of our neighbors' use of their property. We had a greater concern for allowing individuals to pursue happiness in whatever way they saw fit, so long as they were not <u>directly</u> interfering with the liberty or property of others. If somebody wanted to do mechanical work on their car in their driveway, people didn't have a problem with that. If people wanted to paint their house a funny color, that was OK too. If people wanted to put a tall fence around their house, that was just fine. In recent decades, we have become much less tolerant of the individual pursuit of happiness. In general, people have an exaggerated sense of what "harms" them and that often leads to the compromise of liberty. In my view, this is not the kind of externality that should be given any weight whatsoever. Indeed, I find this growing intolerance of the manner in which others would like to pursue their happiness one of the most disturbing trends in our society.

Bella: *Right up there with oppressive epistemology?*

You betcha.

IMPERFECT INFORMATION AND THE LEMONS PRINCIPLE

When economists theorize about markets, and the efficiencies they bring with them, they often assume that there is perfect information about what is being bought and sold in these markets. In the real world, that is never the case. Getting accurate information about what you are going to buy can be challenging. Sometimes the lack of good information can undermine the efficacy of markets. This is particularly true in the market for services. Let's suppose that you pay a mechanic to tell you what is wrong with your car. After diagnosing your car, it is this same mechanic who is likely to receive additional payments for fixing it. Thus, the mechanic has an incentive to tell you something is wrong with your car, even when that may not be the case—or to exaggerate what is wrong with your car—so you will spend extra money in fixing it. It is not very easy for you to know whether your mechanic is telling you the truth, or not. Of course, you could say "thanks very much" and take it to a second mechanics shop to get a second opinion, but that will cost you extra money as well. When you hire someone to do something for you, economists refer to the costs that you incur due to this misalignment of interests as "agency cost". Agency cost includes not only the cost that you incur due to the fact that the quality of the services is compromised by this conflict of interest, but also any costs you incur in trying to monitor the activities of the person you have hired to make sure they are doing a good job. For example, getting a second opinion from another mechanic would be included under the "monitoring" part of agency cost. Taken to an extreme, "agency cost" can constitute fraud. That is, if people you have hired to do some service for you are simply lying to you about what they intend to do for you to get your money, that would constitute fraud.

Agency cost and fraud can tremendously undermine a market and prevent beneficial transactions from occurring. Let's take home improvements. If you contract with someone to put an extension on your house, it is very difficult to know if they will do a good job. They may try to use cheaper materials than you have contracted for, so that they can make greater profits. Of course, you could spend additional money or time to monitor for this kind of bad behavior, but that will cost you more. If you catch your contractors cheating you, you could take them to court for damages, but that is also costly, uncertain and unpleasant. Any way you look at it, you confront some agency cost as a part of such a project. The problem is that if agency costs are high enough, many people who might have contracted to have work done on their house—and would have felt better off from having such work done—may decide not to have such work done because the hassles and uncertainties are so great. This means the contractors also won't get work that they might have gotten, even though they would have liked to do the work at that price. Thus, agency cost and dishonesty undermine the power and efficacy of markets. Dishonesty hurts us all in this way. Honesty brings with it tremendous market efficiencies because it supports beneficial transactions that might not otherwise occur.

Agency cost—and dishonesty-in-dealings—can be so powerful that it undermines markets completely. Let's see how this works. Suppose you buy a new car. The instant you drive it off the new car lot it decreases in value by around 25 to 33%. That is very curious. The car constitutes precisely the same item that it did a moment before. The expected stream of benefits associated with it hasn't changed. The only things which have changed are its ownership and its physical location. Yet it substantially drops in tradable value. There is a market failure here. The market failure has to do with the signal that is sent to potential buyers if you try to sell a car so soon after you have purchased it. Potential buyers wonder why you would want to sell it so soon. One possible explanation is that the car is what we call a "lemon." When we say a car is a "lemon", we mean that it didn't turn out too good in the manufacturing process. For example, perhaps its electrical system has occasional problems whereby it ceases to operate in the middle of traffic, and yet the mechanics can't figure out what is wrong with it. (I had a car like that!) That is a lemon. Because potential buyers do not want to end up with a lemon, and they suspect a seller might not tell them about the fact that it is a lemon, they discount the value of all cars that are being resold so soon after purchase, based on the expectation that they might be receiving a lemon. (The economist who first identified and explained this important problem is George Akerlof.)

There are, of course, ways to work around the lemons problem. For example, let's say you work for the military and have just received a transfer to work in some foreign country, and so you decide to sell your car since it is too expensive to transport it to this other country. But you recently purchased it as a new car, and so you face the lemons problem that it is apt to be heavily discounted by potential buyers. One way around the lemons principle is that you might offer to let a potential buyer have a mechanic inspect it. You might also let them have an extensive test drive. You might also show them your letter of transfer, so that they know why you are selling the car. At the end of the day, we know that these are imperfect mechanisms because people do, in fact, get much lower prices on new cars that are being resold.

Bella: *But what about that lovely new car smell? Aren't people willing to pay a premium for that? I think you are not taking that sufficiently into account! You humans are always underestimating the importance of how something smells.*

Maybe, but I don't think it accounts for such a big difference in price. The lemons problem can be so severe that it destroys a market altogether. Let's suppose, again, that you work for the military and have been transferred overseas. You want to sell your car, and in fact you know that it is a terrific car, and certainly not a lemon, but you have no way to effectively send that signal to the market. As a consequence, potential purchasers lump you in with all the other relatively new cars being resold, and you can only sell your car if you accept 1/3 less than it is really worth. In this situation, you might consider not selling your car at all, precisely because you know that it is worth more than that and isn't a lemon! Perhaps you will consider storing it until you get back from your mission overseas. Perhaps you will lend it to your brother. The point is that you may withdraw from the market. But as more and more of the good quality cars are withdrawn from the market, the relative percentage of lemons remaining in the market increases. As a consequence, potential purchasers put an ever higher discount on any cars that remain in the market, given their now higher expectation of receiving a lemon. But as the prices get lower and lower, the good quality cars continue to withdraw from the market, until there is nothing left but lemons. At this point, the market collapses altogether. This is bad both for people who would like to sell their car as well as people who would like to buy them. Markets are constantly trying to develop ways to get around the lemons problem, which is essentially a signaling problem.

The lemons principle shows the great harm that liars can do to the prowess of markets as a discovery mechanism. It is, of course, not surprising that lying would mess up what is essentially a knowledge process. There are many instances where the government can help support and improve markets by addressing the lemons problem, in particular in its efforts to bring legal actions against fraudsters, address false advertising, enforce contracts through access to the courts and so forth. Another important way to address the problems of agency cost and fraud is called honesty. If people are honest, the economy works much better. Societies that develop and reinforce the value of honesty prosper. Morals have an important economic function.

MORAL SENTIMENTS

The great Scottish economist Adam Smith recognized this. In addition to his most famous book "The Wealth of Nations," he also wrote another book called "The Theory of Moral Sentiments." In this latter book, which he wrote well before he wrote "The Wealth of Nations", he made the point that for society and markets to function well, there needs to be a general acceptance of, and behavior in accordance with, moral principles. In short, if we are all trying to steal from one another, markets don't work very well. Markets do not operate effectively in a moral and legal vacuum. Imagine two tribes who do not trust one another, but who want to trade, say, fish for carved bowls. They know where the boundary is between their territories. But both sides fear violence from the other side. In an effort to begin trade, perhaps, one day, one of them leaves three fish on the border in the hope that someone from the other tribe will see the fish and get the idea. And, sure enough, they come back, and there is a carved wooden bowl where the fishes were. If our trader likes these terms of trade—that is, three fish for one bowl—he may begin to leave fish at the border each day, and later return in the hope of finding a bowl. But you can readily see how inefficient such distrust is. It would be far better if they could get together and simply discuss how many bowls they wanted to trade for how many fish, without any fear that one might hit the other over the head, or simply steal the other one's products. Honesty-in-dealing and law-and-order go a long way to making markets work well. In general, this requires a moral framework as well as government.

THE BUSINESS CYCLE OF BOOM AND BUST

As even a cursory glance at the history of capitalism would reveal, there are times when the economy as a whole seems to get stuck—like a great sailing ship with no wind in its sails. These times are marked by an increase in the number of people who are unemployed—that is, people who would like to work but can't find a job. At one point during the Great Depression in the 1930s in the US, about one in four people were out of work. That is a very tough situation, particularly if you have a family to feed. Indeed, during the Great Depression, there were very long lines of people wherever and whenever folks decided to give away soup or other food to those who were down on their luck. Capitalist economies tend to be characterized by fluctuations in the intensity with which productive facilities and labor are utilized in the economy as a whole. That is, there tend to be alternative periods of boom and bust. The periods of boom tend to be periods of increased real investment in plant and equipment, high economic growth rates, increasing incomes and lots of jobs to go around. The periods of bust tend to have slower economic growth rates, or even declines in the level of economic activity, high levels of unemployment, less real investment and lower incomes.

This oscillation in the economy is driven by a blend of self-reinforcing and self-correcting mechanisms that tend to offset one another to a certain degree. Let's look at the self-reinforcing mechanisms first. When lots of companies are in the process of hiring new workers, this creates more income (overall) for more workers and thus more spending power. As more workers start to spend more, more goods and services are purchased, and inventories of goods begin to become depleted. As business see this general increase in demand, and also decide it's time to replenish their inventories, they order more goods from suppliers. The suppliers then turn to hire yet more workers, and the upward cycle reinforces itself.

Once the upswing is in full motion, and as the economy begins to approach full employment of productive resources, the self-correcting mechanisms begin to kick in. First, it becomes harder to find good workers as full employment is approached; everyone already has a job. At that stage, the employers have to lure the workers away from other jobs by offering higher wages. But this makes the workers more expensive to hire, and so some of the employers become less anxious to do so. With the increased demands for goods and services, some of the goods and services hit production bottlenecks—that is, points where it simply becomes very difficult to increase production in the short run. With the shortages of supply, we begin to see prices rise, which itself begins to choke off some of the excess demand. Also, as the economy heats up, more and more businesses are engaged in new investments, and more and more workers are buying homes, and many of them are seeking loans from banks to do so. With the increased demand for loans, the interest that one has to pay on those loans begins to be increased, but this, in itself, begins to make borrowing less attractive. As all of these mechanisms kick in, the economy begins to slow in its growth. Businesses see that the growth in the demand for their products and services is beginning to slow down. As a result, they cut back on new investments in plant, equipment and so forth. The suppliers of these real investment products thus quickly experience a reduction in demand. They are forced to lay off workers. These workers now have less to spend than they did before. As a consequence, they spend less than before. This means that yet more goods and services do not get purchased that would have been purchased. Inventories of unpurchased goods begin to accumulate. Companies lay off yet more workers. And so the economy begins to contract.

But as the economy begins to contract, self-correcting mechanisms kick into gear once more. As more and more workers become unemployed, some may become willing to work at a lower wage than they were before. This can make it economical for a business to hire them when it might not have otherwise been the case. Businesses also begin to lower prices to try to sell their accumulated inventories. At these lower prices, some people find it worth buying the goods when they might not have otherwise done so. Over time, the excess accumulated inventories begin to dwindle and some of the businesses decide it is time to restock the shelves. And the process turns itself around, and the economy begins to grow once again.

There have been times when the business cycle has been so extreme that the downswing caused massive suffering. The most notable instance of this is what we refer to as the Great Depression, as mentioned above. Unemployment was extremely high and there were cascading bankruptcies among both companies and banks. The banking system itself essentially ceased to operate for a time. A great economist of the day—John Maynard Keynes—developed a theory to explain not only why an economy could collapse, but why it might get stuck there. He argued that you can reach a point that is so desperate that the normal self-correcting mechanisms we discussed above do <u>not</u> kick into gear properly. Let's think about this in terms of competing metaphors. On the one hand, the people who believe the economy is always fully self correcting think of the economy as like a great ship that has a very large and heavy keel. Although a large wave may knock it about a bit, that heavy keel always pulls the ship back upright. That keel is constituted by the forces of supply and demand. Unemployment is nothing more than an excess supply of labor. Thus, as the price of labor—otherwise known as wages—decreases in response to this excess supply of labor, then more workers will end up being hired. Similarly, unused productive capacity of any sort—that is, empty plant and unused equipment—is really nothing more than an excess supply of these resources. As their prices fall, the demand to use them will increase. Moreover, if there is inadequate real investment by companies, then companies will cease borrowing. But as soon as companies cease borrowing, then—in response—banks will lower the interest they charge on loans, and hence borrowing will become more attractive. With borrowing becoming less expensive, real investment will pick up, and more workers will be hired to construct such plant and equipment.

Keynes argued it doesn't always work that way. The metaphor that captures his view of the economy would be that of a lumbering barge with cargo. If a big wave hits the barge and it is tipped over, the cargo slides to one side and keeps the barge tipped over. The cargo is business confidence. The economy gets stuck because the price signals that should be equilibrating it cannot be sent. That is, the businesses see they are in an economic depression, and therefore are not going to build any new plant and equipment to produce more goods and services until they see that demand is picking up—no matter what the interest rate is on money that they might borrow from the banks. As a consequence of this lack of real investment, companies don't hire anybody. As the workers don't get hired, they don't get any income, so they can't spend any money on the goods and services that might have been purchased. The companies see this lack of demand for their products, and thus are reinforced in their beliefs that it a bad time to invest in new plant and equipment and a bad time to hire workers. As a whole, they are trapped. If all the businesses hired at the same time, then the workers would all have income to buy what the businesses produced, so hiring the people would have made eminent sense. But since others aren't hiring, each of the businesses taken in isolation decides that they also will not hire. As a consequence, workers sit idle and their needs and the needs of their families go largely unfulfilled, plant and equipment sit idle, and businesses make no profits.

In that kind of situation, Keynes believed that the government needed to kick start the process by stepping in and simply spending governmental money on any kind of governmental projects. As a consequence, some people would be hired to provide the government with whatever it was purchasing. These workers would have income they otherwise would not have had, and thus would start spending. This would, in turn, lead to other people being hired to produce the things this first group is purchasing. And so on. In sum, this cyclical process that seems built into the economy can lead to considerable human hardship. Historically, politicians and policy makers such as Keynes have tried to figure out ways to soften or smooth the cycle, so that it is not quite so harmful. One of the ways governments have learned to do this is to increase government spending or cut taxes at the times in which the economy is on a downswing. This leads the greater overall demand for goods and services, and thus lessens the downturn in the economy. This is referred to as "fiscal policy". Another possible policy is to increase the money supply during a downturn. With more money in the economy, banks have more to lend, and will tend to do so at lower interest rates. This leads to more people borrowing than they might have otherwise done, and thereby similarly increases overall demand for goods and services at a time when the economy would otherwise be contracting. This is referred to as "monetary policy".

Some have argued that these governmental efforts to ameliorate the business cycle through fiscal and monetary policy can make matters worse. If they are not timed properly, then they may worsen rather than ameliorate the cycle. In addition, governments may use them too often, or too heavily, because it may help incumbent politicians get re-elected if they stimulate the economy just as they are coming up for election, rather than when it really needs it. Monetary policy may fail to stimulate the economy if banks do not want to make loans due to increased economic uncertainty. Fiscal policy may lead to an allocation of productive resources to uses that are not profitable in the medium and long run and thus cannot be sustained without permanent governmental subsidies or excessive governmental debt that may itself compromise economic growth. If the economy's problem is getting productive resources into the right uses, fiscal policy can slow that down. The right economic policy is dependent on the particulars of the situation being addressed.

ALIENATION AND LACK OF SOCIAL COHESION

Karl Marx was a critic of capitalism—perhaps its fiercest critic ever. He argued that capitalism had a number of "contradictions" built into it. What he meant by a contradiction was an aspect of the system that through its very success would ultimately undermine it. To put this more simply, he was saying that in the long run, it is not a stable social system. One of these contradictions was the manner in which, he believed, that capitalism undermines the very social norms and mores that hold a society together. He felt capitalism did this in two ways. First, there is the dynamic process that leads to innovation with some regions growing economically while others decline. As this occurs, workers move to wherever the jobs are, of course. But as workers do this, they tend to move away from the community that they grew up in. As a consequence, communities are no longer stable, as such. No longer do we have two, three or even four generations all living near one another. Rather, each generation gets scattered about to wherever the latest economic growth has been.

This mobility comes at a high cost in terms of social cohesion. People move to places where they don't know their neighbors and they don't know anyone except the people they might meet at work. As a consequence, they stop caring quite so much for the community around them. Old people end up alone with no one to care for them. Young people aren't properly socialized into good behavior by the multiple generations of a closely knit community who might constantly be guiding them to better, more fruitful conduct. This eventually leads to a collapse of the social fabric, an increase in violence and a decay of communities that is both wasteful and sad. Karl Marx shares much with conservatives in seeing the importance of the social fabric for maintaining a healthy society, and, ultimately, helping to make markets themselves function well. This is why conservatives emphasize the importance of values, family, private community organizations, religion, moral, culture, art and tradition in counterbalancing the negative aspects of mobility and the turmoil and chaos that can accompany the creative-destruction that characterizes markets. It is our family, religion, culture and values that stand as a buffer to the markets, and give us our sense of self and dignity and the realization that our ultimate worth can never be measured by a market.

Another contradiction of capitalism that Marx focused on was the manner in which markets can lead us to treat one another as mere "things" and the damaging psychological effect this has on people. That is, in a capitalist economy, we are always focused on how to make more money. The focus on making more money sometimes makes people forget that—within the productive process—they are dealing with other human beings, who have feelings and aspirations and want to live a full, rich life. There is a Charlie Chaplin movie called "Modern Times" that captures this idea visually. Charlie Chaplin works on an assembly line. His job is to screw in two bolts to metal plates that move by on the assembly line. He has a large wrench in each hand, and reaches again and again to tighten one bolt after another, all day long. One can easily see that this kind of work is not intrinsically rewarding. It is not work anyone would want to do, if they could avoid it. Charlie really has become a part of the machine itself, and that is all that is expected of him. Indeed, at one point, he actually gets pulled into the assembly line and is literally pictured as a part of the machine.

Marx's point about these kinds of jobs and working environments was a simple one; it is not likely to produce happy and healthy people. Instead of feeling proud of what they do, and intrinsically rewarded by the experience of work, and therefore ready to do their very best, they will instead feel separated from the process and from others. He called this feeling "alienation". Alienated people don't make good citizens and neighbors. Marx thought that this kind of situation was ultimately unsustainable. That is, he thought people would ultimately rebel from such treatment, and find ways to organize production that were healthier and more intrinsically rewarding. And, of course, it's not that Marx is wrong about alienation being a serious problem. Rather, the issue is that humanity has never found anything quite so wonderfully efficient as is capitalism; nor any system that so well complements our sense of liberty. Experiments with other ways of organizing production, consumption and distribution have always turned out disastrously. Indeed, within capitalism, many companies, in fact, do recognize the importance of these types of issues and have experimented with alternative production methods that are more intrinsically rewarding for workers—for example, having one team of workers move along with a vehicle on an assembly line and participate in multiple stages of the production process. Labor unions as well as governments have also focused on addressing issues of the quality and safety of the work experience and environment.

THE INTERFACE BETWEEN ECONOMICS, POLITICS AND GOVERNMENT

Even though—as we saw in the previous chapter—markets are an extraordinary engine of economic discovery, because markets can and do fail a healthy and productive society must create an exploratory process and interaction between markets, politics and governments that facilitates the discovery of efficient means of addressing market failures. Societies that succeed in finding this right balance will prosper. Those that fail will not prosper.

Suggested Readings

*   James E. Meade The Intelligent Radical's Guide to Economic Policy: The Mixed Economy George Allen & Unwin Ltd. (1975)

12

THE CULT OF EXPERTISM

Great spirits have always found violent opposition from mediocrities. The latter cannot understand it when a man does not thoughtlessly submit to hereditary prejudices but honestly and courageously uses his intelligence.

ALBERT EINSTEIN

It is difficult to get a man to understand something when his salary depends on his not understanding it.

UPTON SINCLAIR

{O}ne of the things a scientific community acquires with a paradigm is a criterion for choosing problems that, while the paradigm is taken for granted, can be assumed to have solutions. To a great extent these are the only problems that the community will admit as scientific or encourage

its members to undertake. Other problems, including many that had previously been standard, are rejected as metaphysical, as the concern of another discipline, or sometimes as just too problematic to be worth the time. A paradigm can, for that matter, even insulate the community from those socially important problems that are not reducible to the puzzle form, because they cannot be stated in terms of the conceptual and instrumental tools the paradigm supplies.

THOMAS KUHN

A foolish faith in authority is the worst enemy of truth.

ALBERT EINSTEIN

DON'T CONSIDER THE SOURCE

To the extent that there was intellectual activity in the Middle Ages in Europe, the Catholic Church dominated it. And there wasn't a lot going on in that regard.

Bella: *They don't call it the Dark Ages for nothing.*

Much of the knowledge that had been attained in the ancient world was lost to Europe. It was only preserved in Islamic countries—which harbored considerably more intellectual activity during these centuries—and in a handful of peripheral European monasteries. In Europe, the Catholic Church was the primary educator. It was the keeper of knowledge. Of course, it was also the ultimate authority on what the Bible meant. Generally, the Bible was in Latin. Few people could read Latin—or read at all for that matter.

Bella: *Dogs were not taught to read either!*

Books themselves were rare and expensive, as they had to be copied by hand. Ideas were largely controlled by the Church. In this period, truth was determined <u>by authority</u>. That is, if you wanted to demonstrate that a proposition was true, you cited Church or biblical authority. Later, during the Renaissance, the list of authorities was expanded to include some of the classical literature of ancient Greece and Rome. Truth <u>flowed</u> from authority. That is, a proposition was considered as demonstrated to be true if it could be traced to or connected to authoritative sources. The epistemological notion here is that truth is a bit like electricity—just as you must have a direct connection to a source of energy in order to produce an electric current, so too you must have a direct connection to an authority to be in possession of the truth.

Bella: *Shocking.*

Such authoritarians—both in medieval times and today—are quite mistaken in their epistemology. Truth can never be determined by appeal to authority; truth has to do with whether a set of words or symbols map onto reality in a way that is informative and accurate. Setting aside religious inspiration, which is a pathway to a different kind of truth, efforts to get at the truth are inevitably associated with weighing evidence and examining the relationship between the statements made with the reality that is being portrayed—not with determining <u>who</u> made the statements. As we have seen, the grandest authorities can be quite wrong while a fool may inadvertently state the truth.

Bella: *Even me?*

Even you, Bella. Indeed, for that matter, even me. In such a case—despite the fact that the words emanate from the mouth of a fool—if they happen to be true, they nonetheless remain true. If Bongo the Clown says that "It usually snows in New England in the winter", the statement remains true even though Bongo is a clown. On the other hand, if a truly august authority such as the Pope states that "Notre Dame's football team will win the national championship in the US this year," there is a pretty good chance that he will be wrong. <u>The source of an idea is irrelevant to its truth or falsity</u>. Period.

Bella: *Full stop?*

Full stop. Never judge the truth or falsity of a statement—or the usefulness or insightfulness of an idea, or the beauty of a work of art—by virtue of its source. Rather, <u>judge it on its merits</u>—that is, say, in the case of science, with respect to how it successfully models reality and yields accurate predictions, or, say, in the case of a work of art for its beauty and meaning and the manner in which it moves you. It has been famously argued by statisticians that monkeys randomly hitting letters on a computer keyboard may happen to type out statements that are true. To point out that the typists are monkeys does not thereby render the typed statements false. The fact that the words were produced by a purely random process does not speak to whether or not the statements produced are true. Indeed, if given enough time, the monkeys would eventually type out Shakespeare's <u>Hamlet</u>; if they did so, it would remain just as powerful and beautiful, despite the fact that it was written by monkeys.

Scientists often stumble upon truth—and artists upon beauty—by accident and happenstance. Recall Leeuwanhoek discovering that hot water could kill microscopic organisms because he had just drunk a very hot cup of coffee and was using the plaque from his teeth as a source for the organisms. When there is an accidental discovery, the important thing is that someone recognize what they have stumbled upon—and not reject it because it was not the result of some pre-ordained and accepted experimental process or derived from an authoritative source. In contrast, the medieval mind associates the truth of a proposition with whether the source of the statement is considered a worthy authority. Bella, could you please pretend you are a medieval thinker for a moment?

Bella: *Yes, your Lordship.*

I like this. Now, let's suppose I ask you, as a medieval thinker, "Is it true that the Sun goes around the Earth?" how do you respond?

Bella: *I ask: "Who said it?"*

Exactly. That is, you inquire as to the source of the idea. So, if I then say: "The Great Church Authority Father Lackadaisical of Laputia said it", then you would reply?

Bella: *"Ah, if thusly spake, it must be true."*

Thus spake Bella. Cultures have epistemologies—that is, deep-seated views on what is, and is not, legitimate in terms of knowledge and how knowledge is properly obtained. These epistemologies shift and change over time, and they are not always aligned well with how knowledge processes actually work—that is, a culture's epistemology may not focus on the true determinants of the growth in knowledge. The dynamic rationality of the sort we have described in this book blossomed in the Enlightenment, and has accounted for the great discoveries of science, the rapid development of technology and the world economy as well as a rapid development and proliferation of great art. Unfortunately, however, as a culture, we are now in the process of withdrawing from the dynamic, rational logic of discovery that defined that bold world.

Bella: *The Sun is setting on the great era of independent thinking.*

Our culture is replacing the logic of discovery with a static authoritarian epistemology that suits the myopic needs of our power elites. Modern thought is returning to the medieval mindset of truth by authority. Call it the new feudalism. Call it naïve positivism.

Bella: *I hope this oppressive regime will not include dogs.*

Modern thinkers are so deeply convinced that truth must come by authority—that is, via the "experts"—that they have a hard time even fathoming the rather obvious truth stated above that the source of an idea is irrelevant to its truth or falsity.

Bella: *The source of a statement is not just a little bit irrelevant to its truth or falsity—it's completely and absolutely irrelevant.*

The modern thinker sputters and responds: "But ... but ... but ... I have to rely on experts, and I <u>do</u> rely on experts, therefore surely that must be because they harbor the truth. I am not a fool!"

Bella: *Well ... the modern thinker <u>is</u> a fool.*

There is one and only one metric of truth, and that is whether the statement, theory or hypothesis fits the reality. Of course, as we have seen, establishing whether or not a statement is true can be quite difficult, but <u>who</u> made the statement is absolutely irrelevant to whether it is true.

Incidentally, so-called "legal thinking"—that is, the manner in which lawyers are taught to interpret the law—operates within this same kind of medieval mindset. That is, from the legal perspective, the proper determination of the current state of the law is dependent on citation to <u>authority</u>, whether it be a statute or case law. Of course, this makes some sense in terms of rule of law. Law is designed to provide a kind of static predictability, so that citizens can know whether their actions are lawful, their contracts enforceable and so forth. Unfortunately, the lawyers' focus on legitimacy as determined by authoritative sources also sometimes puts lawyers in a mode of "thinking" that is largely inconsistent with the pursuit of truth (or beauty or usefulness for that matter) in any arena outside of the law. That is, some of them are so inculcated in the law that they tend to believe in truth by authority as opposed to truth based on a particular kind of concordant relationship between a statement and the reality it purports to represent. In this sense, the term "legal thinking" constitutes an oxymoron (<u>i.e.</u>, an expression that is self-contradictory.)

Bella: *Why are you suddenly taking us on this tangent on the nature of legal thinking?*

Easy target.

Bella: *Ah, I get it—like a slow moving squirrel.*

Unfortunately, the increasing influence of "legal thinking" on our social and political discourse constitutes one of the main drivers taking us back to the medieval mindset of truth by authority.

Bella: *Hey! What should I do if I am not in a position to assess the truth of a statement myself? That is, what if I have to rely on authority? What if I need to get my shots at the veterinarian? I am not really in a position to question whether she is using the right shots.*

That is a profound question. We will come back to that, and to the topic of how to deal with experts and expertise, at the end of the chapter. There are many times in life when it is quite appropriate to rely on someone else's judgment. But note that a decision to rely on someone else's judgment as to truth in certain circumstances should not be confused with, and is not the same as, an epistemological criterion for truth. Indeed, to make the decision to trust someone else's assessment of the truth in a given instance involves altogether different questions. In order to make <u>that</u> decision you need to consider not only the person's arguably superior access to evidence and information, but also their judgment, purpose and incentives in light of the context in which the decision is being taken.

THE NEW FEUDALISM

There are two types of thinkers that characterize the new feudalism and dominate the modern mindset. I call them the "dogmatists" and the "disappointed dogmatists". The dogmatists are those who believe that knowledge is derived from authority—although they would never put it that way. They are, in essence, just like the authoritarian church fathers of the medieval period, although in their modern guise they generally come in the form of naïve positivists. We'll get to the disappointed dogmatists below, but let's start with the dogmatists. (And please note I am <u>not</u> talking about <u>religious</u> dogmatists here; religion is a different topic altogether. Here I am talking about an attitude regarding secular knowledge; I will talk about religion and spirituality in a later chapter.)

Bella: *I do like the dog in **dogmatism**.*

THE DOGMATISTS

For dogmatists of a modern ilk, propositions are determined to be true through a designated process that is conducted, controlled and ordained by experts, who then constitute the one and only legitimate repositories of those accumulated truths; the rest of us are supposed to consume it from them. Thus, in the view of dogmatists, knowledge is like a commodity—a thing that you either have or you don't have, and that you can buy from someone else, but if and only if they are an "expert". You obtain the truth either through <u>being</u> an expert yourself—that is, by virtue of whatever processes have been deemed necessary to produce an expert—or <u>from</u> the experts themselves—who convey the results of their legitimate expertise to you. In sum, truth is by authority. For the modern dogmatist, <u>who</u> says something has everything to do with whether or not it should be deemed true. Indeed, for the dogmatists, to not accept the truth of what the experts tell us is the very epitome of irrationality. To them, such blind acceptance of the dictates of experts is the very essence of being an educated person.

For dogmatists, therefore, truth must be transmitted. That is, propositions must be directly connected to a <u>legitimate</u> or <u>authoritative</u> source if they are properly to be deemed as true. Dogmatists are rigid about what has been determined to be true, and shun all else as nonsense, and possibly dangerous nonsense at that. In general, they even avoid religion because they don't see it as a legitimate source of knowledge and instead worship at the altar of (what they think of as) science, displaying a religious-like adherence to every pronouncement made by scientists, or "experts" of any sort. This is ironic. The history of science has shown that scientists are almost always wrong in some aspect of what they are thinking, and often profoundly wrong. Moreover, scientists and experts of other ilk often have a vested economic interest—either directly or indirectly—in having what they are saying accepted as true; thus, they are biased. Indeed, the faith in expertism that dogmatic secularists display is demonstrably irrational, whereas the same cannot be said for religious faith.

Bella: *In God, we trust. All the rest of you are required to provide evidence and good arguments.*

Indeed, it is far better to place one's faith in God, but demand to see the evidence for yourself when it comes to <u>humans</u> attempting to sell you <u>commoditized "knowledge"</u>. Modern dogmatists have a great deal of faith, but it is not in God. Their faith is that science and experts—through the designated processes for proof and the accumulation of knowledge—can and will capture the truth and wisdom necessary to address <u>all</u> practical human problems, if only that pure process is not corrupted by money and narrow economic interests and if only the rest of us are rational enough to appreciate their commoditized truths.

Bella: *I hope you aren't considering a move to **catmatism** as opposed to dogmatism; that just wouldn't be right.*

Modern dogmatists seek a certain kind of (quasi-holy) purity among their experts. Since they see experts as the only legitimate repositories of accumulated proven truth, many of the modern dogmatists don't want their experts tainted too directly by commercial enterprise and the profit motive. As a consequence, the modern dogmatists tend to trust academics more than, say, spokespersons from the private business sector; that is, the academic tends to rank higher on their epistemological hierarchy. Another result of the dogmatists' mode of thinking—at least for some of them—is a firm and unquestioning belief that financial contributions to political campaigns undermine the objectivity that might otherwise be forthcoming from politicians. To be frank, I can only chuckle at this notion that politicians would undoubtedly be more pure, objective and pliable recipients of expertistic truth if they were not thusly corrupted.

Bella: *Perhaps it is not that money corrupts politicians, but that corrupt politicians permit the influence of money to sway their judgment.*

If you believe that the very essence of rational discourse centers around criticism and the manner in which criticisms are addressed—as I do—then you might conclude that rigid rules that control and limit the private financing of political campaigns are likely to result not so much in a reduction of corruption, but rather in the suppression of alternative ideas and innovations that might stand as criticisms to the status quo. Allowing money to flow freely into whatever political coffers citizens see fit to place it renders it much easier for citizens to organize themselves and to criticize those in power. The alternative is to give those already in power the nod to control the flow of money and ideas. If one has the government regulating and policing the flows of political funding, such control will inevitably be used to entrench those already in power and protect them from needed criticism.

Bella: *Money is <u>not</u> the root of all evil; power is the root of all evil.*

And since money is a check on power, <u>money is a check on evil</u>. When we think about the work of our politicians, it is, of course, relatively easy to spot the bad ideas that result of the influence of money. Campaign contributions are raised by those in the marketplace who want the rules set in a manner that is advantageous to them. For example, it is very difficult for politicians from agricultural states to go against subsidies for agriculture, even if they think this is a bad idea from a policy perspective. There is no doubt that there is much abuse of this sort. But what tends to be missed in the analysis—because it is very difficult to identify—are the many terrible ideas that are <u>not</u> implemented, precisely due to the power of money to generate well-targeted criticism and thereby block bad ideas. Indeed, if you want to see a system chock full of terrible ideas that were not blocked by money, examine the historical record of a communist country, such as, say, the former Soviet Union. No money corrupted their election process, because they didn't have any real election process. The communist officials were free—as a group—to implement whatever good ideas they had, and to do whatever the experts told them to do. Yet, the policy ideas they implemented were horrific and debilitating for the nation. This was precisely because citizens were not free to aggregate their money and criticize those in power.

In politics, money is voice. If we want a diversity of voices in the political sphere to be heard, and we want fruitful criticism, we need to ensure that money flows freely to support whatever ideas and views the citizenry wants it to, and that it is not controlled by the government and those already in power. Many modern dogmatists see money as something that corrupts the purity of reason, rather than something that facilitates independence, criticism, innovation and the further growth of knowledge. To the modern dogmatist, the expertistic processes of determining the truth are delicate and need to be protected. They believe that our purveyors of truth and wisdom must have the cleanliness and pureness of the laboratory; the modern dogmatist envisions the experts in their white smocks and plastic gloves as they garner truths for the rest of us. Those experts must be somewhat removed from the world at large, which is otherwise corrupted by money. Expertism is the new religion, and—after all—a religion must have its demons. For the dogmatists, the money that facilitates criticism of those in power provides the demons. In contrast, for those that believe in the efficacy of free critical discourse, money facilitates expression.

Expertism is our new form of faith and worship, and science—at least, as the dogmatists envision it—is its altar. For them, it stands in contrast to the corruptions of the world. The only battle is to bring others to the new faith in expertism. Our journey to the experts is like a pilgrimage to the oracle of Delphi on Mount Parnassus. We may hope to catch a glimpse of the truths they maintain, but the oracle on Mount Parnassus remains a world apart from the common citizen—hoi polloi, as the Greeks might say. The experts are the new elite. Rationality entails giving all power to them. Or so they would like us to think.

Bella: *Bad, dogmatists, bad!*

THE DISAPPOINTED DOGMATISTS

By way on contrast, disappointed dogmatists are total skeptics. They don't believe in anything. Ironically, they are skeptics because they are purer in their dogmatic demands than the dogmatists. It is because they are so pure that they cannot but reject both dogmatism and rationality—once they perceive that knowledge processes are flawed in the least. This is why I call them disappointed dogmatists.

Disappointed dogmatists have absorbed the fact that knowledge processes are human processes, and, as such, they involve judgments that may well be flawed—and indeed quite often turn out to be flawed. The disappointed dogmatists can see that neither induction nor deduction has the power to prove. And they are clever people who are great at semantic games. They can pull apart the meaning of words until you are not sure what you are talking about anymore. They go by many names: Deconstructionists, Post-modernists, Subjectivists, Anti-rationalists, Nihilists, Dadaists, Moral Relativists and so on—not to mention the ideologies in which truth is believed to be merely a matter of power. I suspect you have encountered these kinds of thinkers; if not, you surely will. They take the wrong lesson from the fact that our epistemological processes are inevitably and intrinsically flawed. They do not realize that rationality does not reside in the static processes of proof but rather—as we have argued in this book—in a dynamic process of improvement through conjecture and criticism. As a consequence of their misplaced and static notions, they reject rationality altogether as an illusion. I must admit that I find the disappointed dog-matists to be even more annoying that the dogmatists.

Bella: *I bark at them.*

That's not a bad tactic. While the dogmatists are short-sighted, elit-ist, turf-conscious and power hungry, the disappointed dogmatists are ar-rogant, smug, self-satisfied and self-serving. The disappointed dogmatists really seem to believe that somehow the fact that one can pull apart the meaning of words and find flaws in epistemological processes implies that there is no such thing as rationality. As a consequence, they believe that argumentation has no purpose or target. They do not comprehend that the back-and-forth of discourse can take you closer to the truth and wisdom, because they do not believe that there is any such thing. As a consequence, they view argumentation as a kind of sport or as bullying. Truth is a matter of choice—or a matter of subjective perspective—or a matter of the will—anything but a matter of evidence. And, as an additional consequence, the disappointed dogmatists don't really take counterarguments seriously. Rather, they simply seek a quick counter to the counter, so that they can show they are cleverer than you are. Ultimately, they view knowledge—to the extent that they believe it can be obtained at all—as a very personal thing, a matter of belief, and as intrinsically flawed as each of us inevitably is. They do not see that the rationality inherent in a group discourse in which conjectures and criticisms are taken seriously has the power to rise above our individual flaws and lead to improvements in our understanding of the world.

The disappointed dogmatists are prideful people; the worst possible embarrassment for them would be to be drawn into a belief that wasn't true. Better, therefore, to believe nothing. This is why they are often atheists. They are much more afraid of the embarrassment of believing something that might <u>not</u> be true, than of the danger of not believing and missing out on the most profound truths of life.

Bella: *They are intellectual cowards!*

Out of this pride and fear, the disappointed dogmatists turn away from all genuine and bold intellectual explorations. If one never takes anything seriously, one will never be fooled. Truly, this is the sin of pride of which the Bible speaks, and it is deemed a sin for good reason. It is pride that dooms the disappointed dogmatists to wander the shadowy valleys of post-modern deconstruction and meaninglessness.

Bella: *The disappointed dogmatists are like children knocking over sand castles and declaring it is thus proven that no one can build with sand, while yet ignoring a great cathedral of sand looming just behind them.*

In the view of disappointed dogmatists, if something cannot be known absolutely, then it cannot be known at all. If they can't have their proofs with the absolutism they seek, then they just won't play in the sandbox of rationality. Indeed, they will proclaim there is no real truth; there is only subjective opinion. Everything is seen as a mere matter of taste and preference.

Bella: *In their view, one dog's "truth" is as good as another's, since no one may be deemed better than anyone else.*

Even words themselves can be broken down to many different meanings—with each person's interpretation equally legitimate, in their view. The disappointed dogmatists are radical subjectivists. They see no transcendent meaning or truth in the world; beyond our individual preferences, it is all ultimately somewhat meaningless—or if there is meaning, it's a meaning that we merely create and impose. But the funny thing about disappointed dogmatists is that they tend to be quite opinionated about what is right and wrong in the world and what is true and not true, even while their own philosophy does not admit of the possibility of such right and wrong answers.

Bella: *Personally, I refuse to take such people seriously.*

Perhaps the greatest irony is that the dogmatists and disappointed dogmatists are all of a piece—they are the yin and yang of the modern cult of expertism. They have all bought into the commoditized notion of knowledge as proven truth—it's only that the dogmatists naïvely believe that science can actually prove, while the disappointed dogmatists believe that science and rationality fail to pass their own test. What unites the dogmatists and the disappointed dogmatists is that they both hold rationality to the wrong standard—a static notion of proof. They are both joined together—cheek by jowl—through this narrow association of rationality with the accumulation of proven truth. The fallacies associated with this static notion of rationality as proven truth run throughout our fragmented culture, and, indeed, generate much of the fragmentation.

Bella: *But wait. I have mulled this over now, and am a bit confused. I thought you were celebrating anti-authoritarianism. Don't you believe in challenging* *authority? Aren't some of these disappointed dogmatists you are attacking really some of the original anti-authoritarians?*

You have mistaken me. I am not promoting <u>anti</u>-authoritarianism <u>per se</u> in this book. I <u>am</u> promoting the benefits of independent thinking as well as the power of conjectures and criticism—and this often entails challenging authority. But the criticisms that are the most powerful are those that are well-targeted—the kind of criticisms that are based in evidence or in the failure of conjectures to perform as advertized. It is this criticism that takes us to new questions and new conjectures and permits us to progress in our thinking and—within science specifically—to progress in our predictive capabilities. In sum, I am a <u>rationalist</u> through-and-through, and I recognize that rationality requires independent thinking and challenging authority. What I reject is naïve positivism, all static views of rationality and the authoritarian attitudes and elitism that attend those viewpoints. Challenging authority for the mere sake of challenging authority is not only adolescent and a waste of time—it's horrendously boring. In contrast, challenging authority through <u>apt</u> criticism empowers you by engaging you in a constructive human process that is both creative and beautiful, and thereby enlarges your soul and permits you to manifest your full humanity. Both the Dogmatists and the Disappointed Dogmatists would deny this from you, because they want to keep it for themselves. And from both of those perspectives, it is essentially a power play—power for them but not for you. So although I am anti-authoritarian, the disappointed dogmatists would nonetheless have no truck for the likes of me; they do not believe in rationality at all.

Bella: *Oh.*

THE ARTIFICIAL FRAGMENTATION OF THE ARTS AND SCIENCES

Our culture is fragmented along the lines of this supposed capacity to establish truth by proof. The world of science is on the one side with the arts and humanities on the other. The two worlds are seen as completely separate and discrete.

Bella: *And ne'er the twain shall meet.*

The social sciences of economics, sociology and anthropology desperately hope they will be deemed to be on the scientific side of the divide, but never quite cut the mustard. If you believe that rationality is the accumulation of proven truth—as is the dominant view in our culture—then a great disciplinary divide arises between those disciplines that seemingly lend themselves to this standard and those that do not. The former are deemed as among the rational, while the latter are viewed as non-rational.

Both sides of this artificial divide seem comfortable with it, and yet both are impoverished by it. The scientists don't see much use at all in that non-scientific non-sense spouted by the arts and humanities. They seem unaware that there is a creative side to the sciences that entails bold conjecturing and individual eccentricity, and which might indeed be enhanced through exposure to the arts and humanities. Indeed, they do not see that science itself is a creative process. And the artists, historians, classicists, writers and thespians don't seem to fully recognize that there is a kind of exploratory discourse that characterizes their disciplines does follow a rational dynamic that is similar in its exploratory and open nature to the sciences. They certainly know that they don't want those scientific nerds traipsing through their backyard.

The modern dogmatists strongly adhere to this cultural fragmentation; for them, it is the very essence of modernity and educated thinking. We must separate the irrational from the rational—giving each its due, of course. They want to recognize that we are emotional animals, but separate that element—along with the wiles of creativity and art—from the purity of reason and science. Science is seen as mechanically accumulating ever more proven truth—a realm in which passion and creativity need not apply. Meanwhile, the arts and humanities is where we are permitted to express ourselves—but where what we express is ultimately meaningless, as it all ultimately comes down to a matter of taste. My biggest problem with this specious epistemology is that, because it does not really reflect the way we actually think, and the way in which knowledge actually develops, we end up lying to ourselves about what we are doing—and artificially cabining parts of our thought processes from one another. The fragmentation of thought that is required by both dogmatism and disappointed dogmatism is bad for your mental health.

The modern dogmatist is often attracted to the distinction that the neurologists have made between left-brain activity and right-brain activity. In simplistic terms, the neurologists' idea is that the left side of the brain is the locus of rational thought, whereas the right side of the brain is the locus of emotional thought. The modern dogmatist sees this biological proposition as vindication of their epistemological fragmentation. To them, rationality involves keeping the right-brain activity separate from the left-brain activity. To them, the structure of their brains mirrors the appropriate division line for the disciplines.

Bella: *It fits in with their notions of purity of reason.*

But do note that—at least as I understand it—from a neurological perspective, if communication between the two sides of the brain is damaged, a person would typically become dysfunctional. And, yet, oddly, the modern dogmatist—through a curious mental discipline—tries to impose a communications barrier between the two sides of his brain on himself and thereby fragment his thinking processes. In contrast to this modern mindset, I believe that both scientific and non-scientific creativity demand a rich interaction among different parts of the brain and, indeed, among different people—one of conjecture, criticism and creative response.[1] The truth is that rationality is not pure—nor should it be. It is a human process, after all.

Bella: *You remain so human centric. Dogs can have mistaken epistemologies as well.*

People—uh ... and dogs—are not the fragmented beings that the dogmatists would have us be. The notion that rationality should be pure derives from the epistemologically mistaken focus on <u>sources</u> of ideas as relating to their truth or falsity. But, as we have noted repeatedly, the source of an idea is absolutely irrelevant to its truth or falsity.

Bella: *Or even to its beauty.*

To attempt to make rationality pure eviscerates it. Rationality and emotion are not opposites and do not sit in polarity to one another. Rationality is, in fact, typically an emotional process. Indeed, have you ever met a good scientist who wasn't passionate about what she did?

Bella: *I can't say that I have.*

As we have emphasized, rationality is a dynamic process of conjectures, criticism, responses to criticism and further conjecturing. The important point here is that it doesn't matter if the source or motivation of these individual components is itself irrational.

Bella: *How can that be?*

A new conjecture might be driven by a sense of beauty, a love of symmetry, a compulsive desire for a more precise partition of a topic, a desire to obtain tenure at a university, or any dream, fantasy, emotion or metaphor. It doesn't matter what generates the conjecture; what matters is the power of the conjecture to better explain the world. That is, we don't (and shouldn't) care where a conjecture comes from—only whether it has greater predictive content. Neither the source of a conjecture, nor the motivation of the proponent of that conjecture, affects its truth or falsity. In fact, powerful scientific conjectures <u>have</u> come from dreams, as one did in the discovery of the ring structure of benzene. Kekule—who discovered the ring structure of benzene—had a dream one night of interlocking snakes biting one another's tails, and that is where he got his great idea, which constituted one of the great breakthroughs in chemistry. Humorously, contemporaries of Kekule were very disturbed by the idea that Kekule had been influenced by a dream, precisely because they wanted to maintain this specious notion of the purity of the scientific process.

And, just as it doesn't matter what motives a conjecture, it also doesn't matter what motivates criticism. For example, criticism might simply be based in one person's dislike of another. The motivation of the critic is <u>irrelevant</u> so long as the criticism is apt in terms of evidence and logic. Even the most cursory look at the history of science shows it to be a passionate affair. This notion that true science and rationality is devoid of passion is, in fact, ludicrous and is part and parcel of the authoritarian epistemology that tries to package and commoditize knowledge—as something for sale by the experts.

Bella: *No passion needed here—thank you very much—we have scientific objectivity for sale.*

A CULTURE OF EPISTEMOLOGICAL DEPENDENCY

The modern dogmatic world view is created and shaped by a cult of expertism, which is regularly reinforced and reproduced by the many experts who make their living by selling expertise. The commoditization and marketing of knowledge by experts—and the corresponding exclusion and alienation of the normal citizen from these processes—is rigorously maintained by the social, professional and academic elites. They guard the boundaries of their profession or discipline or area of expertise, not because it promotes the growth of knowledge, but rather in order to secure and maximize the income and power they garner by virtue of the manner in which they package and sell their expertise. Expertise is typically sold and marketed <u>through</u> the very concept of a discipline or a profession—as if truth or falsity of propositions relates to whether or not the propositions emanated from a discipline or profession. For example, if you are trained in the discipline of economics—that is, you have been ordained with your Ph.D.—then you can open shop and start making money on your expertise—as a professor, consultant, economic prognosticator, expert witness, government employee, policy wonk and so forth. You don't get these positions by virtue of <u>what</u> you know, but by virtue of the processes you have undergone in joining the profession and being deemed an expert.

In feudal times, there were similar collectives of crafts-persons called guilds, and their goals were the same—maximizing the returns to the members of the guild by maintaining control over the exercise of their professional knowledge base. A guild mentality goes hand in hand with an authoritarian epistemology. The one derives from the other. Indeed, authoritarian epistemology (that is, dogmatism) and a guild mentality constitute the twin pillars of the new feudalism. The key to making money off of one's expertise is to ensure that no one but the initiates into the discipline may apply that expertise. Metaphorically speaking, this is done by ensuring that the expert is always required to stand between the normal citizen and whatever reality is being addressed. They are "intermediaries" in this sense. That is, the experts try to make sure that they are always in a position to intermediate between normal persons and whatever issues or decisions those persons need to comprehend and address. Such "intermediation" ensures that the experts will get paid on a regular basis, of course.

Bella: *It's kind of like a toll booth—if you have a certain kind of problem, then you have to pay an expert to get an answer.*

This is a very nice arrangement for the experts, as you can imagine. Thus, for example, it is generally <u>illegal</u> for anyone but a lawyer to provide legal advice, even though an experienced person who has confronted certain legal issues repeatedly might be in a better position to give such advice than would your typical lawyer. But the merits don't matter here; the status of being a lawyer and collecting your rents does. Similarly, it is generally illegal to obtain pharmaceutical medicine without a doctor giving you a prescription, even if you have a recurrent problem that requires the same prescription each and every time. While there are circumstances where such rules are merited, in part they are there simply to maximize the income of the professions. Given that this "intermediation"—that is, the "standing between" the normal person and some aspect of reality—maximizes the returns to a profession or discipline, experts tend to discourage normal citizens from thinking for themselves about the issues. The expert is the one with the answers—and the one that is to be paid! But as more and more areas of life are expertized, taken over and monopolized by some purported profession or disciplines, normal citizens are discouraged from thinking about an ever bigger swath of life. This reinforces the authoritarian epistemology, as normal citizens are repeatedly told: you are not worthy to think about this topic for yourself. You must pay for and consume whatever the experts have to say on it.

Bella: *It's as if they were selling them dog food.*

In this sense, there is a broad effort to render general society ever more ignorant, and thus ever more dependent on the experts. The presentation of evidence and argumentation to the general citizenry—for them to weigh it—is eschewed; rather, the general citizenry is provided with the conclusory statements of the experts that they are simply expected to consume.

Bella: *Did you say the evidence was chewed?*

Eschewed.

Bella: *Gesundheit.*

OMNIPRESENT CONFLICTS OF INTEREST

The key thing to realize about people involved in any profession, including academic disciplines and the sciences, is that they are making money off the ideas or expert services that they are teaching, researching, expressing, implementing or operationalizing. Put simply, experts make their living off their expertise. The problem with this is that the expert's interest in making money from their expertise doesn't necessarily always align well with the interests of the persons who need to benefit from that expertise and who are purchasing those services in some form. This is sometimes referred to as a "conflict of interest." Conflicts of interest abound, and can take many forms, depending on how the experts are compensated for their expertise. For example, a knee surgeon, who gets paid for each knee surgery she does, might have a tendency to see surgery as the best solution to a knee problem even when it is not.

Bella: *If you only have a hammer, everything looks like a nail.*

The surgeon may not even be consciously aware of being influenced in this way, but the danger is there, particularly if she has a payment to make on her yacht.

Bella: *Are we going sailing?*

Alternatively, suppose another knee surgeon is at a teaching hospital, and receives a fixed salary for her services, part of which is in compensation for conducting knee surgeries at the hospital. Let's suppose she gets paid the same salary whether or not she conducts any surgeries. Given that surgery is hard work for a surgeon, she may be inclined to prescribe knee surgery somewhat less often than the surgeon who gets paid per operation. It's not that they won't try to be honest in their decisions. But in the cases that are close calls, one may be more inclined to go the one way, and the other the other way. In general, people tend to be subtly influenced by their incentives.

Bella: *It is* human *nature.*

The same kinds of conflicts of interest hold for practitioners of any discipline or with respect to any area of expertise. It's one of the reasons you have to learn to think for yourself and to think critically. Imagine a car mechanic who makes money from repairs. This mechanic makes more money, the more times she finds that any particular car part—say, a carburetor—needs to be replaced. Now, your average person taking a car to a mechanic doesn't know a carburetor from a carbuncle. Perhaps the mechanic will occasionally be tempted to tell her customers that the carburetor needs to be replaced, even when the old one would have done just fine for quite a while longer—particularly if she has payments to make on her new sofa and wide screen TV.

Bella: *Are all expert decision driven by the need to pay for their luxuries?*

To be sure, there are many fine and earnest practitioners to be found within every profession, discipline and occupation who are not swayed by such conflicts of interest in the least—they do their very best to give you the advice or service that is in your interest in each and every instance regardless of the economic consequences for themselves. But there is also, inevitably, a substantial minority of practitioners in any profession or discipline who are influenced by their own narrow economic interest and will take advantage of the unwary—and, as noted above, may not even be fully aware themselves that they have been influenced by a conflict of interest. The tricky thing for those consuming the services of experts is that they may have little way of knowing whether they have a perfectly honest and earnest expert to whom they are turning for advice, or are encountering an expert who is only looking out for her own narrow economic interests. As a consequence, one needs to be very careful in dealing with experts.

Moreover, all experts have a conflict of interest simply in that they have a desire to protect and enhance their ability to continue to make a living from their expertise. This can lead them to artificially shun criticisms of their ideas or expertise—even if the criticism is apt—simply because they want to protect their reputation as an authoritative expert. Further, they may assert that their expertise is applicable even when it is not, in order to enhance their income. And to protect themselves from competition, they may try to preclude or block other approaches to an issue—approaches that are outside their particular expertise, even when these other approaches are perfectly legitimate and may be effective. Due to this conflict of interest, experts are never in a position to be fully objective about their topic.

Bella: *Does this mean we should never rely on experts?*

Of course not. But it does mean we should be wary. I come back to this topic—and the answer to your question—at the end of the chapter.

Bella: *But what about university professors and academic researches? We can believe them, can't we? I don't see any conflicts of interest there.*

Many people—and dogs, it appears—have this odd idea that because academics are not in a commercial or business environment, their work is not tainted by economic concerns. This is a foolish view. Academics, like anyone else, are concerned to continue to make a living. How the content of their work is received is very much a concern in terms of protecting their livelihood. Indeed, many academics will tell you that they will not take on controversial issues in their work until they have tenure, or that they only dared to do more unconventional and innovative work after receiving tenure. Tenure is where a university or college has guaranteed an academic post to a professor. Professors tend receive tenure, if they do receive it, after a certain number of years in the job. At most universities and colleges, it is based on whether they have a sufficient quality and number of publications within their discipline. While lip service is given to teaching, it is not really considered quite so important at most universities and colleges. That is why some of the academic institutions with the best reputations may have some really terrible teachers; they were good a publishing but bad at teaching, but a priority was placed on the former. Beyond tenure, many academics have concerns throughout their academic careers about raising grant monies and having a professional reputation that will continue to lure attractive offers and opportunities. These concerns tend to reinforce compliance with a narrow academic grid, which sometimes serves to actually stunt the growth of knowledge.

Bella: *But what about famous academics? We should be able to trust them. Once they have become famous within their profession, they don't have any reason to worry anymore, do they?*

This problem of bias becomes even bigger if a person's reputation becomes attached to particular ideas, which is usually the case for a successful academic or scientist. Indeed, that is the very definition of success within a discipline—to have one's name attached to certain kinds of findings or ideas. As a consequence, the most successful academics—and scientists— are apt to be the ones with the strongest interest in maintaining the status quo of ideas within the discipline, rather than challenging those ideas and advancing knowledge, or even permitting others to challenge those ideas. This has been observed across many scientific disciplines. As Thomas Kuhn teaches us, a scientific revolution is often constituted by young scientists challenging an entrenched, and literally aging, scientific establishment. The establishment is usually not won over, but rather—over time—dies off and is replaced by a new generation with a different set of ideas. The point here is that reputation can lead to further bias.

For example, hypothetically, imagine that, say, a particular scientist is celebrated for having developed evidence that the planet is warming due to human-made emissions of carbon dioxide. (And let's explore this hypothetical without taking any view whatsoever on the actual current debate over these issues.) The problem of human-induced global warming is, of course, properly seen as a very important policy area. Let's suppose that massive research funds are made available to our hypothetical scientist and her team to continue their research. The scientist goes around to different organizations and makes speeches about how important the problem is. She is personally celebrated at these events for the importance of her contributions to the science. Now suppose some contrary evidence emerges that is suggestive that she may be wrong about some aspect of her work.

The question is: will she be open-minded and fair in assessing this new evidence? Will she make sure that this evidence is brought to light and properly debated and assessed? One can imagine that in some cases she may not be perfectly objective in assessing the new evidence, or ensuring that it is brought to light. People don't like to be criticized. More particularly, powerful and famous people don't like to be criticized with respect to the very thing that brought them their power and fame. It is human nature. It is clear, however, that this impulse can work against scientific progress. And, notably, this bias is present not despite the fact that this person is a leading practitioner within the discipline, but because she is a leading practitioner. The more established and famous the scientist, the more likely she is to be biased by the need to protect her reputational capital. This is, indeed, why criticism within a community of scientists is such an important value. People tend not to be so great at pressure-testing their own work. It takes a community, it takes criticism, and it takes openness to criticism. The objectivity of science lies not in its results, but in the extent to which there is vigorous debate and criticism that are taken seriously and whereby the ideas continue to be developed and refined.

Bella: *Does reputation always have such a negative effect?*

No. In fact, in the provision of most services, concern for reputation generally has a good influence. For example, if you are in, say, housing construction, you want to have a good reputation, so that others will be inclined to hire you to do yet more work. You want people to believe that you follow through on contracts and that you do a good job. But, ironically, precisely with respect to disciplines whose job is to contribute to the growth of knowledge, concern for reputation can be more pernicious. As we have seen, growth of knowledge requires criticism as well as fruitful response to criticism. But if you are a powerful person within a scientific discipline, and you have made your reputation on the basis of certain findings, and you continue to receive grant moneys for further research based on that reputation and those findings, you may not take kindly to criticism. In fact, you may be tempted to use your considerable influence and power within the discipline to suppress criticism and to attack those who would dare attempt it. Rather obviously, this does not promote the growth of knowledge. Now, mind you, as I indicated above, there are some wonderful people who rise above such temptations, but many do not. This is one of the reasons you can't fully trust the experts. Their concern for their reputation may actually retard the growth of knowledge, and often does.

THE GROWING INFLUENCE OF GUILD CONSCIOUSNESS

As you probably know, Karl Marx was a radical left-wing thinker of the mid 19th century.

Bella: *I didn't know that.*

Well, you <u>are</u> just a dog after all. I need to introduce him because I am going to use one of his ideas.

Bella: *Pleased to meet you Karl.*

Marx had a huge influence on left-wing political and economic thinking as well as a considerable influence on the history of thought in general. Among other things, he influenced and inspired communism as well as some of the world's most oppressive regimes that took away people's freedoms, controlled ideas and murdered vast numbers of their own citizens.

Bella: *Karl sounds like a fabulous fellow.*

Well, one can make a useful distinction between Marx (the thinker) and the acts of his many followers.

Bella: *Ah, yes, our old friend the routinization of charisma.*

To be sure, Marx did have some very bad ideas. But he also had some insightful ones. Indeed, Marx's early writings on the alienation of workers from the process of production are powerful; I particularly recommend his <u>Economic and Philosophic Manuscripts</u>. (Remember: never judge an idea by its source; judge it by its merits.) One of Marx's more insightful concepts is the idea of <u>class consciousness</u>. Marx believed that society's mode of producing goods and services created economic classes. In his view, there was an ownership class—called the capitalists or the bourgeoisie— and a working class, which he called the proletariat.

Bella: *So far, it's hard to argue with that.*

Marx believed that these class distinctions determined much of what and how people thought about the world. That is, the values they held were derived from their social class. Moreover, they developed what he called "class consciousness". That is, they would have values and make decisions consistent with the interests of their class. What Marx was saying is that people generally don't tend to think for themselves; they are conditioned by whatever class they are in to think along certain lines—generally in the interest of their class. Marx was ultimately optimistic however. He believed that the clash of classes would eventually result in a better world that developed more fair and liberating means of producing and distributing goods and services.

This idea of class consciousness contains a very powerful insight into human nature. It is the simple but profound idea that our <u>economic</u> interests shape our values and how we view the world. There is a lot of truth in this. People want to think well of themselves. Indeed, they generally have a <u>need</u> to think well of themselves. Thus, they embrace values that celebrate who they are and the nature of their contribution to the world, and they tend to avoid values that would be inconsistent with or challenge how they make their living. It's not that one cannot transcend one's economic interests, and have independent thoughts and values that challenge those interests, but it is hard to do this. It takes deep, critical and careful thought. Indeed, it takes a willingness to follow the logic of discovery even if it works against your own interests. Many people do not do that. They are not that open to ideas generally. The concept of class consciousness is powerful.

When Marx developed this idea in the mid-19th century, it wasn't a bad description of society—particularly in England where he did quite a bit of his writing and where he is buried (just a short subway ride out of London.) If you read the English literature of the time, you'll find it is all about class, and how the different classes viewed the world differently. For example, read Jane Austen's <u>Pride and Prejudice</u>—a terrific book—to get a feel for the depth of class consciousness. But the world has changed quite a bit since then. In the United States today, there is much less of a sense of class than in 19th century England. Class consciousness does not play as much of a role in our world views, as it may have at one time. In that sense, Marx kind of missed the mark. But Marx's insight here is much deeper than the idea of class consciousness alone. The more fundamental idea is, as I noted above, that our economic interests shape our views and values. He is right about that—at least as regards many people, if not everyone. Thus, while it may <u>not</u> be class consciousness that drives modern viewpoint, it is often the "guild consciousness"—associated with particular types of <u>expertise</u>—that drives the modern world, and defines its many social battle-lines.

Bella: *We have a long way to go before we will even begin to achieve dog consciousness—except in our agreed-upon animus to cats, of course.*

The important point here is a simple one; the experts are <u>not</u> working for your interest—they are working for <u>their</u> interest. However, Marx's insight, as applied here, informs us that the experts, in protecting their own interests as a group, <u>mistake their own interests for a set of universal values</u>. In other words, the experts tend <u>not</u> to even be aware that the manner in which they protect their profits and preclude criticism of their discipline and themselves, and how these defensive reactions may work against the growth of knowledge and the public interest. These illusions render them even more damaging to both democracy and the growth of knowledge than they would be if they were more self-aware.

OUR INCREASING DEPENDENCY AND DECLINING LIBERTIES

If these trends continue, we may be heading into a new dark age in which independent thought is suppressed and the experts-cum-bureaucrats rule. Indeed, this will prove to be the great struggle of the 21st century; societies will ask: how much power do we give to the "experts" and how much do we leave with the people? Our cultural belief in science as an accumulation of proven truth bolsters a cult of expertism that not only undermines the true rational spirit of criticism and conjecture, but also our liberties and our democracy. The vision is that if the experts are the true repositories of accumulated knowledge and wisdom, then best to let them run the world and make the decisions. After all, with 300 plus million people in the United States we can't exactly decide things with a town hall meeting, can we? In such a context, what could be more rational than turning to the experts? Yes, they will say, democracy is important, but—in this view—democracy is seen merely as an exercise in legitimation—that is, it is a binding symbol and an important constraint, but not a reliable model for actual decision-making. In this view, it is the job of the elites to bring the populace along, and to educate them regarding the findings of the experts and the elites. The elites do not look to the People to actually contribute to the dialogue in a meaningful way. They are too numerous and inexpert for that—or so goes the view of modern dogmatism.

This suppression of rational discourse and independent thinking is not by virtue of some grand conspiracy, of course, but rather because an authoritative epistemology which, albeit wrongheaded, suits many people's needs. The experts have deemed the world too complicated to rely on an epistemological model that calls for conjecture, criticism and response to criticism. They don't like to be criticized and they don't like to respond to criticism. Moreover, they believe that a population that is ignorant—at least in the view of the experts—and that indeed must remain largely ignorant given the complexities of the issues we confront is not in a position to criticize the scientific, corporate and bureaucratic elites. The people need the answers handed to them—by the experts who make their living by doing so. Indeed, it is believed (if not said) that the people are too numerous and stupid to have it be otherwise. Thus, the general populace is not invited to criticize the experts, scientific authorities, bureaucrats, politicians and corporate magnates, but to embrace the dictates of the experts. If they do pose challenges to those in power and authority, they are marginalized, and decried as kooks and even "deniers." And, most certainly, those who would dare to criticize are labeled as "unscientific".

Bella: *The Modern Dogmatists say "How dare these peons criticize those who make their money by telling the People what to think?" The supply of self-righteous umbrage among the* human *elites is unending.*

Because the modern dogmatist believes that science involves the accumulation of proven truth, he sees scientists, trained experts and the academic disciplines as having a lock on legitimate knowledge. In light of this, he doesn't see much of a role for debate and criticism—at least not with respect to any topic that lends itself to expert opinion. For the modern dogmatists, then, the role of political fora, governments and media is not to provide a platform that facilitates criticism and debate on the issues, but rather to amplify and spread the views of experts. And the key to making this work is to keep tight control of the message. Indeed, this is the only rational thing to do in their view, since the experts have a corner on truth. It all becomes about "messaging." Of course, this dogmatic and ascendant viewpoint takes away from the capacity of the normal citizen to participate in the democracy in a fruitful and real way.

Modern dogmatism drives the impulse to have the government, media, experts and lawyers—taken together—to encroach ever further on what might have been previously viewed as the prerogatives of normal citizens.

First, the scientific and academic disciplines are always becoming more specialized and expanding their scope. Thus, the areas over which experts claim to have a lock on knowledge are ever expanding. Second, most questions that are posed to experts really involve mixed questions, in that the ultimate decisions being made typically involve a blend of expert knowledge and other economic, political, social, personal and moral concerns. But since modern dogmatism sees the expert as harboring the key input to finding the answer—and the experts go along with this as it expands their power, influence and income—the society tends to look to the experts to weigh the whole package of considerations and provide the final answers—even though their expertise would only speak to some portion of the relevant considerations.

For example, think about an elderly person considering having hip replacement surgery. For an elderly person, such surgery certainly carries many risks. Other considerations include whether the person wants to go through the pain of recovery as well as being inconvenienced by the recovery process. Ultimately, the decision as to whether an elderly person should have a hip replacement involves both technical and personal considerations. The hope would be that the person makes the decision with the advice and input of her doctor. Given the modern tendency toward dogmatism and the cult of the expert, however, the unfortunate propensity is to turn to the professional—in this case a doctor—to make the decision for the person. It should be noted here, as well, that although the vast majority of doctors are honest people who intend the best for their patients, the doctor <u>does</u> often have a conflict of interest, in that he may make more money by doing the operation than if he didn't do it. Unfortunately, some doctors may be influenced by such a conflict of interest, and engage in operations that are not really advisable if all considerations are taken into account. Setting aside conflicts of interest, the doctor may simply not be well positioned, given her particular life experiences, to make the right personal set of trade-offs for the particular patient asking her advice. In general, there are serious costs in overreliance on experts.

The influence of modern dogmatism is apt to lead to the compromise of fundamental liberties. There is a dangerous combination of the experts, who want to be important, and the bureaucrats, who want to be seen to do the "rational" thing by aligning themselves with the experts, and the lawyers, who want to sue people for not doing what the experts said they should, and the politicians, who want to show they have changed the world for the better, and the media, who want to teach the ignorant masses how to lead better lives. Taken together, there is a tendency to encroach ever further on our liberties. In the modern dogmatist view, the experts—the repositories of accumulated truth and wisdom—know better than the people what it is that is good for the people. As a consequence, the thinking goes, we should <u>require</u> the people to do what the experts think they should be doing. Indeed, that is the essence of what they think it means to be "rational".

Bella: *But say goodbye to Lady Liberty and hello to Tyranny. Are the people eating what they should be? Are they doing the right exercises? Are the people thinking the things they are supposed to be thinking? Do they say the right things so as not to offend others? Do they have the right opinions on issues of the environment or race or evolution or public education or religion? Are they thinking what the experts have determined they should believe?*

It is <u>not</u> a long journey to travel from dogmatism to oppression. Indeed, the one leads to the other. My point is not that one should by cynical. Cynicism involves an approach to life in which you distrust human motivation. A cynic looks for, and explains everything, in terms of ulterior—and generally bad—motives.

Bella: *That is the path of the disappointed dogmatist.*

While some people <u>do</u> have bad motives, I believe people generally have good motives, or at least a blend of motives, many of which are good. In general, most people try to do the right thing. This book is not a call to cynicism, although some would label anyone who dares to question as a cynic. Rather, <u>this book is a call for you to reject the intellectual, artistic and personal dependency that the cult of expertism will attempt to foist on you</u>.

Bella: *They won't catch me!*

The New Feudalism would have you set aside your confidence in yourself and in your own thinking. This book is a call to be skeptical of that dependent mindset. It is a call to believe in yourself and your own thinking capabilities. Your personal capabilities are not only important but crucial. I don't ask you to disbelieve and distrust. On the contrary, I ask you to believe in your own starring role in navigating your way through life and to truth, beauty and wisdom. This book is not about cynicism and skepticism—it is about belief in yourself, your own view of the world and your vital connections to others that provide you with opportunities to contribute and create to beauty, truth, goodness, health and prosperity.

HOW TO QUESTION AUTHORITY

Now, let me be clear here: I am <u>not</u> saying in this book that you should ignore experts or never believe what they say. In any undertaking in life, it is good, and it may be quite important, to know what the experts think. Moreover, I have no doubt that <u>there is much more harm to society generally incurred (or imposed) by those who are unaware of or have ignored expert opinion than due to expert opinion being somehow misguided or self-interested.</u> So <u>do seek out expert opinion and do heed it where it is apt.</u> The key point to keep in mind, however, is that expert opinion always has its biases and, indeed, the so-called experts may <u>not</u> always have your best interest at heart. You cannot rely on experts to do <u>your</u> thinking for you. You cannot rely on them to interpret the world for you and to make your decisions. You must educate yourself if you do not want to play someone else's fool. Of course, educating yourself means <u>seeking out expert opinion</u>.

Bella: *So how do you strike the right balance? We can't—each and every one of us—become an expert in everything. What should we do when we have to rely on an expert?*

There isn't the time and resources to be an expert in everything, and nobody would want to be. Indeed, to try to do so would not only be inefficient, it would be a little crazy. (And let me tell you, I am glad that there are accountants in the world; because I can rely on them, I am not required to master the principles of accounting.) And, of course, sometimes you have no practical choice other than to rely on an expert. If you are in an emergency room and have a profusely bleeding wound, you don't have any practical options other than relying on the expertise of the medical personnel who are attending to you. How much you should rely on experts depends in part on how important the consequences of a particular decision, or piece of information, or viewpoint, is to you. First and foremost, however, as I noted previously, <u>do not rely on anything I tell you in this book; I am not taking responsibility for your decisions and your life.</u> Seriously. But I will share with you how I think about it, if and when I have to rely on an expert. When possible and reasonable to do so, I consider the following steps:

- First, understand the <u>question</u> or issue. What exactly am I trying to decide, or understand, or know? What it is that I want or need?
- Second, I ask myself: <u>what is at stake</u> in this particular decision or piece of information? What happens if the expert is wrong?
- Third, I ask myself: <u>what resources do I have</u> to address this issue and how much of those resources do I want to dedicate to it? Do I have the time, resources and opportunity to better inform myself? Is this particular decision or issue worth my time?
- Fourth, I ask myself: does this expert have <u>the right expertise</u> to answer my question or address my issue?
- Fifth: I ask myself whether this expert has the right <u>incentives</u> to answer my question, or address my issue, in a full, honest and truthful manner. Are the expert's interests fully aligned with mine? How does she get paid for her services? Will that tend to bias her advice?
- Sixth, regardless of the incentives, I ask myself: do I <u>trust</u> this particular expert? On the one hand, there may be strong conflicts of interests, and yet it might still be quite reasonable to trust a particular expert. There are many experts with great integrity who will give excellent, highly informed and pertinent advice regardless of the ramifications for themselves. On the other hand, even if it doesn't appear that there are significant conflicts of interest, I may encounter sources of expertise that I simply don't trust. If I have a choice—that is, I are not in an emergency room and bleeding—I consider heeding that internal voice and seeking a different expert.
- Seventh: where practical, I ask what <u>the evidence</u> is for the expert's viewpoint. I ask questions and make sure I understand—as best I can—the basis for the expert opinion. Does the expert share the evidence with me, and explain it well, or does she just expert me to accept her conclusions?
- Eighth: if it is practical and reasonable to do so, I get <u>other expert opinions</u>. Also I ask myself: are there different schools of thought on the issue? Is there a consensus among the experts? If there is disagreement among the experts, what is the evidence for the different and varying opinions?

- Ninth: I ask myself whether there is not also other <u>complementary expertise</u> that I should seek, given the nature of the issue or decision under consideration. Are there other ways to think about this issue? Is this something that only one discipline addresses, or do different disciplines take somewhat different approaches?
- Tenth: to the extent that I can, I <u>do my own research</u>. I don't mean original scientific research, of course, but I consider reading up on the topic myself. It is amazing how quickly one can get on top of complex technical issues with the help of the Internet. The Internet can give one a good sense of the issues as stake, and what questions to ask if one is forced to rely on an expert. It helps me arrive at an informed and independent judgment as to whether I should trust any particular expert. Of course, one has to be careful with the Internet. Many things on the Internet are simply incorrect. So I have to make considered judgments in the use of this information as well.
- Eleventh: I may seek <u>non-expert</u> opinions. How have my peers addressed this same issue? What do my friends think? What does my family think? I might contact others through the Internet who have the same issue or challenge. Is there a network of people, or perhaps a blog on the Internet, where I can interact with other people thinking about this issue? Is there a support group? Again, one also has to be careful with these sources. Others may be in a fundamentally different situation than I am. Or others may not share my values; they are not necessarily looking at what I think is important in a given decision. Or these others may have an agenda of their own that doesn't really reflect my interests. They may simply be delusional. One must be careful and thoughtful.
- Twelfth: I ask yourself what aspects of the issue or decision lend themselves to the input of an expert and which do not. For example, I consider <u>what aspects of the decision or issue involve value judgments or personal preferences</u> and therefore go beyond any expert's expertise and, indeed, call for my input. Has the expert tried to usurp aspects of the decision-making that are properly my own to weigh?

13

THE DEATH OF FORMALISM

I have been thinking about that Zeno's paradox, and I can't solve it.

KATE FISHER

Do I contradict myself? Very well, then I contradict myself, I am large, I contain multitudes.

WALT WHITMAN

How wonderful that we have met with a paradox. Now we have some hope of making progress.

NEILS BOHR

A PARADOX

Bella: *Did you say a pair of ducks? Where? I want to chase them!*

No, I said a "paradox".

Bella: *What's that? Can you chase it?*

Yes. In fact, it is a bit like chasing your tail. The sentence in the box below is a good example of one.

This statement is false.

Bella: *Is that statement true?*

That is the question Bella. There are only two possibilities, of course. That is, either the statement is true or false. Let's explore both possibilities. If the statement is true, then, by virtue of what it is informing us, it must be false. But that is a contradiction. Alternatively, suppose the statement is false. If the statement is false, we can see that it has given us accurate information, which means it is true. But that is also a contradiction. Thus, it can neither be true nor false.

Bella: *How can a meaningful statement be* <u>neither</u> *true nor false?*

You see for yourself that it is so.

Bella: *I get this. Paradoxes* <u>are</u> *just like when I chase my tail around in a circle. I love that. Here I go now!*

PARADOXES ARE IMPORTANT

Paradoxes may seem as though they are merely amusing parlor tricks, designed to provide some transient entertainment to the mind and of no significance beyond that. In contrast, my view is that we should take them seriously. They take us to the edge of intellectual precipices. It is good to know where those precipices are. We should embrace paradoxes for four reasons. First, in some ways, paradoxes constitute traps within the human reasoning process—places where our reasoning power fails us. And once you meet them, you start to notice that they come up again and again in different forms and embodied in different disciplines. Great minds have gotten trapped by them and gone no further in their exploration of a field because they were stumped by a paradox. You need to appreciate and recognize these intellectual traps—first of all, so you can leap beyond them when you need to. Second, paradoxes give us insight on the limits of our mechanical thought processes. They teach us intellectual humility. They show us that we can't solve everything by just thinking hard about it. Third, paradoxes teach us that formal systems do not seem to be able to embrace the contradictory possibilities of reality—that is, they betray the fact that there is a certain poverty in the seeming simple consistencies of formal systems. I will say more on this below, of course. Fourth, paradoxes are entertaining. You can flummox other people with them. Finally, I think paradoxes teach us something about possibilities—that there is something undefined and indefinable about the universe. They teach us something about the freedom within our souls and within the universe. I can't put my finger on it, but I sense it there. Pondering paradoxes is as important as playing tug-of-war with your dog.

Bella: *Wow. That's important.*

ZENO'S PARADOXES

You cannot move.

Bella: *What do you mean? Are you asking me to stay?*

No. I am telling you that you cannot move.

Bella: *But I can move. Just watch me run around and sniff. I am still looking for those two ducks.*

That was mere illusion.

Bella: *How so?*

Let me prove it to you. I am holding my hand above that biscuit. It is about 1 foot away.

Bella: *Don't mess with my biscuit.*

Now, before I can move my hand to touch the biscuit, I would first have to move it to the halfway point between my hand and the biscuit—that is, a point ½ foot away from the biscuit. But before I can reach the point that is ½ foot from the biscuit, my hand would have to first travel half of that distance—that is, I would first have to have my hand reach a point that is ¼ foot from my starting position. But before my hand reaches the point that is a quarter of the distance to the biscuit, my hand would first have to travel to the point which is half way to that point from the starting point—that is, 1/8th of the distance from my starting point to the biscuit. But before I can reach that point, my hand would have to go half the way to it—that is, the point which is 1/16th of the distance from my hand to the biscuit.

Bella: *I am getting less worried about you grabbing my biscuit.*

Now we could continue this analysis forever.

Bella: *Yes, but before we did that, we would have to do the analysis for half of forever.*

The point is that <u>before</u> I make even the tiniest movement with my hand toward the biscuit I would first have to move my hand half of that tiny distance. But that means that I can never get started on the <u>first</u> little movement, because I would have to have already moved halfway to that point, but I can't have already moved halfway to that point because it <u>is</u> the first movement. Thus, I can never move my hand at all.

Bella: *But that is crazy; I move all the time. See me run. I am a wild dog!*

The ancient Greek philosopher Zeno was the first to point out the impossibility of movement. He said that the appearance of such movement—such as you running around in the back yard—is merely an illusion. Like a big motion picture being put on by God.

Bella: *I see. Do you believe this?*

Not really.

Bella: *Then Zeno must be wrong.*

But where is the flaw in his argument? Let me give you another example that Zeno used. You see that turtle out there in the yard?

Bella: *Yes, I do. I want to go catch it.*

But according to Zeno, that is impossible.

Bella: *I don't like this Zeno fellow.*

Let's assume you can run faster than the turtle.

Bella: *But I <u>can</u> run faster than that turtle!*

Then it is a good assumption. Now let's see why it is impossible for you to catch up with the turtle, even though you can run faster. Here you are sitting next to me on the deck. But the turtle is out there in the middle of the yard. So let's say you head in the direction of the turtle and run as fast as you can. In the meantime, the turtle starts running away from you, but at a slower speed than you are running. But before you reach the turtle, you will have to first reach the point at which the turtle begins its movement away from you. But by the time you reach that point, the turtle will have moved at least <u>some</u> distance forward, even though it will not have coved as much distance as you have, since you are running faster. So you keep chasing the turtle. But, again, by the time you reach where the turtle <u>was</u> when you had arrived at the turtle's original position, the turtle will <u>again</u> have moved forward at least some, albeit less distance than you would have covered in the same time. And, of course, this pattern will be repeated each time you try to cover the final distance to the turtle. Thus, you will never reach the turtle.

Bella: *But that makes no sense. Of course, I can catch the turtle. I have done it many times. Your argument doesn't fit what we observe.*

True enough. That is why Zeno said that what you observe is a mere illusion—because it cannot be thus. However, I agree with you that we have to reject Zeno's arguments because they don't fit with what we observe. But yet they do seem compelling. What do you think the problem is here?

Bella: *I think the problem is that <u>you</u> can't run fast enough.*

PARADOXES OF SELF-REFERENCE

> # The statement in the box below is false.

> # The statement in the box above is true.

Look at the two boxes above and the statements therein. They refer to one another. Taken together, they constitute a paradox. Ask yourself: Are these statements true? There are two possibilities for each statement: either it is true or it is false. Work through the possibilities. Assume the statement in the top box is true and see if that leads to a contradiction. Then assume the statement in the top box is false and see if that leads to a contradiction. You will find that any way you try it, it leads to a contradiction, much like the paradox with which I opened the chapter.

Bella: *I am chasing my tail again!*

These are good examples of a whole class of paradoxes based on self-reference. Any time you have a logical or language based system that can refer to itself, you can create these kinds of paradoxes. Suppose someone says "Everything I say is a lie." Is that statement true or false? These paradoxes of self-reference turn out to have some profound importance for mathematics and human thought more generally.

RUSSELL'S PARADOX

The following paradox was developed by the philosopher Bertrand Russell. Father William Sampson, a high school teacher of mine whom I mentioned in the acknowledgments, told it to me when I was in high school. It is my favorite paradox. Let's define a "Group" as any defined collection. Of course, that sort of sounds like what they call a "set" in mathematics. Indeed, you may have already learned set theory. Let's be clear here. I don't want you applying what you have learned from set theory in an unthinking fashion. That is why I am using the less familiar term "Group"—so you will think this through for yourself.

Bella: *But isn't there also an area of mathematics called Group Theory?*

Yes. Ignore that as well for the moment. Just think of a "Group" as a well-defined collection of anything. For example, you might have the Group of All Pencils. To be in that Group, you have to be a pencil. If you are a pencil, you are in the Group. If you are not a pencil, you are not in the Group.

Bella: *I get the idea.*

Now let's try the Group of All Groups. If you are a Group, then you are in that Group. If you are not a Group per se—for example, if you are a Great Dane named Bella—then you are not in the Group of All Groups.

Bella: *Is the Group of All Groups in the Group of All Groups?*

Of course, it is. It is a Group, and therefore fits the criterion to be in that Group. But this brings us to a new concept, which is Self-Including Groups. A Self-Including Group is a Group that includes itself. For example, the Group of All Groups is a Self-Including Group. The Group of All The Things You Can Think Of is also a Self-Including Group, because you can think of it. In contrast, the Group of All Pencils does not include itself.

Bella: *Why not?*

The Group of All Pencils in not in the Group of Self-Including Groups because the Group of All Pencils is not itself a pencil. This brings us to a second type of Group—Non-Self-Including Group. Non-Self-Including Groups are those that do not include themselves. Thus, the Group of All

Pencils is a Non-Self-Including Group. Now, all Groups should either be Self-Including (like the Group of All Groups) or Non-Self-Including (like the Group of All Pencils).

Bella: *What else could they be? Clearly, all Groups have to either include themselves or not include themselves. But I have two obvious questions to ask:*

1. *Is the Group of All Self-Including Groups Self-Including or Non-Self-Including?*
2. *Is the Group of All Non-Self-Including Self-Including or Non-Self-Including?*

Let's take your first question first. As stated above, all Groups must be either Self-Including or Non-Self-Including. So let's explore both possibilities—and see if either leads to a contradiction. Let's first assume that the Group of All Self-Including Groups is Self-Including, and see if it leads to any contradictions. To be in this Group, one has to be self-including. If we go with the assumption that this Group is self-including, we arrive at no contradictions.

Now, in contrast, let's assume that the Group of All Self-Including Groups is non-self-including. If this Group were non-self-including then it wouldn't be included in itself (given that it only includes self-including groups), so there is no contradiction there either. In sum, we can't really tell if the Group of Self-Including-Groups is Self-Including or Non-Self-Including, but neither possibility leads to a contradiction.

THE GROUP OF NON-SELF-INCLUDING GROUPS

On to your second question: is the Group of Non-Self-Including Groups Self-Including or Non-Self-Including? Let's explore the two possibilities and see if either leads to a contradiction. To be in the Group of Non-Self-Including Groups, you need to be non-self-including. So to include itself, this Group would have to not include itself. That is a contradiction. Thus, we must assume that the Group of Non-Self-Including Groups is not Self-Including.

Bella: *I feel like I am chasing my tail again!*

Let's explore the other possibility. Suppose the Group of Non-Self-Including Groups were non-self-including. In this case, it would clearly include itself because it includes all Groups that are non-self-including. But this is <u>also</u> a contradiction. We must therefore assume that the Group of Non-Self-Including Groups is not non-self-including. In sum, we have found a Group that is <u>neither</u> self-including nor non-self-including, since either possibility leads to a contradiction.

Bella: *But how can it be that a Group* <u>neither</u> *includes itself nor does not include itself?*

It's another paradox of self-reference and there is really no getting around it.

THE GRAND QUEST FOR THE ULTIMATE UNIVERSAL AXIOMS

There is a grand vision that haunts much of scientific development. It is the quest for the universal set of axioms from which everything can be deduced and everything explained. Can we find one set of axioms—that is, a limited number of simple scientific (and generally mathematical) statements—from which everything may be explained? One can see that this would be attractive. Let's call this quest "formalism". Much of 18th and particularly 19th and early 20th century science was driven by the formalist vision. Of course, the best place to begin the formalist project would be with mathematics itself. Can we find a set of mathematical axioms from which everything we know in mathematics may be derived, or at least everything we know within some subset of mathematics? For example, Bertrand Russell and Alfred Whitehead tried to do this in a grand mathematical work entitled <u>Principia Mathematica</u>.

GÖDEL'S THEOREM

In one of the most stunning results in the history of mathematics, Kurt Gödel—a German mathematician—demonstrated that it was <u>not</u> possible to provide an axiomatic foundation for number theory that was both <u>consistent</u>—meaning the axiomatic system did not lead to contradictions— and <u>complete</u>—meaning that you could actually use the axioms to derive all the known results within number theory. Of course, to fulfill the formalist vision, one would have to have a system of axioms that was both consistent and complete. First, you must have consistency, of course. That is, you can't have an explanatory system which can demonstrate the same statement to be both true <u>and</u> false, can you? Second, if you don't have completeness, it means that there are known results, that can be demonstrated, but that are not reached by your set of axioms. The proof of Gödel's theorem is beyond the scope and level of difficulty that is appropriate to this book, but the essence of it you already have. What Gödel did was to show that any axiomatic system that was sufficiently rich to capture all of the results of number theory within its scope could be used to create self-referential statements that were contradictory in the very same way that Russell's paradox does above. In other words, Gödel showed that even formal mathematics cannot escape from the paradoxes of self-reference.

THE FAILURE OF THE FORMALIST PROJECT

If even mathematics alone cannot be captured by one set of axioms that is both consistent and complete, there remains no hope for science as a whole to be thusly captured. What we are saying here is that there can never be any one set of consistent axioms that explains all that is known (or, at least, that we think we know.) Another way to say this is that it has been mathematically demonstrated that our knowledge will always be fragmented—that is, that there will be different and mutually inconsistent set of axioms required to model the world we live in.

    Bella: *It's as if God stole Walt Whitman's line: "Do I contradict myself? Very well, then I contradict myself, I am large, I contain multitudes."*

THE FAILURE OF REDUCTIONISM

Closely related to the formalist project is the idea of reductionism. Reductionism is basically the notion that we explain bigger things from smaller things. It is the idea that there is a kind of explanatory hierarchy. It would include notions such that we can use, say, physics principles, and the movement of the smallest atoms, to explain chemical reactions, which in turn we can use to explain, say, biological behavior and, ultimately, say human behavior. That would constitute a true unification of the sciences. Reductionism fails for a number of reasons. First, it fails because of Gödel's theorem. But it also fails because there is no hierarchy of explanation that tracks causality in the real world. That is, what might be considered "higher" levels in any explanatory chain can reach back down and cause different interactions at seemingly lower levels of causality—thus, pulling the explanatory hierarchy asunder. To take a simple example, a human being working with chemicals may cause a chemical reaction to be different than it otherwise would have been by <u>deciding</u> to blend the chemicals at a different temperature. Thus, to <u>fully</u> explain why the chemical reaction occurred as it did, one would have to explain why the human being chose to do what she did. To put this another way, there is, in reality, no consistent logical starting point for explanatory frameworks. The decision of the starting point for our explanatory frameworks has to do with what questions we are asking and what challenges we are addressing rather than with ultimate causal chains in the universe. Finally, the reductionist vision has failed in the sense that science has not become integrated in the fashion it envisions. Rather, actual and successful explanatory frameworks in science are fragmented across different disciplines—with the boundaries among them left a bit unclear, transient and often mutually inconsistent. This is likely the best that humans will ever do, although our knowledge is apt, of course, to continue to deepen, as our predictive abilities continue to grow, and attempting to connect these disparate intellectual frameworks can, itself, generate new and valuable ideas.

Suggested Readings

- Passage on "Achilles and the Tortoise" from Gilbert Ryle's <u>Dilemmas</u> (Cambridge, 1966) at pp 36 to 53.
- Passage on "Gödel's Theorem" from Clifford A. Pickover <u>The Math Book</u> (Sterling, 2009) at pp 362-363.
- "Introduction: A Musico-Logical Offering" of Douglas R. Hofstadter's <u>Gödel, Escher, Bach: an Eternal Golden Braid</u> at pp 3 to 32.

PART 2

COLLECTIVE RATIONALITY (OR DEMOCRACY AS DISCOVERY)

in which I explore collective rationality. I try to make it clear that voting per se is <u>not</u> the essence of democracy and does not lead to social coherence. Rather, I argue that the essence of democracy—at its best—is as an inclusive process of discovery, supported by crucial freedoms and liberal institutions, including the right to vote.

14

THE POLITICAL SPECTRUM

*Election for office when there are just two candidates and just one issue is
a predictable and straightforward story. ... The voters can be ranked
according to how far to the "left" or "right" each one stands on the issue.
If one of the candidates were to adopt an extreme position—appealing
to the right, say—the other candidate could take a less extreme position
and thereby capture the middle voters and all those at the other extreme,
hence a majority. Anticipating this, the former candidate will optimally
attempt to stake out the center, as best the candidate can estimate it. ...
the two candidates are led to squeeze together at the political center.*

EDMUND S. PHELPS

Any fundamental discussion of politics and governance must begin with a
look at what is called the political spectrum. Politics in America is a very
entertaining sport, but you have to know who the teams are. The idea of a
"political spectrum" began with the French Revolution. As it happened, the

folks who had collected together on one side of the room tended to be of one political viewpoint and the folks that had gathered on the other side of the room had a different political viewpoint. So they called the one group "the Left" and the other group they called "the Right"—simply based on where they were standing in the room. But the terms have stuck. The meaning of the political spectrum in terms of "Right" and "Left" has evolved through time and across countries, but still stands as an important indicator light of political inclination. Of necessity, the following descriptions of the political Right and Left are caricatures, and, it should go without saying, that they are <u>my</u> caricatures. They are merely intended to give you a feel for the meaning of the "Left" and the "Right."

THE LEFT

The Left sees the primary economic problem for society <u>not</u> as the production of goods and services that meet our individual and collective needs, but rather as correcting the fact that the good things of life have not been distributed fairly. As a consequence, the Left tends to be more for <u>change</u>, (and occasionally for revolutionary change). They proclaim they are for "the people" and place great emphasis on equality. They tend to distrust business-people and the wealthy. They are generally very supportive of labor unions, and are great believers in the benefits of organizing working and poor people and acting collectively. They tend to trust the governmental regulation of affairs over results that are determined by markets, and in some countries this has been taken to the extreme of the government owning and running everything, which is called Communism. They tend to see the government as the key to solving most social problems, and where they permit markets to operate, they tend to think that they are in need of a great deal of regulation. They often look at politics, and much of life, as a struggle between those who are powerful and those who are not, and they are decidedly on the side of those who are being oppressed. The view of <u>who</u> it is that constitutes the oppressed may change across time and countries, of course. It is often based on classes. You have the working class or the peasants pitted against the upper classes and the business people. There is a great deal of left-wing literature on this topic. The groups that are viewed as oppressed may also be based on race, gender, ethnicity, geographic origin, religion and so forth.

The Left loves the political narrative of the struggle of the oppressed against their rulers. For the most part, it is this narrative, rather than principles, that drive their social and political thinking. More specifically, issues are <u>not</u> necessarily to be resolved through the application of a principle. Rather, issues should be addressed <u>in terms of the struggle</u> by the oppressed against the powerful. The Left looks to who is on each side of a fight to determine how an issue should be properly resolved. The reason they do this is not that they are unprincipled per se. They have principles, but those principles are based in the idea of struggle. The Left believes that only through solidarity can the oppressed ever hope to succeed in their battles against the powerful. They build their political coalitions out of the groups that are perceived to be oppressed, rather than on a set of ideas. This can make them rather difficult to argue with, since they often aren't basing their views on the application of any particular principle, but rather on what is required by the coalition of interests of which they view themselves as a part. If you make an argument based on particular principles, they will sometimes say things like "I just won't go there" or "I don't use those types of intellectual constructs" or "Those are bourgeois ideas"—meaning they are the ideas of wealthy people and not ones which they are willing to entertain. Much of the Left is highly distrustful of religion. They see religion as a tool of the powerful to keep the oppressed in their place. (That being said, for some Left-wing people, it is their interpretation of their religion that provides the basis of their political views.)

Many in the Left are highly distrustful of the influence of money. They think that politics would be more pure, noble, generous and right-minded if politicians didn't have to raise money. They often believe that there should be heavy governmental regulation of the influence of money on politics, or that it should be forbidden altogether. On the other hand, they tend to trust whatever scientists say, as long as the scientists don't obtain their money from big business interests, which they see as corrupting. The Left believes that the solution to many of our social problems is simply through better education of the public. They believe that most people, if they have the right education and environment, would be good people, and that if poor people do bad things, it is because they haven't had the right opportunities in life.

Perhaps most importantly, from the point of view of social and economic organization, the Left believes that <u>anything is possible</u>, as long as we get enough people to simply agree on it and implement it. That is, they do not feel constrained in terms of the best design for society. Rather, they feel unconstrained in the following ways: First, they do not see human nature itself as a constraint. According to the Left, people—and their behavior—are formed by society, not the other way around. That is, if we can just get the design of society right, then people will be good. Second, the Left does not feel constrained by the laws of economics—nor do they really believe that there is any such thing as laws of economics. They see all this "stuff" around us that the economy has produced, and focus on the fact that it is just people doing all these things. They conclude that if we can just organize the people in a different way, we can make the economy run any way we like. The economy is not seen as something outside our control—or as a constraint. To point to the economic causes of a problem is, according to the Left, to fail to recognize the plasticity of society—that is, to fail to recognize that we are not trapped by economic constraints, since we could just condition people to behave differently. The Left believes that—like engineers—we can re-design society any way we like. What this ignores, of course, is the different economic arrangements lead to different incentives for people and therefore different behaviors, some of which may not have been intended by the "social engineers." The Left counters this critique with the proposition that people won't follow selfish incentives if they are properly shaped by their society. Thus, this really goes back to their rejection of "human nature" as a constraint on what Left-wing social engineers might accomplish. In sum and substance, the Left believes in social engineering—that is, the idea we can design society to be any way we like and make it so, if only we can get enough people looking at it the right way. Finally, because the Left believes in social engineering, they do not tolerate a lot of dissent. The social world is <u>not</u> one where we should be on a voyage of discovery through debate.
Bella: *No, indeed.*

When the correct answers are identified, they must be imposed on society. From the Left's perspective, this is required to reshape society for the better. It is all well intended. Of course, there are many different variants of the Left, and, as I noted, my description is a bit of a caricature. But I imagine you get the idea. People on the Left are also sometimes referred to as "liberals", or sometimes as "progressives." In the US, the Democratic Party is thought of as being more to the Left, although people who are even more to the Left than the Democrats tend to think them as much too conservative. Indeed, some Democrats are, in fact, fairly conservative. Historically, on the far Left, you have Marxists, communists and socialists of various stripes. Socialists are considered to be far to the left, but not quite as far as the Marxists and communists. Among the liberals, who are not quite as far to the Left as the socialists (but still pretty far Left), you will find many different variants as well. Some of them are great believers in using the marketplace to allocate resources, and actually do understand how markets work, but see a need for governmental intervention to give everyone equality of opportunity, and perhaps see things like basic medical care as something that should be an economic right. Others on the Left may be very distrustful of markets, and believe that government must take a heavy hand in the planning of all economic activity. Some are more pro-Union than others. And so on.

The epistemological failures of the Left are driven by its narrow focus on its shallow narrative of struggle between groups defined as oppressors and other groups defined as the oppressed. Social, political and economic reality is often much more complex than this simplistic narrative would have it. At times, the Left even appears to believe that truth and wisdom can only find its origin in, and be uttered by, the oppressed—as if they lived in a separate reality from the oppressors and are somehow more human. From an epistemological perspective, the Left also fails to open itself to an exploration of economic laws and the inherent limits of human nature—laws and limits that, in fact, do cabin what is possible. As a consequence, they fail to explore and understand our true potential, and often implement policies that are destructive of the ends they purport to seek. That is a tragedy of enormous proportions. The ultimate epistemological failure of the Left, however, is ironic; they do not really trust open and honest discourse among the People—an exploration involving bold conjectures and pointed criticism—to guide us to a better society. Rather, the Left places its trust in a liberal elite—a vanguard—who they see as reshaping society for the benefit of the ignorant masses. But as Karl Marx himself, who was not so simplistically minded, wisely asked: "Who will teach the teachers?"

Bella: *Despite being the founder of Communism, I think Marx had a hidden conservative streak in him.*

Now, I would like to note that there are many people who constitute exceptions to this epistemological critique of the Left. There are thinkers on the Left who are truly open and deep and stand ready and willing to engage in critical thought. They wouldn't dream of answering an argument with anything other than another argument that would take us collectively deeper into an exploration of our world and what is possible. The best left wing thinkers will open your mind to a different set of arguments that you might not have seen otherwise. The best of the Left is well worth reading and contemplating. What you want to avoid is wasting your time in reading the pure ideologues, who are simply in the business of propagandizing and emoting (except in so far it is important to be aware of these currents of thought). In contrast, you <u>should</u> seek the truly independent thinkers—wherever they are on the political spectrum—who espouse some radical critique, that is, a critique that they see as going to the root of a problem. Whether you agree with them or not, exposure to high quality critical thinking will always advance your own thinking. Remember— never judge an idea by its source; rather, look to its merits.

THE RIGHT

The Right is distrustful of rapid change and, indeed, is not fond of change in general. Change can be destabilizing. They believe in tradition. And they are not always that principled about that! You might ask them: "Why should we do it that way?" and they will reply "We have always done it that way." They often emphasize religion and religious values. The Right is most definitely against social engineering. They distrust "do-gooders"— those who would seek to correct an imperfect world, but inevitably do so at a great cost and with damaging social disruption. They are believers in the "unintended consequences" of efforts at social engineering. That is, they think that new governmental policies—designed to solve one problem— almost always end up creating other unexpected and unintended negative consequences. They believe that the human condition is not perfectible, and that efforts to create a social paradise in this world inevitably lead to social chaos and much greater horrors. They tend to believe there is a natural order to society, and it is the job of those at the top to guide society and keep it stable. They tend to think market-driven outcomes are good and distrust the government to find solutions. While they might admit that sometimes the market fails, they think that government failure—as it tries to substitute for the market—is the greater danger.

The Right believes that civilization is a thin veneer—which is to say we are never all that far from complete social disorder and violence in the streets. They place a high value on social stability. They trust successful businessmen and women. They believe that those who are successful should help those who are not, but this should be done privately, and through private organizations, not through government. They trust science, but only when it is applied to practical and immediate technical problems. They distrust scientists who are trying to restructure society by their own lights. They think human nature has both a good and an evil side, and that the evil side can never be fully suppressed, and has to be dealt with directly and forcefully when it constitutes a threat to the social order or national security.

People on the Right are sometimes referred to as "conservatives." The Republican Party is thought of as being more to the Right, but some conservatives think it is too Leftish for their tastes. And just like there are some conservative Democrats, there are some Republicans who are liberal. Among the conservatives, you have "market conservatives," who are very much focused on economic issues and are great believers in minimizing government intervention in the economy, but otherwise may have what are considered liberal social views. But other conservatives—called "social conservatives"—are more focused on conservative social values and religion. In contrast to market conservatives, some of the social conservatives may not be believers in open markets.

At the extreme Right, many would place various fascist parties, such as the Nazi's of World War II Germany. But there is debate about this. It is noteworthy, in that regard, that the term "Nazi" stands for National Socialist Party. That being said, Adolf Hitler certainly saw the Left in his own country as an enemy (among many), and one of his first priorities was to have many people on the Left imprisoned or killed. There are dictators throughout history, and they are probably defined more by their absolute authority than their political philosophy, but certainly some have had philosophies or perspectives that could be described as Right-wing and others Left-wing. Most certainly, it can be said that both Right-wing and Left-wing perspectives have inspired oppression.

223

Bella: *None of these dictators are supporters of personal liberty, that is for sure.*

The epistemological failures of the Right are tied to unthinking deference to tradition and authority, and not enough belief in the power of critical thinking and of criticism itself to promote beneficial change. Society is well served by criticism as it attempts to think through how it might be improved. The Right is so paralyzed by the fear that well-intended governmental action may have negative unintended consequences that they sometimes forego critical thought altogether. The Right also suffers from an almost mystical devotion to the market. One can join the Right in its appreciation of the power of markets and yet still see that there are occasions where markets do fail, and where governmental mechanisms to address those failures may well be efficacious.

The Right also has an excessive devotion to gradualism. If there is to be any change, they believe it should be in as small increments as possible. But there are times when wholesale change is called for, and some societal changes are linked with others and should, from a policy perspective, be linked. There are times where societies need to take bold action and times in which they need to experiment. The Great Depression is a good example of a time of experimentation was called for; the social and economic problems were so severe that the danger of unintended consequences from some experimentation was outweighed by the possibility that the situation might be improved. It is what is referred to as "desperate times". This is not necessarily to say that all the experiments worked out or were to the best. Pollution is another good example of where heavy governmental involvement is required. Early in my life, the air and the waterways of the US were becoming heavily polluted. Congress took fairly bold legislative action to address this, and was quite successful in doing so. The rivers of America today are much cleaner than they were when I was a youth, and this was done in a manner that did not preclude economic growth at the same time. This was a big change at the point when it was needed; gradualism would have been inappropriate. Appropriate change is not always small and incremental.

Finally, some people on the Right are sometimes simply motivated by an impoverished set of values. That is, some of them are simply narrow minded, bigoted, judgmental, greedy and genuinely lacking in concern for those struggling to make ends meet and for genuine equality of opportunity. That is, some of them simply don't care about poor folks.

Now, be warned that there are lots of variants of both the Right and the Left, and I have caricatured them here, just to give you a sense of it and as a starting place for further discussion. And just as there are deep thinkers on the Left, so too are there deep thinkers on the Right who are well worth reading. In general, avoid ideologues and seek those with a passion for the truth. There are smart and well-meaning people all along the political spectrum. Indeed, people all along the political spectrum have greatly contributed to society and have earned our celebration of them. Notably, also, there are many very nasty people all along the political spectrum. Neither side has a monopoly on either smarts or meanness. And, as noted above, historically, and at the extremes, there have been both Left-wing and Right-wing governments that have been horrifically oppressive. Neither side has had a monopoly on generating political and social horror. Indeed, neither side is intrinsically good or evil, but they do tend to disagree rather vigorously about what is good and bad in the world. In the US today, just beneath the surface of our rhetoric, there is substantial fear of the other side's potential for oppression. That is, people on the Left fear that the Right—if it got sufficient power—is never very far from implementing genuinely oppressive policies. By the same token, people on the Right fear that the Left—if it got sufficient power—is never very far from implementing genuinely oppressive policies.

Bella: *I fear they may both be right.*

Me too. The funny thing is that while each side takes its own fears (of the other side) seriously, they do not take the other side's fear seriously. I guess that is simply because they don't fear themselves. The most profound flaw I see in both groups is a high degree of intolerance for people who think differently than they do. That is most unattractive.

Bella: *A pox on both their houses.*

In fact, most people tend to be somewhere in the middle of the political spectrum. Indeed, most thoughtful people will hold some right-wing views and some left-wing views, and will have well-reasoned arguments for what they believe. That being said, many people are not all that thoughtful about the world they live in. They tend to only read sources of ideas with which they already agree. That is, some media outlets and authors are known to be of the Left or of the Right, and most people tend to gravitate toward simply reading the arguments they already agree with and with which they are comfortable. Don't be that kind of person. Try to find the best writers and thinkers all across the political spectrum; if they are good thinkers who are seeking truth, then they all have something to teach you. Do not limit yourself to exposure to that with which you already agree. If you do, there will be no advancement in your thinking, or deepening of your wisdom. On the other hand, avoid the ideologues who would feed you intellectual mush designed to put your mind to sleep.

Ideology in general—whether of the Right or of the Left—tends to stand in opposition to clear thinking. Ideology involves pre-packaged bundles of political and social thought that provide ideological adherents, <u>who would rather follow than think for themselves</u>, a handy narrative and set of simplistic answers to complicated questions. Ideologies are created by politicians, politically-oriented authors and political activists who are trying to get large numbers of people to act in concert in order to fulfill some political objective. That is not necessarily bad in-and-of-itself, by which I mean to say that propaganda is not <u>always</u> bad; it depends on what you are propagandizing. But do realize that propaganda is just that, and plays no role in advancing and deepening our understanding of the world, and can be quite dangerous in that it may serve to preclude such explorations.

15

FUNDAMENTAL POLITICAL VALUES

In politics, again, it is almost a commonplace, that a party of order or stability, and a party of progress or reform, are both necessary elements of a healthy state of political life; until the one or the other shall have so enlarged its mental grasp as to be a party equally of order and of progress, knowing and distinguishing what is fit to be preserved from what ought to be swept away.

JOHN STUART MILL

America is <u>not</u> simply a geographic location with inhabitants. Nor is it a country defined by its historical culture (such as, say, France). Rather, it is a set of ideas, and an historical struggle as to what those ideas mean. The reason for this is that throughout the history of the country we have all come from different places and different social classes and have had different cultural and religious affiliations. Yet, throughout our history we have had to pull ourselves together to deal with those differences to meet the challenges that we faced as a community and a nation. We have come to realize that the way in which we deal with those differences can be a source of great strength—or of weakness. We are not a country that asks everyone to be the same. Rather, we have turned to ideas, and a rather abstract set of ideas at that, to unite us. I believe it is the very seriousness with which we take these ideas that defines us as a nation, and, in fact, makes America exceptional.

Bella: *What are the most important and fundamental political values or ideas in the United States—the ideas that unite us as a political community and to a certain extent define our national character?*

I have a list of thirteen fundamental political ideas which, I think, most of us would agree are important and upon which we base our political rhetoric and thinking. As Americans, we cherish these ideas, albeit with different Americans thinking some are more important than others and disagreeing with one another as to what these ideas mean and which are most important. While I try to give some ideas as to what I mean by them below, it is the very fact of our disagreements as to their precise content that renders them central to our ongoing political and social debate. These include:

(1) LIBERTY

- This includes a lot of things like:
    - i.   freedom of speech;
    - ii.   freedom of religion;
    - iii. separation of church and state;
    - iv.   freedom to choose where you live;
    - v.   freedom to travel within the country where you like;
    - vi.   freedom to choose your occupation,;
    - vii. freedom to spend your money on what you like;
    - viii. freedom to associate with whom you like;
    - ix.   the right to due process under the law (including the presumption of innocence until proven guilty in a criminal trial);
    - x.   the right to be free from unreasonable search and seizure from the government, and so forth

(2) DEMOCRACY

- By which I mean—at least for purposes of this chapter—the right to vote and having our votes largely determine who represents us in the government and so forth.

(3) EQUALITY AND FAIRNESS

- Which can mean very different, and quite contradictory things, including:
  - i.   equality of outcome
  - ii. equality of opportunity, which can include either:
    1. Precisely equal treatment within particular circumstances (such as, say, having the entrance requirement for a university be based purely on who gets the highest test scores), or, in stark contrast:
    2. Unequal treatment in particular circumstances to ensure that there is approximately equal treatment across a longer time horizon (which might include, say, setting aside certain slots in a university for those who didn't score as high on a test, but who have been previously disadvantaged due to, say, race or social class or learning challenges)
  - iii. equality before the law
  - iv. social equality

(4) PROPERTY

- By which I mean the expectation that you can do what you want with your property (within certain reasonable limits) and that your interest in your property will be protected and enforced by the government, and that it will not be taken away from you by the government, except in the unusual circumstance where there is a compelling public interest in which case you will be fully compensated

(5) ECONOMIC PROSPERITY

- By which one means that the economy is robust and growing and providing opportunities for folks to make a good living

(6) LAW AND ORDER

- Which includes not only physical security and the policing of society, but also that there are effective and affordable mechanisms for sorting through cases and controversies with respect to the law, that the behavior of government and government officials is in accordance to the law (or else there are legal consequences), and that government does not conduct itself in an arbitrary and capricious manner

(7) NATIONAL SECURITY

- By which I mean the country is safe from foreign and domestic enemies

(8) ENVIRONMENTAL CARE

- Which would include controlling pollution and setting aside areas of the country to conserve in a natural state

(9) SOCIAL COHESION AND IDENTITY

- By which I mean the desire to feel close with one's community and patriotic about one's country

(10) TOLERANCE

- By which I mean tolerating people with whom we disagree or with respect to whose behavior, language or decisions we don't approve, but whose behavior, language or decisions falls within wide (but not unreasonable) bounds

(11) PRIVACY

- By which I mean the right to not have others—including the government—view, monitor or know about the details of your life without your permission, unless there is a compelling need for such information (as in, say, the investigation of a murder)

(12) EDUCATION

- By which I mean our faith that a good education is the key to a good life and our belief that everyone should be, at least, somewhat educated

(13) RELIGION (AND, MORE GENERALLY, OUR SENSE OF RIGHT AND WRONG)

- By which I mean the importance we place on people living an ethical and moral life—of course, as to what constitutes such a life there is, most palpably, great disagreement

These values provide the "stuff" of our arguments around the kitchen table as well as the rhetoric of politics. Every politician—and every political party—will select some subset and particular interpretation of these values to emphasize. These are the values that define the American conversation—a conversation with real world ramifications of the greatest import. It is a conversation that has resulted in joy, beauty, humor, glory, productivity and invention as well as tragedy, sadness, unfairness and lost opportunity. But as you probably already suspect, there is a very big challenge associated with these ideas. The challenge is that they are complicated, ill defined and not always consistent with one another. As a consequence, in many applications, we often have to choose one over the other. Moreover, each one of them is often interpreted differently by different people. Indeed, you can rearrange and re-interpret these ideas in a manner that takes you to positions and perspectives that are as different as can be. It is important to understand this for a number of reasons.

First, people employ these abstract ideas in argumentation as if they are absolutes that can never be breached, whereas, in fact, we must compromise on at least some of them quite often in the name of honoring one of the other core values. So don't fall for the rhetorical trick whereby a politician or debater or commentator will make reference to one of these values as if that ends the argument. Also, <u>do</u> realize that the best counterargument to any particular political argument generally lays in one of the other fundamental values to which the speaker has failed to employ.

Second, if you grasp the profound tensions among these different values, and the various ways they may be interpreted, you will never be without a good argument. That will not, of course, make you wise, but it is a good start. Indeed, learning all the different ways in which people interpret these values and creatively blend them <u>will</u> make you wiser. Ultimately, however, true wisdom must run beyond the arguments and achieves a point of rendering judgments about the best trade-offs among these values.

Third, the way in which we blend, interpret and prioritize these ideas makes <u>all</u> the difference. You can creatively blend the above ideas, all of which seem reasonable as taken in isolation, to come up with social and political philosophies which are deeply unfair, oppressive and—indeed—even frightening.

This brings us to my fourth point. These ideas do not in fact unite us as a nation, precisely because they can be twisted around and spun to serve just about any end. No, it is not the ideas that unite us—it is the seriousness with which we take these ideas. It is the fact that we care passionately about what these ideas mean and that we bother to argue about them and struggle with them. That is what brings us together as Americans. It is our conversation—and struggle—to determine what liberty, democracy, equality, property and prosperity mean to us. So long as that conversation remains rich, vibrant and real, and we continue to take it seriously, I believe that we will remain a great nation and a great place to live. This is because such a conversation lifts us up and makes us better people. And it gives us more refined and nuanced ideas about how to live well together. It is the American discovery process.

My final point is that people who disagree with one another politically often think that the other person is simply lacking with respect to one of these fundamental ideas or values. What the disagreement usually signifies, however, is that the two disputants either look at the trade-off among these ideas differently or interpret them in very different ways. To recognize this, to be tolerant of it and to learn from the interaction is <u>not</u> to say that some approaches and perspectives aren't superior to others. I do believe that there are some right and wrong answers here. But recognizing that the source of our passionate differences may reside in different interpretations of fundamental values—rather than a lack of values—can help in understanding and learning from one another and in deepening the conversation.

In sum: when you hear political arguments, it is important for you:

(1) to recognize to which of these fundamental ideas or values the speaker is appealing;

(2) to think about how the speaker is interpreting that idea or value;

(3) to think about which of these fundamental ideas or values she is ignoring; and

(4) to use these categories to stimulate your own thinking in finding the counterarguments to any given political position in order to deepen your own understanding.

Let's analyze some of these fundamental ideas and values to display the kinds of tensions and trade-offs among them to which I am referring.

TENSION #1: DEMOCRACY VERSUS THE OTHER FUNDAMENTAL POLITICAL VALUES

We hold the idea of democracy in the highest possible esteem. Indeed, it is almost as if we view anything that the majority votes upon as having not only a certain legitimacy but as having—of necessity—a degree of sacredness, wisdom and epistemological truth about it. But it just isn't so. The majority can believe in and vote for things that are patently unwise, inefficient, destructive and even downright stupid. While employing the majority vote as a means to settle important political questions—such as, say, who will be the President of the United States—is of fundamental importance, it in no way implies that what the majority decides will be good or fair or even makes any sense at all.

Bella: *But the President of the United States isn't elected by the majority of the citizenry; he or she is elected by a majority of the Electoral College, which is determined by individuals voting in each of the States and territories.*

Yes, but it is a little off the point. The point is that the results of democratic voting <u>can</u> be bad, <u>if</u> it leads to sufficiently egregious violations of some of the other fundamental values in which we also believe. For example, what if the majority vote that everyone must follow the same uniform religious beliefs and practices? Certainly, the majority of the Puritans of New England believed that everyone living in their communities should follow the Puritan's religious beliefs and practices. While they had come to America for religious freedom, it wasn't for religious freedom of the individual, it was for religious freedom for their community and part of that set of ideas was that everyone should worship in the same way—their way. Indeed, if you didn't worship in precisely the way they thought you should, they took away your property and sent you wandering into the woods—if you were lucky. They may even have accused you of being a witch and had you hung. There is clearly a strong tension between the idea of democratic rule and the idea of religious liberty of the individual. My point is simply that what the majority rules can be quite oppressive and violate fundamental liberties.

Let's take a more trivial example to highlight the point. What if, for example, the majority decides that I should sleep on one side of my pillow rather than the other? What's the problem with that? We would all agree that that is inappropriate intrusion upon my life choices, but why do we think that? What lines have we drawn, and based on what concept? Here we begin to get further into the idea of liberty. We clearly think that there are some things that a democratic majority has no business in addressing at all. In that sense, we can say that the idea of liberty is always at cross-purposes with the idea of democracy. To put it more gently, we could say that each complements and sets limits on the other. The one thing we can say is that they do not reside together without constant tension—and where we draw that line between the two is always of fundamental importance.

What if the democratic majority says that I should never leave the state of Virginia because they think I am a smart fellow and that by keeping me in Virginia everyone else there will be better off? Should the democratic majority be able to determine where I reside or whether I can travel from one state to another? What if the democratic majority says that I can never clean shirts for less than 10 cents per shirt, because—in their collective "wisdom"—they believe that that would create ruinous competition for others who clean shirts? Should the democratic majority be permitted to address that issue? Should the democratic majority be able to vote simply that they don't like a particular person—say, Rob Fisher—and decide—through this democratic process—to take away my home or to imprison me without a trial or simply because my views are unpopular? It should be rather clear that we don't always think the purely democratic answer is the right answer. Should the majority in a neighborhood be able to vote on banning anyone in the neighborhood from having a full-sized van—based on the fact that some people—perhaps a majority—don't like how such vans look? Should the majority in a neighborhood be able to say that people can't work on their own cars in their front yards, because the majority doesn't like looking at it? Should the majority in a neighborhood be able to say that people can't paint their houses purple, because the majority thinks it is a silly color? Should the majority in a neighborhood be able to say that no one can buy a house there who belongs to a particular race, because the majority there doesn't feel comfortable living near people of that race? I think we can agree that violations of liberty—such as racial segregation—are repugnant, even if a majority of people vote for it to be so. So let's be clear—democracy can lead to horrific oppression and unfairness. What if the majority thinks that Jewish people are engaged in dangerous conspiracies against the nation and should have their property taken away and be placed in internment camps? What if the democratic majority believes that a part of the population should be enslaved and the majority does, in fact, vote for this and implements it? What if the democratic majority thinks there should be no medical services provided for those over 70 years old, because they believe that is a waste of economic resources? Simply put, what if the majority votes for propositions that are horrible, cruel and patently unfair? We know that this is quite possible from both history and, of course, simple logic.

I am not making an argument against democracy as a form of government. As noted by Winston Churchill, democracy's advantage is that it is the "least worst" system of government—but that doesn't mean that democracies always favor what is fair or good or wise or even merely sensible. As noted above, there is an odd and unstated belief by many people that if a majority votes for a proposition then that somehow that confers some element of special worthiness to the proposition—that it is more likely that it is wise and based in truth. The fact that a majority of a population votes for something confers no wisdom, truth or heightened epistemological status on it whatsoever; it just means that more than half the people—at a given point in time—thought it should be so. The majority of a population can be quite ignorant and have its views based firmly in falsehood. There is no question about that. The majority of the voting population of the states in the pre-civil war American south certainly believed that the institution of slavery should be preserved, and there was nothing fair about that.

Notice that the Constitution of the United States did <u>not</u> establish a country that was intended to be democratic with respect to all decisions. Indeed, it was precisely a recognition of the potential flaws in democracy that led the Founding Fathers to agree upon a Constitution that <u>limits</u> the Federal Government only to the tasks listed in the document. In addition, and more importantly, the Bill of Rights—the first ten amendments to the Constitution—are designed to protect individual freedoms by specifically limiting government in regard to interfering with the exercise of those freedoms. For example, according to the First Amendment to the Constitution, the federal government may <u>not</u> pass any law that impinges on the freedom of the press. Now, if you think about it—it is perfectly <u>un</u>democratic to pronounce that certain types of laws <u>cannot</u> be passed; indeed, you are specifically binding future majorities as to what they can and cannot do. The Bill of Rights is there to protect our liberties <u>from</u> democracy when democracy might be otherwise inclined to overreach.

Just as there are no guarantees that a majority will vote wisely with respect to liberty or fairness, there is also no guarantee that it will do so with respect to policies that would ensure economic prosperity. For example, as we saw in an earlier chapter, prices and profits are key signals that inform private decision makers in the economy about what to produce and how much of it to produce in order to efficiently meet the needs of those willing to pay for goods and services. In contrast, there can be no doubt that if a government decides to strictly control all prices and profits in accordance with what the bureaucrats deem "fair"—as opposed to market signals—the economic system would not perform well and the average level of economic prosperity for citizens would decreased dramatically. The fact that such an approach harms economic prosperity does not mean a majority of citizens might not vote for it, or vote to place someone in office who would take such an approach. There is nothing about the fact that the majority of the population votes for a particular approach to the economy that would suggest that that approach will necessarily be efficient or wise.

TENSION #2: EQUALITY VERSUS THE OTHER FUNDAMENTAL POLITICAL VALUES

Someone who thinks we should all be treated as equals is called an "egalitarian." A radical egalitarian might believe that we should all have precisely the same economic and social benefits from being a citizen. She might argue: "Wouldn't the world be a better place if we all received the same benefits from the economy as one another? And wouldn't that be the fair outcome? We are all born into this world equal as well as equally helpless. Isn't everything that we accomplish in life really ultimately attributable to what others have invested in us at some stage of our development? Why should some ever get more than others?" That's the voice of the radical egalitarian. But most of us share a sense of the importance of equality. Basically, there are four important and very different ideas on the nature of equality. These include:

(1) Equality of outcome;
(2) Equality of opportunity; and
(3) Social equality.
(4) Equality before the law;

EQUALITY OF OUTCOME

Let's look at the first one first—equality of outcome. In the economic realm, this might manifest itself as the idea that we should all be paid exactly the same. Let's say the average income per year for a person in the US is $26,000. In that case, the notion would be that everyone should receive that same $26,000 per year.

Bella: *But would that really work?*

No, it wouldn't. As discussed in an earlier chapter, if we were all paid the same, then there would be too many people applying for the pleasant jobs and not enough people applying for the unpleasant or challenging jobs. Unpleasant jobs simply would not get done, and they may be quite important. Also, who would bother to study hard—and invest in education—to prepare for and obtain jobs that require knowledge from years of study—if everyone got paid the same? We would end up with far too few surgeons. The irony is that equality of outcome would be bad for everyone, as everyone—while perhaps equal in terms of benefits—would live in a society where everyone was impoverished and without fundamental goods and services.

In sum, this notion of equality—that is, equality of outcome—is completely inconsistent with a well-functioning economy. If we are to reward those who are extra productive and who work extra hard, we <u>must</u> pay them more than others who do not make as high a contribution. Otherwise, in many cases, the extra effort and beneficial contributions to the economy will not be forthcoming. That is human nature. Some communist societies have been based on this idea of equality, and while it might be a good way to divide up a cake at a birthday party, with the same size slice for everyone, as we have noted above, it doesn't provide a basis for the economic activity of a nation.

Even from a radical egalitarian point of view, equality of outcome doesn't work; it doesn't take into account the fact that people may have very different needs. For example, a young child with a learning disability should have <u>extra</u> resources devoted to her education over and above someone who doesn't need as much help. Even the communist Karl Marx rejected this shallow notion of equality. His view was "To each according to his <u>need</u>; from each according to his ability"—and we could count that as yet another vision of equality. If you think about it, it is a lovely sentiment, and certainly the way that resources should be allocated within a loving family. The problem with applying it to an economy as a whole is that—like the critique of equality of outcome that we noted above—it doesn't reward individuals for their full contribution to the economy and thus discourages investment in education and training, hard work, innovation, and taking on difficult tasks—all of which are necessary for a healthy economy and to produce the prosperity that we all want. It's like the fable of the ants and the grasshopper. The ants work hard all summer to prepare for the hardships of winter and store away food. In contrast, the grasshopper plays all summer, and when the winter comes has stored no food with which to endure it. If the ants allow the grasshopper in to share their food, the problem is that too many may want to act like the grasshopper and there won't be enough food for anyone.

Bella: *I suppose the grasshopper can earn his keep by playing his fiddle.*

Yes, well then, she better be good at it.

EQUALITY OF OPPORTUNITY

A second notion of equality is equality of opportunity. Equality of opportunity is very different from equality of outcome—indeed, it may be thought of as its opposite. With equality of opportunity, different outcomes are not only permitted, but embraced. The operative metaphor here is that of a footrace. The idea of equality of opportunity is to make sure the race is fair and that we all get to start the race at the same starting line. Thus, the idea here is <u>not</u> that we all get the same benefits, but rather that we all have the same opportunities to learn, to show what we can do, and to compete.

The problem with equality of opportunity is that it is impossible to fully implement in a free society where families make their own choices; thus, we face yet another trade-off and tension among fundamental goals. Some families are more oriented to education than others. Some choose to buy more books for their children than others. Some choose to allocate more of their income to specialized training for their children in, say, piano or ballet or ice skating. Some families have vastly more money to spend on such investments in their children than others. And some families have vastly more wealth to leave to the next generation than others. We are all born into different families, and that—in-and-of-itself—ensures that there will never be equality of opportunity. So there is a tension between liberty and equality of opportunity.

Also, we all begin life with different natural gifts. Each of us is more naturally gifted at some activities than others. Some of us are quick at math and for others it is a struggle, and for yet others they may find that they are slow at learning one aspect of mathematics and yet brilliant at other aspects. Some of us can run faster than others, and are more coordinated, no matter how hard we work at improving athletic skills. Some of us can remember facts really easily and for others that is more challenging. Some of us can read other people's emotions better than other people can. Some of us are better at making jokes and entertaining people than are others. Some of us are more physically attractive than others, and this may advantage them in various profound ways in life. So the starting line is not the same for all of us.

All that being said, equality of opportunity is a highly laudable goal, and a goal that society can make great progress in without foregoing fundamental liberties. For example, as a society, we can, at least, try to level up the playing field a bit by making sure every person can get an education, even if their family is too poor to afford it. This is why the government provides free public education, and makes it a law that every child must receive an education in some form. The government can also provide excellent police protection in all neighborhoods, including poor neighborhoods, which gives everyone in the society a chance to have physical security even if they can't afford to live in a wealthy neighborhood with a bigger tax base. Being able to walk to work or school without being harmed is an important aspect of equality of opportunity. We can also make sure that we are a society that doesn't discriminate on the basis of race or sex or any other irrelevant category.

EQUALITY BEFORE THE LAW

Our third type of equality is equality before the law. This is perhaps the most fundamentally important type of equality, in that we are all afforded equal protection under the law. That is, (1) the law applies equally to everyone; (2) each person is treated the same under the law; and (3) the law's processes and protections are open to all in an equal manner. In truth, there is not a lot to debate here, or at least there should not be. Every decent society should have equal protection under the law and it is enshrined in the US Constitution. What equal protection under the law means can best be seen by contemplating situations that violate the principle. For example, in the normal course of events, if one person attacks another they are arrested and prosecuted under the law for assault. But now let's suppose they were not prosecuted because the prosecutors don't like the people who were attacked. That would be a failure of equal protection under the law.

SOCIAL EQUALITY

To complete our discussion of different types of equality, it is worth mentioning social equality. In our social and daily interactions with others, do we treat others as equals and as having the same full dignity that we consider ourselves entitled to? Throughout history, the concept has flourished in many societies that some people are simply more important than others. It seems to be a part of human nature to define and categorize some subset of humanity as an elite group that is to be accorded some special kind of treatment and acknowledgment. Now, of course, that is fine when it is earned. For example, if troops are coming back from a war, it is perfectly appropriate to celebrate them for their contributions to our peace and prosperity and to accord them special acknowledgment. Acknowledging accomplishment and celebrating our societies healthy values is great. But many people do seem to think they are intrinsically better than others, when they have done nothing to earn such regard, and accordingly treat others as social inferiors. Personally, I do not respect such behavior. I admire the Australian practice in this regard. They call it "cutting down tall poppies."

Bella: *Did you say they cut down tall PUPPIES?!? Those Aussies are barbarians!*

That's poppies, not puppies. Among other things, the practice there is to call everyone by their first names, even if it is a bit daring to do so, just so they are fully aware that we are all equals here, regardless of formal rank. While I don't recommend that you necessarily adopt this practice—that is, there are times when using formal titles is a proper courtesy—I must say that I like the sentiment behind it.

Bella: *Is that why you always call me by my first name?*

What is your last name, anyway?

Bella: *Dog.*

TENSION #3: LIBERTY VERSUS THE OTHER FUNDAMENTAL VALUES

The school of thought that puts the most emphasis on liberty is the "libertarians". Because their viewpoint is relatively pure, a description of libertarianism will give a good sense of the tensions between liberty and the other fundamental political values. Libertarians emphasize liberty as the prime value, pretty much at the expense of almost any of the other fundamental political values—although more moderate libertarians will acknowledge some trade-offs there. The libertarian notion of social justice is, roughly, "To each according to what they can get within a set of minimally constraining rules." Libertarians emphasize individual choice. They believe that the scope for voluntary action for individuals should be maximized. They argue that this is best done by allowing the <u>full</u> and free market reign over the allocation of resources. The line of argument follows Pareto (whom we discussed in previous chapters). If people freely choose to make a trade with one another then, as long as coercion is not involved, we can and should presume that neither party would have made the trade unless they felt, in some broad sense, to be made better off by doing so. Presuming no third party's property rights are infringed by a particular trade, it follows that any hindrance or impediment to trade damages those parties who would like to have engaged in that trade. Any such impediment is, therefore, according to the libertarians, an infringement upon their property rights and their freedom. Thus, absolute freedom of trade between any persons of anything they want to trade at anytime is placed as the ideal of liberty.

Some fairly radical propositions follow. For example, it follows that no government agency should intervene in industrial relations between managers of a business and the workers in terms of setting wages. If a worker freely agrees to exchange his or her labor time for wages from an employer at an agreed upon rate, why should it be any business of any third party, including the government? From the libertarian point of view, a minimum wage set by the government is an infringement on liberty—the liberty of the worker to choose to work at a lower wage. (The worker's incentive to accept a wage lower than the minimum wage would be that she wouldn't otherwise get the job—but the libertarian's point is that it should be her choice, not the government's choice.) In the libertarian view, people should be free to choose on how to dispose of themselves, their own time, and their resources as long as it does not interfere with the property rights of others. It also follows from the libertarian vision that compulsory union membership for workers is an infringement upon their freedom.

The libertarian emphasis on property derives from the English tradition of John Locke. Suppose that there is a society on an island. Around the island are many shells, plenty for everyone. One individual selects a common shell and spends several free hours carving it into a pleasant small statue. The other islanders decide they like the statue. Together, they vote to take it away from the individual who carved it. The Lockean tradition would label this as theft. Locke would have argued on the following basis. If individuals are to be considered free in any sense then they must be allowed control over their own person. Their body must be considered their own to allocate as they please. This insight provides the moral foundation for property. If an individual's time is to be considered as their own then the results of their allocation of that time must also be considered their own. If this is not the case then their time is not their own and they are not free. Personal freedom demands that if we spend time carving a shell into a statue then that statue is our property. Locke tempers the argument with the condition that there must be sufficient resources for others to do the same. In terms of the tale, there must be plenty of other shells available so that others have access as well. If there had been only one shell available then the individual would not have had a right to it even if she did combine it with her free labor time.

Another example that might be found among libertarians in colder climates is that of the snowy parking lot. Suppose there is an empty parking lot except for a thick layer of snow. Assume that there are several shovels readily available. One individual spends several hours clearing a space for her car. Just as she finishes someone else drives up and parks in the spot. Locke would argue that to not consider the parking spot the property of the initial snow shoveler would be a violation of freedom since there are plenty of other spots that the other person could choose to clear. Once you have accepted the above line of argument the libertarian goes on to declare that taxation is the moral equivalent of theft. If freedom is to be respected then the proceeds of our labor processes must be considered as property. It follows that every portion of those proceeds must be considered to be the property of the individual. If to take 100 percent of the proceeds is theft, then to take even 1 percent of the proceeds is theft as well. Taxation is nothing other than the removal of a portion of the proceeds of our labor time through a coercive mechanism. (It is coercive because if you do not pay your taxes you will incur penalties and even physical detention.) The fact that people vote for taxation doesn't change its theft-like character just as the fact that the islanders may vote to take away the carved shell statue does not mean that such an act is not theft. Here we again see the tension between democracy and liberty.

On these grounds a few radical libertarians move to the anarchistic position that there should be no state whatsoever. More moderate libertarians consider government a necessary evil that should be kept as small as possible because its method of allocating resources is based on coercion. Government activity involves forcefully removing income from the private sector and using it for purposes other than those to which it would have been directed. The libertarians argue for a minimal state that would allow the free market its fullest possible reign. Libertarians prefer using "dollar votes" in the market place to allocate resources as opposed to using the political sector.

Milton Friedman, a well-known American economist, was once asked by Australian economist Rod Maddock if allocating resources through the political sector wasn't more fair since in the economic sector there is great inequality in terms of "dollar votes" whereas in the political sector each person receives one vote. Friedman acknowledged the element of inequality but countered that the advantage of "dollar votes" was that the consumer always got what he "voted for" in the sense of receiving his chosen purchase whereas in the political sector the voter only got what the 51 percent or more happened to agree upon. There is a tension between the libertarian notion of justice and any notion of justice which implies intervention into the market place.

One could write numerous books about the tensions among the various political values with which I opened this chapter, but I think you get the idea. Finding our way among the tradeoffs inherent in these values is what the political discovery process is all about. In later chapters, we will turn to that discovery process.

Suggested Readings

- Chapters 1, 2 and 3 of Robert Nozick Anarchy, State and Utopia (Basic Books, Inc., 1974) at pages 3 to 53.
- Arthur M. Okun Equality and Efficiency: The Big Tradeoff (The Brookings Institution, 1975).
- Chapters 1 and 2 of Richard A. Epstein's Takings: Private Property and the Power of Eminent Domain (Harvard University Press, 1985) at pages 3 to 18.

16

NO SUCH THING AS "RACE"

No one has been barred on account of his race from fighting or dying for America—there are not "white" or "colored" signs on the foxholes or graveyards of battle.

JOHN F. KENNEDY

There is not a black America and white America and Latino America and Asian America—there's the United States of America.

BARACK OBAMA

WHAT IS RACISM?

Racism is a deeply flawed mode of interpreting the world that is disconnected from reality. A racist is a person who believes two things: (1) that there are certain groupings of people within society—known as "races"—that are biologically determined, and (2) that some of these races are "superior" to others. Racists apply these beliefs by categorizing people in terms of race and then discriminating among them on that basis. In general, racism manifests itself when some individuals are treated unfairly due to the fact that they are perceived to be of a certain race. Racists are often so deeply convinced of the truth of their perspective that they believe they "see" it confirmed in the world around them. They simply ignore any aspects of reality that might challenge and contradict their views. Instead, they focus selectively and exclusively on aspects of reality that appear to them to be consistent with their warped vision. For example, they will observe someone that they believe to be of a certain race doing a bad thing, and they will say "See, that proves that I am right that that group is inferior." They ignore the fact that any randomly selected group of people will contain some subset that does bad things. What the racist "observes" doesn't demonstrate or confirm his false beliefs—but he thinks it does. He takes it as evidence of the "real" world that others are simply ignoring, and this conviction feeds into his sense of superiority.

    Bella: *Why do people have racist views?*

The answer to that lies in both psychology and history. I believe racist views are held because they make people feel good about who they are, at the expense of someone else. Historically, such ideas have also been used and promulgated by those who are trying to support some unfair or oppressive economic or political regime, or some unfair usurpation from others, or to be able to point to others who are "different" as the cause of various troubles. For example, people of European descent might have felt better about taking the land of American Indians, and breaking treaties with them, when they combined those actions with racist arguments that these native peoples were inferior to them. Racists like to feel like they are better than others, and it is a particularly helpful viewpoint if it justifies in their own minds acts that might otherwise be viewed as unfair.

RACE IS A SOCIAL CONSTRUCT, NOT A BIOLOGICAL REALITY

As noted above, at the very heart of racism is the assertion that some races are superior to others. The question of whether one race is superior to another embodies a number of specious premises. Among the false premises is the notion that race exists from a biological perspective. In fact, from a biological perspective, there is no such thing as race. That is, it not a coherent concept from a biological perspective. "Race" is a socially constructed "reality." From a biological point of view, it is clear that humans are all genetically extremely close to one another. To the extent there is genetic diversity, the most diversity is found <u>within</u> groups that have been labeled as belonging to particular "races". This strongly suggests that the manner in which society classifies people by race does <u>not</u> correspond to an underlying genetic reality. Indeed, the very idea of race is an historical accident—probably largely attributable to the manner in which the Europeans sailed to different far flung points on the planet, and noted that "the people seemed very different" and falsely concluded that they must be a different type or "race" of persons. In fact, what are thought of as "racial characteristics" are actually found in smooth variations—with a wide variety of blends of characteristics—among people around the planet. The notion that there are particular types that we may call races is an illusion.

Bella: *What do you mean that there is no such thing as race? If one looks around, it is pretty obvious that various people have differing skin colors. Isn't that a manifestation of race?*

It is true that different people have different colored skin. And it is also true that the color of your skin is largely determined by your genetic makeup. As we all know, our genetic code is like a map that structures our biological makeup. But for race to exist on a genetic level, there would have to be some special set of linkages within the genetic code that systematically brought together in the characteristics that we refer to as "racial." In fact, there are no such systematic linkages that bind these features together. As noted above, if you take a characteristic that we describe as racial—such as skin color—and look at people all over the planet, you find a smooth distribution of different colored skin through all variations and points in between, with no particular linkage to any other set of characteristics. Indeed, as also noted above, there is tremendous genetic diversity within groups that people would normally describe as belonging to a given race. At the same time, there are often strong genetic similarities across people who would be described as being of separate races. Thus, there is no biological coherence to the notion. Given that there is no such thing as race from a biological perspective, generalizations as to the "nature" of people, who are said to be of a particular race, are intellectually incoherent. Put simply, trying to understand and interpret the world in terms of race is an intellectual dead end.

Bella: *But aren't there associations between certain diseases and particular races? Isn't it true that you are more likely to get certain diseases, and not get others, if you are of a particular race? Doesn't that prove that race exists biologically?*

No, this does not prove that race exists biologically. Certainly, there may be statistical correlations between certain attributes that we describe as racial and certain diseases, and those statistical correlations can help health professionals and others in the fight against various diseases. For example, a person with lighter colored skin may be more likely to get skin cancer than one with darker skin. But a correlation between certain attributes that are sometimes described as racial—such as, say, skin color—does not imply that there is a coherent or stable linkage among the array of characteristics that are proclaimed as constituting a race. To be sure, each of us has a different genetic makeup, and that genetic makeup can affect the incidence of different diseases. This fact does not demonstrate a biological basis for race.

Let's take another example. Sickle cell anemia—a terrible disease—only occurs among people of African descent. One might therefore argue that the possibility of getting this disease is a "racial" characteristic. But the real story is different. In sub-Saharan Africa, there was a genetic change that made people more resistant to malaria. This led to a much higher survival rate—over time—of those with this gene. Unfortunately, this same genetic change also increased the likelihood of sickle cell anemia. Thus, those two characteristics are genetically linked and are only found in descendents of people from sub-Saharan Africa. Thus, if you are one of these people, you are both less likely to get malaria and more likely to get sickle cell anemia. But this does not indicate the existence of "race" per se, but simply of this particular genetic change. For the concept of race to be coherent from a biological perspective it would entail showing some genetic linkage among the many characteristics that are attributed to "race". There are no such linkages. In sum, genetics is important, and the genetic code certainly has a lot to do with our characteristics. But the concept of race is not evidenced within that code.

Bella: *I am a little suspicious of this. How do I know you aren't some kook with way-out views on this? Isn't this just semantics?*

No, it's not just semantics. The concept of race turns out to be a scientific dead-end; that is, it is not a coherent way to organize what we know about the genetic code. That is a fancy way of saying that race doesn't really exist except in some of our imaginations. And if you won't believe me, and you want authority, I'll give you the Encyclopedia Britannica (2007). Here's how they put it:

> Although most people continue to think of races as physically distinct populations, scientific advances in the 20th century have shown that human physical variations do not fit a "racial" model. There are no genes that can identify distinct groups that accord with the conventional race categories. ... Because of the overlapping of traits that bear no relationship to one another (such as skin colour and hair texture) and the inability of scientists to cluster peoples into discrete racial packages, modern researchers argue that the concept of race has no biological validity.[52]

Bella: *Wait a second. Aren't you citing authority there? I thought we weren't supposed to trust authority.*

Reading and citation to authorities is fine. My message in this book is <u>not</u> to not ever trust authority, but rather to question it and think it through for yourself. Besides—I'll use any cheap trick in the name and pursuit of truth.

Bella: *So if the idea of race is a mere social construct, should we simply ignore it in all things?*

THE IMPORTANCE OF RACE

It would be lovely to have a world in which we were completely blind to race, and that is certainly the right approach in your personal and professional dealings with all people. Yet, we find ourselves in a world where we cannot ignore race altogether simply because people <u>do</u> identify themselves and others in terms of race. The concept of race is ingrained in people from their childhood (although different countries and cultures have very different notions of race and ethnicity.) Moreover, people find some benefit and solidarity in such identification. For example, if a person belongs to a group that has been oppressed because of their perceived race, she may well feel some special sense of identification with others who have been similarly oppressed. In fact, she may well embrace the idea of race of something that supports her common cause with these other people against oppression. People often think of themselves as being "white" or "black" or "African-American" or "Hispanic" or "Native American" and so forth.

Bella: *So race really is important?*

Oh yes. As a country, we have had a history in which racial concepts have often been the cause of horrific wrongs. That history is real and the links of solidarity forged by those experiences are real as well. It is important to be aware of how people feel about race and racial issues, how their sense of identity is affected by it and, indeed, what their self-identity is. For example, people with different racial identities may interpret comments you make very differently, especially if they perceive it to be in the context of race. One needs to be aware of racial identities not only to avoid being misunderstood, but also to grasp fully what others are saying. Thus, it is unwise to ignore the idea of race altogether.

Bella: *But this leaves us all in this uncomfortable spot, where we feel we should be blind to race on the one hand and yet sensitive to it on the other.*

This can be a tricky balancing act. The key to success in it is to treat each and every human being as the unique person that they are, never to pre-judge them, and yet be ever ready to comprehend where they are coming from. In sum, it is of fundamental importance that you look at each person as an individual.

Bella: *Why is that?*

First, it is the truth. Every human being is unique. Second, you should do it is out of fairness. It is not right to pre-judge an individual based on any superficial set of characteristics that they might share in part with others. Third, you should do it out of a concern for efficiency. If you do not judge people as individuals, you will fail in facilitating the process by which those individuals may make their best contributions to the world around them. Fourth, you should do it for yourself. If you do not treat others as individuals, you will fail to connect with people. As a result, you will be spiritually and emotionally impoverished. Indeed, you will never fulfill your full potential in this world.

Suggested Readings and Viewings

- DVD Video: BBC's <u>The Incredible Human Journey</u>, presented by Dr. Alice Roberts and described as "Follow in the footsteps of our ancestors and discover how the first humans became you"
- "Race" Encyclopedia Britannica (2007) Volume 18 at pages 844 to 854 (a brilliant essay on the concept of race)

17

A COUNTRY FOUNDED ON EPISTEMOLOGY

Eleven score and fifteen years ago, our country began. It was the beginning of the American Dream. There were the slaves—still slaves. There were the Indians—-still Indians. There were the immigrants—still immigrants. There were the rich—still the rich. None Americans. Yet out of all this America began. It is the country of all countries. Its people are the people of all people. Why? Because of what it is made of. It is not made of documents. It is not made of land. It is made of people and our Dream. Therefore we are America.

SPEECH ON 4 JULY 2011
SAMMY FISHER, AGE 9

I like that speech by my daughter Sammy—which she just decided to jot down one day in anticipation of the celebration of the birthday of the United States. She captures poetically the notion of the American "melting pot" and American exceptionalism. The idea is that the United States has something special about it due to the history of the manner in which so many people were brought together to try to make something new and different. As the speech implies, it certainly wasn't due to all the people being the same. And it wasn't due to a lack of suffering, conflict or unfairness. There has been plenty of that. The speech points to the people and their aspirations—having come together as a kind of unity despite their many deep differences—as the very essence of America.

Bella: *E Pluribus Unum—Out of the Many, One. So how did they do that? Is America special? If so, what is it that makes it special?*

The Founding Fathers of the United States—as part of the Enlightenment—had an understanding of how knowledge grows, and they looked at society itself as a rational mechanism for the exploration and pursuit of happiness. I believe that the Constitution and the other institutions of the United States were founded on the idea of a rational journey of discovery—a journey that would bring our diverse peoples together as one. The Founding Fathers created the framework for our collective rational discourse. How else to pull together the diverse strands making up our nation?

Politics, law and government are about <u>collective</u> choice. Collectively, how do we choose our leaders? Collectively, how do we choose to interpret the concept of liberty? Collectively, how do we determine who owns what, and who gets what? How do we secure, as a People, peace, prosperity and the public good? Indeed, what is the "public good"? As we will see in later chapters, static or formal ways of thinking about collective choice—such as through voting theory—fail to capture and explain what it means to engage in actual politics, law, governance and public policy. In this chapter, I will argue that the proper way to understand these aspects of collective choice are as rational, dynamic explorations that are, or at least should be, driven by a logic of discovery. I also argue that the Founding Fathers understood this and created institutions that would promote such a collective, rational exploration. And that the most important role of voting is in the way in which it stimulates and promotes this rational exploration. Alexander Hamilton put the question as follows:

> It has been frequently remarked that it seems to have been reserved to the people of this country, by their conduct and example, to decide the important question, whether

societies of men are really capable or not of establishing good government from reflection and choice, or whether they are forever destined to depend for their political constitutions on accident and force.[53]

Note that his focus here is <u>not</u> on majority rule <u>per se</u>, but whether a people can establish "good government" from "reflection and choice" and in a manner that is not dependent upon "accident and force." Thus, the goal is not majority rule <u>per se</u>, but rather to see if people can use a representative form of government to achieve <u>good</u> government based on rational reflection.

Bella: *That <u>is</u> a challenge. That's why dogs just leave everything up to the alpha! None of this rational reflection stuff—too messy. How can a group of people be rational in their decision-making?*

The Founding Fathers recognized the problematic nature of majority rule. In Federalist Paper Number 10, James Madison wrote of the experience of the States that: "measures are too often decided, not according to the rules of justice and the rights of the minor party, but by the superior forces of an interested and overbearing majority." The Founding Fathers thought that direct democracy—that is, majority rule applied directly to the decisions of governance—was to be avoided. It was viewed as both unstable and unfair.

Hamilton wrote of the danger that had presented itself in the "petty republics of Greece and Italy" which had experienced a "perpetual vibration between the extremes of tyranny and anarchy." Madison identified the reason for this instability and unfairness was the predominance of what he called "factions" in political affairs. He stated: "By a faction I understand a number of citizens, whether amounting to a majority or minority of the whole, who are united and actuated by some common impulse of passion, or of interest, adverse to the rights of other citizens, or to the permanent and aggregate interests of the community."[54]

How this goal of good government was to be achieved was also well understood. The question was what representative institutions would render governmental processes both rational and stable. And, according to Hamilton, the "<u>science</u> of politics"—his words—provided the answer. In Federalist Paper Number 9, Hamilton wrote: "The science of politics ... like most other sciences, has received great improvement. The efficacy of various principles is now well understood, which were either not known at all, or imperfectly known to the ancients. The regular distribution of power into distinct departments; the introduction of legislative balances and checks; the institution of courts composed of judges holding their offices during good behavior; the representation of the people in the legislature by deputies of their own election: these are wholly new discoveries, or have made their principal progress towards perfection in modern times."

Thus, to facilitate the quest for good government, the Founding Fathers introduced (among other things): (1) the First Amendment; (2) Representative Democracy; (3) Bicameralism; (4) Separation of Powers; and (5) Federalism. When taken together, the uniting vision under all these institutions is to promote informed dialogue and experimentation. Indeed, it is a framework specifically designed to facilitate criticism and the growth of knowledge in our governance as a polity.

THE FIRST AMENDMENT

Congress shall make no law respecting an establishment of religion, or prohibiting the free exercise thereof; or abridging the freedom of speech, or of the press; or the right of the people peaceably to assemble, and to petition the Government for a redress of grievances.
First Amendment to the U.S. Constitution

Bella: *What is the First Amendment really about? It seems to throw together a number of important, but seemingly unrelated things.*

It says that people should be free to exercise their religious beliefs in whatever way they see fit, and that the government should not set up an official, government sponsored religion. It says the press should be free to write what they like. It says people should be free to say what they like—or at least that the government should not set up any law precluding them from doing so. It says that people should have a right to get together as long as they are peaceable about it—that is, not rioting or threatening physical harm to others. It says that the people should be able to complain to the government and ask the government to address problems.

Bella: *So why are all these important things lumped together in the First Amendment? What is this Amendment all about?*

What unifies this Amendment into a coherent whole is an <u>epistemological</u> vision—a vision of how a society best arrives at the truth, and ultimately at a better society. Indeed, just like this book, this Amendment is about criticism and the growth of knowledge. The Founding Fathers understood that knowledge does not derive from governmental or any other kind of authority. Rather, they saw that to arrive at the truth, society had to be free to argue—free to make bold conjectures, free to criticize those conjectures, free to improve upon those conjectures. If a government were to evolve in a manner such that it truly served the people—that is, if it was going to be "of the people, by the people, and for the people"—it would have to always stand subject to both the criticisms of the people and to their bold new ideas. The only way in which this is possible is, of course, to have freedom of speech.

Bella: *If any authority other than individual citizens themselves was to control speech, then there wouldn't be much criticism of that authority, would there? But what about the freedom to bark?*

You exercise that freedom quite well.

FREE SPEECH

Freedom of speech provides the ground in which conjectures can be freely formed and expressed, criticisms articulated, and responses to criticism proposed. If there is to be substantial progress in any field of thought, there must be such openness. Freedom of speech ensures this.

Bella: *But how does freedom of speech work? Won't there be chaos?*

No. The beauty of speech is that it will evoke speech. If wrongheaded views are promulgated, then others will come forth with criticism of those ideas. And yet others will step forward with new views that account for the best in what was in the previously expressed views.

Bella: *That seems kind of naïve. How do you know that the most sensible views will prevail? How do you know that some people, who are evil but very charismatic, will not lead the society to do terrible and wrong things—or, indeed, merely highly inefficient things? How do you stop the spread of ignorant and harmful viewpoints, such as those based on racism? You might just get a lot of barking!*

Many people share your fear. Indeed, I think the view that is implicit in your question is becoming the dominant view, and that we are moving toward losing this most precious of our freedoms. Many people think that freedom of speech doesn't work and that people need the experts to tell them what to think within an environment where views are controlled. For many people, this ties back to their dogmatic epistemological beliefs. Truth is provenance of experts, who will tell the rest of us what to think.

Recently in the US there has been an anti-tax movement known as the Tea Party. They represent a substantial swath of the population. There were some who suggested that the media was irresponsible to be reporting on the views of those in the Tea Party. Clearly, someone who holds this viewpoint does not have a great deal of confidence in the American population generally to sort through differing views on their own. Rather, they prefer that an elite in the media make the decisions as to what kind of views should be presented. Such control by the elites is apt to take the nation far away from a healthy and robust democratic discourse. I trust the people far more than I trust the media.

Bella: *Personally, I always find it kind of insulting when politicians express the view that there needs to be controls on what the masses of the population are exposed to. I consider myself to be among these masses and don't really think I need anybody filtering the ideas to which I am exposed.*

But notice the instinct of such politicians: they see a need for control if society is to reach the right answers. They do not believe in the wild and free interplay of ideas to take us to a better place. The other freedoms protected by the First Amendment include press, assembly, religion and petition.

FREEDOM OF THE PRESS

Freedom of the press goes hand-in-hand with freedom of speech, of course. In its essence, it is the freedom to broadcast speech in some form. With the Internet, this freedom is finding a more powerful outlet than ever before.

Bella: *I love the way that people are using the Internet to organize themselves into groups with common sets of interests, informing one another, challenging authority, and disintermediating the media and the experts. It's the First Amendment to its core.*

FREEDOM OF ASSEMBLY

Freedom of assembly is also closely related, of course. The people you hang out with affect your views. In interaction with these others, you develop and refine your views. Assembly makes your views more powerful and more likely to be heard. Assembly also gives notice to others that there is a grouping of people with particular views. Assembly provides a platform for a group to refine its viewpoint through conjectures, criticism, response to criticism and further refinement. This can rapidly translate into political power.

Bella: *Hey, the pack matters.*

And that is precisely why totalitarian governments tend to ban or strictly control assembly; it constitutes an intrinsic challenge to their regime.

FREEDOM OF RELIGION

According to the First Amendment, the government should not be in the business of establishing a religion. In other words, there is not to be any official religion of the country. Moreover, the Amendment indicates that the government shall also not interfere with people's freedom to exercise their religious beliefs. While this is a fundamentally important freedom in and of itself, it also has an important epistemological role. If the government is free to try to influence or preclude the exercise of religious beliefs, it is deep into the business of telling people what they are supposed to think.

Bella: *This kind of puts the cart before the horse, since in a democracy it is the people who are supposed to tell the government what to think.*

Religion fundamentally shapes who we are and what we think about many topics. Keeping this shaping function outside the halls of government is also a kind of check on governmental excess. It puts people in the healthy habit of not always looking to the government for the answer to every question. Keeping religion separate from the government creates and maintains a separate and distinctly non-governmental type of authority from which healthy criticism of government is apt to emerge on a regular basis.

Bella: *Hence, those who want to see all the answers emanating from the government tend to be against religion.*

FREEDOM TO PETITION THE GOVERNMENT

The freedom to petition the government for the redress of grievances is the very epitome of criticism. If the citizenry doesn't like something—say, the current level of taxation—they are free to let the government know.

Bella: *Seems like a good idea.*

Not to King George III. Put simply, this is the freedom to criticize the government directly—that is, to tell it what you don't like and how that criticism might be addressed.

REPRESENTATIVE DEMOCRACY

In general, it is hard to have a coherent conversation among a very large number of people. Admittedly, this is a rather obvious truth. It is also an important one. It is even more difficult to have a rich discourse about challenging topics if those many people are scattered far and wide. Thus, in order to facilitate a democracy capable of a sophisticated exploration of ideas, the Founding Fathers set up a representative democracy. Instead of voting directly on the issues of the day, in a representative democracy the people elect representatives, whose job it is to go to the capital and to have those exploratory and innovative conversations with his or her other similarly elected colleagues and to vote on the issues and pass laws and thereby govern the country. The advantage of a representative democracy is that the representatives can learn from one another, develop alternative conjectures about the best laws, criticize one another's ideas, and make wise compromises in a way that is not possible for the people as a whole to do directly. They can also take their new-found knowledge back to the people and facilitate further conversation with those whom they represent.

The point to keep in mind about representative government is that it purposely foregoes direct voting on issues by the people. The clear purpose of this is so that the representatives can do something more than simply reflect the current views of the population in their district. Rather, the purpose, as I have indicated above, is to facilitate a richer discussion of policy purposes, trade-offs and compromises under a (somewhat) more manageable number of people. That is, it more directly facilitates a rich discourse of conjectures and criticism. We certainly have the technology today to have everyone in the country vote on just about every political question. We will see in later chapters why this is not likely to result in coherent outcomes.

BICAMERALISM

The curious fact is that the US Congress has <u>two</u> legislative bodies within it—the House and the Senate. Of course, for a bill to become law, it must be passed in both the House and the Senate as well as signed by the President of the United States.

   Bella: *Wouldn't one legislative body be enough?*

   The reason we have two legislative bodies is to make sure that certain kinds of conversations occur and certain voices are represented, as we will see below. The two bodies are quite different. The House is elected every two years. As a result, every single House member stands for re-election every two years. Thus, in any given two year period there is, at least, the theoretical possibility that we could get a completely new House of Representatives. This makes the representatives more directly responsive to changes in the mood of the people in their respective districts than they might be otherwise. As a result, the sometimes rapidly changing moods of the people tend to be reflected in the conversations that the representatives have with one another and in their debates. In addition, the number of House representatives from any given state reflects the number of people in that state. That is, states with higher populations receive greater representations that those in states with a lower population. As a consequence, the House tends to reflect the population trends of the country. If lots of people live in New York, then we will end up having lots of representatives from New York in the House, and they will have a bigger influence than the representative from a state with a smaller population, simply because they are outnumbered when it comes to voting on legislation.

   In contrast, Senators stand for re-election only once every six years, and in any given election year, only about 1/3 of the Senate is up for re-election. As a result, from a theoretical perspective, the most the Senate could turn over in any given year is 1/3 of its members. Also, it is important to note that Senatorial positions are not awarded to states on the basis of population; instead, each state simply gets two senators. As a result, states with very small populations have a much stronger representation in the Senate then they do in the House.

The structure of the Senate ensures that a different set of voices and interests are reflected in deliberations than in the House. First, there is an argument that the Senate ensures a longer term view of the country's welfare is taken into consideration. There is something to this argument. Since a senator has six years after being elected before she has to face the people again, she can take the longer view, and ignore popular sentiment if she thinks it is temporary and irrational. Second, this longer duration in office (without facing re-election) may facilitate Senators in being able to reach compromises with fellow senators since the focus is taken off the short-term. When a senator is up for re-election, she will have a record of almost six years she can point at to give the citizens in her state a sense of her overall performance. Third, the fact that there are two senators per states (as opposed to apportionment by population) means that the voice of the kind of people who live in less populated states (for example, those with a rural or regional perspective) are heard.

Thus, the requirement that a bill has to be passed by both of the legislative bodies in Congress before it becomes law ensures that a lot of different kinds of voices are heard. Moreover, the fact that the House and the Senate ultimately have to pass the same bill often leads to further discussion and negotiation between the two legislative bodies. While all of this can make it difficult to pass legislation, it does ensure that many different kinds of voices are heard in the process and that, therefore, many different kinds of concerns and critiques are considered. It terms of generating the right kinds of criticisms of potential legislation that should be thought about before passing a law, it is a brilliant system. This may explain why it has lasted so long, and how it has been capable of adjusting to the needs of the country given a rapidly changing world.

SEPARATION OF POWERS

The Founding Fathers distrusted absolute political power. With absolute power, one is not required to take into account anyone else's conjectures about the world. With absolute power, one does not have to pay attention to anyone's criticisms. If you have absolute power, there is no need for dialogue or the exploration of ideas. The Founding Fathers wanted a republic driven by ideas—the best ideas. They wanted a republic that would continue to grow and deepen in knowledge. They accomplished this by breaking up the powers of the federal government into different branches and placing checks on power. The Congress was to legislate, the Judicial branch was to adjudicate cases and controversies and thereby interpret the law, and the Executive branch under the President was to implement the law.

THE CHECKS AND BALANCES ON CONGRESSIONAL POWER

The power of the Congress is cabined. To wit:
- While the Congress can pass bills, they only became law when the President signs them, or if they override his or her veto with a supermajority of 2/3rds in both the House and the Senate.
- The laws are not implemented by the Congress, but rather by the executive branch of the government. Thus, the Congress must clearly articulate its ideas in the law, since they are not going to be the one's executing it.
- The laws are not interpreted by the Congress. This, of course, is done by the courts.
- And Congress has no army. It is the executive that controls the military.

THE CHECKS AND BALANCES ON EXECUTIVE POWER

The power of the Presidency is cabined. To wit:
- While the President controls the military and executes the laws, it is the Congress that passes the laws and, as significantly, controls the purse strings. That is, budgets come through Congress. Indeed, the Congress could conceivably leave the President with no funding to even pay for staff to assist him.
- As noted above, Congress can override a Presidential veto.
- Congress has the power to investigate and render its investigations public.

- Congress can impeach the President of the United States (among others), and ultimately boot him or her out of office.
- The Courts have the power to declare Presidential actions as unconstitutional.
- Through litigation, the Courts have the power to review the decisions of the executive branch to ensure that they are lawful.

THE CHECKS AND BALANCES ON JUDICIAL POWER

The power of the Courts is cabined. To wit:
- The Courts do not pass the laws.
- The Courts do not execute the laws.
- The Courts have no army.
- The Congress can pass laws that shape the exercise of judicial power.

There is a great deal that can be said on this topic. My focus here is a simple one. The brilliance of the separation of powers is the manner in which it facilitates a rich and democratic discourse on social policy. It forces each of the branches to clearly articulate not only what it is doing, but why it is doing it. In contrast, imagine if you had a unitary government with the same people passing laws, interpreting laws and executing laws. They would be very tempted to be arbitrary in their application of power. But to maintain their legitimacy, the branches are forced to constantly look over their shoulder, and defend their actions with words that must be seen as in accord with their powers.

If it is to exercise its power, the legislature has an incentive to be clear in the laws it passes—because someone else will be executing them and someone else will be interpreting them. The President must be seen as executing the laws, and therefore must explain his or her actions if he or she is to maintain legitimacy. And if the courts are not to be ignored, they much articulate their reasoning in a compelling enough manner. If they did not, they run the danger of losing legitimacy and being ignored.

This interaction leads to constant learning. Laws are passed. Laws are operationalized. Laws are challenged. Laws are interpreted. Laws are changed in light of what has been learned. This is nothing other than conjectures, criticism and the growth of knowledge in yet another form. The separation of powers forces the federal government into a conversation with itself—that is, among the branches. In doing so, it opens it up the federal government to a richer democratic discourse with the People.

FEDERALISM

The United States has not only a federal government, but also state governments and local governments, such as towns and counties. Under the US Constitution, the federal government is a limited government; it is limited to the governmental powers outlined in the Constitution. Other powers are left to the people and the states. Much of the governance of the US—and with respect to very important issues—occurs at the state and local level as opposed to the federal level. Among other things, states and localities are deeply involved in public education, roads, licensing of professionals, police work, criminal prosecution, parks, zoning, environmental protection, the provision of courts of general jurisdiction and so on.

The Founding Fathers had two epistemological reasons why it was of crucial importance to have a large swath of governmental powers at the state level. First, they thought that this level of government would always be closer to the people. At the state level, it was possible to have a much richer discourse among all the people and to more closely track their views in the details of government. In short, it was easier at that level to have a government that was truly "of the people, by the people and for the people."

An additional epistemological argument for having a substantial portion of government at the state and local level is that the actions of these many governments can serve as experiments for one another. For example, the best way in which to provide public education is enormously complicated and is also a challenge that evolves due to a changing population as well as evolving economy and technology. To have a rigid system imposed at the federal level is not likely to result in as much growth of knowledge about what techniques work as such a system of broad experimentation and learning.

Bella: *If state and local governments are so great for a democracy, why have a federal government at all?*

That is a profound question. And it highlights the deeper question of what types of issues are best dealt with at a state or local level and which types of issues are best dealt at the federal level. This, in turn, raises yet another question, which is what types of issues, if any, are best dealt with at an international level versus a national level. We really need a theory to help us find that optimal layering of governance. For example, one can readily see that having the defense of the nation dealt with at a <u>state</u> level wouldn't work too well. First, there is the obvious danger that the states might go to war with one another.

Bella: *Wait. Didn't that happen anyway? Isn't that called the civil war?*

Well, you have a point there. Nonetheless, a strong national government does substantially lessen the likelihood of such a conflict. But setting the issue of civil war to the side, imagine trying to coordinate fifty different state militias into a defense of the country. Some states might decide to contribute. Others might decide not to contribute. Some might decide to let the other states bear these burdens, and simply enjoy the benefits of the defense efforts of others. All in all, our national defense is unlikely to be as strong as it might need to be. National defense would seem to be something better dealt with at a national level.

This example provides a hint of the kinds of issues that might best be dealt with at the national level. The characteristic of defense that calls for national coordination and control is that it is a strong jointly-shared interest that would be undermined by a wide variety of different approaches among the states. This is not a bad model for determining what should be dealt with at the federal level. Some examples of things that might best be dealt with at the federal level are interstate transportation, the regulation of business commerce the goes across state lines, environmental issues that cut across state lines, and the protection of fundamental human rights. Trying to decide where the best layer of governance is, given the tradeoffs, tends to be very complicated and often controversial. Delving into the full complexity of the issues is beyond the scope of this book.

A MAJOR THREAT TO DEMOCRACY AS DISCOVERY—AD HOMINEM ATTACKS

We have forgotten how to talk to one another. Civil discourse requires listening to one another and responding to argument with argument. It is how we grow, both as individuals and as a people. But today we refuse to truly listen to one another and to be responsive to one another's arguments. Instead, we seek to demonize or marginalize the opposing side. There is a name for this; it is called an <u>ad hominem</u> attack. That is, an ad hominem attack is an attack on the person rather on the arguments. Ad hominem attacks are generally counterproductive to the growth of knowledge. Indeed, they are very damaging to the kind of healthy public discourse that defines a healthy democracy.

Bella: *But if a person is a bad person, or has done something immoral or improper at some stage of their life, isn't that relevant as to whether I should vote for them and, indeed, even to their credibility?*

One problem with that approach is that many people choose <u>not</u> to participate in the discourse—either as citizens or politicians—because they don't want to face an intrusive and unfair attack on their personal life. Thus, we lose the benefit of their ideas. Our society ends up with an impoverished discourse whose bandwidth is taken up with largely irrelevant attacks on individuals, rather than tangling with the issues, which are complicated and worthy of substantial bandwidth. I have no idea whether or not ad hominem attacks are politically effective, but they make me both ashamed for my country and pessimistic about its future. It is not America at its best. I hope we can reach the point where we can disagree intelligently and resolve our political differences through an informed political process that draws on all of our best ideas.

Vigorous, open debate on the merits of the issues is to be celebrated. But personal attacks should be deemed out of bounds. There is more at stake here than just civility. The challenges we face as a country today require that our public discourse be genuinely rich and meaningful. In my view, when people engage in irrelevant personal attacks on politicians along any point of the political spectrum, they are letting the country down and damaging our democracy and our hopes for the future.

The point of this chapter is a simple one. While voting is necessary for a democracy, the most important characteristic of a democracy is that it has foundational institutions, such as we have reviewed above, that generate, facilitate and maintain an inclusive environment in which the citizenry is tapped upon and drawn into a fruitful and responsive discourse about governance, with the result being a process of discovery that moves the society ever toward the goal of "good governance."

Suggested Readings

- Hamilton, Alexander; Madison, James; Jay, John <u>The Federalist Papers</u>

18

POLITICIANS AS ENTREPRENEURS

Let me ... warn you in the most solemn manner against the baneful effects of the spirit of party.

GEORGE WASHINGTON

Politicians can be thought of as like entrepreneurs. As we saw in an earlier chapter, an entrepreneur is an innovative business person who sees a new opportunity that no one else has, and pulls together resources to meet that emerging need or want. Politicians do very much the same thing. They see an opportunity to express certain ideas that will pull together a coalition of people to vote for them and put them into a position of power. Politicians study the political spectrum as it evolves and entrepreneurially position themselves at a point that they believe will maximize the likelihood of obtaining power. As a consequence, politicians have to be careful in what they say. They are constrained to express ideas in a manner and with a design to keep their voting coalition together. Otherwise, they will be voted out of office. This is actually kind of hard to do, because no thinking person has just the right set of views to keep a large group of people happy with them. Thus, politicians are not free to say whatever they think on any topic. Their expression of ideas has to be well crafted to keep their public persona acceptable to a particular voting bloc. This is why politicians often say exaggerated things, or peculiarly bland things, or peculiarly repetitive things, or express things in very odd ways. The ones who can sound natural while conveying their selected message are quite talented. On top of this, anything they say will be quoted selectively and out of context by their political enemies. So they have to be doubly careful what they say. And, of course, the media has a grand time and makes great sport of trying to trip them up and ask them questions that would force them to talk like a normal human being.

Bella: *Pity the poor politician.*

The fact that politicians can't really freely express their views openly like a normal human being makes it very difficult for them to engage in an honest open intellectual dialogue of argument, counterargument, concession to argument, refining of questions, and so forth. To do so is antithetical to their task of shaping a particular image of themselves that will attract a particular voting bloc. This is unfortunate because it makes real debate and dialogue—at least publicly—an unlikely event. Moreover, it makes it peculiarly challenging for politicians themselves to continue to develop in their own thinking. Indeed, they spend so much time in shaping and refining their message, which is directed at particular political ends, that they start convincing themselves, and thus cease to question and challenge their own beliefs. This stunts their further intellectual growth.

Bella: *Let's just hope they did a lot of growing before they got into the profession of being a politician!*

As noted above, politicians have to think strategically about their message, if they want to hold a voting-bloc together to get into office and remain in office. Much of their thinking, therefore, is focused on the political spectrum. There is an economic theory—called clustering theory—that sheds light here on what are apt to be successful political strategies. Imagine there is a single road going through a town in the Appalachian mountains. Everyone in the small town lives along this road on the mountain side, and are fairly evenly distributed along it. Let's suppose also that two different people have decided to open up two different and competing restaurants.

Bella: *The question is where along the road that runs through the town should they put those restaurants, right?*

Right. Let's also suppose that the town has a zoning hearing about the location of new businesses. At the zoning hearing, each restaurant proprietor will have the opportunity to find out where her competitor intends to put her restaurant. In fact, each restaurant proprietor will be able to continually make adjustments to her own zoning request until she finally settles on a location. Imagine the town and the road are broken into zones A through K, and which look like the following—with Zones A and K at either ends of the town, and Zone F in the middle of the town, as follows:

|__A__|__B__|__C__|__D__|__E__|__F__|__G__|__H__|__I__|__J__|__K__|

Economic theory predicts that both restaurants will end up in Zone F, even though this may not be optimal from the villagers' point of view. Let's see why.

Assume that both restaurants want to maximize how many of the villagers they can attract on the basis of locational convenience. Beyond that, let's assume that the two restaurants are expected to be about the same in terms of quality. Now suppose Restaurant One indicates in a zoning hearing that they intend to locate in Zone C and Restaurant Two indicates it will locate in Zone I. From its location in Zone C, Restaurant One would, of course, attract villagers from Zones A and B, as it is a much shorter walk to her restaurant than the other one. Restaurant One should also be able to attract the villagers all the way over to the middle of Zone F—which is in the very middle of the village—since it would also be the shortest walk. Similarly, from its location in Zone I, Restaurant Two should be able to attract the villagers in Zones J and K as well as all those from the middle of Zone F. (To help yourself visualize this, have a penny represent Restaurant One and have a dime represent Restaurant Two and place them both on the chart above, and move them around as we continue the analysis.)

Bella: *I am using two little chewy treats as my markers.*

But the owner of Restaurant One looks at the zoning plans and sees an opportunity. She says to herself: "I can do better than that. Instead of locating way to the left in Zone C, if I move my restaurant (Restaurant One) all the way past the middle of the village and over to Zone H, then I will attract all the villagers from Zones A through H, since my restaurant will be the shortest walk from all those spots. My competitor, Restaurant Two (still in Zone I), will only be able to attract the villagers toward the far right—that is, those in Zones J and K. But the owner of Restaurant Two learns quickly. She decides to leapfrog her competitor—Restaurant One—and move Restaurant Two to Zone G, so now she can get all the villagers from Zones A through F to come to her restaurant, which is now the shortest walk for villagers from those zones.

Restaurant One, still in Zone H, will now only have an advantage in attracting the villagers in Zones H, I, J and K. The owner of Restaurant One sees what is happening, so she leaps to Zone F to get ahead of Restaurant Two. Restaurant Two sees that this is also his best choice. Thus, both restaurants end up right next to each other in Zone F.

Notice that this is not a particularly good placement of the restaurants from the villagers' perspective, assuming the villagers are interested in minimizing how far they have to walk to get to a restaurant. Indeed, the starting points of the two restaurants—in Zones C and I respectively—would have been much better from that perspective. But competitive forces bring them both to a "cluster" in the middle of the town. That is why this is called cluster theory.

The same dynamic holds for politics and the political spectrum. Think of the town in the above example as the political spectrum with left-wing voters in one direction and right-wing voters in the other. Assume that politicians want to obtain as many votes as possible and choose to position themselves along the political spectrum so as to do so. Assume voters on the other hand will vote for whichever politician is closest in position to where they are.

Bella: *What happens?*

Just as in the above example, suppose Politician One positions herself at Zone C and Politician Two positions herself at Zone I. Each will obtain half the votes. But if Politician One shifts toward to the center, say, to Zone E, then she will obtain more than half the votes, since more of the voters will be closer to her on the political spectrum. Politician Two will feel the same pull to the center to maximize the number of votes. One would expect they will both end up in the center with the Left-Wing politician ending up just slightly to the Left of center and the Right-wing just slightly to the Right of center. This is one of the most fundamental dynamics of politics.

This can present particular difficulties for politicians if there is a primary system in which they have to win the nomination of their party before moving to the general election. That is, imagine you are a Republican running for the US Senate in State X. First, you must win the Republican nomination. That is called the primary. In that election process, you are running against other Republicans, and the people voting in this primary are just the Republican citizens. Now, it is pretty safe to say that, on average, Republicans are more conservative than the general population of the state (which inevitably will include some Democrats and Independents). To position yourself to win among the Republicans, according to the theory we presented above, you would do well to place yourself in the middle of the Republicans' political spectrum. So you make statements that indicate to the world that you are right in the middle of the Republicans. Let's suppose that you win the primary. That's great for you, of course, but now you have created a problem for yourself in the general election. To win the general election, you must obtain a majority of the entire population of state X, not just the Republican voters. So to do well in the general election, you want to place yourself in the center of the political spectrum for the overall state. But this means you have to move to the Left from your initial position. Similarly, a Democrat who won the Democratic primary, and is now running against you in the general election, might find herself in an analogous position, but having to move further to the right than she was in her primary. Lo and behold—one does tend to see both left-wing and right-wing politicians move to the center for general elections.

Bella: *Where do they really stand?*

Only the politician herself can know the answer to that question, and even she may not know for sure.

19

YOUR VOTE DOES NOT MATTER

Politics is the art of preventing people from taking part in affairs which properly concern them.

PAUL VALÉRY

ZERO PROBABILITY OF "MAKING A DIFFERENCE"

Your vote does not matter.

Bella: *What do you mean? I don't even have a vote. I am a dog.*

Well, then, I am done with my demonstration, because your vote definitely doesn't matter. But I was actually referring to our reader.

Bella: *Well, how do you know our reader is old enough to vote?*

You have me there. I don't know that he or she is. In that case, I have once again proven that his or her vote doesn't matter. But what I was really trying to get at is the fact that <u>no one's vote matters</u>—at least, it doesn't matter statistically speaking.

Bella: *That is an outrage. People have died defending this country and the freedoms for which it stands. Voting is at the very heart of that. How dare you dishonor so many by saying that voting doesn't matter? Even a dog would be offended.*

I am not saying that voting isn't an important part of democracy. We have discussed the fruitful role of voting. But I am saying something rather stark and shocking here, and that is that no one person's vote really matters. Let me explain my thinking. What is it that makes a vote matter? For the sake of argument, let's say that a vote matters only if it changes a decision that is made. If it doesn't affect the outcome of a decision, then it doesn't matter. Fair enough?

Bella: *I suppose.*

Now, let's suppose there are 25 voters, and they are voting on who gets to walk Bella in the park—Fred or George. Both Fred and George make passionate speeches on why they would be the best person to walk Bella. After the speeches, the vote is taken. Let's suppose there are 15 votes for Fred and 10 votes for George. Clearly, Fred wins.

Bella: *OK.*

Now change the hypothetical slightly and suppose that any one of the voters had been called away just before the vote and, thus, missed their opportunity to vote. You can readily see that the outcome of the vote would have been exactly the same. The new tally would have been either 14 votes for Fred and 10 for George (if the missing person was one who would have voted for Fred) or 15 votes for Fred and 9 votes for George (if the missing person was one who would have voted for George.) In either case, Fred still wins. You can see from this example that no one person's vote really mattered at all.

Bella: *Yes, but what if the vote had been 13 to 12 in favor of Fred. In that case, one vote made the difference to ensure a victory for Fred.*

Yes, that's true. In that case, where one vote makes the difference, we can say that the vote matters. In fact, we can go further than that. We can say that all 13 votes for Fred mattered, because if any one of them hadn't voted, Fred would not have won. I will admit that individual votes can matter, on occasion, <u>when one has a small number of voters</u> and the vote

276

is very close in terms of the two sides. But those are very narrow circumstances, and they really serve to establish my point. If we are talking about voting in a political context in a large country such as the United States, your vote does not matter.

Bella: *How can you say that? I thought we just proved that your vote* can *matter if the margin of victory is one vote.*

Precisely. But if a very large number of people are voting, the probability that the decision will be determined by merely one vote is, for all practical purposes, zero. It is simply not going to happen. Take any recent election year and look at every House and Senate race in every state in the United States and also look at the Presidential race—taking the voting on a state-by-state basis—and you won't see any of these decisions made by a margin of one vote. Therefore, your vote does not matter. The probabilistic expectation that it could matter is practically-speaking zero. Far more people win multimillion dollar lotteries then ever have their vote matter. Think about that.

Bella: *But what about the 2000 Presidential vote in Florida? Wasn't that very close? And didn't the decision of who would be the President of the United States ride on that vote? Doesn't that vote in Florida prove that one person's vote can matter?*

No, indeed. It confirms that your vote can never matter. The Presidential vote in Florida in 2000 was close, but there were still thousands of votes at issue. And in a case where the vote was, in fact, that close, we saw what happened. Court cases were filed and lawyers argued before judges about which votes were legitimate and which were not. We had experts examining individual ballots and arguing about whether or not they had been marked properly. At the end of the day, it was all decided by the Supreme Court of the United States. Not only does your vote not matter, the best your vote can do is to make a race close enough that it is decided by a judge.

MARGINAL COST EXCEEDS EXPECTED BENEFIT

Now, given that your vote cannot matter, I have a second proposition: To vote is irrational.

Bella: *Now you are getting downright unpatriotic.*

I am just stating the facts. If you concede that the probability of your vote mattering is zero, then it is quite simple to demonstrate that voting is irrational—you simply compare the expected benefits of voting with the expected costs. The expected benefits are obviously zero, since there is a zero probability that your vote matters. But it always costs you something to vote.

Bella: *You mean they make you pay money to vote?!?!?*

No. But you have to take time out of your day to do it. You could have been doing something else useful, or remunerative, or pleasurable, or productive with your time. You lose the benefit of whatever else you could have been doing. That is the cost of voting. And you often have to wait in line quite a while before you get to cast your ballot. And you have to get there somehow, and that generally costs a little bit of money, even if it is only the cost of the gasoline. Given the near zero probability that your vote matters, and that it definitely costs you some modest amount to vote, it is crystal clear that voting is irrational. This implies that the only people we have voting are the irrational ones. Are those the people who you want to be deciding who our leaders are?

Bella: *No wonder government is a mess!*

Exactly. The Australians have it figured out. They require, as a matter of law, that all their citizens vote; if you don't vote, then you are fined. That way they at least have all the rational folks voting as well.

SO WHY VOTE?

Bella: *So do you vote?*

Well, as a matter of fact, I do.

Bella: *Does that indicate you are irrational?*

Most certainly.

Bella: *So why do you vote then?*

I think I vote to contribute to something that is larger than myself—and in that way I feel closer to God. But that is a subject for a later chapter. Now, not only does your vote not matter, but political parties work very hard to ensure that that remains the case. Let's see how.

THE GERRYMANDER—OR HOW TO ENSURE THAT VOTING IS NOT REPRESENTATIVE

Each state in the United States elects representatives to the US House of Representatives, which is one of the two legislative bodies in the US Congress. The number of representatives that each state gets depends on the number of people living in the state. As population changes are recorded every ten years through a national census, the number of representatives for each state is adjusted to reflect those population changes. As states end up being allocated a different number of representatives, the boundaries of the congressional voting districts need to be re-drawn. But there is a danger here: boundaries of voting districts can be set to purposefully disadvantage particular sub-groups of the population. When this is done, it is called a "gerrymander". The term comes from the name of a governor of Massachusetts—one Elbridge Gerry. He oversaw the implementation of a redistricting of the state designed to advantage his party. Some of the districts were so exaggerated in shape as to resemble a salamander—hence the term Gerrymander.

Bella: *How do you like my Bellamander pictured below?*

Very nice, Bella.

279

Bella: *So how does this Bellamandering work anyway?*

Well, the idea is that you break up concentrations of the group that you want to politically disadvantage, and lump them in with majorities of the folks you want to advantage, by redrawing the lines between voting districts. Let's take an example to make this clear. Suppose that you have a rectangular shaped state as pictured below:

2/3 Scotch Irish (SI) Protestants and 1/3 English Protestants	All English Protestants (EP)	2/3 Irish Catholics (IC) and 1/3 English Protestants

Suppose also that:
- The western 1/3 of the state is 2/3 Protestants of Scotch-Irish descent and 1/3 Protestants of English descent
- The middle 1/3 of the state is 100% Protestants of English descent
- The eastern 1/3 of the state is made up of 2/3 Catholics of Irish descent and 1/3 Protestants of English descent

Let's suppose also that these different groups, on average, have very different views on politics and different political and economic interests and that—for the sake of simplicity of analysis—are going to vote for someone who is like themselves. And, finally, let's suppose that this state gets awarded three congressional districts. The question is: what difference does it make where the boundaries of the congressional districts are drawn? As we will see, it makes a great deal of difference!

First, let's suppose that the three congressional districts were defined by vertical (that is, north-south) lines that divided the state up into equal thirds. In this case, we can predict that the candidate elected in the western district will be a Scotch-Irish Protestant, in the central district an English Protestant, and in the eastern district an Irish Catholic. More specifically, given the population distributions, the Scotch-Irish Protestant will win by a margin of 2-to-1, the English Protestant will win 100% of the votes in her district and the Irish Catholic will win by a margin of 2-to-1. Now, let's do a little gerrymandering!

Bella: *You mean Bellamandering!*

Sure. Let's suppose that instead of vertical boundaries, we broke the state up into three equal thirds using <u>horizontal</u> boundaries. In the diagram below, I have represented the three horizontal districts. I have reflected the different populations with the initials SI for Scotch Irish, EP for English Protestant and IC for Irish Catholic. (Notice that the population distribution has remained unchanged.) I have shaded in the middle third of the state (from a vertical perspective) for ease of comparison.

SI	SI	EP	EP	EP	EP	EP	IC	IC
SI	SI	EP	EP	EP	EP	EP	IC	IC
SI	SI	EP	EP	EP	EP	EP	IC	IC

With the new boundaries, we now have a northern district, a middle horizontal district and a southern district. Let's see who gets elected now. In the northern district, the winner will clearly be an English Protestant by a vote of 5-to-4. In the middle horizontal district, the winner will also be an English Protestant by a vote of 5-to-4. And in the southern district, the winner will be an English Protestant by a vote of 5-to-4. Thus, simply by re-drawing the boundaries of the electoral districts we go from representation constituted by 1 English Protestant, 1 Irish Catholic and 1 Scotch Irish to representation by 3 English Protestant, given the very same population and population distribution. Whoever draws the electoral boundaries essentially determines the electoral outcomes. Gerrymandering has often been used to disadvantage racial minorities in terms of their representation.

20

NO SUCH THING AS THE "PUBLIC INTEREST"

We live together because social organization provides the efficient means of achieving our individual objectives and not because society offers us a means of arriving at some transcendental common bliss.

JAMES M. BUCHANAN

Bella: *You get the sense from the quote above that Mr. Buchanan is not wild about attending community festivities.*

THE "SOCIAL UTILE"

Folks constantly refer to the "public interest." When you ask someone: "Why is your policy the best policy?", they often reply "Because it is in the public interest."

"Public interest" is an empty term. It's OK to use the term, of course, if you have some real arguments supporting your proposition, such as "My idea is better because it will lead to greater economic growth"—and then have some arguments supporting that. Or you might say "My idea is better because it protects our basic freedom to practice religion in whatever way we see fit"—and then have some arguments to back that up. But simply to assert: "Well, it is the right thing to do because it is in the public interest" is not to make an argument at all. So beware when people start talking about the public interest. It usually means they don't have any substantive arguments or that their arguments are very weak.

Bella: What does the "public interest" really mean?

When we say something is in the "public interest," it implies a preference ordering—just like a rational individual might employ in making her own economic decisions. That is, it implies one can rank things—from best to worst—in terms of one's preferences. For society to have such a preference ordering, we must be able to say (in a meaningful way) that the society prefers Situation X to Situation Y, and that society prefers Situation Y to Situation Z. (And if the society truly has ordered its preferences from best to worst, we would hope to be able to infer from the above information that the society also preferred Situation X to Situation Z.) To say that a particular policy alternative is in the public interest is to imply that the change involved would constitute a movement to a higher ranked preference for the society as a whole.

Bella: But how is it that we can rank alternative states of the world from a public perspective?

One way to do this would be if we had some sort of measuring stick. We would need a unit of account. Let's call it a "social utile." Thus, we might say: "This alternative has more social utility than that one." And, indeed, sometimes you will hear people say that something has "social utility."

Bella: So where do you get this measuring stick? Is it a stick that I can retrieve?

Well, the problem, of course, is that there is no way to measure a social utile. Think about it. In the real world, even if a public policy choice helps the vast majority of the people, there will still be some people who are made worse off by it. The key question is how do you objectively measure these impacts across individuals—and compare and contrast those impacts to come up with a metric of social improvement—given that each of these individuals is a unique human being with only their own life to experience? You can't really do it—at least not without placing your own value judgments in as weights. Put another way, one cannot really measure "social utility" without making <u>personal</u> value judgments that assign weights with which one compares the significance of who was helped by the social change, and by how much, with who was hurt by it and by how much.

For example, let's say that my arm is chopped off in defense of my country, and let's say that the defense action that I took, and in which I lost my arm, saved four civilians from having their arms chopped off (which would have occurred if the invading forces had not been defeated due to my personal heroics.)

Bella: *That's a rather crude example.*

Well, war is horrible, even if sometimes necessary. Now, in the scenario above, we can definitely conclude that I have done a noble thing. And we may well want to celebrate my heroism. Further, we may want to compensate me financially for the fact that I might have a harder time making a living, and also to compensate me for any other lost aspects of enjoyment of life because I have lost a limb in defense of the country. Finally, one might make a pretty compelling argument that having one person lose his arm is better than having four people lose their arms. But what you cannot do is scientifically measure how much better off or worse off society is as a result.

Bella: *Why not?*

Because no one other than me can know, measure or experience what the loss of a limb means <u>to me</u>. And, by the same token, no one can know, measure or experience what the loss of a limb might have meant <u>to those four other people</u>. Indeed, it could be that my only true love, passion and enjoyment in my life was to play the piano, and that, moreover, I was so uniquely talented in it, and so masterful at composition, that if I hadn't lost my arm I would have gone on to create music that would entertain the planet for ages to come. At the same time, it could be that the other four people who would have lost their arms but didn't, had a great deal of <u>other</u> wonderful things going in their lives, and while this harm to them would have been substantial, they would all have still gone on to live quite happy, fulfilling lives.

My point is simply that the answer to these kinds of questions is unknowable. We have no measuring stick that can create a metric that cuts across different people's experiences of life and allows us to compare their value. We cannot <u>directly</u> compare and measure one another's sensibilities about the world—either happy or sad—and certainly cannot use arithmetic to then compare outcomes and see which alternatives fulfills the "public interest." This is <u>not</u> to say that we may not come to some conclusion about what we think is best for society, given some particular choice society confronts, but rather to note that our answer can never be based on direct measurements of social utility.

Let's take one more example. Suppose that each of the 7 billion people on the planet will be made $10 richer <u>if</u> we permit just one person to be horribly tortured. We can certainly all agree, I think, that this is not fair and it would not only be a bad idea but also cruel. The philosophical question, however, is whether the pleasures of that $70 billion dollars of additional wealth—spread across 7 billion people, each with their own preferences—can be <u>objectively</u> measured and compared with the pain and suffering of the torture of that one person? My suggestion is that they cannot. These things are fundamentally incommensurable (that is, they cannot be compared.)

Bella: *But more realistically, suppose the policy is one of free and open trade for the country, and suppose that there is compelling evidence that this will benefit the vast majority of the population.*

Nonetheless, there will certainly be <u>some</u> people who are peculiarly well-suited to work in certain industries that will suffer from the global competition. That is, if you work in an industry that loses out to the foreign competition, and which goes out of business, you may find yourself out of a job. Moreover, if your skills were particularly well suited to that industry, you may find that you can't get a job that pays you as much in another industry. There is no question that at least some people will be worse off from such a policy change. But how does one measure their losses and compare it to the gains of others? Yes, one can put dollar figures on it, but that doesn't make those individuals who are suffering from the change one whit better off. And what do such numbers really mean? How does one legitimately add and subtract the joys and sufferings of different people? Another person's gains can't make up for <u>my</u> suffering; so what is the basis for pretending that one can add and subtract them as if they do? Is my pain of unemployment legitimately offset by your gain of wealth? More generally, does a moment of pain for me count the same as a moment of pain for you?

What if we are trying to build a bridge between two islands and we know that if we succeed then the people on both islands will be much better off economically. But let's say we also know that someone will die in the process of constructing the bridge. This is not such an unreasonable assumption. In the 19th century it was quite typical for people to die in the construction of large bridges, and this remains true even today. Can we say that society is better off if such a bridge is to be built? <u>Is some economic benefit for a large number of people worth the life of one person</u>? How do you measure that? Is there some comparable unit—some measuring stick—across individuals so that we can compare and contrast and definitively be able to say "This alternative is better for society"? That is, is there such a thing as a social utile?

The answer is no. There is no such number. There is no way of measuring such things. Dollars don't do it, because we don't know how to place the right price on each thing, and regardless of the price we pick there is no philosophical basis for asserting that my joy is comparable to your joy and my pain is comparable to your pain and the dollar measure of the one for me is the same as the dollar measure of the other for you. Indeed, although what I can buy for a dollar may mean something to me, it is doubtful if it is exactly comparable to what a dollar of expenditure may mean for you. And though I may be very sympathetic to your pain, I will never actually <u>feel</u> your pain; I only feel <u>my</u> pain, even if it is induced by seeing you in pain. And though I may be happy for you, I will never actually feel <u>your</u> happiness. I only feel my happiness, even if it is happiness in seeing you happy. We are all <u>different</u> beings, and our happiness and sadness cannot coherently be aggregated and measured with numbers—at least not any numbers that have a basis in objective fact. The effort to do so is really based on a mistaken metaphor—some sort of notion that we are all part of a greater creature known as society. But society is not a sentient being, as is each individual human. And though we may be bound together spiritually, we are corporeally distinct. There is no way to directly measure whether one alternative state the world is better than another from a <u>social</u> point of view; society is not one mind experiencing pleasure and pain.

Now, that doesn't mean that we can't come up with ways of making social decisions. We can convince one another that certain social alternatives are superior. We can argue and give reasons for our various policy positions and criticize those positions. In this way, we are more likely to unearth for whom the policy is a benefit and for whom it is not. We can also vote on social decisions. And we can also use the market to help us make some of these tough decisions in a fair way. For example, following up on one of our examples above, we could use a market to help us decide how to allocate the risks of building a bridge. That is, we could pay someone to take the risks inherent in such construction, and let them decide individually whether the price is worth the risk to them. As a society, we also might devise certain ethical rules, religious principles and/or moral valuations whereby we compare and contrast the impact of decisions on different people. But these are not the same thing as a "social utile"—that is, a direct way to measure the "public interest." Our initial point here is simply that we cannot <u>scientifically</u> determine that one alternative is better for society than another through some sort of objective measurement.

Bella: *Well, I concede that there is no such thing as a social utile. But you mentioned voting as a way to make social decisions. Can't we simply use voting to determine a social preference ordering over alternative states of the world and thereby define the "public interest"? Indeed, isn't democracy just a way to determine a social preference ordering over alternative states of the world?*

In general, it turns out that voting cannot give us a coherent preference ordering for society either.

CONDORCET'S PARADOX OF MAJORITY VOTING

In the 1700s, the French thinker Marquis de Condorcet—an acquaintance of Benjamin Franklin's—developed the following paradox of voting to show why a majority is never happy. Suppose there are three people living on an island—Bella, Bobby and Carl.

Bella: *You mean two people and a dog.*

Yes, but it is two people and a voting dog.

Bella: *Now you're talking!*

Suppose also that there are just enough materials to build one hut for the three of them, and they have to decide where they want to build it. There are three spots on the island they are considering for the construction of the hut—the **Beach**, the **Hill** and the **Jungle**. Let's suppose also that their preferences for the location of the hut are different, and are as indicated below. The most preferred location being listed as the highest for each voter and the least preferred location is at the bottom.

Bella	Bobby	Carl
Beach	Hill	Jungle
Hill	Jungle	Beach
Jungle	Beach	Hill

Bella: *I like this! Go beach!!! Boo Jungle!!!*

To follow the analysis below, you will have to carefully track the above chart of individual preferences. Through voting, we are going to try to determine the group's preference.

MAJORITY RULE BY PAIR-WISE COMBINATION

Because Bella, Bobby and Carl want to be democratic about this, they will vote on where to put the hut and follow the will of the majority. More specifically, they intend to do a "run-off" style election. Yet more specifically, they agree to compare the alternatives in pairs, have a vote with respect to each pair, and then follow the majority's will with respect to that pair to determine which is superior from the group's point of view. Once they settle the vote between one pair, they will have a vote between that winner and any other alternatives they have not yet addressed. This manner of voting is called <u>majority rule by pair-wise combination</u>.

Bella: *So let's get to the voting!*

Let's say that Bella, Bobby and Carl first vote on the **Beach** vs. the **Hill**. As you can see from their preferences, both Bella and Carl prefer the **Beach** to the **Hill**, so the **Beach** wins. (Make sure you follow along with the chart to double check each vote.)

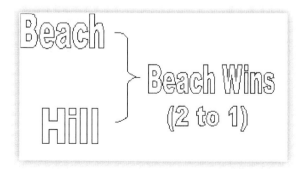

Since the **Hill** has been eliminated, they then have a run-off election comparing the **Beach** to the **Jungle** to determine a final winner. Since both Bobby and Carl prefer the **Jungle** to the **Beach**, the **Jungle** wins. So it looks like the democratic majority—Bobby and Carl, in this case—have determined that the hut will go in the **Jungle**.

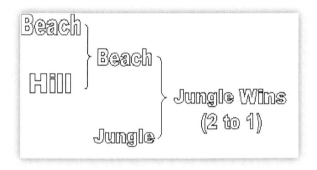

Bella: *But wait!!! Why should we stop the voting there? You say that the* **Jungle** *is the winner. But if you look at the preferences listed above, you will note that both Bobby and I prefer the* **Hill** *to the* **Jungle**. *Bobby and I taken together constitute a majority! So shouldn't the* **Hill** *be declared the winner?*

You have identified the key problem, Bella. In fact, if you study the schedule of individual preferences above, you will see that—no matter which alternative we declare as the winner—<u>there is always a majority that prefers something different than the status quo</u>. Let's run through all the possibilities to prove that is the case.

Let's suppose after some conversation Bella, Bobby and Carl finally tentatively settle on building the hut on the **Beach**. But this turns out to be an unhappy circumstance! Note that a majority—Bobby and Carl—will be forever dissatisfied, in that they know both of them together would have preferred the **Jungle** over the **Beech**.

So let's say that, in light of this discovery, they end up building the hut in the **Jungle**. But this also turns out to be an unhappy circumstance! Notice that a <u>different</u> majority—Bella and Bobby—would have preferred the **Hill** to the **Jungle**. If they settle for the **Jungle**, there will always be a majority who are dissatisfied.

In light of this discovery, let's say they switch to the **Hill** as the place to build their hut. But this <u>also</u> turns out to be an unhappy situation.

There is yet a <u>different</u> majority—Bella and Carl—are dissatisfied with the **Hill** in that they would have both preferred the **Beach**. If they are always determined to follow the will of the majority, they will be on the move from one spot to another for eternity. (See the diagram immediately below.)

Indeed, you can see that there will always be a majority who is unhappy with the status quo. To put this another way, there is no coherent preference ordering for the group. According to the majority (albeit <u>different</u> majorities in each instance), the **Beach** is preferred to the **Hill**, the **Hill** is preferred to the **Jungle**, and the **Jungle** is preferred to the **Beach**. No matter what they pick, there will be a majority that prefers something else.

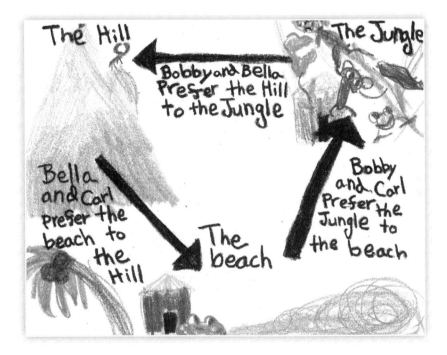

Drawing by Roxy Fisher 1

Bella: *Perhaps that is why people grumble about politics so much—there is always a majority that wants something else!*

Precisely. Indeed, it is worse than you think. A careful analysis of the situation shows that the ultimate outcome of the voting is completely determined by the <u>order</u> in which the pairs of alternatives are compared. Check it out below (and double check with the preferences listed above to be sure you understand why the votes play out the way they do):

<u>Voting Order #1</u>: Start with **Beach** vs. **Hill**, with **Beach** winning, then have a run-off election of **Beach** vs. **Jungle**—with the **Jungle** as the ultimate winner.

<u>Voting Order #2</u>: Start with **Hill** vs. **Jungle**, with **Hill** winning, then have a run-off election of **Hill** vs. **Beach**—with the **Beach** as the ultimate winner.

<u>Voting Order #3</u>: Start with **Beach** vs. **Jungle**, with **Jungle** winning, then have a run-off election of **Jungle** vs. **Hill**—with **Hill** as the ultimate winner.

Bella: *But that is very disturbing. If the determination of the winner is solely dependent upon the order in which the votes are taken, then whoever controls the voting order determines the final outcome. That is not democracy—that is dictatorship! I want to get off this island.*

Exactly. The lesson is that anyone who controls the order in which issues are put before the public—or the precise terms under which a question is posed to the public—has a great deal of control over the outcome. Great power lies within how issues are framed. If you know the preferences of the population, and the manner in which they vary, you can generally frame an issue in a manner that is more likely to secure the outcome you seek.

Bella: *But how dependent is this strange and disturbing outcome on the weird way in which you have set up the preferences?*

It is true that this "cyclical majority" is dependent on the pattern of the individual preferences. But the question then becomes: how common is this pattern of preferences? It turns out that people are likely to order their preferences in these contrasting ways that produce cyclical majorities, if they have multiple and fundamentally different criteria for weighing the social alternatives from one another. Of course, in a diverse, multi-cultural country such as the United States that is exactly what we have.

Bella: *So you have to stop holding out on me here: if voting can't give you a coherent picture of the will of the majority, why is voting important?*

First, permit me to summarize for you what voting is <u>not</u> about. As a society, we have this odd notion that somehow through voting we can extract a coherent picture of how the majority wants the country to be shaped. Indeed, after each election, various pundits compete with one another to interpret the meaning of the People's mandate. This is based on a mistaken metaphor that a democratic majority is kind of like a conscious mind that has a specific image of what it wants. It isn't. Typically, in society, there are many different majorities with many different views on many different things. And, as we saw above, while one majority may support the status quo over some other particular alternative, a <u>different</u> majority would prefer something different than the status quo. The point is a general one. That is, there is no voting system that will provide you with a coherent portrayal of how society should be ordered. (You can take whole courses in college analyzing different types of voting systems and their properties!) While voting is an incredibly important right and an important democratic process, it cannot tell us with any specificity how to coherently shape a good society. Voting is simply too crude a mechanism to convey a clear picture as to the will of the People.

The real purposes of voting are four-fold.

First, and most importantly, the purpose of voting is the manner in which it forces a rich and inclusive discourse of social discovery. The voting process presents an opportunity for the society at large to debate the issues. With elections come choices, and with choices comes debate. The voting process provides this triggering moment for much needed debate and social discourse on the issues. The voting process stimulates politicians to answer to the people, to give reasons for their policies, to criticize one another and to answer criticism. Thus, voting provides a key institution that helps ensure that we have a rich and inclusive discourse on the issues our society confronts. It is part of the engine of discovery that is at the essence of a healthy democracy.

Second, voting gives individual citizens a sense of participation in the political processes of the country. This sense of participation inspires many people to become better informed about the issues, and to contribute to the ongoing debates about issues of public policy. This sense of participation is both a benefit in-and-of-itself, in that people tend to enjoy being part of the process and learning about issues, but it is also beneficial in that they may often contribute to the ongoing debate in important ways. The proverbial political conversations that occur over the kitchen table are genuinely important and have a deep influence on a society.

Third, voting is about social legitimacy and the peaceful transition of power among those who would rule the country. That is, through voting, people come to accept whoever is running the country as legitimate, and even their opponents accept them as legitimate (at least, one hopes they do.) This is a great mechanism for avoiding violence. (Incidentally, it is a most beautiful thing to witness the peaceful transition of power from one US administration to the next, despite the many important disagreements the two sides might have. This smooth and peaceful transition is one of our most precious national assets. It is right that it is celebrated with great pomp and circumstance.)

Fourth, and finally, sometimes voting is simply about getting us to an answer, whether or not the answer is the best one. There are many things in life that simply need an answer, and where simply having an answer is more important than having a perfect answer. This is what Napoleon meant when he said that one bad general is better than two good generals (that is, because the one bad general will make timely choices, whereas the two good generals will argue and argue trying to get the perfect decision, rather than simply making a timely decision.)

In sum, a narrow focus on voting as determining social preferences not only is muddled, but misses the point. At its best, democracy is constituted by a rich participatory dialogue where innovative conjectures about resolutions to social issues are raised, discussed and criticized from all perspectives. Democracy is an inclusive and exploratory process to find better political, legal and governmental approaches to problems. A truly democratic society is not defined narrowly by the mere fact of voting. Voting is necessary but not sufficient for a healthy democracy. A vibrant democracy requires social institutions that create the possibility for and support a rich dialogue of conjecture and criticism on social issues. At its best, democracy provides the foundation for the growth of social and political knowledge through conjectures and criticism. As we saw in an earlier chapter, the good news is that the Founding Fathers of the US already did this.

PART 3

THE SOUND OF A FLOWER BLOOMING

As an experiment, one day I asked my daughter Sammy: *"What is the sound of one hand clapping?"* Without hesitation, she replied: *"It's the sound of a flower blooming."* In this section, we explore economics, evolving technology, networks and spirituality as entry points for our personal interconnections with others. Among other things, we find that the current revolution in information technology empowers individuals to freely enter and more fully partake in the philosophy of discovery that I have espoused in this book. I attempt to provide the beginnings of a foundation for a philosophy of how to live in this rapidly evolving world as a fulfilled and happy person.

21

WAYS OF KNOWING

{L}anguage itself is never completely explicit; words are mere steppingstones for thoughts. When listening to speech, we have continuously to establish logical connections between the words; otherwise, as when our attention flags, they become a mere medley of sounds. Economy in art and humour has its roots in this basic mechanism of communicating thought contents by acoustic or visual signs, and is a purposeful development of this principle. It spaces out the steppingstones at intervals just wide enough to require a significant effort from the receiver of the message; it controls his course not by fixed rails but by focusing his attention on a task which he has to complete by his own exertions. The artist achieves the greatest mastery over the consumer by according him the greatest liberty; he rules his subjects by turning them into accomplices.

ARTHUR KOESTLER

In this chapter, I will briefly discuss three types of knowledge that are outside the scope of traditional "hard science". The first area is tacit knowledge, which is highly personalized knowledge that is not part of an articulated discourse. The second area I'll call practical or disciplinary knowledge. This broad category involves the many disciplines or pursuits that entail a knowledge base but that are not really a science—ranging from history to business to dance to fashion. And third is spiritual knowledge. This overview of non-scientific knowledge will provide you with a keener awareness of the fact that there <u>are</u> types of knowledge that go beyond or are prior to—choose your metaphor—scientific knowledge. Non-scientific knowledge interacts with science in important ways, both through the creativity involved in the generation of innovative scientific conjectures and also in terms of the formulation of criticism that can advance knowledge.

From an epistemological perspective, science must be understood as nested within other types of knowledge with which it has a symbiotic relationship. By focusing on non-scientific knowledge, this chapter highlights the fact that scientific knowledge is ultimately based in, advanced by and utilized by individual seekers of knowledge—who are all quirky individuals just like you. The purpose is to de-commoditize the knowledge process and bring you to the realization that you are, in fact, in the middle of it. I hope you come to understand yourself as something like an epicenter of an epistemological earthquake—emanating creative vibrations to the surrounding environment. I am trying to convince you that you are in the middle of this whole knowledge thing—whether you know it or not. By highlighting non-scientific knowledge, this chapter also focuses our attention on the limits of the arena within which science itself operates. Science, taken in isolation, constitutes a very limited and fragmented view of the world. An awareness of the limited scope of science opens you to seeking other types of knowledge, including spiritual knowledge.

TACIT KNOWLEDGE

Hungarian scientist and epistemologist Michael Polanyi is known for emphasizing the importance of what he called "tacit knowledge," and authored a book by that title. The word "tacit" simply means unspoken. In his writings, Polanyi focused on those personal aspects of knowledge that have not been explicitly articulated but <u>do</u> constitute an important part of what each of us may know as individuals. Take, for example, someone who is very good with animals. Such a person has an unspoken knowledge of how to deal with animals that has been gathered through personal experience. This knowledge is no part of scientific discourse, yet undeniably constitutes a very practical and useful kind of knowledge. We will see that this type of knowledge interacts with scientific discourse in important ways.

Tacit knowledge doesn't just apply to working with animals, of course; it applies to all of the things that you do that involve unspoken knowledge. For example, your ability to talk is dependent on your knowledge of how to use your mouth, lips, tongue, vocal chords, facial muscles and so forth to generate all the different sounds inherent in language. But unless you are a speech therapist, you probably haven't articulated to yourself how to do that, and you would probably have a hard time explaining it to another person. Generally, most people tend to learn how to make the sounds involved in language by mimicking others.

Tacit knowledge is huge—and hugely important to you. It constitutes a lot of who you are, in fact. For example, most of the ways in which we use our bodies involve tacit knowledge. If you are playing soccer, the angle and pressure with which you hit the ball with your foot to get it to go where you want involves tacit knowledge. Athletes call this "muscle memory" precisely in recognition that it is tacit. Your ability to give someone a hug that conveys affection involves tacit knowledge regarding how hard to squeeze. Tacit knowledge guides the expression you put on your face if you come up to someone to ask them for directions. Imagine if—in this context—you put on a facial expression that was very angry or, alternatively, extremely joyful; you would scare the person away! Indeed, this tacit knowledge of facial communication is so deeply buried within our psyches that we have a hard time faking it in a believable way. This is why, for example, good actors generally don't focus on mimicking some particular facial expression in their dramatic performances, but rather focus on their character's inner monologue and, in particular, what the character is trying to accomplish. In this manner, they trust in their tacit knowledge to bring out the expressions that match those internal workings of the mind.

Tacit knowledge goes well beyond muscle memory, of course. Tacit knowledge guides many moment-to-moment decisions that we make. For example, suppose you are trying to convince someone to do something.

The kind of arguments you use, and your tactics, will shift depending on how the person is reacting to them, but you probably couldn't articulate the signals that are guiding you. There are many activities in life where you must trust in your tacit knowledge. This is what people mean when they say: "Just be yourself."

Bella: *It always paralyzes me when people say "just be yourself." I ask myself: Who am I really? Do I really know how to be myself? And what if I don't succeed at being myself? What if to 'be myself' simply implies a paralysis of self-doubt and feigned authenticity that comes so naturally to me? In that case, to be myself would be to not be myself!*

Bella, let it go! We covered paradoxes in the previous chapter.

Bella: *To be or not to be, that is the question.*

Tacit knowledge is the basis of our intuitions. For example, suppose you have an intuition that someone is not trustworthy. There is most likely a basis for that intuition in something that you observed, but you couldn't articulate it exactly and there is no obvious logical basis for it. And, of course, such intuitions can turn out to be incorrect. Nonetheless, there does tend to be some kind of real knowledge there, as some people's intuitions on these topics prove to be correct quite often. Our intuitions about physical space, time, matter, motion and force that we develop as children are tacit knowledge. These intuitions tend to be a pretty good guide to our physical world. Nonetheless, for many people, some of their intuitions about time, space and matter turn out to be quite wrong. Newton's laws are not intuitively obvious to most people (which is why we needed Newton to figure them out), and Einstein's work shows us that many of our intuitions about physics are defied when we go to very small scales, or very large scales, or very high speeds. Even much of your knowledge of yourself is tacit. For example, you may have a sense of the types of movie you like to watch, but have not clearly articulated to yourself why you like, say, mysteries better than science fiction.

Bella: *I like biscuits.*

Tacit knowledge evolves and interacts with the articulated discourses that characterize both science and more informal bodies of knowledge. Typically, our unarticulated intuitions are refined and honed through whatever type of work we do. For example, as an economist, I often have intuitions that there is an economic problem with something before I understand why. This insight is coming from my tacit knowledge. The next step in my thinking is then to analyze carefully the incentives of the people involved in the economic situation I am studying as well as the constraints that cabin their decision making. At this point, my initial intuition is often confirmed and supported by a theory that explains <u>why</u> there is an economic problem where I thought there might be one. Finally, I then look to empirical and anecdotal evidence to see if my theory is confirmed in practice. I am shocked at how often my initial, inarticulate intuitions have guided me in the right direction.

Notice that this reverses the traditional epistemological order of events that we are taught when we are introduced to science. The rhetoric of science has it that we run from: (1) observation to (2) theory to (3) understanding. The actual history of science confirms my own experience—not that I've made any great discoveries—that the order is often reversed, running from: (1) understanding to (2) theory to (3) observation, and that the process is considerably more complicated than the traditional version would have it.

Of course, when I was 18 and just entering college I would not have possessed the depth of tacit knowledge regarding economic issues that I have at age 57, having worked on economic issues for decades. My tacit as well as explicit knowledge have been developed, refined and informed by college courses on economics, graduate school, reading economic articles, thinking about economics while reading the newspaper, and practical life experiences as well as accumulated professional experience as an economist and lawyer. The point is that, over time, I have accumulated much economic knowledge, some of which I am explicitly aware of, and much of which I am not. Thus, many discovery processes for me will begin by simply thinking hard and attempting to articulate what I already know, but don't know that I know. The same will often be the case in your life. Discovery processes, including scientific discoveries, are often initiated or driven by an effort to articulate an idea that has already begun to be developed tacitly. This is why you must both trust your instincts, but also verify them.

This is certainly how Einstein approached his work—that is, going from (1) understanding to (2) theory to (3) observation. For example, he spent a lot of time trying to imagine what you would see if you could run as fast as a light beam. He was aware of the experiments of Michelson and Morley in the 1890s that showed that light always moved at a uniform speed—that is, the speed of light. This, of course, makes no sense from a classical perspective. That is, if one were on a moving platform—going, say, 30 miles per hour—and one threw a baseball from that moving platform in the direction of the movement at, say, 40 miles per hour, then—ignoring air resistance—the ball should end up going 70 miles per hour. But light does not work that way, apparently. Einstein tried to make sense of this.[55] He liked thought experiments. He imagined the difference between how a light moving up and down (vertically) on a rapidly-moving space ship would look to someone on board versus how it would look to someone from a stationary object nearby. From the vantage point of the person standing on the stationary object, the light would appear to have travelled further than it did to the person on board the spaceship. This is because—for the person standing on the stationary object—the light would have a horizontal element to its movement as well as a vertical movement. Einstein reasoned that—if light always travels at the same speed—then it would not be possible for light to go different distances in the same time frame. Thus, if light travels further from the perspective of the person on the stationary object versus the perspective of the person on the space ship, the difference must be due to a different amount of time having gone by. Using basic geometry, he calculated what the difference in time would have to be. He arrived at an equation that predicted the shortening (or "dilation") of time when an object is moving. Later, the implications of this equation were empirically tested. The passage of time recorded on an atomic clock on a satellite was compared with the passage of time recorded by an atomic clock on Earth. It was found that time had, in fact, dilated on the satellite exactly in accordance with Einstein's predictions, which had resulted from his playful thought experiments. Thus, we see that Einstein travelled from (1) understanding to (2) theory to (3) observation.

Much of the knowledge you employ in navigating the world has nothing to do with scientific discourse, of course. You develop it through your experiences, through watching and mimicking, through practice, through storytelling and watching plays, through art, through reading both fiction and non-fiction, and so on. Much of this becomes tacit knowledge. And you would be completely lost without it. You would indeed be as helpless as a baby. The point of this is that you—as a seeker of knowledge—are already situated in the world and full of ideas, notions and intuitions. And this full, very real, person plays a role in science. In contrast, the common rhetoric of science has it that we are supposed to come to science as if we are a "blank slate"—bringing no pre-conceptions whatsoever to the process. We are told that we should trust science to fill our (otherwise empty) minds with objective truth. In fact, we do not come to science as a blank slate, nor should we! If we did so, we would be leaving behind our tacit knowledge. This is like throwing out the baby with the bathwater. That is, in the name of scientific purity, we would have disposed of the scientist herself. This is a profoundly wrong approach to knowledge. We should enter into scientific discourse as the full human beings that we are—with all kinds of intuitions, pre-conceptions, tacit knowledge and, indeed, biases. This is essential precisely because we need our tacit knowledge as an input to the discovery process in terms of generating both conjectures and criticisms and, indeed, even to a certain extent in our capabilities to observe. Scientific creativity is particularly important in terms of developing new conjectures. And, as we have seen, it is the job of criticism—an essential component to the scientific process—to unearth and expose personal biases that turn out to be incorrect. That is, we don't rely on a purging of our souls and minds to obtain objectivity, but rather the process of weighing evidence against our conjectures to sort our error.

PRACTICAL OR DISCIPLINARY KNOWLEDGE

On a general level, in addition to tacit knowledge, there are myriad articulated discourses that constitute ways of knowing that are outside of science. These knowledge bases are complex and interact with scientific thought, but are most decidedly not a direct part of that particular discourse. To take a trivial example, we might all agree that discussions of fashion definitely involve knowledge of a sort. You wouldn't hire a person to be the editor of a fashion magazine unless they were quite knowledgeable in this regard.

Bella: *A mere cursory examination of your attire is suggestive that you are not too knowledgeable in that regard, and yet that there might be valuable knowledge to be had there.*

And you would be right. Fashion discourse, and the knowledge involved, is clearly something quite separate and distinct from science. One of the key ideas in this book is that you can employ the tools of rationality in the exploration and development of bodies of knowledge that are outside the scope of science per se. Such an application of rationality may not yield quite as powerful results as they do in science, but, as we will see, may nonetheless be quite fruitful and important.

We think of physics, biology, chemistry, geology, physical anthropology, mathematics and medicine as "harder" sciences. We view them as more rigorous than history, political science, language studies, sociology, cultural anthropology, geography, business, law, ethics and religious studies. Economics falls somewhere in between the two groups, but certainly closer to the latter. And then there is art, music, dance, poetry, theater, comedy, creative writing and dog training. These clearly involve bodies of knowledge, methods and discipline, and yet we don't know quite where to put them epistemologically.

Bella: *Did you say dog training? What about people training? I have to do a lot of that.*

Despite the fact that these many bodies of knowledge do not constitute what we would call "hard science", we would all agree, I think, that they are often useful and important.

Bella: *Certainly, people training is crucial—otherwise they are just insufficiently responsive.*

My point here is a simple one: what we think of as the "hard" sciences are a small island in the sea of human knowledge. To be sure, it is an especially important island and, in general, there is more rigour on that island. But as I have argued in previous chapters the differences between the "hard" sciences and these other bodies of thought is more one of degree than of kind. <u>They are all susceptible to improvement and refinement through processes of conjectures and criticism.</u> That is the very essence of rationality. Moreover, all these camps of thought can learn from and be inspired by one another.

Bella: *Where possible, we must return to the ideal of the Renaissance Dog—a dog for all seasons and pursuits.*

SPIRITUAL KNOWLEDGE

In a different vein, I believe that there are also spiritual ways of coming to knowledge. (I will discuss this more extensively in a later chapter.) These are also, rather obviously, distinct and separate from scientific discourse. People have been exploring paths to spiritual enlightenment for as long as we have been human. The mystics of the world are on to something. Indeed, it is amusing to me that scientifically (and therefore supposedly empirically) minded people often reject these paths without ever having really tried them—so how would they know if these paths are efficacious or not? Of course, like the application of rationality and the scientific method, spiritual paths may also be fraught with error and misunderstanding. And humans, given their failings, may well try to oppress and control others through religious and spiritual ideas, just as they do through supposedly scientific ideas. But such spiritual failures do not imply a failure of the approach any more than scientific failures imply a lack of rationality.

To be sure, spiritual paths to knowledge are quite different than employing the tools of rationality, but they do not preclude one another, and may indeed enhance one another. They simply constitute somewhat different and complementary realms. Jesus Christ said "Render unto Caesar the things which are Caesar's, and unto God the things that are God's." I believe that He meant this epistemologically. Give the material world its due and give the world of morality, meaning, beauty, emotion and spirituality its due. Whatever your religion may (or may not) be, you are a person both of the corporeal world and the spiritual. Do not deny either.

22

FINDING YOUR EPISTEMOLOGICAL NICHE IN THE KNOWLEDGE ECONOMY

The investigation of nature is an infinite pasture-ground, where all may graze, and where the more bite, the longer the grass grows, the sweeter is its flavor, and the more it nourishes.

THOMAS HENRY HUXLEY

{T}he moment man first picked up a stone or a branch to use as a tool, he altered irrevocably the balance between him and his environment. From this point on, the way in which the world around him changed was different. It was no longer regular or predictable. New objects appeared that were not recognizable as a mutation of something that had existed before, and as each one emerged it altered the environment not for a season, but for ever. While the number of these tools remained small, their effect

took a long time to spread and to cause change. But as they increased, so did their effects: the more the tools, the faster the rate of change.

JAMES BURKE

THE GREAT REVOLUTION

We are in the midst of the most extraordinary technological and economic revolution in the history of humankind—the information revolution. It is largely driven by a basic economic fact—the plummeting costs of information technology, including the cost of computers, information storage, computational power, software and interconnectivity. As a result of these plummeting costs:

(1) economic innovation will be faster than ever before;

(2) goods and services are becoming much more information-intensive;

(3) intermediaries—that is, people who stand between you and what you want—will be bypassed unless they add considerable value;

(4) the economy will be ever more globalized;

(5) business competition will become more intense;

(6) new business models will evolve rapidly;

(7) both private and governmental organizations and institutional structures will evolve more rapidly than ever before;

(8) being heard in society will become a much more open, competitive process;

(9) previously marginalized groups will be empowered;

(10) political and cultural change will be faster than ever before;

(11) culture will become more globalized—in the sense of rapid dissemination and crossing borders quickly—but more fragmented in that it will be driven by those with like interests who choose to connect with one another;

(12) international cooperation will become more important;

(13) totalitarian and communist regimes will be ever more economically disadvantaged, and

(14) more than ever before, the development of economic processes, products and services will be driven by the logic of discovery.

This is the world in which you will live your life. These are big changes. How they will play out is difficult to say. While much of this will be wonderful, not all of it will be. To navigate this world well you will need to be not only extremely well educated but also a critical independent thinker. More than ever before, to prosper you will need to understand how to employ the logic of discovery to constructively collaborate with others in producing value and seeking truth, beauty and happiness. I wrote this book to help prepare you for this world.

Bella: *And one cannot help but wonder how it will all affect dogs.*

This brave new world will be one of rapid change. Conventional thinking will usually be behind the curve. You will have to use technology to build and maintain relationships, track events and keep up with evolving ideas and knowledge in real time. It will be the age of constructive collaboration. You will need to know how to work constructively with other people through formulating conjectures, engaging in constructive criticism, taking criticism seriously and formulating new, more refined conjectures. It will also be an age marked by tension and turmoil. Information technology is creating platforms by which those in authority will regularly be challenged. Don't expect them to be happy about this. While I think this will be a dangerous world, I am largely optimistic. It certainly will be interesting.

Bella: *Is it a good thing to live in interesting times?*

That depends on how interesting they get.

For most goods and services, economic scarcity rules the day. What is consumed by one person may not be consumed by another. If there is a pie to divvy up, for any piece that I eat, there is one less piece for you. If I use a resource to produce one good, then generally I can't use that resource to produce a different good—at least not at that point in time. And the extra resources required to produce an extra unit of a good always has a cost of some significance. There are, however, some major exceptions to these economic rules of scarcity; to wit: knowledge products, information products, information-intensive products and network economics. Knowledge products and information-intensive goods, services and productive processes are increasing in importance in the current era. It is important that you understand their unique qualities. They will substantially shape your future.

THE MARGINAL COST OF AN INFORMATION PRODUCT IS ZERO

An information product is a product or service that predominantly involves information. As you know, we are in the information age where computing power, information storage power and connectivity among computers is extremely inexpensive. As a consequence, the extra cost of replicating and distributing an extra bit of information is very nearly zero. Indeed, for most practical purposes we can call it zero. Put differently, if an informational good or service can be put into a digital format, it can be reproduced and distributed at almost no cost. Now, this is not to say that the <u>initial production</u> of the information is inexpensive. That initial production of the information may be quite expensive, in fact. But it is the reproduction and distribution that is at near zero cost. This is best understood through some examples.

Take, for example, a song. It may take quite a bit of effort to compose a good song. So there is a substantial cost there. But once that song is put into a digital format, it can be reproduced and distributed at essentially a zero cost. You can simply download it into your computer and play it on a hand held device anytime you want. This cost structure is very different than the cost structure for, say, a chair. To produce another chair, one has to get some more materials—pre-cut or shaped wood, glue, bolts and other parts—and put it together. In addition, you have to physically transport the chair to wherever someone wants to buy it. As a consequence, the cost for a "copy" of a chair always remains substantial. In stark contrast, as noted above, the cost for a digital copy of a song is near zero, and for most practical purposes may be resumed to be zero.

Bella: *Does that mean I will get the song for free?*

No. This near zero cost to <u>replicate</u> an information product, such as a song, does <u>not</u> mean that the person selling it will charge you zero for it. After all, the song writer wants to be compensated for the effort and substantial cost of creating the song in the first place, so she has to charge something for it. But the capability of people to replicate an information product at near zero cost can make it difficult to get them to pay money to the creator of the information. Below we will discuss the difficulties of creating a profitable business model in the digital age, but first let's explore some more examples of information products. Take the book you are reading right now as an example. In its digital form, it can be replicated at near zero cost, yet it took me a very large amount of effort to write it.

Bella: *And what about me?*

No, Bella, you cannot be replicated in digital format.

Bella: *I mean what about the time it took me to co-author this book!*

Sorry. Let me rephrase that. It took <u>Bella</u> and I a long time to write this book. Other examples of information products include computer software of any sort, movies, maps, digital photographs, games, professional advice, communication, social websites, data, educational services and so on.

INFORMATION PRODUCTS HAVE CHALLENGING BUSINESS MODELS

In the information age, developing a profitable business model can be quite difficult. Let's go back to our song writer. It is costly to compose a song. If you are going to make a living at this, you need to make some money for your efforts. If you post the song online, and ask people to pay you money for downloading it, they may well do so. But as soon as one person has downloaded it, they can copy it for zero cost and share it with a friend who didn't pay you any money at all. As a consequence, you may not make enough money to pay for your living. You will have to stop writing songs and get another job. In the information age, a lot more goods and services are just like that song. Let's say you write some useful software code, and work very hard to produce it. Once someone else has it, it is quite easy for them to copy it and give it to someone else. It is hard to make money that way.

There are a couple of ways to approach this problem. First of all, finding ways to protect intellectual property rights becomes much more important in this world. Intellectual property is the notion that certain kinds of knowledge or information products belong to the person who discovered or created them. For people to receive compensation for an information or knowledge product that they have created, they have to have some kind of a legal claim to payment. This is what we try to do to protect the songwriters, for example. They receive what is called a copyright, and that means you are <u>not</u> supposed to copy their work without paying the price they have set for it. Now, of course, some people do break the rules and make copies of things they are not supposed to, and thereby reduce the revenues of the songwriters.

There are a number of other tactics that are used to create business models to try and secure profits from information-intensive products. One tactic is the "bundling" of different goods and services. This is where you don't sell the information products separately, but rather sell them for a given price as part of a package of goods and services. For example, there may be a physical product that can be sold, such as a computer, with which informational products, such as software and various services, might be bundled to make the product more competitive. Another version of this tactic is to sell <u>access</u> to various bundled information products—perhaps for a monthly fee.

Another business challenge associated with information products is that the potential buyers don't know its quality until they try it, and so they may not be willing to buy it in the first place. There are some different business tactics to try to address this challenge:

- Give away samples
- Maintain good quality and hope that word spreads among buyers
- Spend so much on advertising that potential buyers realize that you have a lot to lose (in terms of wasted advertising expenditures) <u>if</u> the product doesn't have good quality, as a consequence of which the potential buyers assume it <u>does</u> have good quality; economists call this a "bonding" strategy.

THE INCREASING INFORMATION INTENSITY OF PRODUCTS, SERVICES AND PRODUCTION

The examples given above—software, movies, books and so forth—are all rather obvious in terms of their information-intensity as products or services. However, what is perhaps less obvious is that society is reaching a point where information-technology has become so powerful that information itself can be employed as an economic substitute for actual materials and physical productive capacity. This constitutes a dematerialization of economic value.

Bella: *How can that be? You can't make a chair out of the digital information being shared among computers. And, as you noted yourself, a dog certainly cannot be digitized!*

Let me give you some examples of how information as well as knowledge can become a substitute for actual materials and for physical productive capacity. Steel production involves complicated chemical reactions. Indeed, the precise chemical make-up of steel makes a great deal of difference as to its quality. In recent decades, the production of steel has become revolutionized by computers. As the steel is being produced, computers model its chemical makeup, and adjust the inputs with precision. The result is much higher quality steel as well as steel that can be more finely customized to various purposes. The quality of steel has improved so much, that in many instances much thinner steel can be employed in many uses than before. For example, over time cars have begun to weigh much less because they are using thinner sheets of high quality steel, among many other such improvements. In this manner, information has directly substituted for steel—that is, by having more information at the right time and applying it in the production of steel, much less physical input of actual steel is needed to produce products with steel content. That constitutes a profound economic revolution.

Let's look at an example where information substitutes for physical productive capacity—the production of engine blocks. The "block" of a car's motor involves a very large chunk of metal with many special holes bored into it for the movement of the car pistons, et cetera. Formerly, it cost an enormous amount of money to set up a large machine with special drill bits aligned precisely to transform a block of metal into an engine block with all the proper holes in it. Since these machines were very expensive to build and set up, car companies tended to use the same engine block for many years, even as the rest of the car continued to be re-designed and otherwise improved. They would also use the same engine block across many different types of vehicles.

With advancements in computer technology, the machines that produce engine blocks now have robotic arms that can drill many different types of holes in many different types of blocks. Thus, one machine can now do the work that it used to take a number of distinct machines to do.

Moreover, to have the holes drilled a bit differently simply involves telling the computer what you want. The computer then makes the adjustments—with neither new machinery nor retooling required. This means there is no need for another machine if a different type of block is wanted. You simply reprogram the old machine. In this way, information—in the form of computer programming—has been directly substituted for the production of new block-boring machines. This leads to enormous cost savings. It also opens up the possibility of more rapid technological progress in that car makers are free to try to develop better engine blocks rather than feeling constrained to stick with a particular model. Thus, we have information substituting for productive machinery as well as increasing the pace of innovation. We are really in an "information economy" now, with all of the peculiar economics that goes along with that.

GLOBALIZATION

With increasingly inexpensive information technology, geography disappears. In a digitally interconnected world with information-intensive goods and services, value-add activities can be conducted anywhere in the world and easily sent to any other part of the world. This has led to an intensity of global competition that goes way beyond mere finished goods and services crossing borders. The entire production process for any good or service now often has aspects that are completed all around the globe. The acquisition of raw materials, financing, consumer research, production planning, engineering, design, production, legal advice, marketing, sales and distribution are all done in far flung places. In such a globalized economy, workers in any one part of the world compete with workers everywhere else to contribute economic value. A telephone call center for the sale of goods to Americans need not be placed in the US; it might be in, say, India, and often is. Moreover, an engineer in the US and an engineer in India are in direct competition with one another; there is nothing about their work that requires them to be in the same location as any other aspect of the design, planning and production process.

With this kind of competition among workers everywhere, one would expect workers in poorer countries to gain the most, since they are starting the competition from a lower economic rung and are willing to take lower compensation for their efforts. This should prove true, at least, so long as two conditions are fulfilled: (1) the countries where they reside are sufficiently stable and are able to sustain a relatively predictable environment in which businesses may operate and (2) the people there have sufficient skills to contribute to the global economy. Indeed, as a result of globalization, we have seen spectacular economic growth in countries such as India and China. From a global perspective, this is certainly a good thing. There are a lot less desperately poor people in the world as a result of these changes. Globalization also has tremendous economic benefits for developed countries such as the US. On the other hand, workers in the most developed countries, such as the US, may find that they have much tougher competition than they have ever confronted before. Facing such intense competition and economic dynamism, workers at the bottom of the economic ladder in developed countries may find themselves somewhat less economically secure.

DISINTERMEDIATION

In the old economy, there was a great deal of "intermediation". Intermediation includes all processes where someone stands between you and whatever you want. In business, this intermediation is done by what are called middle-men. These are folks like wholesalers who buy products from suppliers and, in turn, sell these same products to retailers, who in turn sell them to customers. Sometimes this chain of transactions is called the "supply chain". In the information age, it is much easier for people to bypass the traditional middle-men. That is, given the plethora of information available on the internet, it is not so hard for people to go directly to the source of whatever they want. This might involve retailers skipping the middle-men (that is, the wholesalers) and going directly to the suppliers themselves, and thus shortening the supply chain. Or, more radically, it might involve customers going directly to the suppliers themselves, and skipping both the retailers and the wholesalers. The process of bypassing the intermediaries is sometimes called "disintermediation." Disintermediation is occurring on many fronts, not just in business.

In a sense, the media itself—television and newspapers and so forth—are intermediaries between yourself and the events of the day. Technology, however, provides you with the means to go directly to events and judge them for yourself—without the intermediation of the media. If there is, say, a tsunami in another part of the world, you can go right on the Internet and see images being placed there by people who are struggling with the damage. If you want to listen in on a Congressional hearing, you can do that. If there is turmoil in the streets of a middle-eastern country, and you want to know what the man or woman on the street there is thinking, you can go on the internet and read their various postings. In doing so, you are disintermediating the media. Information regarding a recent (and unusual) earthquake in Virginia reached residents of New York City <u>before</u> the rumblings of the earthquake were actually felt—and well before the traditional media were relating the story.

INFORMATION TECHNOLOGY LEADS TO "FLATTER" ORGANIZATIONS

When I first began working at a law firm, I would spend a considerable amount of time each week waiting outside the office of one of the key partners—standing in line with other associates—waiting to run something by him to get his approval. After some time, I left that law firm and worked elsewhere. Later in my career, I came back to that same law firm to work again. By this time, email had been invented. I no longer had to wait outside the partner's office to get sign-off on various decisions. This could all be done through email. This saved me a number of hours per week in terms of productivity. But the ramifications of email went far beyond this particular increase in efficiency. Previously, high-level decisions about legal matters had been discussed by the law partners on the phone, and associates (that is, junior folks like me) were typically not a part of the discussion. That was mainly for technological reasons; it was much easier for one partner to just pick up the phone to talk to another partner. Upon my return to the law firm, however, much of this back-and-forth discussion of the tricky issues was done by email. Since it was the associates who typically had to implement the ideas being discussed in the email correspondence, they were copied on the emails. But this meant they had direct access to the discussions, and could contribute if they had something to add. This brought associates into strategic and tactical discussions at an earlier stage in their careers than otherwise would have been the case. Moreover, given the new technology, a single partner now could effectively oversee many more matters than he or she could have before. And the same is true of any business-person.

As a consequence, in many kinds of activities there is substantially less need for a middle layer of management. By middle management I mean the people at the middle layer of an organization that used to be needed to convey the desires of the top management to the many people at the bottom of the organization that are actually doing directly whatever needs doing and then report back to the senior management as to what was actually getting done. With dramatically improved communications technology, we don't need so many people in the middle-layers of management anymore. In the world we are entering, we just need leaders and doers. This is sometime referred to as a "flatter organization." This simply implies that there aren't as many people in the middle layers, so the overall organization chart looks a bit less like a steep pyramid. Flatter organizational structure is really just a form of disintermediation, but in this case it's not a middle-man that is being bypassed but middle-management, as the leaders of the organization communicate more directly with the many doers in the organization.

While flatter organizations can lead to great improvements in productivity, which in turn leads to increased economic growth and higher incomes on average, this shift might also lead to a more skewed distribution of income with less of a middle class. That is, we may be entering a world where there are very high paying jobs and very low paying jobs—and not a lot in between. Flatter organizational structure may also lead to less mobility between the income classes. That is, it might become harder to work your way up in an organization if there are no middle rungs to the promotional "ladder", so-to-speak. It may turn out that you either come in at the bottom and stay there, or you come in at the top and stay there. This could further disadvantage anyone who does not have a good start in life, despite any inherent talents or a capacity and willingness to work hard.

INFORMATION TECHNOLOGY CHANGES THE BOUNDARIES OF ORGANIZATIONS AND PROCESSES

Information technology is also apt to change what organizations do internally versus what they decide to purchase from outsiders. Every business has to make decisions about which aspects of its production process it hires people to do versus which aspects it is going to purchase from some other business or entity. Suppose your business is to make tables. On the one hand, you may both make tables and then deliver them to retailers. On the other hand, alternatively, you may decide that it makes more sense for your business just to make the tables, but then to enter into a contract with a different entity to deliver the tables to retail outlets. Taking an activity like that and contracting to have some other organization provide the service is called "outsourcing". A good business person will look at the various activities that are needed in their business, and figure out which ones it is best to do internally and which would be best to outsource.

Information technology will have a big impact on these kinds of business decisions. If you can communicate seamlessly with people in other organizations as well as monitor their activities closely with information technology, then it is less expensive and more practical to outsource many aspects of your business. This has already led to radical changes in the way people do business. Aspects of the business model that you would have almost always formerly found to be done in-house are now outsourced. For example, what we think of today as a shoe company may, in fact, no longer produce shoes, but rather simply manage a brand name for shoes that they contract for others to produce. As another example, many small companies now outsource many of the activities involved with administering the various types of compensation and benefits that employees receive. They will hire a company that specialized in human resources to oversee these aspects of its business decision making. The traditional boundaries of businesses and other organizations are becoming more porous, and continue to evolve more rapidly than ever before.

In sum, much the economic activity of the future will be information-intensive and involve rapid change. But "information", "knowledge" and "ideas" are really all the same thing. Their evolution is driven by the same logic of discovery that we have been discussing in this book. To prosper in this new information-intensive world, it is especially important that you understand the logic of discovery and learn how to apply it in these contexts. More specifically, to succeed in this brave new world, you will have to be comfortable with interactive, collaborative processes in which you make conjectures, engage in constructive criticism and refine conjectures in light of the evidence in order to improve ideas—that is where the "value-add" will be as well as both the higher compensation and the fun. Much of this will happen in the context of networks.

NETWORKS

A network is anything that people use where the use of it by any one person increases the value of the use of it by anyone else. Networks are generally characterized by a set of standards and a technology that are required for their use, although standards themselves can be networks on their own. The best example of a network is a telephone system. Let's suppose you have just invented the telephone. And let's suppose initially there are just two people whose phones are connected by a telephone system—you and your friend. At this point, the only use of the telephone is to call your friend. That's nice, of course, but only of modest usefulness, at best.

    Bella: *I think that is quite useful. I'd call you up and tell you to feed me my dinner.*

But let's say people like the idea of the telephone and more are willing to join the network. When one more person gets a telephone and becomes connected to the network, the network becomes more useful to everyone who uses it, since now there are two other people you can call instead of one.

    Bella: *I get it. If you are not there, I'll call someone else to feed me my dinner.*

As more and more people join the telephone network, the network becomes ever more useful to all of them, because they now have ever more people they can call. Today you can call almost anyone at almost any time, and the phone network is vital in terms of how people communicate and organize their lives.

    Bella: *We can even order dog food to be delivered to our door.*

Like information products, there are some weird economics associated with networks. A network is not governed by scarcity in the same way that goods and services normally are. Historically, with typical goods and services, the more of the good I consume, the less remains for you. In stark contrast, networks have this lovely quality that the more people who share in them, the <u>more</u> valuable they become for everyone else. Life is full of networks. Let's start with some obvious ones. The road system is a network. The more roads that are added to the pre-existing network of roads, the more places you can drive to and the more useful the network becomes.

Bella: *A bunch of dogs barking throughout a neighborhood is a network—each letting the next know that a worthy object of barking is strolling down the street. The more, the merrier.*

The more, the noisier.

The railway system is a network as well and the same logic applies— that is, the more lines that become available, the more places you can go to using the system. One of the most important examples today of a network is the Internet. This is a network of computers all around the world in which the computers communicate with one another. In this way, when people want to share information or software, the computers can tap into and use the information or software on the other computers in the network. This is enormously powerful. The Internet facilitates the distribution of information products at near zero cost, and the more computers that hook into it, the more useful it is. It also makes each computer owner a potential broadcaster to the world, if people are interested in what that person has to offer.

ANY KIND OF STANDARD IS A NETWORK

Any kind of a standard is a network. For example, the metric system, by which distances are measured with meters, centimeters, millimeters, kilometers and so forth, is really a network. The more people who use it, the more useful it is. If you were the only person using the metric system, it would be of quite limited usefulness. If two people were using it, it would be more useful, but still not terribly useful. If many people in the world are using this same set of standards, then it is extremely useful. The same is true of just about any standard. The more people who use it, the more useful it is. Standards are networks. Computers, of course, have standards that allow them to communicate with one another—that is, to tell each other what information they want, where the information is, and what the information is. Of course, the more computers that use a standard, the more computers can communicate with one another. Among other things, standards like this are what make the Internet possible.

Not only are computer languages networks, but human ones are as well. Take the English language, for example. The more people who know the English language, the better it is for everyone else who knows it. This is because the more people who know a language, the more will be written and communicated in it, and thus the more useful it will be. Let's take a really simple example of a standard as a network—driving on the right-hand side of the road. If someone is facing you, her right hand is on the same side as your left hand. Using this idea, we have developed a simple rule which many countries use; if we all drive on the right-hand side of the road, then we won't crash into each other (or, at least, not nearly so much as we otherwise might). That's obviously a very handy standard. Clearly, the more people who share this standard, the better.

Bella: *Don't they drive on the left-hand side of the road in some countries?*

Yes, that's true. And it doesn't really matter <u>which</u> side of the road you make as the standard one on which to travel. What is important in this instance is simply that there <u>is</u> a standard. This is how it often is with standards; that is, it is not so important what the standard is, but just that you have one. Of course, the fact that different countries have different standards on this can be a problem. If you visit a country with a different standard, when you are crossing the street you may tend to look the wrong way. In the US, you look to your left as you begin to cross the street, but in, say, Bermuda you need to look to your right. If you don't do this correctly, you may well get hit by a car. In sum, it is very important to be aware of <u>which</u> standard you are working within.

Bella: *Perhaps it's best to get in the habit of looking* <u>both</u> *ways.*

Yes, indeed. At any rate, knowing what network you are in—and what rules it is governed by—is important. I understand that at one point a rocket was sent in the wrong direction because some engineers were using the metric system and others the English System.

NOT ALL STANDARDS ARE CREATED EQUAL

As noted above, in many contexts, the most important thing about a particular standard may simply be that it does exist and is shared by participants. Nonetheless, it is important to recognize that some standards—whether or not embraced by all—may be superior to others in terms of various important considerations. That is, not all standards are created equal. For example, as much as I am attached to the traditional system of weights and measures that are used in the United States, (which is sometimes known as the English System and which uses measurements like inches, feet, miles, pounds, tons and so forth), it must be admitted that it is not nearly so practical as the metric system. This is for at least two reasons. First, the metric system is much more widely used around the world. Second, the metric system is set up more logically and is substantially easier to use from an arithmetic point of view. In sum, while the most important thing about any set of measurement standards is simply that they exist and are shared, the point here is that one might be superior to the other and constitute a better choice. Oddly, however, as we will see below, it doesn't always make sense to switch to an alternative standard, even if that alternative is demonstrably superior! This is because there may be, and often are, substantial costs to switching standards. The gains one might make from switching to an otherwise superior standard are not always sufficient to justify incurring the cost of switching—more on this below.

THE PRECIPITOUS ECONOMICS OF NETWORKS

Because the value of a network increases with the number of people who use it, networks can reach a critical threshold where they suddenly become much more valuable. In turn, this can then further accelerate their popularity. In this situation, the network is in a positive feedback loop—the bigger it gets, the better it gets and the better it gets, the bigger it gets. A threshold in the benefit of participation is reached where the case for joining the network becomes compelling for almost everyone. This can happen quite suddenly. The positive feedback loop continues until the network becomes dominant in whatever niche it fills. A dramatic example is provided by the recent growth in the usage of the English language. The number of people around the globe who speak English has been dramatically increasing in recent decades, perhaps due to the historical importance of the commerce of a number of English-speaking nations. Indeed, English has already become the world's language for business. As ever more people learn English as a second language, it becomes yet more valuable for other people to learn English, and thus they choose to make that investment. I have read about factories where there are multiple different language groups involved—none of which include English—and yet they all use English to talk to one another. Through a positive feedback loop of ever growing benefits with ever greater participation, English has become the second language of choice for people around the world. The Internet seems to be accelerating this process. Online social networks provide another example of such positive feedback loops. As one person sees ever more of her friends join a social networking site, and begin to organize their lives based on it, the benefits of joining increase. Pretty soon, great swaths of society are communicating with one another and sharing aspects of their lives through a given online service.

NETWORKS HAVE SWITCHING COSTS, WHICH IMPLIES SOME RIGIDITY

Another standard that constitutes a network is the layout of the keys on a type-writer. This standard layout is known as "Qwerty", which, as you will see if you look at a computer keyboard, is the order of the keys in the first row of letters on the upper left—that is, Q, W, E, R, T and Y. Of course, the more people who use such a standard, the better, because then everyone can count on keyboards being set up the same way with every keyboard they encounter. Once people learn to type fast with a given layout of keys, they do not want to switch to any other layout—otherwise they would have to relearn typing. The cost of switching from one network to another is called—oddly enough—switching cost.

One of the important things to understand about networks is that, as noted above, they are not always optimal—that is, they do not constitute the best of all possible worlds. In part, this is due to the presence of switching costs. Networks may remain dominant in whatever niche they occupy, even if they don't offer the best potential network. That is, there might be better alternative networks out there, but the majority of people stick with the network in which they are already participating so that they do not have to incur switching costs. The Qwerty arrangement of letters was originally designed for mechanical typewriters where the keys would get jammed if someone typed too quickly. In light of this, the keys were arranged to slow down the typing—that is, with distances between keys that are most commonly used were set further apart from one another than they might be otherwise. With computer keyboards, of course, jamming is no longer an issue. Nonetheless, we continue with the Qwerty keyboard, even though it would be more efficient to create an alternative keyboard set up for speed. As noted above, this is due to the switching cost. Because it is costly to switch networks, a dominant network tends to have staying power, until it is unseated by an alternative that is <u>sufficiently</u> superior that it overcomes the switching costs.

The United States has largely remained on the English System of weights and measures due to switching costs. Even though the metric system probably makes more sense,[57] given the advantages described above, we stick with the English System because we grew up with it, we are used to it, we like it, and many of our tools, machinery, signs and so forth have it built into them. For example, bolts and wrenches in the United States tend to be set in sizes standardized on the basis of inches. As you can imagine, it would be quite an expensive process to switch completely away from that—and for a long time afterward anyone doing mechanical work would need two sets of wrenches—one based on each measurement system.

SCIENCE AND KNOWLEDGE ARE CONSTITUTED BY INTERRELATED NETWORKS

Our lives are dominated by learning and navigating a myriad of complex and overlapping networks. Indeed, science and, more generally, all processes of discovery are really defined by interlocking sets of networks—especially networks when they take the form of standards. As we have seen, science is a <u>collective</u> project driven by a logic of discovery that includes conjectures, criticism and fruitful responses to criticism. The logic of discovery coordinates the ideas and criticisms of a wide array of scientists and generates the progressive network that is science. The more people who participate in science's logic of discovery, and who bring their talents, skills and energy to bear upon it, the more it advances, and the more their peculiar insights and talents complement one another to advance the discovery process. Science, of course, relies heavily on a wide array of standards and a large part of understanding science and contributing to it involves grasping these standards. Indeed, scientific research programs themselves can be thought of as networks, defined by the standards inherent in the positive and negative heuristics. The market economy can be thought of as a network—or interrelated set of networks—as well, of course, as per our discussion in a previous chapter. Networks provide the soil in which the logic of discovery may thrive. The two are closely intertwined.

ART AND CULTURE ARE ALSO DEFINED BY INTERRELATED NETWORKS

Art and culture are also defined by interrelated sets of networks. To become an artist, you learn the techniques that other artists have used and you absorb an art's language and the evocative nature of its tool set through experiencing the art of others. The greater the number of people who share in a particular set of explorations, the more powerful the exploration becomes. Indeed, the greatest art does appear to arrive in clusters of work among artists who influence, empower and embolden one another. They constitute a network.

Culture itself may also be thought of as a complex of interrelated networks. To a large extent, culture is based on a shared set of experiences. These experiences, of course, may take many forms, ranging from shared media, literature, art and humor on the one hand to various types of organizational, economic and family structures, education, sports, religion, morality and so forth on the other. Those shared experiences result in certain shared values, shared presumptions and shared humor. Other things being equal, the more people who share a culture, the more benefits there are to it. That is, the cultural products tend to be richer, as more people contribute to it. Culture facilitates a depth of communication among its participants that may be much more difficult when attempted across different cultures. I have a friend who I am told is much funnier when speaking French than when she is speaking English. Unfortunately, I don't understand French. (The good news is that she is nonetheless quite clever in English.)

Culture, of course, is never a unified monolith. Rather, it tends to be fragmented, and typically entails a complex grid of interlocking networks, each of which may define its own subculture. These subcultures can be quite strong in terms of their influence on people. For example, you may find a German mathematician and a French mathematician have much more in common than do other Germans and French people with one another.

Bella: *Particularly, I have noticed that beards, sandals and pants that are too short appear to be required gear, at least among male mathematicians.*

None of us is really a member of just <u>one</u> culture. Rather, we are defined by the blend of overlapping cultural networks in which we participate. For example, if a person is from, say, the Texas panhandle, her experience of "American" culture will be quite different than if she were, say, from the Bronx in New York City. Her experience of the language itself would be different. If you spend a substantial portion of your time playing, say, high school football in Northern Virginia, you will have a particular set of cultural experiences, which will be quite different than what you would experience if you spent your time, say, learning and performing in a ballet company in Washington, DC. If you are raised in a Jewish family in New York City that has roots in Eastern Europe you will have a very different set of "American" cultural experiences than if you are from a Catholic Hispanic family living in Los Angeles. If your focus in high school is on mathematics and sciences, you may have a very different set of cultural experience than if your focus is on performing in the high school musicals. These varied cultural networks are not exclusive, of course. You can be great in both the high school musical and mathematics. But each of these pursuits has its own language and its own complex of networks that define it, its own set of assumptions, its own values and its own rules of participation and contribution. While each of us may be quite unique, we are very much defined by the set of networks which we have experienced.

Bella: *Am I nothing more than the intersection of the networks in which I participate?*

We choose many of our networks, but then they, in turn, shape us. It's a complex dance. Choose wisely.

Suggested Readings

- Carl Shapiro and Hal R. Varian <u>Information Rules: A Strategic Guide to the Network Economy</u> Harvard Business School Press (1999)
- James Burke's <u>Connections</u> (Little, Brown and Company, 1978)

23

AN EPISTEMOLOGICAL SPACE FOR GOD

The scientist's religious feeling takes the form of a rapturous amazement at the harmony of natural law, which reveals an intelligence of such superiority that, compared with it, all the systematic thinking and acting of human beings is an utterly insignificant reflection. This feeling is the guiding principle of his life and work. ... It is beyond question closely akin to that which has possessed the religious geniuses of all ages.

ALBERT EINSTEIN

There are no satisfying explanations of what consciousness is.

LAURENCE FISHER

Strange is our situation here upon Earth. Each of us comes for a short visit, not knowing why, yet sometimes seeming to divine a purpose.

ALBERT EINSTEIN

Being an atheist requires faith, because there is no conclusive evidence that God does not exist.

LAURENCE FISHER

There are more things in Heaven and Earth, Horatio, than are dreamt of in your philosophy.

WILLIAM SHAKESPEARE

THE HORATIO TRAP

Recall that "epistemological" means having to do with or relating to how you know something. There is a terrible but common epistemological trap that you should try to avoid—one that leads to not only an impoverished spiritual life, but a deadened imagination and a lack of creativity. I am going to call it the Horatio Trap, as inspired by Shakespeare's quote above from the play Hamlet. At the time of Shakespeare, the word "philosophy" meant "science." Thus, in Shakespeare's famous play, the character Hamlet is saying to Horatio that there is more in the world than science has taught him—much more than science has even dreamed of.

Bella: *Such as ghosts, for example.*

The Horatio Trap is to mistake science as the final arbiter of reality. More precisely, it's to take an overly simplistic and falsely materialistic view of science as establishing the limits of what is possible. Those who are caught in this trap tend to harbor a visceral certainty that the universe is as simple and mechanical as they see it. According to their view, we live in a material world with no observable spiritual component. They see only implacable, unfeeling forces at work. They see humanity as a lonely species on a rock floating through space. They see science as the only rational method for determining the truth. They believe that nothing can be known except through science. They see a fundamental tension between science and religion. In their view, religion is nothing more than superstition, and, indeed, sometimes a dangerous superstition, especially if it leads people to harm one another in disputes over religious differences. They believe there is no meaning to our existence, but the meaning we choose to place on any given task before us. They consider themselves the smart ones—the only ones who can ruthlessly face the truths of the universe. Like the positivists, they want to play for the <u>seemingly</u> safe epistemological ground, without understanding that that doesn't exist. They think objectivity is achieved by emptying one's soul rather than filling it. They are proud that they are not drawn into the false comforts of religion—proud that they are smarter than religious folks. In their pride, they turn away from any transcendent meaning that does not derive directly from social preferences or choices. To those who are caught in the Horatio trap, I would say: There's more to life, and to reality itself, than science will ever know, or ever be able to teach you—do not limit yourself to the narrow confines of science. For all his dithering in the play, Hamlet has got that one right. In this chapter, we are going to shift our gaze from scientific to spiritual knowledge. I am trying to create a little epistemological elbow room. I'll make three arguments and an observation in this chapter:

First, I will argue that with respect to the ultimate nature of reality extreme epistemological humility is warranted. The scientific process itself does not permit science to say anything about the spiritual. It is not de-signed to do that. Second, I will argue that there are other ways of knowing than science. In particular, I will argue that we have some direct knowl-edge of the spiritual world through our sense of a conscious self. Third, I will argue that the only <u>rational</u> approach to the spiritual is to explore it in good faith, not to reject it without exploration. Fourth, I will observe the palpable reality of the "networks" of good and evil. I will also observe that networks have the capacity to connect us to others in profound ways.

I'M A LITTLE TEAPOT

Bertrand Russell is a philosopher and mathematician of the early twentieth century. He was aggressively atheistic. (An atheist is a person who doesn't believe in God.) Russell proposed the following amusing hypothesis (concerning an orbiting teapot), by which he intended to make several points regarding religion. Imagine that a little teapot is believed by many to be orbiting the Sun. Suppose we build a telescope that should be large enough to see that teapot, but we fail to see it. At this point, teapot believers will say that the teapot is just a little smaller than we expected, but it is still there. Russell acknowledges that there is no way that science could ever disprove the teapot hypothesis. But it is also clear to Russell, and he hopes to his readers, that despite the fact that the hypothesis cannot be disproven, it is nonetheless ridiculous and useless. Obviously, by means of this lovely example, Russell is attempting to draw a parallel between those who believe in God and those who believe in orbiting teapots. He is making fun of those who believe in God and implicitly suggesting that—like an orbiting teapot—they are both quaint and ridiculous in their belief.

The parallel is correct in one sense. Russell is quite right that the tools of science cannot directly speak to the existence of God, or the arguable lack of His existence. And that is a profoundly important point. Questions of God are <u>not</u> scientific questions, and science cannot speak to them. But his example goes beyond that. By selecting an orbiting teapot as his example, he is also suggesting—if not saying so directly—that to believe in God is like believing in an orbiting teapot. But these two hypotheses are only the same in that they are beyond the reach of science, and the differences are telling. Most people have believed in God, or in multiple gods, as far back as we have been human. I do not know of too many people who believe in orbiting teapots. Also, the idea of God is generally tied to some sense of transcendent morality—that is, the notion that there is a difference between right and wrong that transcends the mere preferences and choices of any individual. This is a fundamentally important belief that ties into daily decision making for most people. I don't know of anyone who has posited that an orbiting teapot provides them with their moral compass in life and to whom they pray. And the idea of God is also generally tied to ideas about how and why everything exists—one of the deepest mysteries of all. I don't even think any physicists have yet hypothesized that a teapot is our cosmological origin. The manner in which belief in God may be distinguished from a teapot are myriad and profound as well as ultimately <u>suggestive</u> that <u>there may be some non-scientific (but not necessarily irrational) ways at which the great majority of people arrive at such knowledge or faith</u>. Mr. Russell chooses the orbiting teapot as his example precisely because it is laughable. But the idea of God is not laughable. Thus, the metaphor is of limited use. Given the differences noted above, it is Mr. Russell who ultimately appears as a bit ridiculous here—with his visceral views concerning beliefs that his cherished tools of science cannot speak to one way or the other, as even he admits. And yet he <u>insists</u> there is no God, simply because that is how it feels to him. Who is being childish here? We can all agree, at least, that Mr. Russell has irrationally closed his mind to spiritual possibilities.

EPISTEMOLOGICAL HUMILITY AS TO THE ULTIMATE NATURE OF THINGS

Our intuitive understanding of the world is based on and limited by what is immediately available to our senses. Yet, wondrously, scientific progress has taken us to the very point where our intuition begins to fail us. What we have come to learn through scientific progress is that <u>the ultimate nature of reality is nothing like the world we perceive</u>. This should lead us to a certain amount of humility when we endeavor to intuit the ultimate nature of reality. For instance, we know that the world of subatomic particles does <u>not</u> work like the world we see around us. We also know that the world of very fast moving things—approaching the speed of light—does <u>not</u> work like the imminent world of our daily experience. We know that time itself is a relative concept and that space curves and that the location of the tiniest particles is not definitive, but probabilistic in its essence. The universe is nothing if not weird. In this sense, we can truly say that the world we perceive around us is an illusion.

Bella: *Don't bring that Zeno guy back up again.*

Put simply, the mystics have had it right all along. Now, it is not that it is not real, of course, but, rather, that the secrets by which it operates are <u>not</u> revealed on the surface. Yet our personal experience of things—which drives our intuitions—<u>is</u> limited to the superficial. As a consequence, whatever the nature of reality is, we do <u>know</u> that we will never fully grasp it intuitively, simply because we are incapable of going that far beyond the limited world of our immediate senses. We may well model it, and make predictions about it, but that is not the same thing as intuitive understanding. This should make us suspicious of our intuitions, <u>especially when they begin to limit our imagination and our sense of the possible</u>. It should, indeed, bring us to an appreciation of the mystery that surrounds us. One of the great lessons of science is that you should <u>not</u> limit your imagination to what you can see in this world. Reality goes far beyond our direct experience. The universe is not limited to the kinds of interactions that characterize and define our daily lives. Nor should our imaginations be, whether involved with corporeal or spiritual conjecturing.

THE EPISTEMOLOGICAL LIMITS OF SCIENCE

As we have seen, science is not really about determining or demonstrating truth per se. Rather, what science is—and what science is truly great at—is increasing the predictive content of scientific models and frameworks over time through a process of bold conjecturing, rigorous criticism, theoretical adjustment and competition among research programs. Now, certainly scientists are trying to get at truth when they are trying to improve their models. So it's not that truth is not important, or that it isn't the goal. Furthermore, a series of models based on actual truth is apt to be a better basis for further scientific developments than one that is not. So truth matters to science. I am not making the argument that science is only about predictive prowess (although many do). But predictive content—that is, being able to make accurate predictions—is what drives science, and it is crucial to understand that it is not the same thing as truth. In sum, science is good at developing models with predictive content; it is not very good at establishing truth per se.

Indeed, as we have seen, there are many times in the history of science where we have accepted some particular scientific model because it yielded greater predictive powers than previous scientific views, and yet, subsequently, the model was refuted—that is, deemed false—and replaced by a new set of ideas. As we have seen, that process—of conjectures and refutations—is what science is all about. The fact that a scientific model has excellent predictive powers does not tell us it is true—any more than, say, a map with which we might make useful predictions of which way to turn your car to get to your destination represents the full reality of the world around us. While the map may have excellent predictive content, it would be foolish to mistake the map for the actual terrain. A building, as represented on the map, may be flat, but that doesn't mean the building itself is flat. Science is like a map. We keep it because—and only because—it has good predictive content and is therefore useful. But, as we have emphasized again and again in this book, it doesn't actually authoritatively determine the truth. Indeed, it cannot tell us the actual nature of the world we live in, or what may lay beyond our map, with all its limitations. To believe it can do so is a fallacy.

For example, suppose a scientist declares that since the Big Bang can be explained by the principles of physics, God doesn't exist. Well, of course, that doesn't follow at all. The fact that physicists can find equations consistent with what they think might have happened, doesn't tell us anything about whether God had a role in it. Indeed, to think it tells us anything about God is completely illogical. We can build mathematical models that have predictive power and that can help us advance technologically. But don't confuse that with the notion that we actually fully understand that reality. We don't. The nature of reality will always remain mysterious to you and to me and to everyone else. Epistemological humility in this regard is appropriate, (and let me note pointedly here that atheism is <u>not</u> epistemologically humble). Never believe that because a scientific equation has well modeled the world (for now) that somehow the mystery has been taken out of reality. Horatio cannot imagine there is a world beyond his immediate sense perception. Don't mistake the map for the terrain, as does Horatio. Let's look at how and why the Horatio trap developed.

SCIENCE AVOIDS THE SPIRITUAL FOR GOOD REASON; IT DOESN'T MEAN YOU SHOULD

In ancient times, humans explained many phenomena by reference to various spiritual or god-like presences. Thunder and lightning weren't perceived as the result of a release of electrical charge, but rather as resulting from the activity of the god Thor. As science began to develop, many things came to be explained in terms of natural forces, and other scientific concepts. These scientific explanations were presented as substitutes to the explanations based on gods and spirits, and were indeed largely intended to replace those explanations. And certainly that is a wonderful thing to do—that is, to develop concepts that explain and ultimately give people predictive powers with respect to events in nature. If you can develop ideas and models with which to make predictions about reality, then you can develop technology to make this a better life in a material sense.

Thus, <u>in terms of yielding direct scientific benefits to humankind</u>, a scientific model with predictive content is always to be preferred—at least for scientific purposes—to an explanation of phenomena that relies on spirits and gods. But keep in mind—that doesn't mean that the scientific explanation is true—it just means it works well for our limited human purposes. Indeed, scientists can never rule out the proposition, say, that invisible sprites control everything we observe, but happen to have followed certain patterns thus far—the patterns being what we call scientific laws. Nor can science rule out that we are dreaming all of this, and the dream is directly orchestrated by God. Nor can science rule out the proposition that God intervenes in the affairs of this world regularly in answer to prayer.

This is not a trivial philosophical debating point. The stark truth is that we don't know the nature of reality, and we have no way of directly testing the truth or falsity of these propositions. Such propositions are not part of the body of science, not because they might not be true, but simply because they are not useful for making scientific predictions. The desire to develop technologically useful knowledge, and to be able to make predictions about the natural world, led those who are scientifically minded to always prefer an explanation or a scientific model that doesn't involve spirits and gods. (As to actual spirits and gods, science simply cannot say one way or another.) The attitude that spirits and gods were to be avoided in scientific explanations soon came to be viewed as a tension between science and religion—even though this is not logically necessary. The view was that the more that science came to explain, the less there was for religion to explain, and that really smart, and fully rational people, ultimately would reject science and replace it with science. Thus, the atheist proudly pronounces: "I do <u>not</u> believe in God. I am a rationalist. I am really smart." And what he means by this is "I am much smarter than you folks who believe in God." The epistemological hubris of the message never ceases to stun me. There are popular, very aggressive books whose message seems to be little more than this prideful proclamation. With a passionate pronouncement of his lack of faith, the atheist feels really good about how smart he is, (albeit he may also feel a little alone in the universe).

Bella: *We should all take a moment to nod to the atheist and say "you are really smart"—to make him feel better about himself.*

Like Horatio, the atheist has fallen victim to a logical fallacy. The fact that humans can develop concepts and models with predictive power in no way directly tells us anything about the existence of God, or the lack there-of. Period. How could it? And what an odd notion it is, if you really think about it. "Hey, I have a map of reality with predictive content, therefore there is no God." This is what is referred to in logic as a "non sequitur." (A "non sequitur" is something that does not follow; that is, the conclusion does not follow as a necessary consequence of the premises.)

Bella: *But are you saying that is it unreasonable to question the existence of God.*

No, I am not saying that. It is the very essence of reasonableness to question everything, and if you do not question the spiritual side of life you will not be properly exploring it. What I object to is the absurd proposition that somehow rationality, or the predictive successes of science, is on the side of the atheist. I also object to the aggressiveness with which some atheists suggest that rationality is somehow on their side, when this constitutes nothing but a non sequitur. The odd thing is that many people do find this fallacious line of reasoning to be convincing. Somehow the success of science suggests to them that there is no God—as if the intellectual constructs we use to explain phenomenon somehow preclude a deeper truth.

Given the illogical nature of this position, I can't help but imagine that—from a psychological perspective—something else is going on. For many atheists, I believe the view is largely driven by pride. The assertive atheist would rather run the risk of missing the more profound truths of life altogether by not believing in the spiritual, than to bear the pain of the possibility that he might believe something that is not true and would thus have been fooled. The atheist is so passionately determined to ensure that he is not personally fooled in any way by anyone, that he assumes the universe is purely driven by materialistic elements that are immediately accessible to his senses and limited imagination. In this, he is like the positivist (and many positivists are, in fact, atheists to boot). The false safety of a short-sighted vision is to be preferred to an encompassing view that may capture more of the truth, but may also be mistaken in part. Pride is defined as a sin precisely because it leads to this turning away from the universe's possibilities. Pride closes the mind as well as the soul. Now don't get me wrong—I do want scientists—in their capacity as scientists—to continue to try to explain things without reference to spirits and gods. That is how our human powers over the world will be advanced. But science has no authority whatsoever with respect to spiritual matters. Here it is truly overstepping its bounds.

Bella: *Aren't you being a little hard on atheists?*

I have no problem with someone who does not believe in God. It is not something one can force oneself to do; nor should one. Spirituality always entails a struggle and is generated by seeking the truth of our existence. Spirituality dares to question and dares to conjecture. What I have a problem with is the notion that somehow the successes of science and rationality argue against God. There is no basis to that argument whatsoever. And the assertion that those who believe in God are somehow irrational is nothing but ugly demagoguery.

Bella: *Are there <u>other</u> ways of knowing than science?*

NON-SCIENTIFIC PATHS TO KNOWLEDGE

I think so. This brings us back to our discussion in one of our earlier chapters. As a beginning point, there is our direct "sense experience" of the world. As our <u>personal</u> sense experience, this is purely outside the scope of science <u>per se</u>. When I look around the room I am sitting in, I see things, I identify things, and I think about them. There is a chair. There is my wife Lisa drinking coffee and reading the newspaper. This is certainly knowledge, in as strong a sense—or even a stronger sense—than anything that science has to offer.

Bella: *Is it fallible? Can I make mistakes within it?*

Certainly. But direct knowledge is no different than science in that regard. Indeed, the sensual human being—directly absorbing the world through her senses and thoughts—is necessary for science itself, for she constitutes the very being that is engaged in scientific experimentation, conjecturing, observation and criticism. But the point here is that that being, and her knowledge and understanding of the world, precedes science and is separate from science, even if heavily influenced by science and even if essential to science itself. A small child, living, say, in a remote tribe in the jungle, has a definite sense of the world without having ever heard a word about what we in the modern world would call science. Indeed, even my friend, here, Bella the Dog, has a sense experience and knowledge of the world—without a smidge of science.

Bella: *Absolutely! And proud of it. Could you throw that red ball?*

So wherever you are reading this, take a moment to look around your environment. Look at the things or people or animals around you. Experience them. Contemplate them. .... That experience you just had is <u>not</u> science, but it is knowledge. It is a direct experience of the world through your senses. I don't deny that what you see and think about might not be influenced by scientific ideas you have learned; but I do claim that that experience itself conveys information to you about the world and is truly beyond science.

So, for starters, we know that there is knowledge outside of science. There is direct knowledge—direct experience. Science itself, of course, has to rely on this as a foundation—even though it would rather not. All scientists are people. Individual's direct experience of the world may be somewhat different from one person to another. In contrast, science is about establishing ideas that transcend any one individual. So this individualized experience of the world makes scientists kind of nervous. They try to get past the individual by describing the scientist as someone who is peculiarly objective and who leaves his or her biases behind. But, of course, no one ceases to be a human being when they participate in science, and, of course, they don't really leave their personal biases behind. And while certainly it is good to try to be as objective as one can be, it is nonetheless very important to keep in mind that it is people who conduct science—inevitably flawed and biased people since we are all flawed and biased. To a certain extent, science itself cannot escape this flawed foundation. But my basic point here is that the observer—that is, you—has an experience of the world that is direct and is outside of science <u>per se</u>. You will recall our extended discussion of tacit knowledge earlier in the book.

Bella: *Alright. So there is knowledge outside of science. But what about knowledge of the spiritual? That is different, isn't it? Can there be direct knowledge of that? How do we get in touch with the spiritual?*

DIRECT ACCESS TO A NON-MATERIAL REALITY

To a certain extent, I believe so. But let's take it one step at a time. Now, as you look around and observe the room, I want you not only to look at, think about, and experience what is around you, but this time I want you to suddenly switch the gaze of your inner eye to the observer of this environment—that is, you-as-you in the process of observing the world around you. As I am sure you can tell, there is a "you" there. That is, you have a direct experience of yourself as a person—a person that is doing the observing—in the midst of the observing. Ask yourself: What is that? What am I experiencing that I think of as myself—the self that is doing the observing, and the thinking, and the feeling? Surely you do have this experience—because I am quite sure you do not confuse the flux of things that you are experiencing externally with yourself as a being. That is, you do make a distinction between the self (that is you) and everything else around you.

So what is that? What is the sensual experience of the you that is inside your body? Is it a thing? I would say no. It cannot be a thing, precisely because it is an experience—it is a sense of self. Our consciousness of self is not a thing. So what is it? It is something outside the realm of "thingness." It is certainly not "material", since a conscious experience of self is not constituted by any "stuff". I would suggest to you that is it spiritual. Indeed, when conceived of clearly, I don't think it can be properly seen as anything but spiritual in its essence. Now you may argue that there is a physical mechanism—called the body—that renders that experience possible. I agree with you. My body is where my "self" is housed (at least, I strongly suspect that it is). But the experience itself is certainly not a thing. And that experience does exist. It is a sentient reality beyond all things—which is what, I think, is meant by the spiritual.

Now, I will admit that some people don't find this line of argument compelling. But I have to say, I don't understand their perspective. When I contemplate the fact that I have a "self" that is conscious of the world, and that is aware of itself, I cannot come to any other conclusion than that that very awareness—in-and-of-itself and <u>as an experience</u>—is not a material phenomenon, but a spiritual one. Now, even if you agree with me, this doesn't prove, say, that that spirit can continue outside the body. But it does give me a direct window into the fact that there are aspects of reality that are not material. To me, that seems undeniable. It is also an experience that is completely <u>beyond</u> the realm of science. It is not that science might not try to study the phenomenon, but the personal experience, and the personal knowledge of that experience, is simply beyond science altogether. The tools of science cannot measure it, cabin it or frame it in any way. But there it is.

Bella: *All my inner-eye can see is that red ball that I want to get.*

The next thing to contemplate is the fact that there seems to be connection points between this non-material world of the perceiving self and the physical world. That is, I can look at a chair, think about it, and experience myself in the act of thinking about the chair, and then I can <u>decide</u> to go pick it up. Please look at some small object around you. Think about that object. And then experience your "self" in the act of thinking about the object. Then decide to do something with the object—perhaps pick it up, or slide it across a table. Now, decide to do some other thing with some other object, but be careful to experience yourself as the decider as you are doing this. Is it not the case that the "decider" that you experience is the same as the "observer" and the "thinker" that you experience as your "self"? Of course, it is.

Bella: *But what does this show us?*

It shows us that there is a direct connection between the non-material world of the sentient self and the material world of things. That is, the spiritual being that is myself can decide to take action and directly intervene in the physical world and change it. Now, some would argue that my "decision" was an illusion, and that the material world itself—in the form of my brain—was behind that decision. But I don't care about that. That is not my point. My point is that—regardless of an underlying material world that might render my sentient self possible—the sentient "self" itself—as experienced by my self—is clearly <u>not</u> material, and yet it can intervene in the material world and change it. Wow. I conclude that the spiritual (i.e., non-material world of personal awareness) and the material world interact. Could it be that there are other spiritual essences that exist and that can affect the material world?

Bella: *But it wasn't the spiritual world that effected that physical change in the world, it was your hand, which is very much a physical object.*

But that begs the question of how my hand received the message from my sentient <u>non-physical</u> self to move the object. We have a choice here. Either we accept that our sense of a sentient self and our sense of the will to act are both illusions—and are purely physical phenomenon—or, at some point, there must be some kind of communication between the non-physical world of our sentient self exerting its will and the physical world of which my hand is a part. That communication between the spiritual world and the physical world implies that the one can change the other. I don't think one can construct a coherent life working with the premise that our will power is an illusion, so I reject that route. The only alternative is that there is some communication between the non-material world and the material world. That it should be so is not really very surprising, but the contemplation of that fact helps to open one's mind to other possibilities. Although we take our sentient selves—the self that has the experience of the world—for granted, because it is always there, I believe it gives us a direct window into another world of possibilities—that is, the spiritual.

Now, this sentient non-material self has a direct experience of the world through our senses. No doubt, this direct experience of the world is heavily influenced by culture, ideas and science. Nonetheless, it is clearly a different path to "knowledge" than science itself—and, indeed, a path to a different kind of knowledge that complements the scientific. The question is: what are its limits? We certainly know that it is susceptible to being fooled. Like science, it is not exactly authoritative. But it does exist. Clearly, also, it reaches beyond what science can reach, and is different in kind. And its method, of course, is not the same as science, though it may be capable of deepening and improvement through rational discourse as well as other experiences.

Some people believe that this sentient self can connect to the world and gain knowledge <u>beyond direct sense experience</u>. This is a key question, of course, and I am not trying to convince you of that one way or the other. On its face, however, the notion that the non-material spiritual essence that constitutes our sentient selves might have some means of connecting to other spiritual essences beyond the known senses is certainly plausible. Indeed, many people throughout the ages have believed that through meditation, contemplation, prayer, and, most importantly, through living a moral life, one can reach deep insights about reality and about God. Many people have even specifically outlined the path that one should follow to achieve this enlightenment. Many people believe that God may inspire us if we open ourselves to Him.

Of course, none of these paths is part of the scientific toolbox—but how pathetic are those who turn away from these possibilities simply for that reason! Love is not a part of that limited toolbox. Should we turn away from that reality? Kindness is not a part of that limited toolbox. Should we turn away from that as well? Concepts of moral right and wrong are not part of that toolbox. Do they have no place in our universe? Beauty is nowhere to be found in the sandbox of positivist science. Shall we leave art behind as well? The scientific toolbox is an odd object to choose to worship. Even odder is to restrict the explorations that constitute your life solely to the unstable contents of science, since there is nothing in the scientific toolbox itself that suggests that you should do so. To reject spirituality is the very zenith of irrationality.

Bella: *But how do we know whether spiritual knowledge is possible?*

THE RATIONAL EXPLORATION OF THE SPIRITUAL SIDE OF LIFE

I cannot give a definitive answer to that question. But I can say that to reject the possibility out-of-hand is irrational. I can also say that it is perfectly rational to be open to the spiritual and to explore it. Different approaches to spirituality or religion are characterized by different beliefs, of course. It is difficult to know what is true within this realm and what is false. But I think that that is the wrong starting point. Do not seek proof—or belief—as your starting point. To do so is kind of like saying: "I refuse to start down the path to wisdom until I am wise." Just as we found that the positivist's focus on proof is mistaken as an approach to science, so too it is with the spiritual. In science, we found that the better approach was a dynamic and bold conjecturing that actively explored the ramifications of scientific assumptions by testing their efficacy in ordering the world around us. I believe that this is also, in its essence, the better way to explore the spiritual and the religious—that is, by incorporating these principles into our lives and discovering where they take us. The religious and spiritual ideas that we learn from others constitute our initial bold conjectures for how to live a life. Just as bold conjectures in science reach beyond the known, so too it should be the case in the spiritual realm. We do not arrive at spiritual beliefs through static contemplation of their truth or falsity, but rather through a dynamic exploration of their content—by living in accordance with them.

Thus, just as you come to understand scientific ideas by exploring them, so too with religion, you must partake in the journey if you are to understand and find what is there. It is a choice. You can't successfully say to yourself: "I wish I was a good person." That is meaningless. Rather, you must try to <u>live</u> as a good person would, and struggle with what that implies in your daily decisions, and in your most important decisions, and through that you will become good and come to understand what goodness is. <u>With respect to the spiritual, you are the research program</u>. Indeed, living a good life is perfectly analogous to conducting research within a research program. The point is not whether or not the interrelated assumptions that define the research program are true or not. That cannot be known. And so it is with a spiritual life: the question is not whether or not you have identified and established as true certain religious principles, but rather <u>how much and what you are learning</u> through exploring the ramifications of those principles through a moral and spiritual life. Are you growing spiritually? That is the question. What have you discovered by living in accordance with religious principles? That is the exploration. This is not to say that the truth of these religious principles is not important, but rather that those truths are best explored and understood through active participation in them.

Bella: *So what can we discover, if anything, through meditation, prayer, contemplation, religious study, moral discourse and attempting to live an ethical and spiritually meaningful life?*

Throughout the millennia, many have claimed that there are special things you can come to understand through this route. You will never know if you do not try. Science cannot give you the answer. If any scientist or scientifically minded person says it can, he is misleading you. Nothing in our scientific box of tools can speak to this one way or the other. As my brother once put it: "Just because a hammer is only good for hammering nails doesn't mean that a screw driver and screws don't exist." So it is with the false battle of science against religion and mysticism. Thus, like science, in the realm of spirituality, the proof must be in the pudding, so-to-speak. That is, the various paths to religious or spiritual knowledge are not to be gained through passive consumption; rather, they must be actively explored if they are to bear fruit. If spiritual knowledge is to be attained, like any other type of knowledge, it involves directed personal effort and hard work.

My own belief is that if we open ourselves to God, then we do gain a different kind of knowledge. I think it is an area—like science—where many mistakes can be made, of course. And I certainly don't think you should embrace it in an unquestioning manner. Just the opposite—you should continually question it all and struggle with it. Just as criticism is central to the growth of scientific knowledge, so too it is for spiritual knowledge. And just as the criticism of a research program assists you in further articulating and applying the particular scientific vision, so too the point of criticism in the spiritual realm is to take you deeper into it, and to make it your own—but not to reject the realm altogether. The reason you do not give up your efforts is because you are seeking those deep insights that are fundamental to living a good, and indeed even a coherent, life. The only rational way to explore and assess these non-scientific paths to knowledge is on their own terms. It is pretty silly saying there is nothing to spirituality if you haven't explored it yourself. That's just plain ignorant.

Bella: *But what if it is all a scam? What if I have been fooled? What if I believe in something that isn't there?*

You are no fool to explore the possibilities of this world. Understand that you will never reach the bottom of it all. You will never reach a final point of complete and absolute understanding. No person ever has or ever will—at least not in this life. But we do know that you can grow as a person through exploration and, indeed, we also know that it is only through exploration that you can grow. What is foolish, therefore, is closing yourself to the possibilities of this world before you have explored them for yourself. The only way one comes to know the possibilities of religion and the spiritual in your own life, and to what truths they may carry you, is to live them. Understanding the needs of our spirit, understanding the difference between right and wrong, understanding our spiritual connection to others and to God, and what this all means for our life is not a matter of waiting for belief and faith to come to you. To discover goodness, you must go to it, and actively explore it. You must live it, or at least try your very best to do so. Indeed, you must generate it from inside you. And the same is true with faith. I have heard people say:

> Oh, I wish I had a strong faith, like so-and-so. They seem
> so happy within their faith. I have so many doubts.

Faith is not about final and firm answers, and it is not something you wait for. It is an exploratory choice. But by that I do not mean that it is a choice you make as to whether and what to believe—like you were selecting beliefs from a menu. No, faith is the commitment to deeply explore spirituality and goodness as a part of your life. When you think of it that way—to me—faith is a no brainer. Do not wait to pray until you are sure your belief in God is firm. Rather, pray because that act constitutes an exploration of your connection to something almighty that you are connected to, but that you can't fully grasp. Pray to explore what is beyond yourself, and you may well discover what is beyond yourself. This is only way to integrate these modes of knowing and understanding into your life. Why should you make this choice? What is in it for you? You should make this choice because your life will not be full, integrated and coherent unless you do it. You will not be fully happy, healthy and good person without doing it. You will not love as deeply if you do not do it. And, most importantly perhaps, you will never know for yourself what is there. Again, I am not saying that you must <u>believe</u> to enjoy these fruits. I am saying that you must <u>explore</u> to enjoy them.

For as long as we have been human, our spiritual side has been central to what it means to be human. It holds us together and defines who we are like nothing else does. If you want to fully experience all that life has to offer, and fully experience your own potential, you must explore this realm for yourself. You can't wait for it to come to you. It won't. You must go to it. I am not telling you precisely what you will find there. I am not asking you to believe. Belief is not required. Belief is an afterthought. It is not the essence of the project. The point is the application of a moral framework to your life and the resultant spiritual growth and deepening. What I am telling you is that there will be enormous returns to this personal journey. It is required for a good life. And I know you will not be <u>fully</u> you without taking that part of life seriously.

BANNED CONCEPTS

There is nothing that irritates the modern academic thinker more than the concepts of "good" and "evil". Let's focus on evil for a moment. As an academic, if you ever dared to suggest that even part of an explanation for something may lay in evil—or even spoke of it in a context of professional discourse—you would be laughed right out of the profession. And I suppose that attitude is OK when the point of an academic discourse is to see how much can be explained in terms of some narrow set of explanatory variables that doesn't include the concept of evil. But, of course, an academic prohibition on the concepts of good and evil in order to focus on a more limited set of explanatory variables doesn't mean that good and evil are not important concepts in understanding the world.

We live in a most peculiar culture. While our professions (setting religion aside) and our highest centers of learning implicitly ban the concepts of good and evil, our popular culture (not to mention religion) embraces it. Typical parents expend enormous effort in teaching their children the difference between "right" and "wrong". In addition, much of our narrative entertainment—in the forms of movies, TV shows, novels, and books for children—portray the struggle between good and evil. There are "good guys" and "bad guys" at the heart of most of our narratives. And while the skilled, more artistic author may choose to make the good guys have flaws—and show them struggling with their own bits of badness—and similarly the bad guys might not be portrayed as thoroughly bad—to make them a little more interesting—nonetheless, the reader still quickly gleans who is who.

Bella: *So who is correct here—the professionals or the People?*

I think the popular view holds the deeper wisdom here. Good and evil are palpable, real forces in the world. To navigate this world, you need to develop a good sense of them. That is why the concepts are central to our stories. There is a good reason that not only religion but also our literature and popular media focuses so heavily on the struggle between good and evil. It is because this struggle is central to who we are.

Bella: *But where do good and evil reside?*

In the hearts of men and women, of course. But good and evil have a reality that goes beyond any one human being. The transcendent realities of good and evil may be thought of as networks.

THE NETWORK OF GOODNESS

Let's first look at goodness as a network. I'll define goodness for these purposes as whenever a person uses their time, energy and/or resources to do something kind, sweet, useful, good, loving, considerate or beneficial for someone else that they are not otherwise required or compelled to do.

The most general type of good act is when someone does some small thing at her own expense for the benefit of another person. By "small thing" here, I mean an act that doesn't take a lot in terms of resources, cost, energy or time of the first person. And typically this small act benefits the recipient to a substantially higher degree than the cost it imposes on the giver. For example, a man is reading a book as he walks down the street and is about to step out in front of a moving car. I see him and yell "Stop! Be careful." He does stop and his life is saved. One can see that the smallest act on my part generated this enormous benefit for another human being. Or, say, an elderly lady drops her groceries, and you pick them up and carry them to her car. This entails only a little trouble on your part, but the lady is substantially better off due to your act of kindness. Clearly the benefit to her is higher than the direct cost to you.

For the moment, let's assume that this is the typical scenario—that is, acts of goodness typically result in greater benefit to the recipient than cost to the giver. Let's see why this creates a network of goodness. Suppose we live in a world where people are willing to engage in "good" acts—with each of us contributing to the goodness when we feel moved to do so. We are all better off in that world. The reason is that each of us will occasionally be in a situation in which we need some small bit of help, and, in at least some of those situations, someone will generously give us that help, with the result that the benefit to us is greater than the cost to them. In our turn, and in other circumstances, we may ourselves end up in the position where we can give to another person, with the result that the benefit to them is greater than the cost to us. The point is that every time someone does this, there is a net gain in welfare—since the giver incurs less cost than the receiver's benefit. Of course, the more people who enter into this "goodness" network, the better it works for everybody and the more instances there are of such a net gain.

Most human beings seem to be wired to appreciate the benefits of this network of goodness and have a willingness to enter into it—particularly if they have been the recipient of the benefits of this network a sufficient number of times when they are young. Put simply, if people are good to you, you tend to develop into a good person.

Thus, if you contribute to this network, you make it stronger in two ways. First, you make it stronger in that there is an additional person (yourself) participating in it, thus increasing the likelihood for all that they will encounter these opportunities for net gain. Second, however, is that by entering this network through engaging in a good act, you also increase the likelihood that the recipient of your generosity will join the network. Good begets good. Now, all of this is abstracting from the special feelings of happiness we may receive by virtue of engaging in a kind act, and knowing ourselves to have done so. That adds even more benefit to belonging to the goodness network.

The goodness network does have a weakness, which is that, in general, folks can obtain the benefits of the network without joining it. That is, people who choose not to engage in any acts of goodness may well continue to be recipients of goodness from others. These people benefit from the good acts of others, but never contribute to those others. In general, the inability of a network to preclude those who are not members of the network from enjoying its benefits may render it weak. But in the case of the goodness network, this is counterbalanced by the propensity of people to join the network if they are sufficient recipients of good acts themselves, especially at a formative stage of their life, and hopefully even afterwards. What makes the goodness network especially strong is that participating in it changes us. We begin to incorporate goodness into who we are—that is, we make it part of our identity. And, as noted above, being a recipient of goodness lures people into the goodness network.

Thus, when you do something good, it reverberates throughout the network of goodness—like an echo chamber. First, you make someone else's life a little better. Second, you refresh someone else's faith and hope in their fellow human beings, and render them more likely to continue to engage in good acts. When they do, the reverberations continue. You may also be the recipient of such feedback effects. Other people do some good act for you, making your life a little better. Your faith and hope in your fellow human being is refreshed and you engage in further kind acts that you might not have done otherwise. When you engage in a good act, its effects and ramifications always run far beyond what you can perceive and comprehend. You become a force for good.

Bella: *May the force be with you.*

And with you. In sum, you can see that the power of goodness is something that lies in the hearts of men and women, and yet is also something that transcends them—precisely because goodness is a network. And when one carefully ponders the network-like nature of goodness, one cannot escape the conclusion that goodness is a very real force in the world. It really is quite odd that it is rejected as an explanatory concept by many professionals and academics. Goodness has direct real world ramifications.

Of course, goodness doesn't always take the form that I described above. That is, it isn't always the case that folks do things that are at a small cost to themselves to generate a benefit that is larger for the recipient. Sometimes people are <u>more</u> generous than that. That is, they make substantial sacrifices for the benefit of others. And, of course, people don't do this in order to receive future expected returns from the goodness network to which they have contributed—they do it simply because it is the right thing to do. Some people dedicate their whole being and all or nearly all of their resources to assisting others. This doesn't just include those who are recognized and celebrated as saintly—the Mother Theresa's of the world—but many people who otherwise simply appear to be living fairly normal lives—except for the fact that they are so very dedicated to doing good for others. This might include a parent who works two jobs so that she can educate her children so that they might have opportunities that she never did. Or it might include someone who works extraordinarily long and intense hours at a national security post because he knows that his work can save lives. Or it might include a homeschooling mom who dedicates every fiber of her being to educating her children in a manner that will permit them to manifest every talent they might have. Most of these saints are unsung heroes, but they are actually all around you. Appreciate them. They, of course, constitute the core of the goodness network and ensure its survival from generation to generation.

THE NETWORK OF EVIL

Evil, of course, is a network as well. Evil begets evil. It is sometimes referred to as the cycle of violence. Evil doers do not seem content with just doing evil themselves. They seem to also want to draw others into it. Certainly, those doing evil can do much greater evil if they have co-conspirators. And once you fully enter the network of evil, it is hard to extract yourself. That is the wisdom of forgiveness, of course—to help people extract themselves from the network of evil. The epitome of evil is the precise converse of goodness; that is, it is when the evil doer does some substantial harm to someone else to gain just a small benefit for themselves. For example, say, a bully might shove someone down on the ice causing them physical harm just for the amusement of seeing them fall. That is evil. Of course, an evil person will always harm someone else if it brings the evil doer a great benefit. But what is really disturbing about evil—and most socially detrimental—is that evil doers will cause grave harm to another for only a small or even purely psychic benefit to themselves.

There are three important things to keep in mind about the network of evil. First, there are genuinely evil people in the world. You need to be wary of them. There are not a lot of them, but they are there and they are dangerous. Second, all of us have some evil in us. It is human nature. We have to directly confront that bit of evil within us, struggle with it, and actively choose good over evil. We do this by taking responsibility for ourselves and our actions and recognizing and acknowledging when we have failed in that struggle. It is that struggle that makes us good. Third, always remember that evil begets evil. Like goodness, it creates a ripple through humanity. The consequences of a seemingly small bad act may well become magnified in the network of evil. This is why struggling to always be good and kind—even in the smallest things—is so very important.

A GLIMPSE OF THE SACRED

Networks pull you out of yourself and connect you to others—not just the networks of goodness and evil, but all the networks. By participating in networks, we share in the creation of value that extends beyond ourselves. Just by participating as an individual, we make the whole greater than it would be otherwise. It is within networks that I catch a glimpse of the sacred—particularly within knowledge networks. Participating within a discourse about any topic—trying to extend our understanding of something in collaboration with others—draws one into a myriad of rippling thoughts and ideas that penetrate and reverberate through society and connect you to the greatest thinkers that have ever been in the past and that will ever be in the future. In it, I see something not only beautiful but also sacred. When people speak of the Holy Spirit, this is what I think of.

WHERE DOES TRANSCENDENT MORALITY RESIDE IF NOT WITH GOD?

For a moment, permit me to turn from philosophical argumentation to simply expressing my own beliefs. More deeply than anything, perhaps, I believe that there is morality <u>in the universe</u>. Good and evil are palpable realities. They exist. And whatever good and evil are, their existence transcends who we are as individuals. I think we <u>experience</u> these transcendent connections—of good and evil—all the time. Loving acts beget joy and evil acts beget unnecessary sorrow. This good and evil in the world existed before any one of us did, and will exist after we are gone. I believe it is a mistake to ignore this palpable experience of good and evil. I believe that you can't properly make morally-informed decisions without these concepts, or, indeed, properly confront the struggle within your own soul between good and evil. Moreover, I don't believe that you can be fully sympathetic to others—and thus fully manifest your own capacity to love and to forgive—without directly observing, confronting and taking responsibility for your own failures in that internal struggle. And, to me, this all points in the direction of a Supreme Being, and a meaningful universe.

I don't believe that we can coherently navigate our world without putting it into a moral framework and context. "What is the right thing to do here?" That is a meaningful question to almost all of us. But what is it that gives the question its meaning? Everything we do is within networks of moral relations. To believe in God is merely to posit that there is a foundation to this daily experience. It is to say that these words "What is the right thing to do here?" are genuinely meaningful—albeit meaningful in a way in which we are too small as individuals to fully grasp and in a way that will forever escape the clutches of the humble tools of science.

I believe that if I did something truly horrible to another human being, on purpose, then I would be severing myself from some type of transcendent goodness, and that that act of severance would have profoundly bad consequences, and that this goes beyond just who and what I am. Rather, it touches on a deep moral order. Do you believe that? The only alternative hypothesis here is that such acts are merely a matter of tastes and choices.

For example, in my view, when we designate Adolf Hitler as an evil man because of his efforts to destroy Jewish people as a group (among other evils), it is <u>not</u> a matter of preference or taste. That is, when I refer to Hitler as evil, I am saying something more about Hitler than that I personally find his actions distasteful. I am saying that the "wrong" here is something more than an arbitrary cultural convention. It is a reality that is bigger than any one human, bigger than any group of humans, and, indeed, bigger than humanity itself. If you agree with this—that is, you agree that good and evil transcend individuals—then you have to ask yourself, where do good and evil reside? How is it that they exist outside myself? This is where God comes in.

An atheist reminds me of a small child walking alone in a dark forest, who is driven to his peculiar beliefs by an emotional need. The child knows that some have suggested that there are wolves in the forest. The child hears a sound, but says to himself: "There is no wolf there, if I can't see it." Just as the child will not accept that there may be a wolf there without seeing it first, so too the atheist will not believe in God unless he sees Him first. The child fears the wolf, and hopes it is not there. The atheist fears belief itself. That is, out of pride, the atheist fears a mistaken belief more than mistaken disbelief, as in the first case, he has been fooled whereas in the second case, he merely misses the point. But reality does not mold itself in response to either our fears or our pride. That is, just as the wolf is little concerned with the child's state of denial, so too the presence of God is not cabined by the atheist's pride.

Bella: *But don't some simply embrace atheism out of despair? Aren't you too hard on them?*

You are right, Bella. And, indeed, the serious atheist is already on a spiritual journey, simply by virtue of the fact that she is taking the question of God's existence seriously. My hope for her is simply that she can move beyond the false trap of seeking proof—and even belief—and take her spiritual explorations into the realm of action.

Suggested Readings

- Armstrong, Karen The Great Transformation: The Beginning of Our Religious Traditions
- C. S. Lewis The Complete Signature Classics: Mere Christianity; The Screwtape Letters; The Abolition of Man; The Great Divorce; The Problem of Pain; Miracles; A Grief Observed Harper One (2002)

24

NAVIGATING YOUR JOURNEY

The unexamined life is not a life worth living for a human being.

SOCRATES

There is a tide in the affairs of men,
Which, taken at the flood, leads on to fortune;
Omitted, all the voyage of their life
Is bound in shallows and in miseries.

WILLIAM SHAKESPEARE

Tend your own garden.

VOLTAIRE

Field of Gourds

The human condition is a strange one. Each of us is alone in our thoughts—alone in the dialogue of our mind—alone in our deaths. No one else can fully share or grasp who or what you are. Karl Marx said "Nothing human is alien to me." But I am not so sure. Rather, I think each of us is uniquely shaped by our personal experience. No one else will ever experience life in quite the way that I do or that you do. There does seem to be an unbridgeable gulf that separates any two human beings. This sense of fundamental aloneness drives much of art and storytelling. We so desperately want to reach one another. Perhaps ironically, it is our efforts to bridge this gulf that generate the finest moments in life. The ever-present mystery constituted by the "other"—and the desperate efforts to connect to that other—result in surprises and successes that not only keep us wanting more, but bring joy and meaning to our lives. Through these efforts, we discover that, despite our visceral sense of aloneness and our individual uniqueness, we are, in fact, nonetheless deeply connected to one another in many ways. We are connected to one another—and fundamentally shaped—by our networks of ideas, language, art and culture and our efforts at discovery as well as our struggles with good and evil. To have a good life and to navigate it well, it is important to understand the complex interplay between our essential aloneness and our interconnectedness and to make good choices in how one interacts through these connections.

More particularly, this book is about connecting with others through the power of rational discourse. It is the logic of discovery that permits one to be larger than oneself—to create with others in a fashion that goes beyond one's individual capabilities—and thereby transcends our individual isolation. Much of the beauty and wonder of life is in this interactive dance among people, where each takes his or her moment, but then cedes a moment to the next person, only to be inspired by that and take another moment for himself or herself. The dance makes us larger than ourselves—takes us outside of ourselves. Through this dance, we become one with others within the exploration. This is the rumba of great conversation, the tango of friendship, the samba of science, the shimmy of art, the jitterbug of politics and the promenade of law. It is the back and forth of life. It is how we bridge that gulf of aloneness.

Bella: *So how do you partake of this great dance of life? I'm ready!*

Like any dance, a lot of it is question of rhythm. You have to develop a sense of when it is the moment for your contribution, and when it is the moment for another's contribution. When others are contributing, you must listen very carefully, fully and with your whole self. This keeps you within the dance and prepares you for when the movement of the dance requires your commitment. And, of course, the dance, at its most beautiful, loses this sense of back-and-forth and emerges as a unity—a unity that is larger than yourself, and yet in which you fully partook and continue to partake. Therein lay happiness and fulfillment.

In sum, the most important thing in life is to open your heart and mind to others by connecting with them through creative processes. And by creative processes, I mean anything constructive—building a family, constructing a work of art, exploring an idea, or collaboratively enjoying a moment together. To succeed at this requires an occasional silence within your soul. Know when it is another person's moment. Celebrate their moment. Give yourself to them. Let them shine. Be with them fully. To a certain degree, this means letting go of your own ego. Always remember that everyone is dazzling in some way, even if their dazzle might be quiet and understated. Be curious enough to look for it. Know also when it is your moment. Let yourself shine. Be honest and open. Show yourself for who you are. And let others, who want to celebrate with you, be in your moment. Don't be afraid to celebrate yourself. That is your gift to those who love you. And you are here on this Earth to be dazzling. Don't be afraid to be confused by life. If you are not confused, you are not paying attention. Those moments of confusion are opportunities. Something or someone (maybe yourself) is trying to tell you something that you may not be fully ready to hear. Confusion constitutes an openness to new things. If you find yourself emotionally confused, take a deep breath, take in the moment, and say: "How grand! I am confused. Something new is coming into my life." Here are my final bits of gratuitous advice. Take them for what they are worth, as any independent thinker would. "Neither a borrower nor a lender be." Just kidding. That's Shakespeare's advice, of course.

1. Dare to use your own intelligence. ... as Kant instructed.
2. Embrace rationality as a dynamic process of discovery.
3. Never be afraid to show ignorance by asking a question.
4. Be opinionated and bold.
5. **Master history and tradition.** While we learn by challenging authority, there is a discipline needed here as well. In order to be positioned to challenge authority in a fruitful and interesting way, you need to understand what has been done before you. All ongoing explorations have a history and a tradition, which reveal the challenges, conjectures and criticisms that have shaped them. By mastering the tradition, you can tap into accumulated wisdom. This puts you in a position to be critical, creative and constructive.
6. **Recognize that while disciplines are fragmented and partial in their perspective, you don't have to be.** Creativity, beauty, reason, truth and God are all cross-disciplinary. Do not be bound in your own thinking by artificial and conventional constraints that are designed merely to protect and legitimize institutional power and maximize rents. Seek wisdom by blurring and traversing the boundaries of disciplines.
7. **Avoid destructive energy and the network of evil.** While you should think for yourself and explore the world, there are explorations that may appear alluring (at least to some), but which can result in enormous harm. For example, I have known people who took illegal drugs, as a sort of rebellious act I think, and who destroyed their minds in the process. You need to be careful in what you choose to explore. If you want to go wild and break rules, then do it through creating outrageous art, poetry and music or articulating wild ideas. You can express yourself—and even create outrage—in ways that are both beautiful and constructive.
8. **Pursue spiritual knowledge through action, not by seeking belief.** Just as rationality demands a commitment to the exploration of ideas through a certain set of tools and methods, so too does spirituality. You do not come to know God by sitting around mulling over whether particular religious statements are true or not—although that can be a good thing to do. Rather, spirituality and goodness are things to be actively explored as ways of choosing and living. By engaging in loving and kind acts, you learn to love more

deeply and you come to experience your spiritual connections to others. Because this exploration is collective in nature, embracing a traditional religion may be the best path to spirituality for you. Or it may not. While you need to find your own way, choosing to explore traditional beliefs may help you in doing so.

9. **If you find your spirit in a bad place, try these:**
   a. <u>Exercise</u>. If you work the body, the mind tends to become healthier.
   b. <u>Create something</u>. Find something beautiful or meaningful or loving or artistic or scientific that you can <u>do</u>. Find something you can contribute to that will lift you out of yourself. Do something for someone else. That is the true path to happiness and satisfaction.
   c. <u>Find someone to help you</u>. You are not alone in this world even though it may feel like it at times. The marvelous fact is that we are connected to others, in more ways than we can fathom. Don't be afraid to ask a friend for help. Also, <u>do</u> seek expert advice and counseling if and when you need it. Being an independent thinker does not mean forgoing the help of experts, if you are in need. It takes courage to ask for help.
   d. <u>Turn to God and ask for help</u>. The implicit admission that you cannot do it all on your own is powerful and will open you to new paths. If you are an atheist, then do this as a tantalizing and bold experiment.
10. **Let virtue be your shield and truth your sword.** I think I got this from some Disney movie, but it's excellent advice.

I'll close with a poem by my daughter Roxy, which she wrote as part of an essay on 11/11/11 when she was 11.

And then lastly you'll know how each and every one of us is like a gourd—special and different—each a different shape or size or color, all waiting for a secret use, waiting to be unfolded. ...

My essay is coming to a close,
but I have one more thought
which I hope you'd like to know—
the something hidden deep within gourds
way deep down way below.
They are imperfect it is true—

all warty and knobby and colorful and striped,
but I think they are a bit like me and you.
They are all different and strange,
but looking at them makes a person change.
It makes a person think and feel
and see that everyone, even gourds,
have feelings that are real
and each of us is like a gourd.
This is not a statement to be ignored.
There is always someone who says:
"This kid makes me frown."
"He is a lunatic, an idiot, a clown."
Sometimes it is even a tiny voice you have created yourself.
He sits on your shoulder, the curmudgeonly elf
But each person and gourd has a secret, a wonder, a pride
You just have to look deep inside

This book constitutes my field of gourds; I hope you like them. Bella—
anything to add?

Bella: *Woof!*

But this, above all: to thine own self be true.

Bella: *Hey, isn't that another line from Shakespeare?*

MY READING LIST

My criterion for this list is books that have heavily influenced the thinking in this book, or which I want to read or re-read as I continue thinking about these topics.
On Science, History of Science, Mathematics, Philosophy of Science and Philosophy:

❖ Asimov, Isaac Asimov's Chronology of Science and Discovery Harper & Row, Publishers, New York (1989)

❖ Baggini, Julian and Fosl, Peter S. The Philosopher's Toolkit: A Compendium of Philosophical Concepts and Methods, Second Edition, Wiley-Blackwell (2010)

❖ Ball, Keith Strange Curves, Counting Rabbits and other Mathematical Explorations Princeton University Press (2003)

❖ Bateson, Gregory Steps to an Ecology of Mind: Collected Essays in Anthropology, Psychiatry, Evolution and Epistemology Paladin (1973)

❖ Becker, Carl L. The Heavenly City of the Eighteenth-Century Philosophers Second Edition Yale University Press (2003, originally 1932)

❖ Bell, E.T. Men of Mathematics Simon & Schuster New York (2008, originally 1937)

❖ Bernstein, Peter L. Against the Gods: The Remarkable Story of Risk John Wiley & Sons Inc., (1998)

❖ Boorstin, Daniel J. The Discoverers Random House, New York (1983)

❖ Brown, James Robert <u>The Laboratory of the Mind: Thought Experiments in the Natural Sciences</u> Routledge London and New York (1993)

❖ Bryson, Bill <u>A Short History of Nearly Everything</u> Broadway Books (2003)

❖ Burke, James <u>Connections</u> Little, Brown and Company (1978)

❖ Burtt, E.A. <u>The Metaphysical Foundations of Modern Science</u> Dover Publishers, Inc. Mineola, New York (2003, originally 1932)

❖ Carroll, Sean <u>From Eternity to Here: The Quest for the Ultimate Theory of Time</u> Dutton (2010)

❖ Courant, Richard and Robbins, Herbert <u>What Is Mathematics?: An Elementary Approach to Ideas and Methods</u> Oxford University Press (1978)

❖ Cox, Brian and Jeff Forshaw <u>Why Does E=mc2? (and why should we care?)</u> DA CAPO Press (2009)

❖ Davies, Paul <u>About Time: Einstein's Unfinished Revolution</u> Simon & Schuster New York (1995)

❖ Davies, Paul <u>God & The New Physics</u> Simon & Schuster (1983)

❖ Davies, Paul <u>The Cosmic Blueprint: New Discoveries in Nature's Creative Ability to Order the Universe</u> Simon & Schuster Inc., (1988)

❖ Davies, Paul <u>The Edge of Infinity</u> Simon & Schuster New York (1982)

❖ Davies, Paul <u>The Mind of God: The Scientific Basis for a Rational World</u> Simon & Schuster (1992)

❖ De Kruif, Paul <u>Microbe Hunters</u> Harcourt Inc. (1996) (originally published 1926).

❖ Einstein, Albert <u>The Meaning of Relativity</u> Fifth Edition Princeton University Press (1956)

❖ Feyerabend, Paul <u>Against Method</u> Verso (1978)

❖ Foucault, Michel <u>The Order of Things: An Archaeology of the Human Sciences</u> Vintage Books (1973)

❖ Gamow, George <u>One, Two Three ... Infinity: Facts and Speculations of Science</u> Dover Publications Inc. (1974)

❖ Greene, Brian <u>The Elegant Universe: Superstrings, Hidden Dimensions, and the Quest for the Ultimate Theory</u> Vintage Books (2003)

❖ Greene, Brian <u>The Fabric of the Cosmos: Space, Time, and the Texture of Reality</u> Vintage Books (2005)

❖ Hakim, Joy <u>The Story of Science: Einstein Adds a New Dimension</u> Smithsonian Books (2007)

❖ Hawking, Stephen <u>A Brief History of Time: From the Big Bang to Black Holes</u> Bantam Books (1990)

❖ Holmes, Richard <u>The Age of Wonder</u> Vintage Books (2008)

❖ Hughes, Bettany <u>The Hemlock Cup: Socrates, Athens and the Search for the Good Life</u> Alfred A. Knopf New York (2011)

❖ Isaacson, Walter <u>Einstein: His Life and Universe</u> Simon & Schuster (2007)

❖ Kline, Morris <u>Mathematics and the Search for Knowledge</u> Oxford University Press (1985)

❖ Koestler, Arthur <u>Insight and Outlook: An Inquiry into the Common Foundations of Science, Art and Social Ethics</u> University of Nebraska Press (1949)

❖ Koestler, Arthur <u>The Act of Creation: A Study of the Conscious and Unconscious in Science and Art</u> Dell Publishing Co., Inc., New York (1964)

❖ Kuhn, Thomas <u>The Copernican Revolution: Planetary Astronomy in the Development of Western Thought</u> Harvard University Press (1992)

❖ Kuhn, Thomas <u>The Structure of Scientific Revolutions</u> Second Edition, Enlarged The University of Chicago Press (1970)

❖ Lakatos, Imre and Alan Musgrave (Eds) <u>Criticism and the Growth of Knowledge</u> Cambridge University Press (1970)

❖ Lakatos, Imre <u>Proofs and Refutations: The Logic of Mathematical Discovery</u> Cambridge University Press (1976)

❖ Lindberg, David C. <u>The Beginnings of Western Science: The European Scientific Tradition in Philosophical, Religious, and Institutional Context, Prehistory to A.D. 1450</u> Second Edition The University of Chicago Press (2007)

❖ Lindley, David <u>Where does the Weirdness Go?: Why Quantum Mechanics Is Strange But Not As Strange As You Think</u> BasicBooks (1996)

❖ Livio, Mario <u>The Equation That Couldn't Be Solved: How Mathematical Genius Discovered the Language of Symmetry</u> Simon & Schuster New York (2005)

❖ MacKay, Charles <u>Extraordinary Popular Delusions and the Madness of Crowds</u> Crown Trade Paperbacks, New York (1980—originally 1842)

❖ March, Robert H. <u>Physics for Poets</u> Contemporary Books Inc., Chicago (1983)

❖ Martineau, John, Editor, <u>Sciencia: Mathematics, Physics, Chemistry, Biology and Astronomy for All</u> Walter & Company, New York

❖ Montford, A. W. <u>The Hockey Stick Illusion: Climategate and the Corruption of Science</u> Stacey International (2010)

❖ McCoy, Roger M. <u>Ending in Ice: The Revolutionary Idea and Tragic Expedition of Alfred Wegener</u> Oxford University Press (2006)

❖ Pickover, Clifford A. <u>Archimedes to Hawking: Laws of Science and the Great Minds Behind Them</u> Oxford University Press (2008)

❖ Pickover, Clifford A. <u>The Math Book</u> Sterling, New York (2009)

❖ Pickover, Clifford A. <u>The Physics Book</u> Sterling, New York (2011)

❖ Popper, Karl R. <u>Conjectures and Refutations: The Growth of Scientific Knowledge</u> Routledge and Kegan Paul, London (1972)

❖ Popper, Karl R. and John C. Eccles The Self and Its Brain: An Argument for Interactionism Routledge & Kegan Paul (1977)

❖ Russell, Bertrand History of Western Philosophy Simon & Schuster (2007, originally 1945)

❖ Ryle, Gilbert Dilemmas Cambridge University Press (1966)

❖ Senechal, Marjorie Quasicrystals and geometry Cambridge University Press (2009)

❖ Snow, CP The Two Cultures Cambridge University Press (1998, originally 1959)

❖ Spencer, Roy W. The Great Global Warming Blunder: How Mother Nature Fooled the World's Top Climate Scientists Encounter Books, New York (2010)

❖ Stewart, Ian The Story of Mathematics: From Babylonian Numerals to Chaos Theory Quercus (2008)

❖ Taleb, Nassim Nicholas Fooled by Randomness: The Hidden Role of Chance in Life and in the Markets Second Edition Random House New York (2005)

❖ Watson, James D. The Double Helix: A Personal Account of the Discovery of the Structure of DNA Simon & Schuster (1996, originally 1968)

❖ Wegener, Alfred The Origin of Continents and Oceans Translated by John Biram, Dover Publishers, Inc. New York (1966)

❖ Westfall, Richard S. The Construction of Modern Science: Mechanisms and Mechanics Cambridge University Press (1977)

❖ Wiker, Benjamin D. The Mystery of the Periodic Table Ignatius Press (2003)

❖ Yount, Lisa A Alfred Wegener: Creator of the Continental Drift Theory Makers of Modern Science Series Chelsea House Publishers (2009)

On God and Religion:

❖ Armstrong, Karen The Great Transformation: The Beginning of Our Religious Traditions Anchor Books (2007)

❖ Armstrong, Karen A History of God: The 4,000 Year Quest of Judaism, Christianity and Islam Ballantine Books (1994)

❖ Lewis, C.S. The Complete C. S. Lewis Signature Classics Harper One (2002)

❖ Meyer, Stephen C. Signature in the Cell: DNA and the Evidence for Intelligent Design Harper One (2009)

On Art:

❖ Gablik, Suzi Has Modernism Failed? Thames and Hudson (1984)

On Ideology, Politics, Economics and Government:

❖ Abrams, Robert Foundations of Political Analysis: An Introduction to the Theory of Collective Choice Colombia University Press (1980)

❖ Berkin, Carol A Brilliant Solution: Inventing the American Constitution Houghton Mifflin Harcourt (2003)

❖ Bryce, Robert Power Hungry: The Myths of "Green" Energy and the Real Fuels of the Future Public Affairs, New York (2010)

❖ Gladwell, Malcolm The Tipping Point: How Little Things Can Make a Big Difference Little, Brown and Company New York (2002)

❖ Hamilton, Alexander; Madison, James; Jay, John The Federalist Papers SoHo Books (2011)

❖ Hayek, F.A. The Road to Serfdom The Collected Works of F. A. Hayek, Volume II, Ed. By Bruce Caldwell, The University of Chicago Press (2007, originally 1944)

❖ Kirk, Russell The Conservative Mind BN Publishing (2008)

❖ Friedman, Milton Capitalism and Freedom Fortieth Anniversary Edition, University of Chicago Press (2002)

❖ Franklin, Benjamin <u>Autobiography</u> The Library of America (1997)

❖ Levitt, Steven D. and Dubner, Stephen J. <u>Freakonomics: A Rogue Economist Explores the Hidden Side of Everything</u> HarperCollinsPublishers (2005)

❖ Levitt, Steven D. and Dubner, Stephen J. <u>Superfreakonomics: Global Cooling, Patriotic Prostitutes, and Why Suicide Bombers Should Buy Life Insurance</u> HarperCollinsPublishers (2009)

❖ Little, I.M.D. <u>A Critique of Welfare Economics</u> Second Edition Oxford University Press (1970)

❖ Meade, James Meade <u>The Intelligent Radical's Guide to Economic Policy: The Mixed Economy</u> George Allen & Unwin Ltd. (1975)

❖ Mill, John Stuart <u>On Liberty</u> from the collection <u>Utilitarianism, On Liberty and Considerations of Representative Government</u> E. P. Dutton & Co. Inc. (1972)

❖ Nozick, Robert <u>Anarchy, State and Utopia</u> Basic Books, Inc. (1974)

❖ Obama, Barack <u>The Audacity of Hope: Thoughts on Reclaiming the American Dream</u> Crown Publishers, New York (2006)

❖ Okun, Arthur M. <u>Equality and Efficiency: The Big Tradeoff</u> The Brookings Institution Washington, DC (1975)

❖ Olson, Mancur <u>The Logic of Collective Action: Public Goods and the Theory of Groups</u> Harvard University Press (1971)

❖ Phelps, Edmund S. <u>Political Economy: An Introductory Text</u> W.W. Norton & Company, New York (1985)

❖ Popper, Karl R. <u>The Open Society and Its Enemies: The Spell of Plato</u> Princeton University Press (1971)

❖ Schumpeter, Joseph A. <u>Capitalism, Socialism and Democracy</u> Harper Torchbooks (1975)

❖ Shapiro, Carl and Hal R. Varian <u>Information Rules: A Strategic Guide to the Network Economy</u> Harvard Business School Press (1999)

❖ Weber, Max <u>The Protestant Ethic and the Spirit of Capitalism</u> Penguin Classics (2002)

❖ Wilson, Edmund <u>To The Finland Station: A Study in the Writing and Acting of History</u> Farrar, Straus and Giroux (1972—originally, 1940)

❖ Wilson, James Q. <u>Bureaucracy: What Government Agencies Do and Why They Do It</u> Basic Books (1989)

(ENDNOTES)

1 Gregory Bateson <u>Steps to an Ecology of Mind: Collected Essays in Anthropology, Psychiatry, Evolution and Epistemology</u> Paladin (1973) at 48.

2 <u>What is Enlightenment</u> (1785) at 169. Quoted from Karl Popper's <u>Conjectures and Refutations: The Growth of Scientific Knowledge</u> at 177.

3 <u>The Order of Things</u>, 1970, from the preface at xv.

4 <u>Id</u>.

5 Skinner, B.F. <u>Science and Human Behavior</u> The Free Press (1953) at 13.

6 I took this photograph in Adelaide, South Australia, in 1979.

7 As classics professor Ken Rothwell explained to me in comments on this book, one view is that logic began with mathematics in the fifth century BC. A man named Hippocrates of Chios—not the medical doctor—appears to have been the first to use a theorem and to try to lay out systematic proofs.

8 Karl Popper makes this argument.

9 Barry Marshall Interview and Biography of from the Academy of Achievement, A Museum of Living History, Washington, DC (online). This is my source for most of the following information of Dr. Marshall and Dr. Warren and their discovery of the role of helicobacter pylori in peptic ulcers.

10 <u>Id</u>.

11 <u>Id</u>.

12 <u>Id</u>.

13 <u>Id</u>.

14 <u>See</u> Michio Kaku blog "Breaking the Speed of Light and Contemplating the Demise of Relativity", September 30, 2011, 6:02 am.

15 Id.

16 See Adam Frank "Scientists Report Breaking the Speed of Light, But Can It Be True? The Two-Way—NPR's News Blog, Category: Science September 22, 2011.

17 See Michio Kaku blog "Breaking the Speed of Light and Contemplating the Demise of Relativity", September 30, 2011, 6:02 am.

18 Id.

19 Id.

20 See BBC News Science & Environment, Nobel win for crystal discovery, 5 October 2011, by Jennifer Carpenter

21 Id.

22 Id.

23 Marjorie Senechal Quasicrystals and geometry Cambridge University Press (1995) at 3.

24 Ian Sample "Nobel Prize in Chemistry for dogged work on 'Impossible' quasicrystals" The Guardian Wednesday 5 October 2011.

25 Marjorie Senechal Quasicrystals and geometry Cambridge University Press (1995) at 1.

26 Alfred Wegener The Origin of Continents and Oceans Translated from the Fourth Revised German Edition by John Biram Dover Publications, Inc. (1966).

27 Lisa Yount Alfred Wegener: Creator of Continental Drift Theory Makers of Modern Science Chelsea House Publishers (2009) at 127.

28 Id. at 127-128.

29 Id. at 135.

30 See Imre Lakatos Proofs and Refutations: The Logic of Mathematical Discovery (Cambridge University Press, 1976) Edited by John Worrall and Elie Zahar.

31 See George Gamow One, Two, Three ... Infinity: Facts and Speculations of Science at pages 45 through 48 in the chapter on "Unusual Properties of Space".

32 Thomas Kuhn The Structure of Scientific Revolutions, Second Edition, The University of Chicago Press at 111.

33 I believe I may have originally obtained this example from the writings of Lakatos, but I don't remember where specifically.

34 See David C. Lindberg The Beginnings of Western Science: The European Scientific Tradition in Philosophical, Religious, and

Institutional Context, Prehistory to A.D. 1450 The University of Chicago Press (2007) at page 82.

35 See Paul de Kruif _Microbe Hunters_ Harcourt, Inc. (1996) (originally published in 1926) at page 27.

36 Id.

37 This account comes from Paul de Kruif _Microbe Hunters_ Harcourt, Inc. (1996) (originally published in 1926) in Chapter 2.

38 Paul de Kruif _Microbe Hunters_ Harcourt, Inc. (1996) (originally published in 1926) at page 37.

39 Id. at Chapter 1. The information on Leeuwanhoek in the following paragraph is from this source.

40 Id. at Chapter 3.

41 Interestingly, as classics professor Ken Rothwell noted in comments on this book, in antiquity they managed to figure out that wine (i.e., alcohol) was a good antibacterial agent.

42 See Imre Lakatos "The Methodology of Scientific Research Programmes" _Criticism and the Growth of Knowledge_ Eds. Imre Lakatos and Alan Musgrave. The methodological concepts in this chapter—and throughout my book—are heavily influenced by Lakatos and the other authors in this wonderful collection on the philosophy of science.

43 As noted in a previous endnote, I believe I may have originally obtained this example from the writings of Lakatos, but I do not remember specifically.

44 As noted above, I borrowed this example, and the point I am making, but do not remember where I originally read it.

45 Again, I read this series of examples and arguments somewhere, but don't recall where.

46 Interestingly, in ancient times, Aristarchus of Samos had also developed a heliocentric theory. Many of the same objections that were raised concerning Copernicus' theory were raised at that time. See G. E. R. Lloyd, _Greek Science After Aristotle_ (1973), at page 53ff. Thanks to classics professor Ken Rothwell for this reference.

47 Ironically, simplicity was one of Ptolemy's goals; see G. E. R. Lloyd, _Greek Science after Aristotle_ (1973), at page 53ff. Ptolemy followed Plato in obsessively thinking that the circle was the perfect geometrical shape for an orbit. Thanks to classics professor Ken Rothwell for this reference.

48 Burtt, E. A. <u>The Metaphysical Foundations of Modern Science</u> Dover Publications, Inc. (2003), first published in 1924, at 36.

49 <u>See</u> Imre Lakatos "The Methodology of Scientific Research Programmes" <u>Criticism and the Growth of Knowledge</u> Eds. Imre Lakatos and Alan Musgrave at 104.

50 I would love to conduct research on the relationship between the epistemology of that I am describing in this book and the manner in which the left and right sides of the brain communicate.

51 Classics professor Ken Rothwell tells me that "this was being complained about already in the fourth century BC."

52 <u>Encyclopedia Britannica</u> (2007) Volume 18 at page 844.

53 Federalist Paper No. 1

54 Federalist Paper Number 10

55 <u>See</u> Hewitt, Paul G <u>Conceptual Physics: The High School Physics Program</u> at pages 218-222 for an excellent presentation on Einstein's thinking on these points and this example.

56 A fabulous source for understanding the economics of information products and networks is Carl Shapiro and Hal R. Varian <u>Information Rules: A Strategic Guide to the Network Economy</u> Harvard Business School Press (1999).

57 My brother, an engineer, tells me that while physicists prefer the metric system, many engineers prefer the English System, the foot being an intuitively appealing and natural measure with which there is no corresponding analogue in the metric system.